Pathways to Machine Learning and Soft Computing

Jer-Guang Hsieh
Jyh-Horng Jeng
Yih-Lon Lin

I-Shou University, Taiwan

Ying-Sheng Kuo

Open University of Kaohsiung, Taiwan

美商EHGBooks微出版公司
www.EHGBooks.com

EHG Books 公司出版
Amazon.com 總經銷
2018 年版權美國登記
未經授權不許翻印全文或部分
及翻譯為其他語言或文字
2018 年 EHGBooks 第一版

ISBN-13：978-1-62503-442-7

Acquire knowledge extensively,
inquire into it accurately,
think over it carefully,
sift it clearly, and
practice it earnestly.

from: Chung-Yung
the Doctrine of the Mean
(one of the Four Confucian Classics)

Preface

The field of machine learning and soft computing is vast, diverse, and fascinating. It can be viewed as judicious mixture of computational intelligence and applied statistics. Currently, this is an active research area. What is machine learning? Broadly speaking, the goal of machine learning is to find a general rule that explains experimental data (or observational data) given only a sample of limited size. What is soft computing? In our views, soft computing is the spirit of the computation invented for our "soft" world. The learning machines addressed in this book include artificial neural networks, generalized radial basis neural networks, fuzzy neural networks, support vector machines, and Wilcoxon learning machines. They are different in their origins, network configurations, and objective functions. More emphasis is put on support vector machines and Wilcoxon learning machines in this book. The powerful evolutionary computation techniques addressed in this book include the genetic algorithm and the particle swarm optimization. The approaches to learning problems introduced in this book are non-parametric (or distribution-free) in the sense that they do not make any probabilistic assumptions on the processes generating the experimental data and they do not make any assumptions of the functional form, e.g., linearity, of the discriminant or predictive functions. This provides a great deal of flexibility in designing an appropriate learning machine for the problem at hand.

The audiences of this book are machine learning beginners who wish to know the basics of machine learning theory and implement their machine learning algorithms. With sound background in machine learning and soft computing, it will become much easier to get into the more specialized area of deep learning or more general area of artificial intelligence. This book was based partly on our lecture notes for the fundamental machine learning courses offered at National Sun-Yat-Sen University, I-Shou University, and Feng Chia University since 2003. It aims at providing practical and simple algorithms for solving standard machine learning problems, and hence is not a comprehensive research monograph. No sophisticated mathematics is used in this book. Associated with each given learning problem, simple algorithms are provided. We hope that the algorithms provided are clear enough so that the readers can write their own computer codes without difficulty. The exercises provided at the end of each chapter should be treated as an integral part of the book. The readers are encouraged to do these exercises, especially those computer projects.

There is an extensive literature on machine learning and soft computing. We have not attempted to compile a comprehensive list. Except for some selective references that are of historical significance, most references cited are sources we have used frequently. Some references might have been unintentionally missed. In those cases, please let us be informed. This book contains a random number of mistakes. Any suggestions will be more than welcome. We will do our best to improve the content of the book.

The readers can download the data sets and R codes used in this book from the website http://m-learning.isu.edu.tw/index.php?gid=20. An integrated SVM toolbox written in Visual C++ can be freely downloaded from the website: http://m-learning.isu.edu.tw/index.php?gid=13. For more vivid graphical display, the numerical examples are restricted to data sets of low dimensions. This certainly does not mean that the methods discussed in this book are applicable only to problems of low dimensions.

Finally, we wish to express our sincere acknowledgement to Professor Tsu-Tian Lee, President of National Taipei University of Technology, for his long-lasting support and friendship. We are deeply grateful for the financial support from National Science Council, Taiwan, over the last twenty years.

J. G. Hsieh, J.H. Jeng,
Y.L. Lin, and Y.S. Kuo
Kaohsiung, Taiwan

About the Authors

Jer-Guang Hsieh received the Ph.D. degree in electrical engineering from Rensselaer Polytechnic Institute, Troy, New York, U.S.A., in 1985. He was with the Department of Electrical Engineering, National Sun Yat-Sen University, Kaohsiung, Taiwan, from 1985 to 2008. Currently, he is a Chair Professor at the Department of Electrical Engineering, I-Shou University, Kaohsiung, Taiwan. He is also a Chair Professor at the Department of Automatic Control Engineering, Feng Chia University, Taichung, Taiwan. Dr. Hsieh is the recipient of the 1983 Henry J. Nolte Memorial Prize of Rensselaer Polytechnic Institute. He won the Distinguished Teaching Award in 1988 and Best Prize for competition of the microcomputer design package for teaching and research in 1989, both from the Ministry of Education of the Republic of China. He won the Young Engineer Prize from the Chinese Engineers Association in 1994. He is a member of the Phi Tau Phi Scholastic Honor Society of the Republic of China and a violinist of Kaohsiung Chamber Orchestra. His current research interests are in the areas of nonlinear control, machine learning and soft computing, and differential games.

Jyh-Horng Jeng received the B.S. and M.S. degrees in mathematics from Tamkang University, Taiwan, in 1982 and 1984, respectively, and the Ph.D. degree in mathematics (Information Group) from The State University of New York at Buffalo (SUNY, Buffalo) in 1996. He was a Senior Research Engineer at the Chung Shan Institute of Science and Technology (CSIST), Taiwan, from 1984 to 1992. Currently, he is a Professor at the Department of Information Engineering, I-Shou University, Taiwan. His research interests include multimedia applications, AI, soft computing and machine learning.

Yih-Lon Lin received the B.S. degree from the Department of Electronic Engineering, I-Shou University, Kaohsiung, Taiwan, in 1997 and the M.S. and Ph.D. degrees from the Department of Electrical Engineering, National Sun Yat-Sen University, Kaohsiung, Taiwan, in 1999 and 2006, respectively. Currently, he is an Associate Professor at the Department of Information Engineering, I-Shou University. His research interests include neural networks, fuzzy systems, and machine learning.

Ying-Sheng Kuo received the B.S. degree in Mechanical Engineering from Feng Chia University, Taichung, Taiwan, in 1988 and the M.S. and

Ph.D. degrees in Mechanical Engineering from National Cheng Kung University, Tainan, Taiwan, in 1991 and 1995, respectively. Currently, he is an Associate Professor at the General Education Center, Open University of Kaohsiung, Kaohsiung, Taiwan. His research interests include machine learning, soft computing, and computational fluid dynamics.

Brief Sketch of the Contents

The book starts with the introduction to machine learning. More emphasis is put on supervised learning, including classification learning (or pattern recognition) and function learning (or regression estimation). Bias-variance dilemma, which occurs in every machine learning problem, is illustrated through a numerical example.

Since machine learning problems usually involve some finite-dimensional optimization problems, solid background in optimization theory is crucial for sound understanding of the machine learning processes. We will briefly review some fundamental concepts and important results of finite-dimensional optimization theory in Chapter 2.

The true beginning of the mathematical analysis of learning processes started by the proposition of the Rosenblatt's algorithms for perceptrons, followed by the proposition of the Widrow-Hoff algorithms for Adalines (adaptive linear neurons). To our astonishment, these algorithms have already provided us hints for kernel-based learning machines of classification and regression if we consider the dual forms of their algorithms. The concept of the kernel is the basis of the support vector machines.

Linear classification problems are studied in Chapter 3. A linear classifier can be represented as a single-layer neural network with a hard limiting output activation function. The Rosenblatt's Perceptron Algorithms for linearly separable training data sets are introduced. Large margin for a linear classification provides the maximum robustness against perturbation. This motivates the introduction of maximal margin classifiers. To allow some misclassifications for linearly inseparable data, we will introduce slack variables for classification problems. Based on this, soft margin classifiers (or linear support vector classifiers) are studied.

Linear regression problems are studied in Chapter 4. A linear regressor can be represented as a single-layer neural network with a linear output activation function. The Widrow-Hoff algorithms, also called the delta learning rules, are derived for finding the least squares solutions. To smooth the predictive functions and to tolerate the errors in corrupted data, we will consider the ridge regression and linear support vector regression.

Three popular and powerful learning machines, i.e., artificial neural networks, generalized radial basis function networks, and fuzzy neural networks are introduced in Chapter 5. All three learning machines can be represented as multi-layer neural networks with a hidden layer, and the activation functions of the hidden nodes are nonlinear and continuously differentiable. Simple back propagation algorithm, which is a direct generalization of the delta learning rule used in Widrow-Hoff algorithm for Adalines, is introduced. The invention of the back propagation learning rules is a major breakthrough in machine learning theory.

At first glance, it might seem strange why we spent so much effort dealing with linear classification and linear regression problems, because our world is truly nonlinear in whatever sense. It will be seen that the commonly used learning machines, including those introduced in Chapter 5, nonlinearly transform in a peculiar way the input vectors to a feature space and perform generalized linear regression in feature space to produce the output vectors. Amazingly, it is rather trivial to go from linear classification and regression to kernel-based nonlinear classification and regression by applying the so called "kernel trick". It simply replaces the inner products by kernels. Such kernel-based approach results in the invention of support vector machines. The idea of a kernel generalizes the standard inner product in the finite-dimensional Euclidean space. The kernels are studied in Chapter 6.

To numerically solve the kernel-based classification and regression problems, we introduce an elegant and powerful sequential minimal optimization technique in Chapter 7.

Every learning problem has some (machine) parameters to be specified in advance. This is the problem of model selection, which is studied in Chapter 8. Two powerful evolutionary computation techniques, i.e., genetic algorithm and particle swarm optimization, are applied for tuning the parameters of support vector machines.

In a broad range of practical applications, data collected inevitably contain one or more atypical observations called outliers; that is, observations that are well separated from the majority or bulk of the data, or in some fashion deviate from the general pattern of the data. As is well known in linear regression theory, classical least squares fit of a regression model can be very adversely influenced by outliers, even by a single one, and often fails to provide a good fit to the bulk of the data. Robust regression that is resistant to the adverse effects of outlying response values offers a half-way house between including outliers and omitting them entirely. Rather than omitting outliers, it dampens their influence on the fitted regression model by down-weighting them. It is desirable that the robust estimates provide a good fit for the majority of the data when the data contain outliers, as well as when the data are free of them. A learning machine is said to be robust if it is not sensitive to outliers in the data.

The newly developed Wilcoxon learning machines will be studied in Chapter 8. They were developed by extending the R-estimators frequently used in robust regression paradigm to nonparametric learning machines for nonlinear learning problems. These machines are based on minimizing the rank-based Wilcoxon norm of total residuals and are quite robust against (or insensitive to) outliers. It is our firm belief that the Wilcoxon approach will provide a promising methodology for many machine learning problems.

Glossary of Symbols

$:=$ defined by

$\varnothing:$ empty set

$x \in A:$ x is an element of the set A

$A \subseteq B:$ A is a subset of B

$A \cap B:$ intersection of sets A and B
       (set of all common elements in A and B)

$A \cup B:$ union of sets A and B
       (set of all elements in A and B)

$A \setminus B:$ difference of sets A and B
       (set of all elements in A not in B)

$X \times Y:$ Cartesian product of two sets X and Y

$B(x,r):$ closed ball of radius r centered at x

$\underline{n}:$ set of integers $1, 2, ..., n;$ $\underline{n} = \{1, 2, ..., n\}$

$\underline{\bar{n}}:$ set of integers $0, 1, 2, ..., n;$ $\underline{\bar{n}} = \{0, 1, 2, ..., n\}$

$\Re:$ set of all real numbers

$\Re^n:$ space of all real n-tuples

$\Re^{m \times n}:$ set of all $m \times n$ real matrices

$\|x\|_1:$ 1-norm of vector x; $\|x\|_1 = |x_1| + ... + |x_n|$

$\|x\|_2:$ 2-norm of vector x; $\|x\|_2 = \sqrt{|x_1|^2 + ... + |x_n|^2}$

$\|x\|:$ 2-norm of vector x; $\|x\| = \sqrt{|x_1|^2 + ... + |x_n|^2}$

$\|x\|_\infty:$ infinity (or maximum) norm of vector x; $\|x\|_\infty = \max_{i \in \underline{n}}\{x_i\}$

$\|v\|_W:$ Wilcoxon norm of v

$\langle x, y \rangle:$ Euclidean (or usual) inner product of x and y

$\text{sgn}(\cdot):$ sign function

$f : A \rightarrow B:$ f is a function from A to B

$\nabla_w L:$ gradient of L with respect to w

$K(x, x'):$ kernel of x and x'

$x^T:$ transpose of vector x

$A^T:$ transpose of matrix A

$A^{-1}:$ inverse of a nonsingular matrix A

$R(A):$ column space of matrix A

$\sigma(A)$:   set of all eigenvalues of the square matrix A

sup: supremum (least upper bound)

inf: infimum (greatest lower bound)

$\deg(p)$:   degree of a polynomial p

$j = \arg\max_i\{y_i\}$:

the index such that y_j achieves the maximum among all i

$j = \arg\min_i\{y_i\}$:

the index such that y_j achieves the minimum among all i

$L_2(X)$:   set of all square integrable functions defined on X

$L_\infty(X)$:   set of all essentially bounded functions defined on X

l_1:   set of all absolute summable sequences

l_2:   set of all square summable sequences

Contents

Preface
About the Authors
Brief Sketch of the Contents
Glossary of Symbols

Chapter 1:   Introduction 1

    1.1   What is Machine Learning? 1
    1.2   Supervised Learning 6
    1.3   Successful Learning 9
    1.4   Brief History 10
    1.5   Notes and References 12

Chapter 2:   Finite-dimensional Optimization 13

    2.1   Preliminaries 13
    2.2   Nonlinear Programming 21
    2.3   Illustrative Examples 31
    2.4   Exercises 33
    2.5   Notes and References 35

Chapter 3:   Linear Classification 37

    3.1   Nearest Mean Classifier 37
    3.2   Hyperplane 40
    3.3   Linear Classifier 41
    3.4   Rosenblatt's Perceptron Algorithms 47
    3.5   Rosenblatt's Algorithm for Nonlinear Classifier 54
    3.6   Maximal Margin Classifier 62
    3.7   Slack Variable for Classification 70
    3.8   1-norm Soft Margin Classifier 73
    3.9   2-norm Soft Margin Classifier 81
    3.10   Illustrative Examples 87
    3.11   Exercises 90
    3.12   Notes and References 96

Chapter 4:   Linear Regression 97

4.1   Linear Least Squares Regressor 97
4.2   Widrow-Hoff Algorithm for Least Squares Regressor 101
4.3   Recursive Algorithm for Linear Least Squares Regressor 105
4.4   Widrow-Hoff Algorithm for Nonlinear Regressor 109
4.5   Ridge Regressor 112
4.6   Recursive Algorithm for Ridge Regressor 117
4.7   Dual Problem of Ridge Regression 121
4.8   Slack Variable for Regression 125
4.9   1-norm Soft Regressor 129
4.10   2-norm Soft Regressor 142
4.11   Illustrative Examples 152
4.12   Exercises 153
4.13   Notes and References 160

Chapter 5:   Multi-layer Neural Networks 161

5.1   Cover's Theorem 161
5.2   Artificial Neural Network 164
5.3   Generalized Radial Basis Function Network 182
5.4   Fuzzy System as a Nonlinear Map 191
5.5   Fuzzy Neural Network 196
5.6   Illustrative Examples 205
5.7   Exercises 211
5.8   Notes and References 216

Chapter 6:   Kernel-based Support Vector Classification and Regression 221

6.1   Kernel and Mercer's Theorem 221
6.2   Commonly Used Kernels 227
6.3   Kernel-based Support Vector Classifier 232
6.4   Kernel-based Support Vector Regressor 239
6.5   Multi-class Classification 249
6.6   Exercises 254
6.7   Notes and References 256

Chapter 7:   Sequential Minimal Optimization Techniques 259

7.1   SMO for Maximal Margin Classifier 259
7.2   SMO for 1-norm Soft Margin Classifier 265
7.3   SMO for 2-norm Soft Margin Classifier 269
7.4   SMO for Ridge Regressor 272
7.5   SMO for 1-norm Soft Regressor 276
7.6   SMO for 2-norm Soft Regressor 280
7.7   Illustrative Examples 284
7.8   Exercises 287
7.9   Notes and References 289

Chapter 8:   Model Selection 291

8.1   Genetic Algorithm 292
8.2   Particle Swarm Optimization 298
8.3   GA-based SVM Parameter Settings 300
8.4   PSO-based SVM Parameter Settings 303
8.5   Illustrative Examples 305
8.6   Exercises 310
8.7   Notes and References 313

Chapter 9:   Wilcoxon Learning Machines 317

9.1   Wilcoxon Norm 317
9.2   Linear Wilcoxon Regressor 319
9.3   Wilcoxon Artificial Neural Network 324
9.4   Wilcoxon Generalized Radial Basis Function Network 328
9.5   Wilcoxon Fuzzy Neural Network 332
9.6   Kernel-based Wilcoxon Machine 336
9.7   Illustrative Examples 341
9.8   Exercises 345
9.9   Notes and References 347

Index 349

Chapter 1   Introduction

1.1   What is Machine Learning?

An important task in almost all science and engineering is fitting models to data. The first step in mathematical modeling of a system under consideration is to use the first principles, e.g., Newton's laws in mechanics, Kirchhoff's laws in lumped electric circuits, or various laws in thermodynamics. As the system becomes increasingly complex, it is more and more unlikely to obtain a precise description of the system in quantitative terms. What we desire in practice is a reasonable yet tractable model. It may also happen that there is no analytic model for the system under consideration. This is particularly true in social science problems. However, in many real situations, we do have some experimental data (or observational data), either from measurement or data collection by some means. This raises the necessity of a theory concerning the learning from examples, i.e., obtaining a good mathematical model from experimental data. This is what machine learning all about.

Machine learning can be embedded in the broader context of knowledge discovery in databases (KDD), originated in computer science. See Hand, Mannila, and Smyth (2001) and Kantardzic (2003). The entire process of KDD is interactive, which is shown in Figure 1.1.1. The machine learning belongs to the fourth component of KDD. Application of machine learning methods to large databases is called data mining.

Our view of machine learning and soft computing is shown in Figure 1.1.2. The items inside the circle represent some commonly used learning machines, those outside the circle represent various tools necessary for solving machine learning problems, and those inside the rectangle denote some possible applications of machine learning and soft computing.

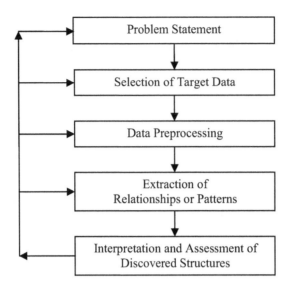

Figure 1.1.1: Process of knowledge discovery in databases.

The learning machines addressed in this book include Artificial Neural Networks (ANNs), Generalized Radial Basis Function Networks (GRBFNs), Fuzzy Neural Networks (FNNs), Support Vector Machines (SVMs), and Wilcoxon Learning Machines (WLMs). More emphasis is put on SVMs and WLMs. In statistical terms, the aforementioned learning machines are nonparametric in the sense that they do not make any assumptions of the functional form, e.g., linearity, of the discriminant or predictive functions. This provides a great deal of flexibility in designing an appropriate learning machine for the problem at hand. In our view, SVM theory cleverly combines the convex optimization from nonlinear optimization theory, kernel representation from functional analysis, and distribution-free generalization error bounds from statistical learning theory. The WLMs were recently developed by extending the *R*-estimators frequently used in robust regression paradigm to nonparametric learning machines for nonlinear learning problems. We firmly believe that WLMs will provide promising alternatives for many machine learning problems. The powerful Evolutionary Computation (EC) techniques addressed in this book include the Genetic Algorithm (GA) and the Particle Swarm Optimization (PSO).

Machine Learning & Soft Computing

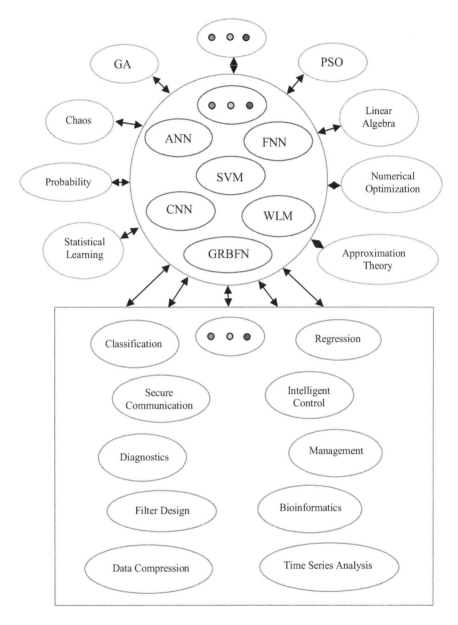

Figure 1.1.2: Brief sketch of machine learning and soft computing.

Our basic belief in machine learning is that we believe there is a process that explains the data we observe. Though we do not know the details of the process underlying the generation of data, we know that it is not completely random. See Alpaydin (2010).

What is a machine learning problem? The goal of machine learning is to find a general rule that explains experimental data given only a sample of limited size. There are three major categories of machine learning, namely supervised learning, unsupervised learning, and reinforcement learning, as shown in Figure 1.1.3. See Herbrich (2002) and Alpaydin (2010).

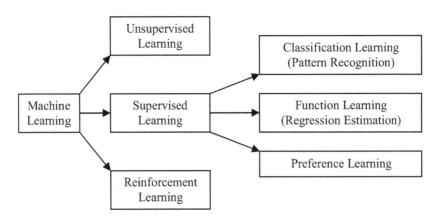

Figure 1.1.3: Main categories of machine learning.

In the supervised learning problem, we are given a sample of input-output pairs, called training sample. The task is to find a deterministic function that maps any input to an output such that disagreement with future input-output observations is minimized.

There are three major types of the supervised learning. The first type is the classification learning, also called pattern recognition. The outputs of a classification problem are categorical variables, also called class labels. Usually, there is no ordering between the classes. Credit scoring of loan applicants in a bank, classification of handwritten letters and digits, optical character recognition, face recognition, speech recognition, and classification of news in a news agency belong to classification problems.

The second type of the supervised learning is the function learning, also called regression estimation. The outputs of a regression problem are continuous variables. Prediction of the stock market share values, weather forecasting, and navigation of an autonomous car belong to regression problems.

The third type of the supervised learning is the preference learning. The outputs of a preference learning problem are ranks in the order space. One may compare whether two elements are equal or, if not, which one has higher rank of preference. Arrangement of WEB pages such that the most relevant pages are ranked highest belongs to preference learning problems.

In the unsupervised learning, we are given a sample of objects without corresponding target values. The goal is to extract some structure or regularity from the experimental data. Finding a concise description of the data could be a set of clusters (cluster analysis) sharing some common regularity in each cluster, or a probability density (density estimation) showing the probability of observing an event in the future. Image and text segmentation, novelty detection in process control, grouping of customers in a company, and alignment in molecular biology belong to unsupervised learning problems.

In some applications, the output of the system is a sequence of actions. A single action is not important; what is important is the strategy or policy that is the sequence of correct actions to reach the goal. In the reinforcement learning, we are given a sample of state-action-reward triples. The goal is to find a concise description of the data in the form of a strategy or policy (what to do?) that maximizes the expected reward over time. Usually no optimal action exists in a given intermediate state; an action is good if it is part of a good policy. In such a case, the learning algorithm should be able to assess the goodness of policies and must identify a sequence of actions, learned from past, so as to maximize the expected reward over time. Playing chess and robot navigation in search of a goal location belong to reinforcement learning problems. See Sutton and Barto (1998), Herbrich (2002), and Alpaydin (2010).

1.2 Supervised Learning

Only supervised learning problems are addressed and more emphasis will be put on the classification and regression problems in this introductory text. The flow chart of the supervised learning is schematically shown in Figure 1.2.1.

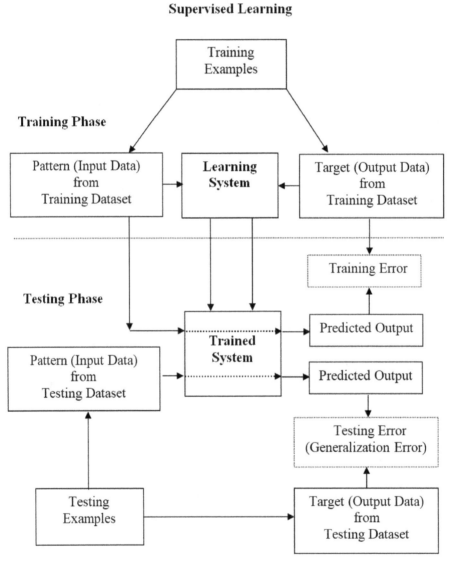

Figure 1.2.1: Flow chart of supervised learning.

The experimental data we have at hand are usually divided as training data set and testing data set. There are two phases of the whole supervised learning process. In the training phase, the training data set is used to train the learning machine. Even after training, the predicted outputs for the training patterns may not be exactly the same as those of the training targets. This results in the training error. In the testing phase, the testing data set is used to validate the trained learning machine. Because the testing examples are not used in training phase, the testing error, also called generalization error, results from inaccurate prediction of the trained system to the testing patterns. Typically, the generalization error is our main concern for most of real learning problems.

It should be noted that small training error doesn't imply good generalization for previously unseen data. In particular, in more technical terms, a learning machine with too high capacity (or too much flexibility) typically leads to the very undesirable effect of overfitting. One important reason is that the experiment data are usually noisy. Interpolation of such noisy data may result in bad generalization for previously unseen data. On the opposite side, a learning machine with too low capacity (or flexibility) typically leads to the very undesirable effect of underfitting. It should be noted that any learning machine almost learns nothing from too few training examples. To get some flavor of these statements, an illustrative example is provided in the following.

Example 1.2.1: Suppose two sets of noisy data, each of size 11, are generated from the function $y = g(x) := 2.5\sin(2x) + x$ corrupted by adding random values from a uniform distribution defined on $[-1, 1]$. Let f_3, f_5, and f_{10} be approximating functions which are polynomials of degrees 3, 5, and 10, respectively. The usual least squares method is employed to find the approximating functions. Simulations results are shown in Figure 1.2.2.

The polynomial of degree 10 has 11 adjustable parameters, which is exactly the same as the number of training examples. In the current case, the class of polynomials of degrees no greater than 10 has high capacity. It is observed that the predictive functions resulting from polynomials of degree 10 interpolate the noisy training examples perfectly but perform rather bad for points not in the training set, namely, the training errors are zeros but with big generalization errors. This is a typical indication of overfitting, which results in very bad generalization capability. We may as well say that it models (or memorizes) not only the true function but also the noise. The predictive functions are oscillatory and are quite different for two different training data sets.

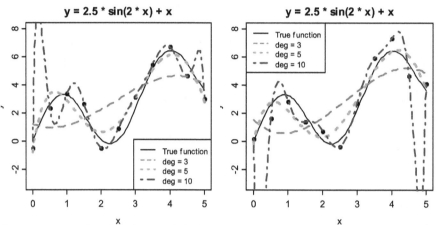

Figure 1.2.2: Fitted polynomials for data set 1 (left) and data set 2 (right).

The polynomial of degree 3 has only four adjustable parameters. In the current case, the class of polynomials of degrees no greater than 3 has low capacity. It is observed that the predictive functions resulting from polynomials of degree 3 do not interpolate the noisy training examples but with big training errors. This is a typical indication of underfitting. We may as well say that it not only filters out or smoothes the noise but also the true function. The predictive functions are not so oscillatory and are not so different for two different training data sets.

For the polynomials of degree 5, the predictive functions do not interpolate the noisy training examples and the training errors are reasonable. For the generalization capability of previously unseen points, it performs best among the three approximating functions. The predictive functions are not so oscillatory and are not so different for two different training data sets.

From the simulation of this example, as the order of the polynomial increases, small change in data set incurs a greater change in the resulting polynomial; thus variance increases. However, complex models have a better fit to the underlying function; thus bias decreases. In statistics, this is termed the bias-variance dilemma (or bias-variance tradeoff), which is true for all machine learning problems.

1.3 Successful Learning

In any machine problem, there are four important factors that must be taken into serious account for a successful learning: (1) quality of training data; (2) feature extraction; (3) model selection; and (4) algorithm utilized for training the learning machine. See Kantardzic (2003) and Alpaydin (2010).

If the experimental data were obtained by imprecise measurement or careless data collection, its quality is usually bad. There are several indicators of data quality:

Are the data accurate?
Are the data consistent?
Are the data complete?
Are the data timely?
Are the data well understood?

In many real learning problems, the feature extraction, which depends heavily on the domain knowledge, is extremely important. These features will be used as the patterns or inputs in the learning problem. Feature extraction includes the feature selection and feature composition. In feature selection, or subset selection, we are interested in finding an appropriate subset of features at hand, for instance, a subset containing small number of dimensions that contribute significantly to accuracy. In feature composition, we are interested in finding a new set of features, which are combinations of the original features, that is more informative for the current problem. For instance, in many medical data sets, weight and height are two inputs. But for some medical diagnostic analysis, a new feature, called the body-mass index (BMI), which is a weighted ratio between weight and height, is more important.

The model selection includes the choice of the learning machine and the determination of machine parameters. It reflects our prior knowledge of the problem, which is called the "inductive bias." An immediate method for model selection is by trial and error. This will be successful only when one has good knowledge about the learning problem under consideration. Another method commonly employed is the method of cross validation (specifically, the k-fold method). First randomly split the data set into several, say m, parts of approximately equal size. Perform m training runs. Each time, one of the m parts is left out and used as an independent validation set for optimizing the parameters. Taking into consideration both the average training and testing error rates, we would choose the parameters with acceptable results on average over the m runs. See Schölkopf and Smola (2002).

For a given learning problem, usually there are various numerical algorithms for solving the associated optimization problem. The algorithm utilized for training the learning machine should be good enough, fast enough, and cheap enough in terms of, for example, space and time complexity.

1.4 Brief History

In Table 1.4.1, we give a list of brief history of machine learning and soft computing. Our viewpoints might be narrow. Only some researchers are mentioned and others are omitted. This doesn't mean that those researchers' contributions are not important.

The evolutionary computation field has been considered by many authors to include the following areas, i.e., Genetic Programming (GP), Evolution Strategy (ES), Evolutionary Programming (EP), Genetic Algorithm (GA), Particle Swarm Optimization (PSO), Differential Evolution (DE), Artificial Bee Colony (ABC), and Cuckoo Search (CS). Only GA and PSO will be briefly touched in this book.

It is important to realize that the spirit of soft computing is the Law of Sufficiency: If a solution is good enough, fast enough, and cheap enough, then it is sufficient. In almost all real-world applications, we are looking for, and satisfied with, sufficient solutions. Hybrids of various soft computing approaches with other computational intelligence tools such as neural networks are becoming more prevalent. See Kennedy and Eberhart (2001).

Table 1.4.1: Brief history of machine learning and soft computing.

Year(s)	Name(s)	Event Description
1936	Fisher	Discriminant analysis
1943	McCulloch Pitts	First mathematical model for the artificial neuron
1958	Rosenblatt	First model of learning machine (perceptron) for classification; True beginning of the mathematical analysis of learning processes
1958	Friedberg	Genetic Programming (GP)
1960	Widrow Hoff	Adaptive linear neuron (Adaline) for regression by using the delta learning rule
1962	Novikoff	First (convergence) theorem about the perceptron
1962	Holland	Genetic Algorithm (GA)
1963	Tikhonov	Regularization method for solutions of ill-posed problems
1965	Zadeh	Fuzzy mathematics
1965	Rechenberg Schwefel	Evolution Strategy (ES)
1966	Fogel Owens Walsh	Evolutionary Programming (EP)
1969	Minsky Papert	Simple biologically motivated learning systems (perceptrons) were incapable of learning an arbitrarily complex problem. (negative result)
1971	Vapnik Chervonenkis	Statistical learning theory
1982	Hopfield	Hopfield network
1982	Vapnik	Introduction of regularization theory into machine learning
1986	Rumelhart Hinton Williams Le Cun	Error back-propagation algorithm (generalized delta learning rule) for multi-layer neural networks (direct generalization of perceptrons)
1988	Chua Yang	Cellular Neural Network (CNN)
1989	Poggio Girosi	Radial Basis Function Network (RBFN)

1989~1991	Goldberg Davis	Popularization of genetic algorithm
1991	Koza	Improvement of genetic programming
1992	Vapnik	Support Vector Machine (SVM)
1995	Kennedy Eberhart	Particle Swarm Optimization (PSO)
2009	Yang Deb	Cuckoo Search (CS)

1.5 Notes and References

For data mining, see Hand, Mannila, and Smyth (2001) and Kantardzic (2003).   For general introduction to machine learning, see Alpaydin (2010), Herbrich (2002), Kecman (2001), and Schölkopf and Smola (2002).

Alpaydin, E. (2010). Introduction to Machine Learning. Second Edition. MIT Press, Cambridge, Massachusetts.

Hand, D., H. Mannila, and P. Smyth (2001). Principles of Data Mining. MIT Press, Cambridge, Massachusetts.

Herbrich, R. (2002). Learning Kernel Classifiers: Theory and Algorithms. MIT Press, Cambridge, Massachusetts.

Kantardzic, M. (2003). Data Mining. Wiley-Interscience, New Jersey.

Kecman, V. (2001). Learning and Soft Computing. MIT Press, Cambridge, Massachusetts.

Kennedy, J. and R.C. Eberhart (2001). Swarm Intelligence. Morgan Kaufmann, San Francisco, California.

Schölkopf, B. and A.J. Smola (2002). Learning with Kernels: Support Vector Machines, Regularization, and Beyond. MIT Press, Cambridge, Massachusetts.

Sutton, R.S. and A.G. Barto (1998). Reinforcement Learning: An Introduction. MIT Press, Cambridge, Massachusetts.

Chapter 2   Finite-dimensional Optimization

Since machine learning problems usually involve some finite-dimensional optimization problems, solid background in optimization theory is crucial for sound understanding of the machine learning processes.   We will briefly review some fundamental concepts and important results of finite-dimensional optimization theory in this chapter. In the first section, we will introduce the concepts of local and global minimizers.   The classical result of Weierstrass Theorem is presented next.   The convex sets, convex functions, and related properties are then reviewed.   The standard problems of nonlinear programming are presented in the second section.   The Karush-Kuhn-Tuker Theorem (KKT Theorem) plays a fundamental role to the nonlinear programming theory.   The dual optimization problems of the primal optimization problems are then reviewed.   This concept will be very useful for the kernel-based learning machines to be developed in later chapters.   Some numerical examples are provided in the third section to illustrate the use of the optimization techniques.   The material of this chapter will be used very often in later chapters.

2.1 Preliminaries

Definition 2.1.1: Suppose $f : K \subseteq \Re^n \to \Re$.   A point $x^* \in K$ is said to be a

(a) **local minimizer** of f over K if there exists an $\varepsilon > 0$ such that $f(x^*) \leq f(x)$ for all $x \in K \cap B(x^*, \varepsilon)$.

(b) **strict local minimizer** of f over K if there exists an $\varepsilon > 0$ such that $f(x^*) < f(x)$ for all $x \in (K \cap B(x^*, \varepsilon)) \setminus \{x^*\}$.

(c) **global minimizer** of f over K if $f(x^*) \leq f(x)$ for all $x \in K$.

(d) **strict global minimizer** of f over K if $f(x^*) < f(x)$ for all $x \in K \setminus \{x^*\}$.

Before stating the useful Weierstrass Theorem, we introduce some concepts from topology. Let $E \subseteq \Re^n$. A point $x \in E$ is said to be an **interior point** of E if there is a ball $B(x, \varepsilon)$ such that $x \in B(x, \varepsilon) \subseteq E$.

A set $E \subseteq \Re^n$ is said to be

∧∧ an **open set** if all points of E are interior points;
∧∧ a **closed set** if its complement is open;
∧∧ a **bounded set** if there is a positive constant $M > 0$ such that $\|x\| < M$ for all $x \in E$.
∧∧ a **compact set** if it is both closed and bounded.

Proposition 2.1.1: (Weierstrass Theorem)

Let $f : D \to \Re$ be continuous on a compact set $D \subseteq \Re^n$. Then f attains a minimum and a maximum on D, i.e., there are points z_1 and z_2 in D such that

$$f(z_1) \le f(z) \le f(z_2) \text{ for all } z \in D.$$

Examples 2.1.1:

(a) Let $D = \Re$ and $f(x) := 5x^3$, $x \in \Re$. Then f is continuous, but D is not compact (closed but not bounded). Since $f(D) = \Re$, f evidently attains neither a minimum nor a maximum on D.

(b) Let $D = (-1, 1)$ and $f(x) := x^3$, $x \in (-1, 1)$. Then f is continuous, but D is not compact (bounded but not closed). Since $f(D) = (-1, 1)$, f evidently attains neither a minimum nor a maximum on D.

(c) Let $D = [-1, 1]$ and let

$$f(x) := \begin{cases} 0, & x \in \{-1, 1\} \\ x^3, & -1 < x < 1. \end{cases}$$

Then D is compact, but f fails to be continuous at -1 and 1. Since $f(D) = (-1, 1)$, f evidently attains neither a minimum nor a maximum on D.

(d) Let $D = [-1, 1]$ and let

$$f(x) := \begin{cases} 1, & x \text{ is rational, } x \in [-1, 1], \\ 0, & x \text{ is irrational, } x \in [-1, 1]. \end{cases}$$

Then D is compact but f is discontinuous at any point on D. Nonetheless, f attains a minimum at every irrational point and a maximum at every rational point.

Example 2.1.2: Consider the following maximization problem:

maximize $\quad \lambda u_1(x_1) + (1 - \lambda) u_2(x_2)$

subject to $\quad x_1 + x_2 \leq w, \; x_1 \geq 0, \; x_2 \geq 0,$

where u_1 and u_2 are continuous, $\lambda \in (0, 1)$, and $w > 0$. It is easy to see that the feasible set D, consisting of all x satisfying the constraints, is a compact set for each $w > 0$, and the objective function is continuous for each $\lambda \in (0, 1)$. The Weierstrass Theorem assures the existence of a solution to this family of optimization problems.

Definition 2.1.2: Let X be a vector space over the field F. A subset $K \subseteq X$ is said to be **convex** if $\lambda x + (1 - \lambda)y \in K$ for all $x, y \in K$ and $\lambda \in [0, 1]$.

The empty set $\emptyset$ is defined to be convex. Geometrically, a set is convex if, given any two points in the set, every point on the line segment joining these two points is also a member of the set. Therefore, any singleton $\{x\}$ is convex and so is every linear manifold. Figure 2.1.1 shows some convex and nonconvex sets in two-dimensional plane.

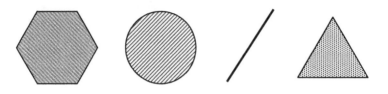

Figure 2.1.1(a): Convex sets.

Figure 2.1.1(b): Nonconvex sets.

Definition 2.1.3: We say that $x = \sum_{i=1}^{n} \lambda_i x_i$, $n < \infty$, is a (finite) **convex combination** of elements x_i if $\sum_{i=1}^{n} \lambda_i = 1$ and $\lambda_i \geq 0$ for all $i \in \underline{n}$.

It is not difficult to prove the following fact:

> A subset $K \subseteq X$ is convex
> $\Leftrightarrow$ every (finite) convex combination of elements $x_i \in K$ belongs to K.

Definition 2.1.4: A point x_0 in a convex set K is an **extreme point** of K if there are no two distinct points $x_1, x_2 \in K$ such that $x_0 = \alpha x_1 + (1-\alpha)x_2$ for some $\alpha \in (0,1)$, i.e., if a relation of the form $x_0 = \alpha x_1 + (1-\alpha)x_2$, $x_1, x_2 \in K$, $\alpha \in (0,1)$, holds only when $x_1 = x_2 = x_0$.

Roughly speaking, x_0 is an extreme point of a convex subset K if it is not an interior point of any interval with endpoints in K. For example, the vertices of a square in the plane are extreme points, but the other boundary points are not extreme. The extreme points of a circular disk are all points on the boundary. A linear variety consisting of more than one point has no extreme points. See Figure 2.1.2 for some illustrations.

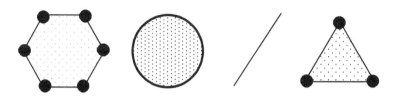

Figure 2.1.2: Extreme points (shown in **bold**).

Definition 2.1.5: Let K be a convex set of a vector space X and $f : K \to \Re$. Then f is said to be

(a) **convex** if for every $\alpha \in (0, 1)$, $x, y \in K$, we have

$$f[\alpha x + (1 - \alpha)y] \leq \alpha f(x) + (1 - \alpha)f(y).$$

(b) **strictly convex** if for every $\alpha \in (0, 1)$, $x, y \in K$, $x \neq y$, we have

$$f[\alpha x + (1 - \alpha)y] < \alpha f(x) + (1 - \alpha)f(y).$$

(c) **concave** if $-f$ is convex, i.e., if for every $\alpha \in (0, 1)$, $x, y \in K$, we have

$$f[\alpha x + (1 - \alpha)y] \geq \alpha f(x) + (1 - \alpha)f(y).$$

(d) **strictly concave** if $-f$ is strictly convex, i.e., if for every $\alpha \in (0, 1)$, $x, y \in K$, $x \neq y$, we have

$$f[\alpha x + (1 - \alpha)y] > \alpha f(x) + (1 - \alpha)f(y).$$

(e) **affine** if it is convex and concave, i.e., if for every $\alpha \in (0, 1)$, $x, y \in K$, we have

$$f[\alpha x + (1 - \alpha)y] = \alpha f(x) + (1 - \alpha)f(y).$$

Geometrically, a function is convex if the line joining any two points on its graph lies nowhere below the graph, or, thinking of a function in two dimensions, it is convex if its graph is bowl shaped. Similarly, a function is concave if the line joining any two points on its graph lies nowhere above the graph, or, thinking of a function in two dimensions, it is concave if its graph is bell shaped. An affine function defined on $\Re^n$ can be written as $f(x) = a^T x + b$ for some vector a and scalar b. Figure 2.1.3 shows some convex and nonconvex functions and Figure 2.1.4 shows some concave and nonconcave functions.

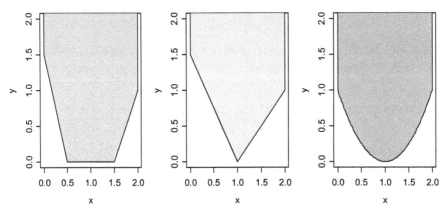

Figure 2.1.3(a): Convex functions (epigraph: shaded region).

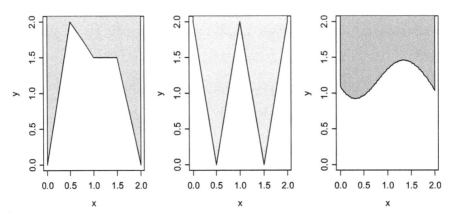

Figure 2.1.3(b): Nonconvex functions (epigraph: shaded region).

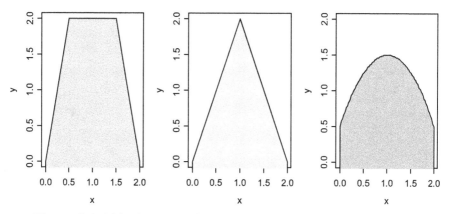

Figure 2.1.4(a): Concave functions (subgraph: shaded region).

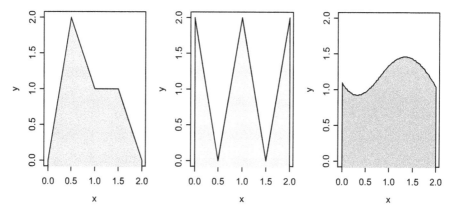

Figure 2.1.4(b): Nonconcave functions (subgraph: shaded region).

Proposition 2.1.2: Let K be a convex set of a vector space X and $f : K \to \Re$. Then the following statements are equivalent.

(a) f is convex;

(b) For every convex combination $x = \sum_{i=1}^{n} \alpha_i x_i$, $\sum_{i=1}^{n} \alpha_i = 1$, $x_i \in K$, $\alpha_i \geq 0$, $i \in \underline{n}$, we have $f\left(\sum_{i=1}^{n} \alpha_i x_i \right) \leq \sum_{i=1}^{n} \alpha_i f(x_i)$;

(c) The epigraph $G_p(f) := \{(x, \lambda) \in K \times \Re : f(x) \leq \lambda\}$ is a convex subset of $X \times \Re$.

The equivalence of (a) and (c) should be clear from Figure 2.1.3. Similarly, we have a corresponding result for concave functions.

Proposition 2.1.3: Let K be a convex set of a vector space X and $f : K \rightarrow \Re$. Then the following statements are equivalent.

(a) f is concave;

(b) For every convex combination $x = \sum_{i=1}^{n} \alpha_i x_i$, $\sum_{i=1}^{n} \alpha_i = 1$, $x_i \in K$,

$\alpha_i \geq 0$, $i \in \underline{n}$, we have $f\left(\sum_{i=1}^{n} \alpha_i x_i \right) \geq \sum_{i=1}^{n} \alpha_i f(x_i)$;

(c) The subgraph $G_s(f) := \{(x, \lambda) \in K \times \Re : f(x) \geq \lambda\}$ is a convex subset of $X \times \Re$.

The equivalence of (a) and (c) should be clear from Figure 2.1.4.

Proposition 2.1.4: Suppose K is a convex subset of $\Re^n$ and $f : K \rightarrow \Re$ is convex. Then the minimal set $M(f)$ where f achieves its minimum is convex (i.e., $M(f)$ is the set of all gobal minimizers of f), and any local minimizer of f is a global minimizer. Moreover, if f is strictly convex, then $M(f)$ contains only one element.

The preceding proposition may be rephrased as saying that for convex functions, all local minimizers are located together in a convex set and all local minimizers are global minimizers. See Figure 2.1.3(a) for illustration.

Proposition 2.1.5: Suppose K is a bounded closed convex subset of $\Re^n$ and $f : K \rightarrow \Re$ is convex. If f has a maximum over K, it is achieved at an extreme point of K.

See the two functions in Figure 2.1.5.

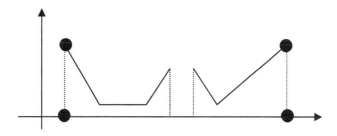

Figure 2.1.5: Maximization of a convex function over an interval.

2.2 Nonlinear Programming

Suppose $\Omega \subseteq \mathfrak{R}^n$ is a domain. Let f, g_i, h_j $i \in \underline{k}$, $j \in \underline{m}$, be real-valued functions defined on Ω. Consider the following **primal optimization problem**:

(P)   minimize $f(w)$
               subject to $g_i(w) = 0$, $i \in \underline{k}$,
                          $h_j(w) \geq 0$, $j \in \underline{m}$, $w \in \Omega$.

Here f is called the **objective function**, $g_i(w) = 0$, $i \in \underline{k}$, are called the **equality constraints**, and $h_j(w) \geq 0$, $j \in \underline{m}$, are called the **inequality constraints**. For simplicity, we will use $g(w) = 0$ to indicate $g_i(w) = 0$, $i \in \underline{k}$, and $h(w) \geq 0$ to indicate $h_j(w) \geq 0$, $j \in \underline{m}$. Thus the problem (P) can be shortly written as

(P)   minimize $f(w)$
               subject to $g(w) = 0$, $h(w) \geq 0$, $w \in \Omega$.

Feasible region or **feasible set** of the problem (P) is the set defined by

$$R_p := \{w \in \Omega : g(w) = 0, h(w) \geq 0\}.$$

Any point $w \in R_p$ is called a **feasible point**. An **optimal solution** $w^* \in R_p$ is a feasible point such that

$$f(w^*) \le f(w) \quad \text{for all} \quad w \in R_p .$$

The value of the objective function at an optimal solution is called the **value of the problem**. Maximization problem can always be converted into a minimization problem by reversing the sign of $f(w)$.

An optimization problem (P) is called a

∧∧ **linear program** if the objective function and all constraints are affine.
∧∧ **nonlinear program** if the objective function or some of the constraints are general nonlinear functions.
∧∧ **equality-constrained program** if all constraints are equality constraints.
∧∧ **inequality-constrained program** if all constraints are inequality constraints.
∧∧ **linearly-constrained program** if all constraints are affine.
∧∧ **bounded-constrained program** if only constraints have the form $w_i \ge l_i$ or $w_i \le u_i$, where l_i and u_i are lower and upper bounds on the ith component of w.
∧∧ **quadratic program** if the objective function is quadratic while the constraints are all affine.
∧∧ **convex program** if the objective function is convex and the feasible set is convex.

Proposition 2.2.1: A sufficient condition for the feasible region R_p to be convex is that the equality constraints g_i, $i \in \underline{k}$, be affine and that the inequality constraints h_j, $j \in \underline{m}$, be concave.

Proof: Let w_1 and w_2 be two feasible points and let $w := \lambda w_1 + (1-\lambda)w_2$, $\lambda \in [0,1]$. Since each g_i, $i \in \underline{k}$, is affine, there is a vector a_i and a scalar b_i such that $g_i(w) = a_i^T w + b_i$. Then we have

$$\begin{aligned}
g_i(w) &= g_i[\lambda w_1 + (1-\lambda)w_2] = a_i^T[\lambda w_1 + (1-\lambda)w_2] + b_i \\
&= \lambda(a_i^T w_1 + b_i) + (1-\lambda)(a_i^T w_2 + b_i) \\
&= \lambda g_i(w_1) + (1-\lambda)g_i(w_2) \\
&= 0 + 0 = 0 .
\end{aligned}$$

Since each h_j, $j \in \underline{m}$, is concave, we have

$$h_j(w) = h_j[\lambda w_1 + (1 - \lambda)w_2] \geq \lambda h_j(w_1) + (1 - \lambda)h_j(w_2) \geq 0 + 0 = 0.$$

Thus $w := \lambda w_1 + (1 - \lambda)w_2$ is feasible for each $\lambda \in [0, 1]$, i.e., the feasible set is convex. This completes the proof.

An inequality constraint $h_j(w) \geq 0$ is said to be **active** at $w*$ if $h_j(w*) = 0$; otherwise, it is said to be **inactive**. For notational ease, define

$$\phi_i := \begin{cases} g_i, & i = 1, ..., k, \\ h_{i-k}, & i = k+1, ..., k+m. \end{cases}$$

Then the feasible set is given by

$$R_p := \{w \in \Omega : \phi_i(w) = 0, i = 1, ..., k, \phi_j(w) \geq 0, j = k+1, ..., k+m\}.$$

The **active set** $A(w)$ at any feasible point w is the set of all indices of the active constraints, i.e., the union of $\{1, ..., k\}$ and the indices of the active inequality constraints, i.e.,

$$A(w) := \{1, ..., k\} \cup \{j \in \{k+1, ..., k+m\} : \phi_j(w) = 0\}.$$

We say that the **linear independence constraint qualification** (LICQ) holds at a feasible point w if the set of active constraint gradients $\{\nabla \phi_i : i \in A(w)\}$ is linearly independent.

The (generalized) **Lagrangian** is defined as

$$L(w, \alpha, \beta) := f(w) - \sum_{i=1}^{k} \alpha_i g_i(w) - \sum_{j=1}^{m} \beta_j h_j(w),$$

where α_i, β_j, $i \in \underline{k}$, $j \in \underline{m}$, are Lagrange multipliers. We may also write

$$L(w, \alpha, \beta) = f(w) - \alpha^T g(w) - \beta^T h(w),$$
$$\alpha := [\alpha_1 \quad \cdots \quad \alpha_k]^T \in \Re^k, \quad g(w) := [g_1(w) \quad \cdots \quad g_k(w)]^T \in \Re^k,$$
$$\beta := [\beta_1 \quad \cdots \quad \beta_m]^T \in \Re^m, \quad h(w) := [h_1(w) \quad \cdots \quad h_m(w)]^T \in \Re^m.$$

The following Karush-Kuhn-Tuker Theorem (KKT Theorem) is fundamental to the nonlinear programming theory.

Proposition 2.2.2: (KKT Theorem) (First-order Necessary Conditions)

Assume f, g_i, $i \in \underline{k}$, and h_j, $j \in \underline{m}$, are continuously differentiable. Suppose the finite $w^* \in R_p$ is a local minimizer of the program (P) and that the LICQ holds at w^*. Then there are vectors $\alpha^* \in \Re^k$ and $\beta^* \in \Re^m$ of Lagrange multipliers with components α_i^*, $i \in \underline{k}$, and β_j^*, $j \in \underline{m}$, respectively, such that the following KKT conditions are satisfied:

$$0 = \nabla_w L(w^*, \alpha^*, \beta^*) = \nabla f(w^*) - \sum_{i=1}^{k} \alpha_i^* \nabla g_i(w^*) - \sum_{j=1}^{m} \beta_j^* \nabla h_j(w^*),$$
$$g_i(w^*) = 0, \quad i \in \underline{k},$$
$$h_j(w^*) \geq 0, \quad j \in \underline{m},$$
$$\beta_j^* \geq 0, \quad j \in \underline{m},$$
$$\beta_j^* h_j(w^*) = 0, \quad j \in \underline{m}.$$

The last relations of the preceding proposition are known as **complementarity conditions**. Points satisfying the KKT conditions are called **critical points** of the program.

Corresponding to any inequality constraint, we have $\beta_j^* \geq 0$, $j \in \underline{m}$. However, corresponding to any inactive constraint h_j, we must have $\beta_j^* = 0$. The signs of α_i^*, $i \in \underline{k}$, corresponding to the equality constraints, are immaterial.

Proposition 2.2.3: Assume f, g_i, $i \in \underline{k}$, and h_j, $j \in \underline{m}$, are continuously differentiable. If KKT conditions and LICQ are satisfied at a feasible point w^*, then the Lagrange multipliers are unique.

Proof: Suppose $(w*, \alpha*, \beta*)$ and $(w*, \xi*, \eta*)$ both satisfy the KKT conditions. Without loss of generality, assume active inequality constraints are h_j, $j = 1, ..., r$, $r \leq m$. Thus we have $h_j(w*) > 0$ for all $j = r+1, ..., m$. By the complementarity conditions, we have $\beta_j^* = \eta_j^* = 0$ for all $j = r+1, ..., m$. Then from

$$\sum_{i=1}^{k} \alpha_i^* \nabla g_i(w*) + \sum_{j=1}^{m} \beta_j^* \nabla h_j(w*) = \sum_{i=1}^{k} \xi_i^* \nabla g_i(w*) + \sum_{j=1}^{m} \eta_j^* \nabla h_j(w*),$$

we have

$$\sum_{i=1}^{k} \alpha_i^* \nabla g_i(w*) + \sum_{j=1}^{r} \beta_j^* \nabla h_j(w*) = \sum_{i=1}^{k} \xi_i^* \nabla g_i(w*) + \sum_{j=1}^{r} \eta_j^* \nabla h_j(w*),$$

or

$$\sum_{i=1}^{k} \left(\alpha_i^* - \xi_i^*\right) \nabla g_i(w*) + \sum_{j=1}^{r} \left(\beta_j^* - \eta_j^*\right) \nabla h_j(w*) = 0.$$

By LICQ, we have $\alpha_i^* = \xi_i^*$, $i \in \underline{k}$, and $\beta_j^* = \eta_j^*$, $j = 1, ..., r$. This completes the proof.

The Lagrange multiplier represents the sensitivity of the optimal value to a given constraint. See Sensitivity Theorem in Luenberger (1984). Consider the family of problems:

$$\text{minimize} \quad f(w)$$
$$\text{subject to} \quad g(w) = c, \; h(w) \geq d, \; w \in \Omega.$$

Under some mild conditions, for sufficiently small ranges of $c \in \mathfrak{R}^k$ and $d \in \mathfrak{R}^m$ near the zero vector, the problem will have a solution point $w(c, d)$ near $w(0, 0) := w*$. For each of these solutions, there is a corresponding optimal value $f(w(c, d))$, and this value can be regarded as a function of c and d, the right-hand sides of the constraints. It can be proved that

$$\left.\frac{\partial f\big(w(c,d)\big)}{\partial c}\right|_{\substack{c=0\\d=0}} = \alpha(0,0) := \alpha *, \quad \left.\frac{\partial f\big(w(c,d)\big)}{\partial d}\right|_{\substack{c=0\\d=0}} = \beta(0,0) := \beta *.$$

The **dual problem** for (P) is defined as the following maximization problem:

(D)   maximize $J_d(\alpha, \beta)$

               subject to $\beta \geq 0$,

where $J_d(\alpha, \beta) := \inf_{w \in \Omega} L(w, \alpha, \beta)$ is called the **dual function**. The value of the objective function at the optimal solution is called the **value of the problem**. The feasible region of (D) is given by

$$R_d := \big\{(\alpha, \beta) \in \Re^k \times \Re^m : \beta_j \geq 0, \ j \in \underline{m}\big\}.$$

Proposition 2.2.4: (Weak Duality Theorem)

Let $w \in R_p$ be a feasible point of the primal problem (P) and $(\alpha, \beta) \in R_d$ be a feasible point of the dual problem (D). Then we have $J_d(\alpha, \beta) \leq J_p(w) := f(w)$.

Proof: Since $g_i(w) = 0$, $i \in \underline{k}$, and $\beta_j \geq 0$, $h_j(w) \geq 0$, $j \in \underline{m}$, we have

$$J_d(\alpha, \beta) := \inf_{u \in \Omega} L(u, \alpha, \beta) \leq L(w, \alpha, \beta)$$

$$= f(w) - \sum_{i=1}^{k} \alpha_i g_i(w) - \sum_{j=1}^{m} \beta_j h_j(w) \leq f(w).$$

This completes the proof.

From the weak duality theorem, we immediately have the following corollary.

Corollary 2.2.1: The value of the dual problem (D) is bounded above by the value of the primal problem (P), i.e.,

$$\sup\{J_d(\alpha, \beta): \beta \geq 0\} \leq \inf\{J_p(w) = f(w): g(w) = 0, h(w) \geq 0\}.$$

Corollary 2.2.2: If $J_p(w*) = f(w*) = J_d(\alpha*, \beta*)$, where $w* \in R_p$ and $(\alpha*, \beta*) \in R_d$, then $w*$ and $(\alpha*, \beta*)$ solve the problems (P) and (D), respectively. In this case, we have $\beta_j^* h_j(w*) = 0$ for all $j \in \underline{m}$.

Proof: From the weak duality theorem, we have

$$J_p(w) := f(w) \geq J_d(\alpha, \beta) \text{ for any } w \in R_p \text{ and } (\alpha, \beta) \in R_d.$$

This implies that

$$\inf_{w \in R_p} f(w) \geq J_d(\alpha*, \beta*) = f(w*),$$

which shows that $w*$ solves the problem (P). By the same token, we have

$$\sup_{(\alpha, \beta) \in R_d} J_d(\alpha, \beta) \leq f(w*) = J_d(\alpha*, \beta*),$$

which shows that $(\alpha*, \beta*)$ solves the problem (D). From

$$f(w*) = J_d(\alpha*, \beta*) = \inf_{w \in \Omega} \left[f(w) - \sum_{i=1}^k \alpha_i^* g_i(w) - \sum_{j=1}^m \beta_j^* h_j(w) \right],$$

we have

$$\sum_{i=1}^k \alpha_i^* g_i(w*) + \sum_{j=1}^m \beta_j^* h_j(w*) = 0.$$

Since $w* \in R_p$ and $(\alpha*, \beta*) \in R_d$, we have

$$g_i(w*) = 0, \ i \in \underline{k}, \ \beta_j^* \geq 0, \ h_j(w*) \geq 0, \ j \in \underline{m}.$$

Hence we have $\beta_j^* h_j(w*) = 0$ for all $j \in \underline{m}$. This completes the proof.

In general, the values of the primal problem (P) and dual problem (D) may not be the same. The difference between these two values is usually called the **duality gap**.

Proposition 2.2.5: (Strong Duality Theorem)

Suppose in the primal problem (P):

(a) Ω is convex;
(b) f is convex, g_i, $i \in \underline{k}$, are affine, and h_j, $j \in \underline{m}$, are concave;
(c) There is a feasible $\overline{w}$ such that $g_i(\overline{w}) = 0$, $i \in \underline{k}$, $h_j(\overline{w}) > 0$, $j \in \underline{m}$, and 0 is an interior point of $g(\Omega) := \{g(w) : w \in \Omega\}$.

Then the duality gap is zero.

A **saddle point** of the Lagrangian for the primal problem (P) is a triple (w^*, α^*, β^*), with $w^* \in \Omega$ and $\beta^* \geq 0$, such that

$$L(w^*, \alpha, \beta) \leq L(w^*, \alpha^*, \beta^*) \leq L(w, \alpha^*, \beta^*)$$
for all $w \in \Omega$ and $\beta \geq 0$.

Note that w here is not required to satisfy the equality or inequality constraints.

Proposition 2.2.6: The triple (w^*, α^*, β^*), with $w^* \in \Omega$ and $\beta^* \geq 0$, is a saddle point of the Lagragian for the primal problem (P) if and only if

(a) w^* solves the primal problem (P);
(b) (α^*, β^*) solves the dual problem (D);
(c) There is no duality gap, i.e., $J_p(w^*) = f(w^*) = J_d(\alpha^*, \beta^*)$.

By combining Proposition 2.2.1 and Proposition 2.1.4, we immediately have the following result.

Proposition 2.2.7: Assume f is convex, g_i, $i \in \underline{k}$, are affine, and h_j, $j \in \underline{m}$, are concave. Then the problem (P) has as its solution a convex set, if a solution exists. This solution is unique if f is strictly convex.

Proposition 2.2.8: Assume that

(a) f, g_i, $i \in \underline{k}$, and h_j, $j \in \underline{m}$, are continuously differentiable;

(b) f is convex, g_i, $i \in \underline{k}$, are affine, and h_j, $j \in \underline{m}$, are concave;

(c) There is a feasible $\overline{w}$ such that $h_j(\overline{w}) > 0$ for all $j \in \underline{m}$.

If $w^* \in R_p$ is a global minimizer of the program (P), then KKT conditions are satisfied.

The condition (c) is called the **Slater's condition**.

Proposition 2.2.9: Assume that

(a) f, g_i, $i \in \underline{k}$, and h_j, $j \in \underline{m}$, are continuously differentiable;

(b) f is convex, g_i, $i \in \underline{k}$, are affine, and h_j, $j \in \underline{m}$, are concave.

If KKT conditions are satisfied for some (w^*, α^*, β^*), then w^* is a global minimizer of the program (P).

By combining the last two propositions, we have the following result.

Proposition 2.2.10: Assume that

(a) f, g_i, $i \in \underline{k}$, and h_j, $j \in \underline{m}$, are continuously differentiable;

(b) f is convex, g_i, $i \in \underline{k}$, are affine, and h_j, $j \in \underline{m}$, are concave;

(c) There is a feasible $\overline{w}$ such that $h_j(\overline{w}) > 0$ for all $j \in \underline{m}$.

Then w^* is a global minimizer of the program (P) if and only if there are vectors $\alpha^* \in \mathfrak{R}^k$ and $\beta^* \in \mathfrak{R}^m$ of Lagrange multipliers such that the KKT conditions are satisfied.

Lagrangian treatment of convex optimization problem leads an alternative dual description, which often turns out to be easier to solve than the primal problem since handling inequality constraints directly is more difficult. The following is a standard example.

Example 2.2.1: Suppose $Q = Q^T \in \Re^{n \times n}$ is a symmetric positive definite matrix, $A \in \Re^{m \times n}$, $b \in \Re^n$, and $c \in \Re^m$ are given, but $w \in \Re^n$ is unknown. Consider the following primal quadratic optimization problem:

$$\begin{aligned}
\text{minimize} \quad & 2^{-1} w^T Q w + b^T w \\
\text{subject to} \quad & Aw \leq c
\end{aligned}$$

Assume the feasible region is not empty. The Lagrangian is given by

$$L(w, \beta) := 2^{-1} w^T Q w + b^T w - \beta^T (c - Aw).$$

Now we calculate the dual function $J_d(\beta)$. Given any β, minimization of L yields

$$0 = \frac{\partial L}{\partial w} = Qw + b + A^T \beta \quad \Rightarrow \quad w = -Q^{-1}(b + A^T \beta).$$

Hence the dual function is given by

$$\begin{aligned}
J_d(\beta) &:= 2^{-1} w^T Q w + (\beta^T A + b^T) w - \beta^T c \\
&= 2^{-1} [Q^{-1}(b + A^T \beta)]^T Q [Q^{-1}(b + A^T \beta)] - (\beta^T A + b^T) Q^{-1}(b + A^T \beta) - \beta^T c \\
&= 2^{-1}(b^T + \beta^T A) Q^{-1}(b + A^T \beta) - (b^T + \beta^T A) Q^{-1}(b + A^T \beta) - \beta^T c \\
&= -2^{-1}(b^T + \beta^T A) Q^{-1}(b + A^T \beta) - \beta^T c \\
&= -2^{-1} \beta^T A Q^{-1} A^T \beta - \beta^T (c + A Q^{-1} b) - 2^{-1} b^T Q^{-1} b \\
&:= -2^{-1} \beta^T P \beta - \beta^T d - 2^{-1} b^T Q^{-1} b,
\end{aligned}$$

where $P := A Q^{-1} A^T$ and $d := c + A Q^{-1} b$. Thus the dual problem becomes:

$$\begin{aligned}
\text{maximize} \quad & -2^{-1} \beta^T P \beta - \beta^T d - 2^{-1} b^T Q^{-1} b \\
\text{subject to} \quad & \beta \geq 0
\end{aligned}$$

Thus the dual of the primal quadratic program is another quadratic program but with simpler constraints.

2.3 Illustrative Examples

In this section, we provide some numerical examples to illustrate the use of the results of preceding sections. See Nocedal and Wright (2006).

Example 2.3.1: Solve the following optimization problem:

$$\text{minimize} \quad 2x_1 + 3x_2$$
$$\text{subject to} \quad x_1^2 + x_2^2 \leq 4, \quad x_2 \geq 0.$$

Solution: Since the feasible set is compact and the objective function is continuous, a global minimum exists by Weierstrass Theorem. The Lagrangian is given by

$$L = 2x_1 + 3x_2 - \beta_1\left(4 - x_1^2 - x_2^2\right) - \beta_2 x_2.$$

The KKT conditions are given by

$$0 = \partial L/\partial x_1 = 2 + 2\beta_1 x_1, \quad 0 = \partial L/\partial x_2 = 3 + 2\beta_1 x_2 - \beta_2,$$
$$x_1^2 + x_2^2 \leq 4, \quad x_2 \geq 0,$$
$$\beta_1 \geq 0, \quad \beta_2 \geq 0,$$
$$\beta_1\left(4 - x_1^2 - x_2^2\right) = 0, \quad \beta_2 x_2 = 0.$$

The case $\beta_1 = 0$ is impossible. Hence we have $\beta_1 > 0$, $x_1 < 0$, and $x_1^2 + x_2^2 = 4$. The case $\beta_2 = 0$ is also impossible, since the second equation cannot be satisfied. Hence we have $\beta_2 > 0$ and $x_2 = 0$. This implies that $x_1 = -2$, $\beta_1 = 1/2$, and $\beta_2 = 3$. At $(-2, 0)$, since $\nabla \phi_1^T = \begin{bmatrix} -2x_1 & -2x_2 \end{bmatrix} = \begin{bmatrix} 4 & 0 \end{bmatrix}$ and $\nabla \phi_2^T = \begin{bmatrix} 0 & 1 \end{bmatrix}$ are linearly independent, LICQ holds. Thus $(-2, 0)$ is the global minimizer. The result is consistent with Proposition 2.2.10.

Example 2.3.2: Solve the following optimization problem:

$$\text{minimize} \quad -\left(x_1 - 2\right)^2 + 3x_2^2$$
$$\text{subject to} \quad x_1^2 + x_2^2 \geq 4$$

Solution: Since $x_1^2 + x_2^2 \geq 4$, we have $\nabla \phi^T = [2x_1 \quad 2x_2] \neq 0$, implying that LICQ holds everywhere. The Lagrangian is given by

$$L = -(x_1 - 2)^2 + 3x_2^2 - \beta(x_1^2 + x_2^2 - 4).$$

The KKT conditions are given by

$$0 = \partial L / \partial x_1 = -2(x_1 - 2) - 2\beta x_1,$$
$$0 = \partial L / \partial x_2 = 6x_2 - 2\beta x_2 = 2x_2(3 - \beta),$$
$$x_1^2 + x_2^2 \geq 4, \quad \beta \geq 0, \quad \beta(x_1^2 + x_2^2 - 4) = 0.$$

If $\beta = 0$, then $x_1 = 2$ and $x_2 = 0$. If $\beta = 3$, then $x_1^2 + x_2^2 = 4$, $x_1 = 1/2$, $x_2 = \pm\sqrt{15}/2$. If $\beta > 0$ but $\beta \neq 3$, then $x_2 = 0$, $x_1^2 + x_2^2 = 4$, $x_1 = \pm 2$. When $x_1 = 2$ and $x_2 = 0$, we have $\beta = 0$. When $x_1 = -2$ and $x_2 = 0$, we have $\beta = -2$, a contradiction. However, none of these critical points are global minimizers. Indeed, there is no global minimizer, since $f(x_1, 0) \to -\infty$ as $x_1 \to \infty$.

Example 2.3.3: Solve the following optimization problem:

$$\begin{aligned} \text{minimize} \quad & 2x^2 + 3y^2 \\ \text{subject to} \quad & (x - 1)^3 = y^2 \end{aligned}$$

Solution: Since $(x - 1)^3 = y^2 \geq 0$, we have $x \geq 1$. Moreover, $x = 1$ if and only if $y = 0$. It is clear that $(1, 0)$ is the global minimizer. Note, however, that at this point, we have

$$\nabla \phi^T = [3(x - 1)^2 \quad -2y]_{x=1, y=0} = 0,$$

implying that LICQ is not satisfied. The Lagrangian is given by

$$L = 2x^2 + 3y^2 - \alpha[(x - 1)^3 - y^2].$$

The KKT conditions are given by

$$0 = \partial L / \partial x = 4x - 3\alpha(x - 1)^2,$$

$$0 = \partial L / \partial y = 6y + 2\alpha y, \quad (x-1)^3 = y^2$$
$$\Rightarrow \quad y(3+\alpha) = 0$$
$$\Rightarrow \quad y = 0 \quad \text{or} \quad \alpha = -3.$$

If $y = 0$, then $x = 1$, but the first equation cannot be satisfied. If $\alpha = -3$, then we have $9x^2 - 14x + 9 = 0$, which has no real solution. Thus, there is no critical point of L. Of course, the unique global minimizer does not appear as part of any critical points of the Lagrangian.

2.4 Exercises

Solve the following nonlinear programming problems.

Exercise 2.4.1:

$$\begin{aligned} &\text{minimize} && 2x_1 + 3x_2 \\ &\text{subject to} && x_1^2 + x_2^2 = 4 \end{aligned}$$

Exercise 2.4.2:

$$\begin{aligned} &\text{minimize} && \left(x_1 - \frac{3}{2}\right)^2 + \left(x_2 - \frac{1}{2}\right)^4 \\ &\text{subject to} && 1 - x_1 - x_2 \geq 0, \quad 1 - x_1 + x_2 \geq 0, \\ & && 1 + x_1 - x_2 \geq 0, \quad 1 + x_1 + x_2 \geq 0. \end{aligned}$$

Exercise 2.4.3:

$$\begin{aligned} &\text{maximize} && x_1 x_2 \\ &\text{subject to} && x_1^2 + x_2^2 \leq 4 \end{aligned}$$

The following exercise shows that the first-order KKT conditions are not sufficient to guarantee the existence of a local optimum, even though the constraint qualification holds everywhere.

Exercise 2.4.4:

$$\text{minimize} \quad -x^3$$

subject to $\qquad x \geq 0$

The following exercise shows that the critical points of the Lagrangian may not be the global optima simply because the global optimum does not exist, even though the constraint qualification holds everywhere.

Exercise 2.4.5:

$$\text{maximize} \qquad 2x + 3y$$
$$\text{subject to} \qquad xy \geq 6$$

The following exercise shows that for a local optimum, if the constraint qualification is violated, then there may not exist appropriate multipliers such that KKT conditions hold, i.e., this local optimum need not appear as part of any critical points of the Lagrangian.

Exercise 2.4.6:

$$\text{maximize} \qquad 3x^3 - 5x^2$$
$$\text{subject to} \qquad (2 - x)^3 = y^2$$

The following exercise shows that if the constraint qualification holds everywhere, but the Lagrangian has no critical point, then the problem has no optimum.

Exercise 2.4.7:

$$\text{minimize} \qquad x^2 - y^2$$
$$\text{subject to} \qquad x + y = 2$$

The following exercise shows that if the finite global optimum is guaranteed to exist and LICQ holds at critical points of the Lagrangian, then the global optimum can be found by comparing the objective values for critical points of the Lagrangian.

Exercise 2.4.8:

$$\text{minimize} \qquad x^2 - y^2$$

$$\text{subject to} \qquad x^2 + y^2 = 4$$

2.5 Notes and References

The materials on finite-dimensional optimization provided in this chapter are quite standard, and can be found in any optimization textbook. The classical result of Weierstrass Theorem can be found in Apostol (1974) and Sundaram (1996). The materials on convex sets and convex functions were quoted from Aubin (1977), Kantorovich and Akilov (1982), Taylor and Mann (1983), Luenberger (1984), Nocedal and Wright (2006), and Cristianini and Shawe-Taylor (2000). The materials on nonlinear programming were quoted from Nocedal and Wright (2006), Sundaram (1996), and Bazaraa, Sherali, and Shetty (1993). Example 2.1.2 was taken from Sundaram (1996). Exercise 2.4.2 was taken from Nocedal and Wright (2006). Other good references on optimization theory are Fletcher (1987), Bertsekas (1999), Boyd and Vandenberghe (2004), Brinkhuis and Tikhomirov (2005), Ruszczynski (2006), and Bonnans etc. (2006).

Apostol, T.M. (1974). Mathematical Analysis. Addison-Wesley, Massachusetts.

Aubin, J.P. (1977). Applied Abstract Analysis. Wiley, New York.

Bazaraa, M., D. Sherali, and C. Shetty (1993). Nonlinear Programming: Theory and Algorithm. Second Edition. Wiley, New York.

Bertsekas, D.P. (1999). Nonlinear Programming. Second Edition. Athena Scientific, Massachusetts.

Bonnans, J. F., J. C. Gilbert, C. Lemarechal, and C. A. Sagastizabal (2006). Numerical Optimization. Second Edition. Springer, Berlin.

Boyd, S. and L. Vandenberghe (2004). Convex Optimization. Cambridge University Press, Cambridge, United Kingdom.

Brinkhuis, J. and V. Tikhomirov (2005). Optimization: Insights and Applications. Princeton University Press, Princeton, New Jersey.

Cristianini, N. and J. Shawe-Taylor (2000). An Introduction to Support Vector Machines. Cambridge University Press, Cambridge, United Kingdom.

Fletcher, R. (1987). Practical Methods of Optimization. Second Edition. Wiley, Chichester, United Kingdom.

Kantorovich, L.V. and G.P. Akilov (1982). Functional Analysis. Pergamon, Oxford, United Kingdom.

Luenberger, D.G. (1984). Introduction to Linear and Nonlinear Programming.   Second Edition. Addison-Wesley, Massachusetts.

Nocedal, J. and S.J. Wright (2006). Numerical Optimization. Second Edition. Springer, New York.

Ruszczynski, A. (2006). Nonlinear Optimization. Princeton University Press, Princeton, New Jersey.

Sundaram, R.K. (1996). A First Course in Optimization Theory. Cambridge University Press, Cambridge, United Kingdom.

Taylor, A.E. and W. Mann (1983). Advanced Calculus. John Wiley and Sons, New York.

Chapter 3　Linear Classification

In this chapter, we will discuss the linear classification problems. We start with a simple binary classification algorithm, i.e., the nearest mean classifier, which contains many important features of the algorithms developed later on. The concept of hyperplanes and linear classification problems are briefly touched. A linear classifier can be represented as a single-layer neural network with a hard limiting output activation function. Then, the Rosenblatt's Perceptron Algorithms, in both primal form and dual form, for linearly separable training data sets will be provided. This is the first model of learning machine (perceptron) for classification, which is the true beginning of the mathematical analysis of learning processes. Three natural strategies dealing with linearly inseparable data sets will be proposed. In particular, the dual form of the Rosenblatt's Perceptron Algorithm provides us a hint to construct kernel-based nonlinear classifiers. Large margin for a linear classification provides the maximum robustness against perturbation. The maximal margin classifiers for linearly separable training set are then introduced. To deal with the linearly inseparable data, we will introduce slack variables for classification problems. Based on the concepts of large margin and slack variables for classification, soft margin classifiers (or linear support vector classifiers) are studied in detail.

3.1 Nearest Mean Classifier

Let $X \subseteq \Re^n$ and $Y := \{1, -1\}$. Suppose we are given a non-trivial training set

$$S := \left\{ \left(x_q, d_q \right) \right\}_{q=1}^{\gamma} \subseteq X \times Y.$$

At the very beginning for the introduction of linear classification, we introduce a binary classification algorithm, i.e., the nearest mean classifier, that is one of the simplest possible. The basic idea of the algorithm is to assign a previously unseen pattern to the class with closer mean. First, compute the means of the two classes. Define

$$I_S^+ := \left\{ q \in \underline{l} : d_q = 1 \right\}, \quad I_S^- := \left\{ j \in \underline{l} : d_j = -1 \right\},$$

$$c_+ := \frac{1}{m_+} \sum_{q \in I_S^+} x_q, \quad c_- := \frac{1}{m_-} \sum_{j \in I_S^-} x_j,$$

where m_+ and m_- are the number of examples with positive and negative labels, respectively. We assign a new point $x \in X$ to the class whose mean is closest. See Figure 3.1.1 for illustration.

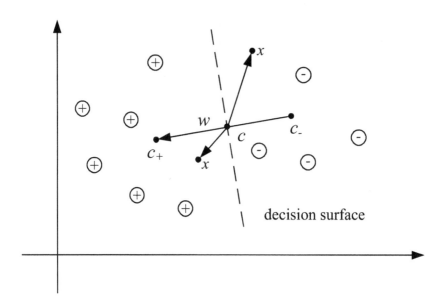

Figure 3.1.1: Nearest mean classification.

Now, we have

$$\begin{aligned}
\|x - c_-\|^2 - \|x - c_+\|^2 &= \langle x - c_-, x - c_- \rangle - \langle x - c_+, x - c_+ \rangle \\
&= [\langle x, x \rangle - 2\langle x, c_- \rangle + \langle c_-, c_- \rangle] - [\langle x, x \rangle - 2\langle x, c_+ \rangle + \langle c_+, c_+ \rangle] \\
&= 2\langle x, c_+ \rangle - 2\langle x, c_- \rangle + \|c_-\|^2 - \|c_+\|^2 \\
&= 2[\langle x, c_+ - c_- \rangle + 2^{-1}(\|c_-\|^2 - \|c_+\|^2)].
\end{aligned}$$

Define

$$w := c_+ - c_-, \quad c := \frac{1}{2}(c_+ + c_-), \quad b := \frac{1}{2}(\|c_-\|^2 - \|c_+\|^2).$$

Then, the decision function is given by

$$g(x) = \text{sgn}\left[\langle x, c_+ - c_- \rangle + 2^{-1}\left(\|c_-\|^2 - \|c_+\|^2\right)\right] = \text{sgn}\left[\langle w, x \rangle + b\right],$$
$$x \in X.$$

Hence, the discriminant function is given by

$$f(x) := \langle w, x \rangle + b$$

and the decision boundary or decision surface is given by

$$0 = f(x) = \langle w, x \rangle + b,$$

which is a hyperplane in $\Re^n$ with normal vector w and bias b. Since $f(c) = 0$, the decision boundary is the bisector of the line segment joining the two means. Points to the right and to the left of the decision boundary belong to different classes.

Same conclusion can also be reached in another way. We compute the class of x by checking whether the vector $x - c$ encloses an angle smaller than $\pi/2$ in magnitude with the vector w. Thus, the decision function is given by

$$\begin{aligned}
g(x) &:= \text{sgn}\left[\langle x - c, w \rangle\right] = \text{sgn}\left[\langle x, w \rangle - \langle c, w \rangle\right] \\
&= \text{sgn}\left[\langle x, w \rangle - 2^{-1}\langle c_+ + c_-, c_+ - c_- \rangle\right] \\
&= \text{sgn}\left[\langle w, x \rangle + 2^{-1}\left(\|c_-\|^2 - \|c_+\|^2\right)\right] = \text{sgn}\left[\langle w, x \rangle + b\right].
\end{aligned}$$

It is instructive to rewrite the decision function in terms of the input patterns, namely,

$$g(x) = \text{sgn}\left[\frac{1}{m_+}\sum_{q \in I_S^+}\langle x, x_q \rangle - \frac{1}{m_-}\sum_{q \in I_S^-}\langle x, x_q \rangle + b\right],$$

where

$$b = 2^{-1}\left[\frac{1}{m_-^2}\sum_{q,j \in I_S^-}\langle x_q, x_j \rangle - \frac{1}{m_+^2}\sum_{q,j \in I_S^+}\langle x_q, x_j \rangle\right].$$

Note that the training data enter the algorithm only through the entries of the Grammian matrix $G := \left(\langle x_q, x_j \rangle \right) \in \mathfrak{R}^{l \times l}$. Moreover, the decision rule can be evaluated using just inner products between the test point x and the training points x_q's, i.e., $\langle x, x_q \rangle$. These facts will be the key of the kernel-based approach to the design of nonlinear learning machines.

3.2 Hyperplane

Since the linear classification problems always involve the hyperplanes, we will study some fundamental properties of the hyperplanes on a finite-dimensional space in this section.

A hyperplane $H_{w,b}$ in $\mathfrak{R}^n$ can be written as

$$w_1 x_1 + w_2 x_2 + ... + w_n x_n + b = \langle w, x \rangle + b = 0,$$
$$x_i, w_i, b \in \mathfrak{R}, \quad x := [x_1 \quad \cdots \quad x_n]^T, \quad w := [w_1 \quad \cdots \quad w_n]^T \in \mathfrak{R}^n.$$

Usually, w is called the weight vector and b is called the bias. Define

$$f_{w,b}(x) := w_1 x_1 + w_2 x_2 + ... + w_n x_n + b = \langle w, x \rangle + b, \quad x \in \mathfrak{R}^n.$$

Then, we have

$$H_{w,b} = \left\{ x \in \mathfrak{R}^n : f_{w,b}(x) := \langle w, x \rangle + b = 0 \right\}.$$

Note that w is a normal vector perpendicular to $H_{w,b}$, while varying the value of b moves the hyperplane parallel to itself. The hyperplane thus defined is an affine subspace (linear manifold) of dimension $n-1$. It divides $\mathfrak{R}^n$ into two half spaces. For simplicity, sometimes we use (w, b) to represent the hyperplane $H_{w,b}$. If we define

$$g_{w,b}(x) := \|w\|^{-1} f_{w,b}(x), \quad x \in \mathfrak{R}^n,$$

then the same hyperplane can also be represented as

$$H_{w,b} = \left\{ x \in \Re^n : g_{w,b}(x) := \left\langle \|w\|^{-1}w, x \right\rangle + \|w\|^{-1}b = 0 \right\}.$$

Let p be any given point of $H_{w,b}$, i.e., $p \in H_{w,b}$. Then, for any $x \in H_{w,b}$, we have

$$\langle w, x - p \rangle = 0 \quad \text{or} \quad \langle w, x \rangle - \langle w, p \rangle = 0.$$

Thus, we have $b = -\langle w, p \rangle$ for any given $p \in H_{w,b}$.

Suppose we are given a hyperplane $H_{w,b}$ and a $y \in \Re^n$. We wish to calculate the distance $d(y, H_{w,b})$ of y to $H_{w,b}$. Let p be any given point of $H_{w,b}$, i.e., $p \in H_{w,b}$. Then, the orthogonal projection of $y - p$ onto the subspace spanned by w is given by

$$\left\langle \frac{w}{\|w\|}, y - p \right\rangle \frac{w}{\|w\|}.$$

This implies that

$$d(y, H_{w,b}) = \left\| \left\langle \frac{w}{\|w\|}, y - p \right\rangle \frac{w}{\|w\|} \right\| = \left| \left\langle \|w\|^{-1}w, y - p \right\rangle \right|$$

$$= \|w\|^{-1} \left| \langle w, y \rangle - \langle w, p \rangle \right| = \|w\|^{-1} \left| \langle w, y \rangle + b \right|$$

$$= \left| \left\langle \|w\|^{-1}w, y \right\rangle + \|w\|^{-1}b \right| = \left| g_{w,b}(y) \right|.$$

Therefore, if $f_{w,b}(y) > 0$, i.e., $g_{w,b}(y) > 0$, then $d(y, H_{w,b}) = g_{w,b}(y)$; if $f_{w,b}(y) < 0$, i.e., $g_{w,b}(y) < 0$ and $d(y, H_{w,b}) = -g_{w,b}(y)$.

3.3 Linear Classifier

Let $X \subseteq \Re^n$ and $Y := \{1, -1\}$. Suppose we are given the training set

$$S := \left\{ \left(x_q, d_q \right) \right\}_{q=1}^{N} \subseteq X \times Y .$$

The training set S is said to be **linearly separable** if there is a hyperplane that correctly classifies the training data. It is said to be **trivial** if all the training examples belong to the same class.

For a given hyperplane $H_{w,b}$, recall

$$f_{w,b}(x) := \langle w, x \rangle + b , \quad g_{w,b}(x) := \left\langle \| w \|^{-1} w, x \right\rangle + \| w \|^{-1} b , \quad x \in \Re^n .$$

By convention, we assign $y_q = +1$ if $f_{w,b}(x_q) > 0$, or equivalently, $g_{w,b}(x_q) > 0$; $y_q = -1$ if $f_{w,b}(x_q) < 0$, or equivalently, $g_{w,b}(x_q) < 0$; $y_q = +1$ if $f_{w,b}(x_q) = 0$, or equivalently, $g_{w,b}(x_q) = 0$.

For any **discriminant function** of the classification problem, it is desirable that similar patterns are mapped to similar classes. This is satisfied if we use $f_{w,b}$ stated above, since, by Cauchy-Schwarz inequality, we have

$$\left| f_{w,b}(x_q) - f_{w,b}(x_j) \right| = \left| \left\langle w, x_q - x_j \right\rangle \right| \le \| w \| \cdot \| x_q - x_j \| ;$$

that is, whenever two data points are close (small $\| x_q - x_j \|$), their difference in the real-valued output of a hypothesis is also small. See Herbrich (2002).

The following definitions are quoted from Cristianini and Shawe-Taylor (2000). The **functional margin** $\mu_q(w, b)$ and **geometric margin** $\eta_q(w, b)$ of an example (x_q, d_q), $q \in \underline{l}$, with respect to the hyperplane $H_{w,b}$ are defined by, respectively,

$$\mu_q(w, b) := d_q \cdot \left[\left\langle w, x_q \right\rangle + b \right] = d_q \cdot f_{w,b}(x_q),$$
$$\eta_q(w, b) := d_q \cdot \left[\left\langle \| w \|^{-1} w, x_q \right\rangle + \| w \|^{-1} b \right] = d_q \cdot g_{w,b}(x_q).$$

Obviously, we have $\eta_q(w, b) = \|w\|^{-1}\mu_q(w, b)$, $q \in \underline{l}$. Note that $\mu_q > 0$ (or $\eta_q > 0$) implies correct classification of the example (x_q, d_q) by the hyperplane $H_{w,b}$. Thus, for a general case μ_q (or η_q) may be negative. The **functional margin** $\mu_S(w, b)$ and **geometric margin** $\eta_S(w, b)$ of a hyperplane $H_{w,b}$ with respect to the training set S are defined by, respectively,

$$\mu_S(w, b) := \min_{q=1}^{l} \mu_q(w, b), \quad \eta_S(w, b) := \min_{q=1}^{l} \eta_q(w, b),$$

where $\mu_q(w, b)$ and $\eta_q(w, b)$, $q \in \underline{l}$, are the functional margin and geometric margin of the example (x_q, d_q) with respect to the hyperplane $H_{w,b}$, respectively. Note that when $\|w\| = 1$, the functional margin and the geometric margin are the same. The **margin** γ_S of a training set S is defined to be the maximum geometric margin over all hyperplanes, i.e.,

$$\gamma_S := \max_{w,b} \min_{q=1}^{l} \left[d_q \cdot g_{w,b}(x_q) \right] = \max_{w,b} \min_{q=1}^{l} \left[d_q \cdot \left(\langle \|w\|^{-1} w, x_q \rangle + \|w\|^{-1} b \right) \right].$$

A hyperplane realizing this maximum is called a **maximal margin hyperplane** or **optimal hyperplane**. The margin of a linearly separable training set is positive. See Figure 3.3.1 for illustration. It is clear that points distant from the maximal margin hyperplane can have larger perturbations without destroying the correct classification of the data. It is termed as the robustness of the maximal margin hyperplanes.

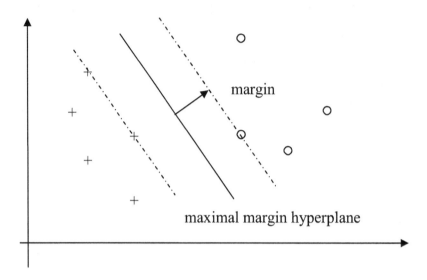

Figure 3.3.1: Robustness property of maximal margin hyperplane.

Proposition 3.3.1: The training set S is linearly separable if and only if there exist a vector $w* \in \mathfrak{R}^n$, $\|w*\| = 1$, a number $b* \in \mathfrak{R}$, and a positive number $\gamma > 0$ such that

$$d_q \cdot \left[\langle w*, x_q \rangle + b*\right] \geq \gamma > 0 \quad \text{for all} \quad q \in \underline{l}.$$

In this case, we have $\gamma_S \geq \eta_S(w*, b*) \geq \gamma > 0$, i.e., the margin of the training set S is at least γ. If, in addition, there is some $j \in \underline{l}$ such that $d_j \cdot \left[\langle w*, x_j \rangle + b*\right] = \gamma$, then the geometric margin of the hyperplane $H_{w*, b*}$ with respect to the training set S is γ.

Proof: ($\Leftarrow$) By hypothesis, we have

$$\eta_q(w*, b*) := d_q \cdot \left[\langle w*, x_q \rangle + b*\right] \geq \gamma > 0 \quad \text{for all} \quad q \in \underline{l}.$$

Thus, the hyperplane $H_{w*, b*}$ correctly classifies the training data, i.e., the training set S is linearly separable.

($\Rightarrow$) Suppose that the training set S is linearly separable. By definition, there is a hyperplane $H_{w,b}$ that correctly classifies the training data. Thus, we have

$$\mu_q := d_q \cdot \left[\left\langle w, x_q \right\rangle + b\right] > 0 \quad \text{for all} \quad q \in \underline{l},$$

or

$$\eta_q := d_q \cdot \left[\left\langle \|w\|^{-1} w, x_q \right\rangle + \|w\|^{-1} b\right] > 0 \quad \text{for all} \quad q \in \underline{l}.$$

Set

$$w^* := \|w\|^{-1} w, \quad b^* := \|w\|^{-1} b, \quad \gamma := \min_{q=1}^{l} \eta_q$$

$$\Rightarrow \quad d_q \cdot \left[\left\langle w^*, x_q \right\rangle + b^*\right] \geq \gamma > 0 \quad \text{for all} \quad q \in \underline{l}.$$

The last two statements are obvious. This completes the proof.

Suppose the nontrivial training set S is linearly separable. Then, there exist a vector $w^* \in \Re^n$, $\|w^*\| = 1$, a number $b^* \in \Re$, and a positive number $\gamma > 0$ such that

$$d_q \cdot \left[\left\langle w^*, x_q \right\rangle + b^*\right] \geq \gamma > 0 \quad \text{for all} \quad q \in \underline{l}.$$

Define

$$U := \max_{q=1}^{l} \|x_q\|.$$

We now show that $|b^*| \leq U$.

If $d_q = 1$, then we have

$$\left\langle w^*, x_q \right\rangle + b^* > 0, \quad b^* > -\left\langle w^*, x_q \right\rangle \geq -\|w^*\| \cdot \|x_q\| = -\|x_q\|.$$

If $d_j = -1$, then we have

$$\left\langle w^*, x_j \right\rangle + b^* < 0, \quad b^* < -\left\langle w^*, x_j \right\rangle = \left\langle -w^*, x_j \right\rangle \leq \|w^*\| \cdot \|x_j\| = \|x_j\|.$$

Define

$$I_S^+ := \{q \in \underline{l} : d_q = 1\}, \quad I_S^- := \{j \in \underline{l} : d_j = -1\}.$$

From the preceding analysis, we have

$$-\left\|x_q\right\| < b^* < \left\|x_j\right\|, \quad q \in I_S^+, \quad j \in I_S^-$$

$$\Rightarrow \quad -U := -\max_{q=1}^{l}\left\|x_q\right\| \le -\min_{q \in I_S^+}\left\|x_q\right\| < b^* < \min_{j \in I_S^-}\left\|x_j\right\| \le \max_{j=1}^{l}\left\|x_j\right\| := U.$$

This proves that $\left|b*\right| \le U$.

The perceptron, i.e., the decision function for the classification problem, can be represented as a single-layer neural network as shown in Figure 3.3.2.

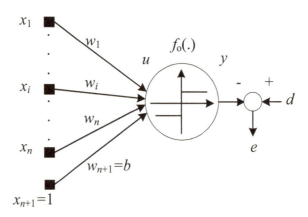

Figure 3.3.2: Single-layer neural network representation of a perceptron.

In this network, x is the input of the network, d is the desired output of the network, u is the input of the neuron, y is the output of the neuron, $f_o(\cdot)$ is the activation function of the neuron defined as the sign function (also called the hard limiting function), and e is the error (or residual). Define

$$z := \begin{bmatrix} x \\ 1 \end{bmatrix} \in \mathfrak{R}^{n+1}, \quad x_{n+1} = 1, \quad \beta := \begin{bmatrix} w \\ b \end{bmatrix} \in \mathfrak{R}^{n+1}, \quad w_{n+1} = b.$$

From the network, we have

$$u = w_1 x_1 + \ldots + w_n x_n + b = \langle w, x \rangle + b = \langle \beta, z \rangle,$$
$$y = f_o(u) = \text{sgn}(u),$$
$$e = d - y.$$

3.4 Rosenblatt's Perceptron Algorithms

In this section, we present the Rosenblatt's Perceptron Algorithms in both primal form and dual form. The perceptron is the first model of learning machine for classification, which is the true beginning of the mathematical analysis of learning processes.   First, we provide the primal form of the Rosenblatt's Perceptron Algorithm.

Algorithm 3.4.1: (primal form)

Data: training set $S := \{(x_q, d_q)\}_{q=1}^{l} \subseteq X \times Y$ and a learning rate $\eta > 0$

Goal: (w, b) defining a linear discriminant function that correctly classifies the training set

Step 1: $w \leftarrow 0; \ b \leftarrow 0; \ k \leftarrow 0;$

Step 2:   Choose $R \geq U := \max_{q=1}^{l} \|x_q\|;$

Step 3:   repeat
$\qquad$ for $q = 1$ to l
$\qquad\qquad$ if $d_q \cdot [\langle w, x_q \rangle + b] \leq 0$, then
$\qquad\qquad\qquad$ $w \leftarrow w + \eta d_q x_q; \ \ b \leftarrow b + \eta d_q R^2; \ \ k \leftarrow k+1;$
$\qquad\qquad$ end if
$\qquad$ end for
$\qquad$ until no misclassification within the *for* loop
$\qquad$ return $k, \ (w, b)$, where k is the number of mistakes during
training

In the preceding algorithm, assuming that the mistake occurred at the qth training example, after updating we can only change the value of the discriminant function $f(x)$ by $\eta d_q \langle x_q, x \rangle + \eta d_q R^2$, which requires just one evaluation of f with all training examples. Thus, we have the following alternative learning algorithm.

Algorithm 3.4.2: (primal form)

Data: training set $S := \left\{ \left(x_q, d_q \right) \right\}_{q=1}^{l} \subseteq X \times Y$ and a learning rate $\eta > 0$

Goal: (w, b) defining a linear discriminant function that correctly classifies the training set

Step 1: $w \leftarrow 0$; $b \leftarrow 0$; $y_q \leftarrow 0$ for all $q \in \underline{l}$.

Step 2:   Choose $R \geq U := \max_{q=1}^{l} \left\| x_q \right\|$;

Step 3:   repeat
        for $q = 1$ to l
           if $d_q \cdot y_q \leq 0$ then
               $w \leftarrow w + \eta d_q x_q$; $b \leftarrow b + \eta d_q R^2$; $k \leftarrow k + 1$;
               for $j = 1$ to l
                    $y_j \leftarrow y_j + \eta d_q \left\langle x_q, x_j \right\rangle + \eta d_q R^2$;
               end for
           end if
        end for
        until no misclassification within the *for* loop
        return k, (w, b), where k is the number of mistakes during
training

Note also that the algorithms presented above are mistake-driven procedures. Though the algorithms start at $w = 0$, it is not necessary to do so. Moreover, the perceptron algorithms may give different solutions depending on the order in which the training examples are processed. In case where the training set is not linearly separable, the algorithms will not converge. The following theorem due to Novikoff was the first (convergence) theorem about the perceptrons and was one of the first theoretical justifications of the idea that large margins yield better classifiers in terms of the number of mistakes during learning.

Proposition 3.4.1: (**Novikoff's Theorem**)

Suppose S is a nontrivial training set and there exist a vector $w* \in \mathfrak{R}^n$, $\|w*\| = 1$, a number $b* \in \mathfrak{R}$, and a positive number $\gamma > 0$ such that

$$d_q \cdot \left[\langle w*, x_q \rangle + b* \right] \geq \gamma > 0 \quad \text{for all} \quad q \in \underline{l}.$$

Then, the number of mistakes made by the on-line perceptron algorithm on the training set S is at most $(2R/\gamma)^2$.

Proof: For simplicity of analysis, we set the following augmented vectors

$$z_q := \begin{bmatrix} x_q \\ R \end{bmatrix} \in \mathfrak{R}^{n+1}, \quad \beta_j := \begin{bmatrix} w_j \\ R^{-1}b_j \end{bmatrix} \in \mathfrak{R}^{n+1}, \quad \beta* := \begin{bmatrix} w* \\ R^{-1}b* \end{bmatrix}.$$

Note that $\beta_0 = 0$ and it is updated at each mistake. Let β_{j-1} be the augmented vector prior to the jth mistake. Then we have

$$d_q \cdot \left[\langle w_{j-1}, x_q \rangle + b_{j-1} \right] \leq 0, \quad w_j = w_{j-1} + \eta d_q x_q, \quad b_j = b_{j-1} + \eta d_q R^2.$$

In terms of the augmented vectors, we have

$$d_q \cdot \left[\langle \beta_{j-1}, z_q \rangle \right] = d_q \cdot \left[\langle w_{j-1}, x_q \rangle + b_{j-1} \right] \leq 0,$$

$$\beta_j := \begin{bmatrix} w_j \\ R^{-1}b_j \end{bmatrix} = \begin{bmatrix} w_{j-1} + \eta d_q x_q \\ R^{-1}(b_{j-1} + \eta d_q R^2) \end{bmatrix}$$

$$= \begin{bmatrix} w_{j-1} \\ R^{-1}b_{j-1} \end{bmatrix} + \eta d_q \begin{bmatrix} x_i \\ R \end{bmatrix} = \beta_{j-1} + \eta d_q z_q.$$

Moreover, the hypothesis gives, for all $q \in \underline{l}$,

$$d_q \cdot \left[\langle z_q, \beta* \rangle \right] = d_q \cdot \left[\langle w*, x_q \rangle + b* \right] \geq \gamma > 0.$$

Now, we have

$$\langle \beta_j, \beta* \rangle = \langle \beta_{j-1} + \eta d_q z_q, \beta* \rangle = \langle \beta_{j-1}, \beta* \rangle + \eta d_q \langle z_q, \beta* \rangle$$
$$\geq \langle \beta_{j-1}, \beta* \rangle + \eta \gamma .$$

By induction, we have

$$\langle \beta_j, \beta* \rangle \geq \langle \beta_{j-1}, \beta* \rangle + \eta \gamma \geq \langle \beta_{j-2}, \beta* \rangle + 2\eta \gamma$$
$$\geq ... \geq \langle \beta_0, \beta* \rangle + j\eta\gamma = j\eta\gamma .$$

We also have

$$\|\beta_j\|^2 = \langle \beta_j, \beta_j \rangle = \langle \beta_{j-1} + \eta d_q z_q, \beta_{j-1} + \eta d_q z_q \rangle$$
$$= \langle \beta_{j-1}, \beta_{j-1} \rangle + 2\eta d_q \langle \beta_{j-1}, z_q \rangle + \eta^2 d_q^2 \langle z_q, z_q \rangle$$
$$\leq \|\beta_{j-1}\|^2 + \eta^2 \|z_q\|^2 = \|\beta_{j-1}\|^2 + \eta^2 \left(\|x_q\|^2 + R^2 \right)$$
$$\leq \|\beta_{j-1}\|^2 + \eta^2 \left(R^2 + R^2 \right)$$
$$= \|\beta_{j-1}\|^2 + 2\eta^2 R^2 .$$

By induction, we have

$$\|\beta_j\|^2 \leq \|\beta_{j-1}\|^2 + 2\eta^2 R^2 \leq \|\beta_{j-2}\|^2 + 2 \cdot \left(2\eta^2 R^2 \right)$$
$$\leq ... \leq \|\beta_0\|^2 + j \cdot \left(2\eta^2 R^2 \right) = 2j\eta^2 R^2$$

$$\Rightarrow \quad \|\beta_j\| \leq \sqrt{2j}\eta R .$$

Combining the above inequalities, we have

$$j\eta\gamma \leq \langle \beta_j, \beta* \rangle \leq \|\beta_j\| \cdot \|\beta*\| \leq \sqrt{2j}\eta R \left[\|w*\|^2 + (b*/R)^2 \right]^{1/2}$$
$$\leq \sqrt{2j}\eta R (1+1)^{1/2} = \sqrt{j} 2\eta R$$

$$\Rightarrow \quad \sqrt{j} \leq \gamma^{-1} 2R , \quad j \leq (2R/\gamma)^2 .$$

This completes the proof.

For a linearly separable training set, the Novikoff's Theorem proves that the perceptron algorithm converges in a finite number of iterations. It is interesting to note that the estimate of the number of mistakes provided by the Novikoff's Theorem is independent of the learning rate. Furthermore, any positive scaling of the training examples will not affect the number of iterations taken by the perceptron algorithm. It will not change the estimate of the number of mistakes provided by the Novikoff's Theorem. Indeed, suppose $z_q := \alpha x_q$, where $\alpha > 0$, then

$$d_q \cdot \left[\langle w^*, x_q \rangle + b^* \right] \geq \gamma > 0 \quad \text{for all} \quad q \in \underline{l},$$
$$\Rightarrow \quad d_q \cdot \left[\langle w^*, \alpha x_q \rangle + \alpha b^* \right] \geq \alpha \gamma > 0 \quad \text{for all} \quad q \in \underline{l}.$$

Moreover, we have

$$\max_{q=1}^{l} \left\| \alpha x_q \right\| = \alpha \cdot \max_{q=1}^{l} \left\| x_q \right\| = \alpha \cdot R.$$

Hence, we have

$$\left(\frac{2\alpha R}{\alpha \gamma} \right)^2 = \left(\frac{2R}{\gamma} \right)^2.$$

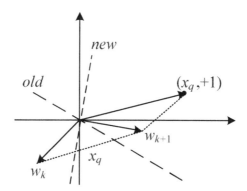

Figure 3.4.1: Geometric interpretation of the perceptron algorithms.

The geometric interpretation of the Rosenblatt's algorithms can be seen from Figure 3.4.1. Notice that the normal vector w points in the region with positive function values. In Figure 3.4.1, x_q of positive class is misclassified by the current linear classifier having normal vector w_k. The updating law moves w_k into $w_{k+1} = w_k + \eta d_q x_q$. This means that $d_q x_q$ "attracts" the old hyperplane. After this updating step, the misclassified point x_q is correctly classified by the new hyperplane. Geometrically, the perceptron algorithm performs a walk through the primal parameter space with each step made in the direction of decreasing training error. See Herbrich (2000).

In the primal form of Algorithm 3.4.1, starting from $w_0 = 0$, the final weight is of the form

$$w = \sum_{q=1}^{l} \eta \alpha_q d_q x_q,$$

and α_q, $q \in l$, is the number of mistakes when using (x_q, d_q) as training example. Then, we have

$$f_{w,b}(x) := \langle w, x \rangle + b = \left\langle \sum_{j=1}^{l} \eta \alpha_j d_j x_j, x \right\rangle + b = \sum_{j=1}^{l} \eta \alpha_j d_j \langle x_j, x \rangle + b,$$

$$\mu_q := d_q \cdot f_{w,b}(x_q) = d_q \cdot \left[\langle w, x_q \rangle + b \right] = d_q \cdot \left[\sum_{j=1}^{l} \eta \alpha_j d_j \langle x_j, x_q \rangle + b \right].$$

This means that the decision rule can be evaluated using just inner products between the test point x and the training points x_j's, i.e., $\langle x, x_j \rangle$. This motivates the dual form of the Rosenblatt's Perceptron Algorithm.

Algorithm 3.4.3: (dual form)

Data: training set $S := \{(x_q, d_q)\}_{q=1}^{l} \subseteq X \times Y$ and a learning rate $\eta > 0$

Goal: (α, b) defining a linear discriminant function that correctly classifies the training set

Step 1: $\alpha \leftarrow 0$; $b \leftarrow 0$;

Step 2:   Choose $R \geq U := \max\limits_{q=1}^{l} \|x_q\|$;

Step 3:   repeat

         for $q = 1$ to l

$$\text{if } d_q \cdot \left[\sum_{j=1}^{l} \eta \alpha_j d_j \langle x_j, x_q \rangle + b\right] \leq 0 \text{ then}$$

$$\alpha_q \leftarrow \alpha_q + 1; \quad b \leftarrow b + \eta d_q R^2;$$

         end if

        end for

       until no misclassification within the *for* loop

       return (α, b)

Note that the training data only enter the algorithm through the entries of the Grammian matrix $G := \left[\langle x_q, x_j \rangle\right] \in \mathfrak{R}^{l \times l}$. In the preceding algorithm, the integer

$$\|\alpha\|_1 := \alpha_1 + \alpha_2 + \ldots + \alpha_l$$

is equal to the number of mistakes. By Novikoff's Theorem, we have $\|\alpha\|_1 \leq (2R/\gamma)^2$.

In the dual form of Algorithm 3.4.3, assuming that the mistake occurred at the qth training example, we only increase the α_q by 1 and bias b by $\eta d_q R^2$ with other α_j, $j \neq q$, unaffected. This can only change the value of the discriminant function $f(x)$ by $\eta y_q \langle x_q, x \rangle + \eta d_q R^2$, which requires just one evaluation of f with all training examples. Thus, we have the following alternative learning algorithm.

Algorithm 3.4.4: (dual form)

Data: training set $S := \left\{(x_q, d_q)\right\}_{q=1}^{l} \subseteq X \times Y$ and a learning rate $\eta > 0$

Goal: (α, b) defining a linear discriminant function that correctly classifies the training set

Step 1: $\alpha \leftarrow 0$; $b \leftarrow 0$; $y_q \leftarrow 0$ for all $q \in \underline{l}$.

Step 2:   Choose $R \geq U := \max\limits_{q=1}^{l} \|x_q\|$;

Step 3:   repeat
    for $q = 1$ to l
      if $d_q \cdot y_q \leq 0$ then
        $\alpha_q \leftarrow \alpha_q + 1$; $b \leftarrow b + \eta d_q R^2$;
        for $j = 1$ to l
          $y_j \leftarrow y_j + \eta d_q \langle x_q, x_j \rangle + \eta d_q R^2$;
        end for
      end if
    end for
    until no misclassification within the *for* loop
    return (α, b)

3.5 Rosenblatt's Algorithms for Nonlinear Classifier

Let $X \subseteq \mathfrak{R}^n$ and $Y := \{1, -1\}$. Suppose we are given a non-trivial training set

$$S := \left\{ \left(x_q, d_q \right) \right\}_{q=1}^{l} \subseteq X \times Y.$$

What if the training examples are not linearly separable in the input space $\mathfrak{R}^n$? There are three natural strategies:

(a) The first strategy is to nonlinearly transform the data to another space. If the transformed data is linearly separable in the new space, called the feature space, then we may apply the techniques for linearly separable data. This results in a linear classifier in the new space but a nonlinear classifier in the original space. See Figure 3.5.1 for illustration.

(b) In the second strategy, we still perform linear classification in the original space but we allow some misclassifications of the original data. This results in a linear classifier in the original space. The rationale behind this approach is that some data may be noisy and are outliers of the training data set. Correct classification or interpolation of all training data may not be so meaningful. The second strategy will be discussed after we introduce the slack variables.

(c) The third strategy is to combine the previous two. First, nonlinearly transform the data to another feature space. Then, perform the linear classification but allow some misclassifications of the transformed data. This results in a linear classifier in the new space but a nonlinear classifier in the original space. The third strategy will be discussed when we discuss the nonlinear classifiers.

In this section, we consider the first strategy.

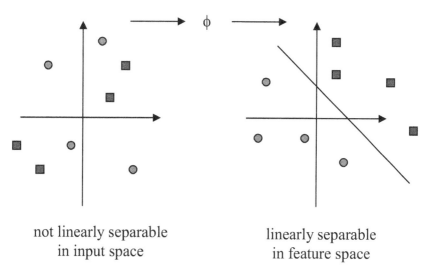

not linearly separable
in input space

linearly separable
in feature space

Figure 3.5.1: Nonlinear transformation of data.

Example 3.5.1: (NXOR problem)

Suppose the training examples are given by Table 3.5.1.

Table 3.5.1: Original training examples.

pattern	label
$(x_1 \quad x_2)$	d
$(0 \quad 0)$	1
$(0 \quad 1)$	-1
$(1 \quad 0)$	-1
$(1 \quad 1)$	1

Clearly, the training data set is not linearly separable in the input space $\Re^2$. Suppose we define a nonlinear map $\phi : \Re^2 \to \Re^3$ as

$$\phi(x_1, x_2) := \begin{bmatrix} \phi_1(x_1, x_2) \\ \phi_2(x_1, x_2) \\ \phi_3(x_1, x_2) \end{bmatrix} := \begin{bmatrix} x_1 \\ x_2 \\ |x_1 - x_2| \end{bmatrix}.$$

Then, the training examples are transformed into $\Re^3$ as shown in Table 3.5.2.

Table 3.5.2: Transformed training examples.

transformed pattern	label
$(\phi_1 \quad \phi_2 \quad \phi_3)$	d
$(0 \quad 0 \quad 0)$	1
$(0 \quad 1 \quad 1)$	-1
$(1 \quad 0 \quad 1)$	-1
$(1 \quad 1 \quad 0)$	1

Obviously, the transformed examples are linearly separable in $\Re^3$. There are infinitely many suitable discriminant functions defining separating hyperplanes in $\Re^3$, which are of the form

$$f(x) = w_1 \phi_1(x) + w_2 \phi_2(x) + w_3 \phi_3(x) + b$$
$$= w_1 x_1 + w_2 x_2 + w_3 |x_1 - x_2| + b.$$

Each is a nonlinear discriminant function in the original input space $\mathfrak{R}^2$ and can be represented as a two-layer neural network as shown in Figure 3.5.2.

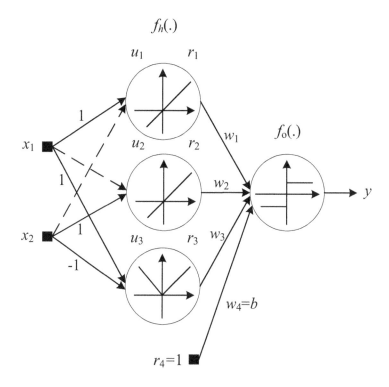

Figure 3.5.2: Two-layer neural network.

For instance, we may take

$$f(x) = -x_1 - x_2 - 3\left|x_1 - x_2\right| + 2.5.$$

The contour plot and the decision boundary are shown in Figure 3.5.3.

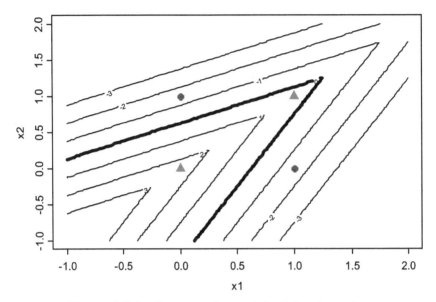

Figure 3.5.3: Contour plot and decision boundary.

The approach used above is interesting for two reasons. First, by transforming nonlinearly the linearly inseparable training examples to a feature space, the transformed training examples becomes linearly separable in the feature space and the final discriminant function is a nonlinear function in the original input space. Second, instead of the original single-layer neural network, we now have a two-layer neural network with a hidden layer. One of the activation functions of the hidden neuron is nonlinear.

The whole idea of the preceding example is best seen from the dual representation of the discriminant function. Before doing this, let us have the following important definition of a kernel.

Definition 3.5.1: Let $(F, \langle .,. \rangle)$, called the **feature space**, be a real inner product space and $X \subseteq \Re^n$. A **kernel** is a real-valued function on $X \times X$ such that

$$K(x, z) := \langle \phi(x), \phi(z) \rangle, \quad x, z \in X,$$

where ϕ, called the **feature map**, is a mapping from X to F.

Very often, it is more practical and easier to define the kernel function directly, serving as a similarity measure between objects, and then specify the corresponding feature map if necessary. In most applications of the kernel methods, the feature map is not needed for obtaining the final solution. Some popular kernels are, for $x, z \in \Re^n$,

polynomial kernel:
$$K(x, z) := (\langle x, z \rangle + c)^d = (x^T z + c)^d, \quad c \geq 0, \quad d \geq 2;$$

Gaussian kernel:
$$K(x, z) := \exp(-\sigma^{-2}\|x - z\|^2);$$

Mahalanobis kernel:
$$K(x, z) := \exp\left[-\sigma_1^{-2}(x_1 - z_1)^2 - \ldots - \sigma_n^{-2}(x_n - z_n)^2\right].$$

In the dual form of the Rosenblatt algorithms for the linear classifier, the training data only enters the algorithms through the inner product $\langle x_j, x_q \rangle$ and the final discriminant function depends only upon the inner product $\langle x_j, x \rangle$. This motivates us to consider the mapping of x in input space into $\phi(x)$ in feature space. Thus, we have

$$\langle \phi(x_j), \phi(x_q) \rangle = K(x_j, x_q) \quad \text{and} \quad \langle \phi(x_j), \phi(x) \rangle = K(x_j, x).$$

Moreover, since

$$\|\phi(x_q)\|^2 = \langle \phi(x_q), \phi(x_q) \rangle = K(x_q, x_q),$$

we may choose

$$R \geq U := \max_{q=1}^{l} \sqrt{K(x_q, x_q)}.$$

Hence, the nonlinear discriminant function becomes

$$f_{w,b}(x) = \sum_{j=1}^{l} \eta \alpha_j d_j \langle \phi(x_j), \phi(x) \rangle + b = \sum_{j=1}^{l} \eta \alpha_j d_j K(x_j, x) + b,$$

and the functional margin of qth example becomes

$$\mu_q := d_q \cdot f_{w,b}(x_q) = d_q \cdot \left[\sum_{j=1}^{l} \eta \alpha_j d_j \langle \phi(x_j), \phi(x_q) \rangle + b \right]$$

$$= d_q \cdot \left[\sum_{j=1}^{l} \eta \alpha_j d_j K(x_j, x_q) + b \right].$$

We have the following algorithm.

Algorithm 3.5.1

Data: training set $S := \{(x_q, d_q)\}_{q=1}^{l} \subseteq X \times Y$ and a learning rate $\eta > 0$

Goal: (α, b) defining a nonlinear discriminant function that correctly classifies the training set

Step 1: $\alpha \leftarrow 0; \ b \leftarrow 0;$

Step 2:   Choose $R \geq U := \max_{q=1}^{l} \sqrt{K(x_q, x_q)};$

Step 3:   repeat
      for $q = 1$ to l

$$\text{if } d_q \cdot \left[\sum_{j=1}^{l} \eta \alpha_j d_j K(x_j, x_q) + b \right] \leq 0 \text{ then}$$

$$\alpha_q \leftarrow \alpha_q + 1;$$
$$b \leftarrow b + \eta d_q R^2;$$

      end if
      end for
      until no misclassification within the *for* loop
      return (α, b)

In the preceding algorithm, assuming that the mistake occurred at the qth training example, we only increase the α_q by 1 and bias b by $\eta d_q R^2$ with other α_j, $j \neq q$, unaffected. This can only change the value of the discriminant function $f(x)$ by $\eta d_q K(x_q, x) + \eta d_q R^2$, which requires just one evaluation of f with all training examples. Thus, we have the following alternative learning algorithm.

Algorithm 3.5.2

Data: training set $S := \{(x_q, d_q)\}_{q=1}^{l} \subseteq X \times Y$ and a learning rate $\eta > 0$

Goal: (α, b) defining a nonlinear discriminant function that correctly classifies the training set

Step 1: $\alpha \leftarrow 0$; $b \leftarrow 0$; $y_q \leftarrow 0$ for all $q \in \underline{l}$.

Step 2: Choose $R \geq U := \max_{q=1}^{l} \sqrt{K(x_q, x_q)}$;

Step 3: repeat
  for $q = 1$ to l
    if $d_q \cdot y_q \leq 0$ then
      $\alpha_q \leftarrow \alpha_q + 1$;
      $b \leftarrow b + \eta d_q R^2$;
      for $j = 1$ to l
        $y_j \leftarrow y_j + \eta d_q K(x_q, x_j) + \eta d_q R^2$;
      end for
    end if
  end for
  until no misclassification within the *for* loop
  return (α, b)

Example 3.5.2: (Example 3.5.1 continued)

We now apply the kernel method to Example 3.5.1. Figures 3.5.4 shows the contour plots and the decision boundaries by using polynomial kernels given by

$$K(x, z) = (x_1 z_1 + x_2 z_2 + c)^2.$$

The readers are encouraged to write down the corresponding discriminant function for each case.

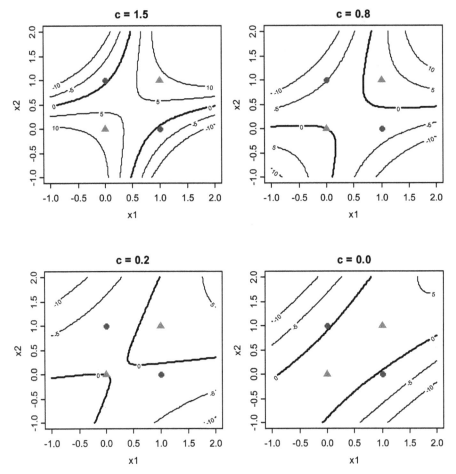

Figure 3.5.4: Contour plots and decision boundaries by using polynomial kernels.

3.6 Maximal Margin Classifier

In this section, we study the maximal margin classifiers.   Let $X \subseteq \mathfrak{R}^n$ and $Y := \{1, -1\}$.   Suppose we are given a non-trivial training set

$$S := \left\{ \left(x_q, d_q \right) \right\}_{q=1}^{l} \subseteq X \times Y.$$

Define

$$I_S^+ := \left\{ q \in \underline{l} : d_q = 1 \right\}, \quad I_S^- := \left\{ j \in \underline{l} : d_j = -1 \right\}.$$

Proposition 3.6.1: Assume the margin of a linearly separable training set S is $\gamma_S > 0$. Then there exist $w* \in \mathfrak{R}^n$, $\|w*\| = 1$, and $b* \in \mathfrak{R}$, realizing the maximal margin hyperplane, such that

$$d_q \cdot \left[\left\langle w*, x_q \right\rangle + b*\right] \geq \gamma_S > 0 \quad \text{for all} \quad q \in \underline{l},$$

$$\left\langle w*, x_{j*} \right\rangle + b* = \gamma_S \quad \text{for some} \quad j* \in I_S^+,$$

$$\left\langle w*, x_{k*} \right\rangle + b* = -\gamma_S \quad \text{for some} \quad k* \in I_S^-.$$

Proof: Without loss of generality, assume $\left\langle w*, x_{j*} \right\rangle + b* = \gamma_S$ for some $j* \in I_S^+$ but $\left\langle w*, x_k \right\rangle + b* \leq -\gamma < -\gamma_S$ for all $k \in I_S^-$, where $\gamma > \gamma_S$. Let $k* \in I_S^-$ such that $\left\langle w*, x_{k*} \right\rangle + b* = -\gamma$. Define

$$\gamma_m := 2^{-1}(\gamma_S + \gamma), \quad \Delta\gamma := \gamma_m - \gamma_S > 0, \quad \tilde{b} := b* + \Delta\gamma.$$

Then, for all $j \in I_S^+$ and $k \in I_S^-$, we have

$$\left\langle w*, x_j \right\rangle + \tilde{b} = \left\langle w*, x_j \right\rangle + b* + \Delta\gamma \geq \gamma_S + \Delta\gamma = \gamma_m,$$

$$\left\langle w*, x_k \right\rangle + \tilde{b} = \left\langle w*, x_k \right\rangle + b* + \Delta\gamma \leq -\gamma + \Delta\gamma = -\gamma_m,$$

and

$$\left\langle w*, x_{j*} \right\rangle + \tilde{b} = \left\langle w*, x_{j*} \right\rangle + b* + \Delta\gamma = \gamma_S + \Delta\gamma = \gamma_m,$$

$$\left\langle w*, x_{k*} \right\rangle + \tilde{b} = \left\langle w*, x_{k*} \right\rangle + b* + \Delta\gamma = -\gamma + \Delta\gamma = -\gamma_m.$$

We thus have obtained a bigger geometric margin $\gamma_m > \gamma_S$, which is a contradiction. This completes the proof.

Suppose there exist $w* \in \mathfrak{R}^n$, $\|w*\| = 1$, $b* \in \mathfrak{R}$, and $\gamma > 0$ such that

$$d_q \cdot \left[\left\langle w*, x_q \right\rangle + b*\right] \geq \gamma > 0 \quad \text{for all} \quad q \in \underline{l},$$

$$d_j \cdot \left[\left\langle w*, x_j \right\rangle + b*\right] = \gamma \quad \text{for some} \quad j \in \underline{l}.$$

Then, the geometric margin of the hyperplane $H_{w*, b*}$ with respect to the training set S is γ. Define $w_0 := \gamma^{-1} w*$ and $b_0 := \gamma^{-1} b*$, then we have

$$d_q \cdot \left[\langle w_0, x_q \rangle + b_0 \right] \geq 1 \quad \text{for all} \quad q \in \underline{l},$$
$$d_j \cdot \left[\langle w_0, x_j \rangle + b_0 \right] = 1 \quad \text{for some} \quad j \in \underline{l}.$$

Now, the functional margin of the hyperplane H_{w_0, b_0} $(= H_{w*, b*})$, with respect to the training set S becomes 1. In this case, H_{w_0, b_0} is called a **canonical hyperplane**.

It is important to note that $\gamma := \|w_0\|^{-1} = \left[\sqrt{\langle w_0, w_0 \rangle} \right]^{-1}$. Hence, for a given non-trivial linearly separable training set S, maximization of the margin of S is equivalent to minimizing the Euclidean norms of the weight vectors w_0 of canonical hyperplanes H_{w_0, b_0}. Thus, consider the following **primal** optimization problem:

(P0) minimize $\dfrac{1}{2} w^T w$

  subject to $d_q \cdot \left[\langle w, x_q \rangle + b \right] \geq 1 \quad \text{for all} \quad q \in \underline{l}.$

The problem (P0) is a standard quadratic convex program. Suppose $(w*, b*)$ solves the (primal) optimization problem (P0). Then, the maximal margin hyperplane is given by $f*(x) = \langle w*, x \rangle + b* = 0$ with margin $\gamma_S = \|w*\|^{-1}$.

Now, we consider its dual problem. The Lagrangian is given by

$$L(w, b, \alpha) := 2^{-1} w^T w - \sum_{q=1}^{l} \alpha_q \left(d_q w^T x_q + d_q b - 1 \right),$$

where $\alpha := [\alpha_1 \quad \cdots \quad \alpha_l]^T \in \mathfrak{R}^l$ is the vector of Lagrange multipliers. The dual function is defined by

$$J_d(\alpha) := \min_{w,b} L(w, b, \alpha).$$

Clearly, we have

$$0 = \frac{\partial L}{\partial w} = w - \sum_{q=1}^{l} \alpha_q d_q x_q, \quad 0 = \frac{\partial L}{\partial b} = -\sum_{q=1}^{l} \alpha_q d_q$$

$$\Rightarrow \quad w = \sum_{q=1}^{l} \alpha_q d_q x_q, \quad \sum_{q=1}^{l} \alpha_q d_q = 0$$

$$\Rightarrow \quad 2^{-1} w^T w = 2^{-1} \left[\sum_{q=1}^{l} \alpha_q d_q x_q^T \right] \cdot \left[\sum_{j=1}^{l} \alpha_j d_j x_j \right]$$

$$= 2^{-1} \sum_{q=1}^{l} \sum_{j=1}^{l} \alpha_q \alpha_j d_q d_j x_q^T x_j \, ,$$

$$-\sum_{q=1}^{l} \alpha_q d_q w^T x_q = -\sum_{q=1}^{l} \alpha_q d_q \left[\sum_{j=1}^{l} \alpha_j d_j x_j^T \right] x_q$$

$$= -\sum_{q=1}^{l} \sum_{j=1}^{l} \alpha_q \alpha_j d_q d_j x_q^T x_j \, ,$$

$$-\sum_{q=1}^{l} \alpha_q d_q b = -b \sum_{q=1}^{l} \alpha_q d_q = 0$$

$$\Rightarrow \quad J_d(\alpha) := \min_{w,b} L(w, b, \alpha) = \sum_{q=1}^{l} \alpha_q - 2^{-1} \sum_{q=1}^{l} \sum_{j=1}^{l} \alpha_q \alpha_j d_q d_j x_q^T x_j \, .$$

Thus, the **dual** problem can be stated as follows:

(D0)   maximize $$\sum_{q=1}^{l} \alpha_q - \frac{1}{2} \sum_{q=1}^{l} \sum_{j=1}^{l} \alpha_q \alpha_j d_q d_j \langle x_q, x_j \rangle$$

subject to $$\sum_{q=1}^{l} \alpha_q d_q = 0 \quad \text{and} \quad \alpha_q \geq 0 \quad \text{for all} \quad q \in \underline{l}.$$

The problem (D0) is a standard quadratic concave program. Note that the dual problem is cast entirely in terms of the training data. Moreover, the objective functional to be maximized depends only on the input patterns in the form of a set of inner products, $\langle x_q, x_j \rangle$, $q, j \in \underline{l}$.

Moreover, the relation $w* = \sum_{q=1}^{l} \alpha_q^* d_q x_q$ shows that the hypothesis can be described as a linear combination of the training points. The application of optimization theory naturally leads to the dual representation; compare this with the dual form of the Rosenblatt's perceptron algorithm.

Suppose $\alpha*$ solves the (dual) optimization problem (D0). Then, we have $w* = \sum_{q=1}^{l} \alpha_q^* d_q x_q$ and the margin is given by $\gamma_S = \|w*\|^{-1}$. The KKT conditions of our optimization problem are given by, for all $q \in \underline{l}$,

$$\alpha_q^* \Big[d_q \langle w*, x_q \rangle + d_q b * - 1 \Big] = 0, \quad d_q \Big[\langle w*, x_q \rangle + b * \Big] - 1 \geq 0, \quad \alpha_q^* \geq 0.$$

Define $I_{sv} := \{ q \in \underline{l} : \alpha_q^* > 0 \}$. Then, we have

$$w* = \sum_{q=1}^{l} \alpha_q^* d_q x_q = \sum_{q \in I_{sv}} \alpha_q^* d_q x_q .$$

Let $k \in I_{sv}$, then $\alpha_k^* > 0$. From the KKT conditions, we have

$$d_k \Big[\langle w*, x_k \rangle + b * \Big] = 1.$$

Since $d_k = \pm 1$, we have $d_k^2 = 1$, and hence

$$\langle w*, x_k \rangle + b* = d_k .$$

This implies that

$$b* = d_k - \langle w*, x_k \rangle = d_k - \left(\sum_{q \in I_{sv}} \alpha_q^* d_q x_q, x_k \right) = d_k - \sum_{q \in I_{sv}} \alpha_q^* d_q \langle x_q, x_k \rangle .$$

The optimal discriminant function is thus given by

$$f*(x) = \langle w*, x \rangle + b* = \sum_{q \in I_{sv}} \alpha_q^* d_q \langle x_q, x \rangle + b*.$$

Obviously, the Lagrange multiplier associated with each point quantifies how important a given training data point (x_q, d_q) is in forming the final solution. Points that have zero α_q^* have no influence. For any $q \in I_{sv}$, we have $\alpha_q^* > 0$. From the KKT conditions, we have

$$d_q [\langle w*, x_q \rangle + b*] = 1.$$

This implies that the functional margin of (x_q, d_q) with respect to the maximal margin hyperplane is one and therefore lies closest to the maximal margin hyperplane.

A pattern x_q, with $q \in I_{sv}$ and $d_q = 1$, is called a **positive support vector**. Similarly, a pattern x_q, with $q \in I_{sv}$ and $d_q = -1$, is called a **negative support vector**. The positive and negative support vectors are guaranteed to exist by Proposition 3.6.1. In conceptual terms, the support vectors are those data points that lie closest to the decision surface and are therefore the most difficult to classify.

The fact that only a subset of the Lagrange multipliers is nonzero is referred to as **sparseness**, and means that the support vectors contain all the information necessary to reconstruct the optimal hyperplane.

Note that in general we have

$$I_{sv} := \{q \in \underline{l} : \alpha_q^* > 0\} \subseteq \{q \in \underline{l} : d_q [\langle w*, x_q \rangle + b*] = 1\}.$$

For any $q \in I_{sv}$, we have $d_q [\langle w*, x_q \rangle + b*] = 1$, i.e.,

$$d_q \left[\left\langle \sum_{j \in I_{sv}} \alpha_j^* d_j x_j, x_q \right\rangle + b* \right] = 1 \text{ or } d_q \sum_{j \in I_{sv}} \alpha_j^* d_j \langle x_j, x_q \rangle = 1 - d_q b*$$

$$\Rightarrow \quad \|w*\|^2 = \langle w*, w* \rangle = \left\langle \sum_{q \in I_{sv}} \alpha_q^* d_q x_q, \sum_{j \in I_{sv}} \alpha_j^* d_j x_j \right\rangle$$

$$= \sum_{q,j \in I_{sv}} \alpha_q^* \alpha_j^* d_q d_j \langle x_q, x_j \rangle$$

$$= \sum_{q \in I_{sv}} \alpha_q^* d_q \sum_{j \in I_{sv}} \alpha_j^* d_j \langle x_q, x_j \rangle = \sum_{q \in I_{sv}} \alpha_q^* (1 - d_q b*)$$

$$= \sum_{q \in I_{sv}} \alpha_q^* - b* \sum_{q \in I_{sv}} \alpha_q^* d_q = \sum_{q \in I_{sv}} \alpha_q^* + 0$$

$$= \sum_{q \in I_{sv}} \alpha_q^* .$$

Thus, the margin is given by

$$\gamma_S = \|w*\|^{-1} = \left(\sum_{q \in I_{sv}} \alpha_q^* \right)^{-1/2} .$$

Moreover, from the above derivation, we have

$$\sum_{q,j \in I_{sv}} \alpha_q^* \alpha_j^* d_q d_j \langle x_q, x_j \rangle = \|w*\|^2 = \sum_{q \in I_{sv}} \alpha_q^* .$$

This implies that value of the problem (D0) is given by

$$J_d(\alpha*) = \sum_{q=1}^{l} \alpha_q^* - \frac{1}{2} \sum_{q=1}^{l} \sum_{j=1}^{l} \alpha_q^* \alpha_j^* d_q d_j \langle x_q, x_j \rangle$$

$$= \sum_{q \in I_{sv}} \alpha_q^* - \frac{1}{2} \sum_{q,j \in I_{sv}} \alpha_q^* \alpha_j^* d_q d_j \langle x_q, x_j \rangle$$

$$= \frac{1}{2} \sum_{q \in I_{sv}} \alpha_q^* .$$

Now, we discuss a stopping criterion, based on KKT conditions, for any algorithm of finding the maximal margin classifier.

If $\alpha_q^* = 0$, then we have

$$d_q [\langle w*, x_q \rangle + b*] \geq 1 \quad \Rightarrow \quad d_q f * (x_q) \geq 1.$$

If $\alpha_q^* > 0$, then we have

$$d_q[\langle w^*, x_q \rangle + b^*] = 1 \;\Rightarrow\; d_q f^*(x_q) = 1.$$

Suppose α_q, $q \in \underline{l}$, is the current value of the dual variable. The current primal variables and discriminant function can thus be calculated. Then, reasonable KKT stopping conditions are given by

$$\begin{aligned}
&\alpha_q \geq 0, \;\; q \in \underline{l}, \\
&d_q f(x_q) \geq 1 \;\; \text{if} \;\; \alpha_q = 0, \\
&d_q f(x_q) = 1 \;\; \text{if} \;\; \alpha_q > 0.
\end{aligned}$$

We may define p_q, $q \in \underline{l}$, to be the measure of dissatisfaction of the KKT stopping conditions for the qth example as

$$\begin{aligned}
&p_q := \max[0, 1 - d_q f(x_q)] \;\; \text{if} \;\; \alpha_q = 0, \\
&p_q := |d_q f(x_q) - 1| \;\; \text{if} \;\; \alpha_q > 0.
\end{aligned}$$

Then, reasonable stopping criteria based on KKT stopping conditions are

$$p_{ave} := \frac{1}{l} \sum_{q=1}^{l} p_q \leq \delta \;\; \text{or} \;\; \|p\|_\infty := \max_{q \in \underline{l}} \{p_q\} \leq \delta,$$

where δ is a pre-specified tolerance.

Let α_q, $q \in \underline{l}$, be the current value of the dual variable. Then, the current primal variables, i.e., current weight and bias, are calculated as

$$w = \sum_{q=1}^{l} \alpha_q d_q x_q, \;\; b = d_k - \langle w, x_k \rangle = d_k - \sum_{q=1}^{l} \alpha_q d_q \langle x_q, x_k \rangle,$$

for any $\alpha_k > 0$. There is no guarantee that these primal variables are feasible, i.e.,

$$d_q \cdot \left[\langle w, x_q \rangle + b \right] = d_q \cdot \left[\sum_{j=1}^{l} \alpha_j d_j \langle x_j, x_q \rangle + b \right] \geq 1 \quad \text{for all} \quad q \in \underline{l}.$$

Hence, it may not always be possible to use the feasibility gap or the percentage duality gap as an indicator of the stopping criterion.

3.7 Slack Variable for Classification

In this section, we introduce the slack variables for classification problems. This will be useful when we consider the soft margin classifiers in later sections.

Let $\gamma > 0$ be given. The **(margin) slack variable** ξ_q of an example (x_q, d_q) with respect to the hyperplane $H_{w,b}$ and target margin γ is defined by

$$\xi_q := \max\left(0, \gamma - d_q \cdot \left[\langle w, x_q \rangle + b \right] \right).$$

From the definition, we have

$$\xi_q \geq 0 \quad \text{and} \quad \xi_q + d_q \cdot \left[\langle w, x_q \rangle + b \right] \geq \gamma .$$

See Figure 3.7.1 for illustration. Clearly, ξ_q measures the amount by which the example (x_q, d_q) fails to have margin γ with respect to the hyperplane $H_{w,b}$.

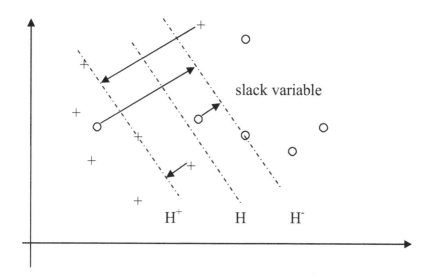

Figure 3.7.1: Slack variables for classification problems.

For simple geometric interpolation, we assume that $\|w\| = 1$. Let H^+ (resp., H^-) be the hyperplane in the positive (resp., negative) region parallel to H and γ distance apart. Thus, we have

$$H^+ := \{x \in \Re^n : \langle w, x \rangle + b - \gamma = 0\},$$
$$H^- := \{x \in \Re^n : \langle w, x \rangle + b + \gamma = 0\}.$$

The open region between H^+ and H^- is called the **region of separation**. We give some deeper analysis of the slack variables.

Case 1:   Suppose $d_q \cdot \left[\langle w, x_q \rangle + b \right] \geq \gamma > 0$, then $\xi_q = 0$. In this case, (w, b) correctly classifies (x_q, d_q) and $d(x_q, H) \geq \gamma$.

Case 2:   Suppose $d_q = 1$ and $0 < d(x, H) = \langle w, x_q \rangle + b < \gamma$. In this case, (w, b) correctly classifies (x_q, d_q) and

$$0 < \xi_q = \gamma - d(x_q, H) = d(x_q, H^+) < \gamma.$$

Case 3: Suppose $d_q = -1$ and $-\gamma < -d(x, H) = \langle w, x_q \rangle + b < 0$. In this case, (w, b) correctly classifies (x_q, d_q) and

$$0 < \xi_q = \gamma - d(x_q, H) = d(x_q, H^-) < \gamma.$$

Case 4: Suppose $\langle w, x_q \rangle + b = 0$. Then $x_q \in H$ and $\xi_q = \gamma > 0$.

Case 5: Suppose $d_q = 1$ but $-d(x_q, H) = \langle w, x_q \rangle + b < 0$. In this case, (w, b) misclassifies (x_q, d_q) and

$$\xi_q = \gamma + d(x_q, H) = d(x_q, H^+) > \gamma.$$

Case 6: Suppose $d_q = -1$ but $d(x_q, H) = \langle w, x_q \rangle + b > 0$. In this case, (w, b) misclassifies (x_q, d_q) and

$$\xi_q = \gamma + d(x_q, H) = d(x_q, H^-) > \gamma.$$

From the preceding analysis, we have the following conclusion.

(a) Suppose $\xi_q = 0$. Then, (x_q, d_q) is correctly classified by (w, b) and lies outside the region of separation. See Case 1. Moreover,

(a1) if $d_q = 1$ and $\langle w, x_q \rangle + b = \gamma$, then $x_q \in H^+$;

(a2) if $d_q = -1$ and $\langle w, x_q \rangle + b = -\gamma$, then $x_q \in H^-$.

(b) Suppose $0 < \xi_q < \gamma$. Then, the data x_q falls inside the region of separation but on the right side of the decision surface. See Case 2 and Case 3.

(c) Suppose $\xi_q = \gamma$. Then, we have $x_q \in H$. See Case 4.

(d) Suppose $\xi_q > \gamma$. Then, (x_q, d_q) is misclassified by (w, b). See Case 5 and Case 6.

To put in another way, we have the following conclusion.

(i) Suppose $d_q = 1$. If $H^+ : (w, b - \gamma)$ correctly classifies (x_q, d_q), then $\xi_q = 0$; otherwise, $\xi_q = d(x_q, H^+)$.

(ii) Suppose $d_q = -1$. If $H^- : (w, b + \gamma)$ correctly classifies (x_q, d_q), then $\xi_q = 0$; otherwise, $\xi_q = d(x_q, H^-)$.

From the preceding analysis, the quantity defined by

$$\|\xi\|_1 := \sum_{q=1}^{l} \xi_q \quad \text{or} \quad \|\xi\|_2^2 := \sum_{q=1}^{l} \xi_q^2$$

measures the total amount by which the training set fails to have margin γ, and takes into account any misclassifications of the training data.

3.8 1-norm Soft Margin Classifier

Recall that the second strategy presented in Section 3.5 for linearly inseparable data sets. We perform linear classification in the original space but we allow some misclassifications of the original data. This results in a linear classifier in the original space. The rationale behind this approach is that some data may be noisy and are outliers of the training data set. Correct classification or interpolation of all training data may not be so meaningful. Based on the concepts of large margin and slack variables for classification, in this and the next sections, we present the soft margin classifiers for linearly inseparable data sets along this approach. This is compared to the hard-margin maximal margin classifiers for linearly separable data sets. First, we consider the 1-norm soft margin classifiers.

Let $X \subseteq \mathfrak{R}^n$ and $Y := \{1, -1\}$. Suppose we are given a non-trivial (possibly not linearly separable) training set

$$S := \{(x_q, d_q)\}_{q=1}^{l} \subseteq X \times Y.$$

Let $\gamma > 0$ be given. Recall that the slack variable ξ_q of an example (x_q, d_q) with respect to the hyperplane $H_{w,b}$ and target margin γ is defined by

$$\xi_q := \max\left(0, \gamma - d_q \cdot \left[\langle w, x_q \rangle + b\right]\right).$$

Hence, we have

$$\xi_q \geq 0 \quad \text{and} \quad \xi_q + d_q \cdot \left[\langle w, x_q \rangle + b\right] \geq \gamma.$$

Scaling by γ the preceding inequalities, we have

$$\gamma^{-1}\xi_q \geq 0 \quad \text{and} \quad \gamma^{-1}\xi_q + d_q \cdot \left[\langle \gamma^{-1}w, x_q \rangle + \gamma^{-1}b\right] \geq 1,$$

i.e.,

$$\gamma^{-1}\xi_q \geq 0 \quad \text{and} \quad d_q \cdot \left[\langle \gamma^{-1}w, x_q \rangle + \gamma^{-1}b\right] \geq 1 - \gamma^{-1}\xi_q.$$

Now, we use $\|\xi\|_1 := \sum_{q=1}^{l} \xi_q$ to measure the amount by which the training set fails to have margin 1, and takes into account any misclassifications of the training data.

Consider the following primal optimization problem (with $C > 0$):

(P1)   minimize $\dfrac{1}{2}w^T w + C\sum_{q=1}^{l}\xi_q$

           subject to $d_q \cdot \left[\langle w, x_q \rangle + b\right] \geq 1 - \xi_q$ and $\xi_q \geq 0$

                        for all $q \in \underline{l}$.

The problem (P1) is a standard quadratic convex program. The regularization (or smoothing) parameter $C > 0$ controls the tradeoff between complexity of the machine and the number of non-separable points. The optimization problem (P1) includes the optimization problem for linearly separable data as a special case by setting $\xi_q = 0$ for all $q \in \underline{l}$.

Suppose $(w*, b*, \xi*)$ solves the preceding primal optimization problem. Then, the decision surface or optimal hyperplane is given by $f*(x) = \langle w*, x \rangle + b* = 0$.

Recall that if $\xi_q^* = 0$, then (x_q, d_q) is correctly classified by $(w*, b*)$ and lies outside the region of separation; if $0 < \xi_q^* < 1$, then the data x_q falls inside the optimal region of separation but on the right side of the optimal decision surface; if $\xi_q^* = 1$, then x_q lies in the optimal hyperplane; and if $\xi_q^* > 1$, then (x_q, d_q) is misclassified by $(w*, b*)$. The margin of the training set is $\gamma_S = \|w*\|^{-1}$.

Now, we consider its dual problem. The Lagrangian is given by

$$L(w, b, \xi, \alpha, \mu) := 2^{-1} w^T w + C \sum_{q=1}^{l} \xi_q$$
$$- \sum_{q=1}^{l} \alpha_q \left(d_q w^T x_q + d_q b - 1 + \xi_q \right) - \sum_{q=1}^{l} \mu_q \xi_q ,$$

where $\alpha := [\alpha_1 \quad \cdots \quad \alpha_l]^T \in \Re^l$ and $\mu := [\mu_1 \quad \cdots \quad \mu_l]^T \in \Re^l$ are the vectors of Lagrange multipliers. The dual function is defined by

$$J_d(\alpha, \mu) := \min_{w, b, \xi} L(w, b, \xi, \alpha, \mu).$$

Clearly, we have

$$0 = \frac{\partial L}{\partial w} = w - \sum_{q=1}^{l} \alpha_q d_q x_q , \quad 0 = \frac{\partial L}{\partial b} = -\sum_{q=1}^{l} \alpha_q d_q ,$$

$$0 = \frac{\partial L}{\partial \xi_q} = C - \alpha_q - \mu_q , \quad q \in \underline{l}$$

$$\Rightarrow \quad w = \sum_{q=1}^{l} \alpha_q d_q x_q , \quad \sum_{q=1}^{l} \alpha_q d_q = 0 , \quad \alpha_q + \mu_q = C , \quad q \in \underline{l}$$

$$\Rightarrow \quad \frac{1}{2}w^T w = \frac{1}{2}\left[\sum_{q=1}^{l}\alpha_q d_q x_q^T\right]\cdot\left[\sum_{j=1}^{l}\alpha_j d_j x_j\right]$$

$$= \frac{1}{2}\sum_{q=1}^{l}\sum_{j=1}^{l}\alpha_q \alpha_j d_q d_j x_q^T x_j \; ,$$

$$-\sum_{q=1}^{l}\alpha_q d_q w^T x_q = -\sum_{q=1}^{l}\alpha_q d_q\left[\sum_{j=1}^{l}\alpha_j d_j x_j^T\right]x_q$$

$$= -\sum_{q=1}^{l}\sum_{j=1}^{l}\alpha_q \alpha_j d_q d_j x_q^T x_j \; ,$$

$$-\sum_{q=1}^{l}\alpha_q d_q b = -b\sum_{q=1}^{l}\alpha_q d_q = 0 \; ,$$

$$C\sum_{q=1}^{l}\xi_q - \sum_{q=1}^{l}\alpha_q \xi_q - \sum_{q=1}^{l}\mu_q \xi_q = 0$$

$$\Rightarrow \quad J_d(\alpha) = J_d(\alpha, \mu) := \min_{w,b,\xi} L(w, b, \xi, \alpha, \mu)$$

$$= \sum_{q=1}^{l}\alpha_q - \frac{1}{2}\sum_{q=1}^{l}\sum_{j=1}^{l}\alpha_q \alpha_j d_q d_j x_q^T x_j \; .$$

Since $\alpha_q \geq 0$, $\mu_q \geq 0$, and $\alpha_q + \mu_q = C$ for all $q \in l$, we have $0 \leq \alpha_q \leq C$, which is often called the **box constraints**. Hence, the dual optimization problem can be stated as follows:

(D1) maximize $\quad \sum_{q=1}^{l}\alpha_q - \frac{1}{2}\sum_{q=1}^{l}\sum_{j=1}^{l}\alpha_q \alpha_j d_q d_j \langle x_q, x_j \rangle$

subject to $\quad \sum_{q=1}^{l}\alpha_q d_q = 0$ and $0 \leq \alpha_q \leq C$ for all $q \in l$.

Note that neither the slack variables ξ_q nor their Lagrange multipliers μ_q appear in the dual problem. Because of the box constraints, the influence of the individual pattern (which could be an outlier) gets limited.

Suppose $\alpha*$ solves the dual problem (D1). Then, we have $w* = \sum_{q=1}^{l} \alpha_q^* d_q x_q$ and the margin is given by $\gamma_S = \|w*\|^{-1}$. The KKT conditions become, for all $q \in \underline{l}$,

$$\alpha_q^* \left[d_q \langle w*, x_q \rangle + d_q b* - 1 + \xi_q^* \right] = 0,$$
$$d_q \langle w*, x_q \rangle + d_q b* - 1 + \xi_q^* \geq 0,$$
$$\alpha_q^* \geq 0,$$
$$\mu_q^* \xi_q^* = 0, \quad \xi_q^* \geq 0, \quad \mu_q^* \geq 0.$$

A new set of KKT conditions is possible. From $\mu_q^* = C - \alpha_q^*$ and $\mu_q^* \xi_q^* = 0$, we have $\left(\alpha_q^* - C \right) \xi_q^* = 0$ for all $q \in \underline{l}$. Hence, the new set of KKT conditions become, for all $q \in \underline{l}$,

$$\alpha_q^* \left[d_q \langle w*, x_q \rangle + d_q b* - 1 + \xi_q^* \right] = 0,$$
$$d_q \langle w*, x_q \rangle + d_q b* - 1 + \xi_q^* \geq 0,$$
$$\left(\alpha_q^* - C \right) \xi_q^* = 0, \quad \alpha_q^* \geq 0, \quad \xi_q^* \geq 0.$$

Define $I_{sv} := \{ q \in \underline{l} : \alpha_q^* > 0 \}$. Then, we have

$$w* = \sum_{q=1}^{l} \alpha_q^* d_q x_q = \sum_{q \in I_{sv}} \alpha_q^* d_q x_q.$$

Choose any $k \in I_{sv}$ such that $0 < \alpha_k^* < C$. From the KKT conditions, we have $\xi_k^* = 0$ and

$$d_k \left[\langle w*, x_k \rangle + b* \right] = 1 - \xi_k^* = 1 - 0 = 1 \quad \text{or} \quad d_k b* = 1 - d_k \langle w*, x_k \rangle.$$

Since $d_k = \pm 1$, we have $d_k^2 = 1$, and hence

$$b* = d_k - \langle w*, x_k \rangle = d_k - \sum_{q \in I_{sv}} \alpha_q^* d_q \langle x_q, x_k \rangle.$$

The optimal discriminant function is thus given by

$$f^*(x) = \langle w^*, x \rangle + b^* = \sum_{q \in I_{sv}} \alpha_q^* d_q \langle x_q, x \rangle + b^*.$$

For any $q \in I_{sv}$, we have $\alpha_q^* > 0$. From the KKT conditions, we have

$$d_q \left[\langle w^*, x_q \rangle + b^* \right] = 1 - \xi_q^*.$$

A pattern x_q with $q \in I_{sv}$ is called a **support vector** even if $\xi_q^* > 0$.

There are several cases that deserve special consideration. First, suppose $0 < \alpha_q^* < C$, then

$$\xi_q^* = 0 \quad \text{and} \quad d_q \left[\langle w^*, x_q \rangle + b^* \right] = 1,$$

which says that the functional margin of (x_q, d_q) with respect to the decision hyperplane is one and therefore lies closest to the decision hyperplane for all those data with $0 < \alpha_q^* < C$. Next, suppose $\alpha_q^* = C$, then ξ_q^* may assume a nonzero value. Now, suppose $\alpha_q^* = C$ and $\xi_q^* = 0$, then $d_q \left[\langle w^*, x_q \rangle + b^* \right] = 1$. Finally, suppose $\alpha_q^* = C$ but $\xi_q^* > 0$, then $d_q \left[\langle w^*, x_q \rangle + b^* \right] = 1 - \xi_q^* < 1$. Note that we do not preclude the possibility of $\alpha_q^* = 0$ (implying $\xi_q^* = 0$) and $d_q \left[\langle w^*, x_q \rangle + b^* \right] = 1$.

From another viewpoint, we first suppose $\xi_q^* > 0$, then $d_q \left[\langle w^*, x_q \rangle + b^* \right] < 1$ by definition and $\alpha_q^* = C > 0$, which implies that x_q must be a support vector. Consequently, if an example with $\xi_q^* > 0$ is left out of the training set, the decision hyperplane would change. Next, suppose $\xi_q^* = 0$ but $d_q \left[\langle w^*, x_q \rangle + b^* \right] > 1$, then $\alpha_q^* = 0$, which says that x_q is not a support vector. Finally, suppose $\xi_q^* = 0$ and

$d_q \big[\langle w^*, x_q \rangle + b^* \big] = 1$, then α_q^* may assume any value in $[0, C]$, which says that x_q may or may not be a support vector.

From above, we have

$$\|w^*\|^2 = \langle w^*, w^* \rangle$$

$$= \left\langle \sum_{q \in I_{sv}} \alpha_q^* d_q x_q, \sum_{j \in I_{sv}} \alpha_j^* d_j x_j \right\rangle$$

$$= \sum_{q, j \in I_{sv}} \alpha_q^* \alpha_j^* d_q d_j \langle x_q, x_j \rangle$$

$$= 2 \sum_{q \in I_{sv}} \alpha_q^* - 2 J_d(\alpha^*).$$

Thus, the margin is given by

$$\gamma_S = \|w^*\|^{-1} = \left[\sum_{q, j \in I_{sv}} \alpha_q^* \alpha_j^* d_q d_j \langle x_q, x_j \rangle \right]^{-1/2}$$

$$= \left[2 \sum_{q \in I_{sv}} \alpha_q^* - 2 J_d(\alpha^*) \right]^{-1/2}.$$

Now, we discuss the stopping criteria for any algorithm of finding the 1-norm soft margin classifier. First, we present a stopping criterion based on the KKT conditions.

If $\alpha_q^* = 0$, then we have $\xi_q^* = 0$ and

$$d_q \big[\langle w^*, x_q \rangle + b^* \big] \geq 1 - \xi_q^* = 1 - 0 = 1 \ \Rightarrow \ d_q f^*(x_q) \geq 1.$$

If $0 < \alpha_q^* < C$, then we have $\xi_q^* = 0$ and

$$d_q \big[\langle w^*, x_q \rangle + b^* \big] = 1 - \xi_q^* = 1 - 0 = 1 \ \Rightarrow \ d_q f^*(x_q) = 1.$$

If $\alpha_q^* = C$, then we have

$$d_q \langle w*, x_q \rangle + d_q b* - 1 + \xi_q^* = 0$$
$$\Rightarrow d_q [\langle w*, x_q \rangle + b*] = 1 - \xi_q^* \leq 1$$
$$\Rightarrow d_q f*(x_q) \leq 1.$$

Suppose α_q, $q \in \underline{l}$, is the current value of the dual variable. The current primal variables and discriminant function can thus be calculated. Then, reasonable KKT stopping conditions are given by

$$0 \leq \alpha_q \leq C, \quad q \in \underline{l},$$
$$d_q f(x_q) \geq 1 \quad \text{if} \quad \alpha_q = 0,$$
$$d_q f(x_q) = 1 \quad \text{if} \quad 0 < \alpha_q < C,$$
$$d_q f(x_q) \leq 1 \quad \text{if} \quad \alpha_q = C.$$

We may define p_q, $q \in \underline{l}$, to be the measure of dissatisfaction of the KKT stopping conditions for the qth example as

$$p_q := \max[0, 1 - d_q f(x_q)] \quad \text{if} \quad \alpha_q = 0,$$
$$p_q := |d_q f(x_q) - 1| \quad \text{if} \quad 0 < \alpha_q < C,$$
$$p_q := \max[0, d_q f(x_q) - 1] \quad \text{if} \quad \alpha_q = C.$$

Then, reasonable stopping criteria based on KKT stopping conditions are

$$p_{ave} := \frac{1}{l} \sum_{q=1}^{l} p_q \leq \delta \quad \text{or} \quad \|p\|_\infty := \max_{q \in \underline{l}} \{p_q\} \leq \delta,$$

where δ is a pre-specified tolerance.

Next, we present another stopping criterion based on the feasibility gap, defined as the percentage duality gap. Let α_q, $q \in \underline{l}$, be the current value of the dual variable. The current weight, bias, and discriminant function can thus be calculated. However, note that the slack variables ξ_q are not specified when moving from the primal to the dual. We may choose the current slack variables to ensure that the primal variables are all feasible. Hence, we define the current slack variable as, $q \in \underline{l}$,

$$\xi_q := \max\left(0, 1 - d_q \cdot \left[\langle w, x_q \rangle + b\right]\right)$$

$$= \max\left(0, 1 - d_q \cdot \left[\sum_{j=1}^{l} d_j \alpha_j \langle x_j, x_q \rangle + b\right]\right)$$

$$= \max\left[0, 1 - d_q \cdot f(x_q)\right].$$

Then, we have

$$J_p(w, \xi) - J_d(\alpha)$$

$$= \frac{1}{2} \sum_{q=1}^{l} \sum_{j=1}^{l} \alpha_q \alpha_j d_q d_j x_q^T x_j + C \sum_{q=1}^{l} \xi_q - J_d(\alpha)$$

$$= -J_d(\alpha) + \sum_{q=1}^{l} \alpha_q + C \sum_{q=1}^{l} \xi_q - J_d(\alpha)$$

$$= \sum_{q=1}^{l} \alpha_q - 2J_d(\alpha) + C \sum_{q=1}^{l} \xi_q,$$

$$J_p(w, \xi) + 1 = J_d(\alpha) + \sum_{q=1}^{l} \alpha_q - 2J_d(\alpha) + C \sum_{q=1}^{l} \xi_q + 1$$

$$= \sum_{q=1}^{l} \alpha_q - J_d(\alpha) + C \sum_{q=1}^{l} \xi_q + 1.$$

A reasonable stopping criterion is given by

$$\frac{J_p - J_d}{J_p + 1} = \frac{\sum_{q=1}^{l} \alpha_q - 2J_d(\alpha) + C \sum_{q=1}^{l} \xi_q}{\sum_{q=1}^{l} \alpha_q - J_d(\alpha) + C \sum_{q=1}^{l} \xi_q + 1} \leq \delta,$$

where δ is a pre-specified tolerance.

3.9   2-norm Soft Margin Classifier

In this section, we continue the study on soft margin classifiers. Specifically, we study the 2-norm soft margin classifiers.

Let $X \subseteq \Re^n$ and $Y := \{1, -1\}$. Suppose we are given a non-trivial (possibly not linearly separable) training set

$$S := \left\{ (x_q, d_q) \right\}_{q=1}^{\gamma} \subseteq X \times Y.$$

Now, we use $\|\xi\|_2^2 := \sum_{q=1}^{l} \xi_q^2$ to measure the amount by which the training set fails to have margin 1, and takes into account any misclassifications of the training data.

Consider the following primal optimization problem (with $C > 0$):

(P20)   minimize $\dfrac{1}{2} w^T w + \dfrac{C}{2} \sum_{q=1}^{l} \xi_q^2$

subject to $d_q \cdot \left[\langle w, x_q \rangle + b \right] \geq 1 - \xi_q$

and $\xi_q \geq 0$ for all $q \in \underline{l}$.

Suppose ξ_q, $q \in \underline{l}$, in problem (P20) are unconstrained and we have, for some fixed w and b,

$$d_q \cdot \left[\langle w, x_q \rangle + b \right] \geq 1 - \xi_q, \quad \xi_q < 0, \text{ for some } q \in \underline{l}.$$

By setting $\varsigma_q = 0 \geq 0$, then, for the same w and b,

$$d_q \cdot \left[\langle w, x_q \rangle + b \right] \geq 1 - \xi_q \geq 1 - 0 = 1 - \varsigma_q.$$

However, the new choice would lower the cost functional. Hence, the non-negativity constraint on ξ_q can be removed. Thus, we consider the following simpler primal optimization problem:

(P2)   minimize $\dfrac{1}{2} w^T w + \dfrac{C}{2} \sum_{q=1}^{l} \xi_q^2$

subject to $d_q \cdot \left[\langle w, x_q \rangle + b \right] \geq 1 - \xi_q$ for all $q \in \underline{l}$.

Suppose $(w*, b*, \xi*)$ solves the preceding primal optimization problem. Then, the decision surface or optimal hyperplane is given by $f*(x) = \langle w*, x \rangle + b* = 0$.

Now, we consider its dual problem. The Lagrangian is given by

$$L(w, b, \xi, \alpha) := \frac{1}{2} w^T w + \frac{C}{2} \sum_{q=1}^{l} \xi_q^2 - \sum_{q=1}^{l} \alpha_q \left(d_q w^T x_q + d_q b - 1 + \xi_q \right),$$

where $\alpha := [\alpha_1 \quad \cdots \quad \alpha_l]^T \in \mathfrak{R}^l$ is the vector of Lagrange multipliers. The dual function is defined by

$$J_d(\alpha) := \min_{w, b, \xi} L(w, b, \xi, \alpha).$$

Clearly, we have

$$0 = \frac{\partial L}{\partial w} = w - \sum_{q=1}^{l} \alpha_q d_q x_q,$$

$$0 = \frac{\partial L}{\partial b} = -\sum_{q=1}^{l} \alpha_q d_q,$$

$$0 = \frac{\partial L}{\partial \xi_q} = C \xi_q - \alpha_q, \quad q \in \underline{l}$$

$$\Rightarrow \quad w = \sum_{q=1}^{l} \alpha_q d_q x_q, \quad \sum_{q=1}^{l} \alpha_q d_q = 0, \quad \xi_q = \frac{1}{C} \alpha_q, \quad q \in \underline{l}$$

$$\Rightarrow \quad \frac{1}{2} w^T w = \frac{1}{2} \left[\sum_{q=1}^{l} \alpha_q d_q x_q^T \right] \cdot \left[\sum_{j=1}^{l} \alpha_j d_j x_j \right]$$

$$= \frac{1}{2} \sum_{q=1}^{l} \sum_{j=1}^{l} \alpha_q \alpha_j d_q d_j x_q^T x_j,$$

$$-\sum_{q=1}^{l} \alpha_q d_q w^T x_q = -\sum_{q=1}^{l} \alpha_q d_q \left[\sum_{j=1}^{l} \alpha_j d_j x_j^T \right] x_q$$

$$= -\sum_{q=1}^{l} \sum_{j=1}^{l} \alpha_q \alpha_j d_q d_j x_q^T x_j,$$

$$-\sum_{q=1}^{l}\alpha_q d_q b = -b\sum_{q=1}^{l}\alpha_q d_q = 0,$$

$$\frac{1}{2}C\sum_{q=1}^{l}\xi_q^2 - \sum_{q=1}^{l}\alpha_q \xi_q = -\frac{1}{2C}\sum_{q=1}^{l}\alpha_q^2$$

$$\Rightarrow\quad J_d(\alpha) := \min_{w,b,\xi} L(w, b, \xi, \alpha)$$

$$= \sum_{q=1}^{l}\alpha_q - \frac{1}{2}\sum_{q=1}^{l}\sum_{j=1}^{l}\alpha_q \alpha_j d_q d_j x_q^T x_j - \frac{1}{2C}\sum_{q=1}^{l}\alpha_q^2 .$$

Hence, the dual optimization problem can be stated as follows:

(D2)   maximize $\displaystyle\sum_{q=1}^{l}\alpha_q - \frac{1}{2}\sum_{q=1}^{l}\sum_{j=1}^{l}\alpha_q \alpha_j d_q d_j \langle x_q, x_j\rangle - \frac{1}{2C}\sum_{q=1}^{l}\alpha_q^2$

subject to $\displaystyle\sum_{q=1}^{l}\alpha_q d_q = 0$ and $\alpha_q \geq 0$ for all $q \in \underline{l}$.

Suppose $\alpha*$ solves the dual problem (D2). Then, we have $w* = \displaystyle\sum_{q=1}^{l}\alpha_q^* d_q x_q$ and the margin is given by $\gamma_S = \|w*\|^{-1}$. The KKT conditions become, for all $q \in \underline{l}$,

$$\alpha_q^*\left[d_q\langle w*, x_q\rangle + d_q b* - 1 + \xi_q^*\right] = 0,$$
$$d_q\langle w*, x_q\rangle + d_q b* - 1 + \xi_q^* \geq 0,$$
$$\alpha_q^* \geq 0.$$

Define $I_{sv} := \{q \in \underline{l} : \alpha_q^* > 0\}$.   Then, we have

$$w* = \sum_{q=1}^{l}\alpha_q^* d_q x_q = \sum_{q \in I_{sv}}\alpha_q^* d_q x_q .$$

Let $k \in I_{sv}$, then $\alpha_k^* > 0$.   From the KKT conditions, we have

$$d_k\left[\langle w*, x_k\rangle + b*\right] = 1 - \xi_k^* = 1 - C^{-1}\alpha_k^*$$

or

$$d_k b^* = 1 - C^{-1}\alpha_k^* - d_k \langle w^*, x_k \rangle.$$

Since $d_k = \pm 1$, we have $d_k^2 = 1$, and hence

$$b^* = d_k \left(1 - C^{-1}\alpha_k^*\right) - \langle w^*, x_k \rangle = d_k \left(1 - C^{-1}\alpha_k^*\right) - \sum_{q \in I_{sv}} \alpha_q^* d_q \langle x_q, x_k \rangle.$$

The optimal discriminant function is thus given by

$$f^*(x) = \langle w^*, x \rangle + b^* = \sum_{q \in I_{sv}} \alpha_q^* d_q \langle x_q, x \rangle + b^*.$$

For any $q \in I_{sv}$, we have $d_q \left[\langle w^*, x_q \rangle + b^* \right] = 1 - \xi_q^*$, i.e.,

$$d_q \left[\left\langle \sum_{j \in I_{sv}} \alpha_j^* d_j x_j, x_q \right\rangle + b^* \right] = 1 - \xi_q^*$$

or

$$d_q \sum_{j \in I_{sv}} \alpha_j^* d_j \langle x_j, x_q \rangle = 1 - \xi_q^* - d_q b^*$$

$$\Rightarrow \quad \|w^*\|^2 = \langle w^*, w^* \rangle$$

$$= \left\langle \sum_{q \in I_{sv}} \alpha_q^* d_q x_q, \sum_{j \in I_{sv}} \alpha_j^* d_j x_j \right\rangle = \sum_{q, j \in I_{sv}} \alpha_q^* \alpha_j^* d_q d_j \langle x_q, x_j \rangle$$

$$= \sum_{q \in I_{sv}} \alpha_q^* d_q \sum_{j \in I_{sv}} \alpha_j^* d_j \langle x_q, x_j \rangle = \sum_{q \in I_{sv}} \alpha_q^* \left(1 - \xi_q^* - d_q b^*\right)$$

$$= \sum_{q \in I_{sv}} \alpha_q^* - \sum_{q \in I_{sv}} \alpha_q^* \xi_q^* - b^* \sum_{q \in I_{sv}} \alpha_q^* d_q$$

$$= \sum_{q \in I_{sv}} \alpha_q^* - \sum_{q \in I_{sv}} \alpha_q^* C^{-1} \alpha_q^* - 0$$

$$= \sum_{q \in I_{sv}} \alpha_q^* - C^{-1} \sum_{q \in I_{sv}} \left(\alpha_q^*\right)^2.$$

Thus, the margin is given by

$$\gamma_S = \|w*\|^{-1} = \left[\sum_{q\in I_{sv}} \alpha_q^* - \frac{1}{C}\sum_{q\in I_{sv}}(\alpha_q^*)^2\right]^{-1/2}.$$

Moreover, from the above derivation, we have

$$\sum_{q,j\in I_{sv}} \alpha_q^*\alpha_j^* d_q d_j\langle x_q, x_j\rangle = \|w*\|^2 = \sum_{q\in I_{sv}} \alpha_q^* - \frac{1}{C}\sum_{q\in I_{sv}}(\alpha_q^*)^2.$$

This implies that value of the problem (D2) is given by

$$J_d(\alpha^*) = \sum_{q=1}^{l} \alpha_q^* - \frac{1}{2}\sum_{q=1}^{l}\sum_{j=1}^{l}\alpha_q^*\alpha_j^* d_q d_j\langle x_q, x_j\rangle - \frac{1}{2C}\sum_{q=1}^{l}(\alpha_q^*)^2$$

$$= \frac{1}{2}\sum_{q\in I_{sv}} \alpha_q^*.$$

Now, we discuss a stopping criterion, based on KKT conditions, for any algorithm of finding the 2-norm soft margin classifier. If $\alpha_q^* = 0$, then we have $\xi_q^* = C^{-1}\alpha_q^* = 0$ and

$$d_q\left[\langle w^*, x_q\rangle + b^*\right] \geq 1 - \xi_q^* = 1 - 0 = 1 \ \Rightarrow\ d_q f*(x_q) \geq 1.$$

If $\alpha_q^* > 0$, then we have $\xi_q^* = C^{-1}\alpha_q^*$ and

$$d_q\langle w^*, x_q\rangle + d_q b^* - 1 + \xi_q^* = 0$$
$$\Rightarrow\ d_q\left[\langle w^*, x_q\rangle + b^*\right] = 1 - \xi_q^* = 1 - C^{-1}\alpha_q^*$$
$$\Rightarrow\ d_q f*(x_q) = 1 - C^{-1}\alpha_q^*.$$

Suppose α_q, $q \in l$, is the current value of the dual variable. The current primal variables and discriminant function can thus be calculated. Then, reasonable KKT stopping conditions are given by

$$\alpha_q \geq 0, \ q\in l,$$
$$d_q f(x_q) \geq 1 \ \text{if} \ \alpha_q = 0,$$

$$d_q f(x_q) = 1 - C^{-1} \alpha_q \text{ if } \alpha_q > 0.$$

We may define p_q, $q \in \underline{l}$, to be the measure of dissatisfaction of the KKT stopping conditions for the qth example as

$$p_q := \max[0, 1 - d_q f(x_q)] \text{ if } \alpha_q = 0,$$
$$p_q := |1 - d_q f(x_q) - C^{-1} \alpha_q| \text{ if } \alpha_q > 0.$$

Then, reasonable stopping criteria based on KKT stopping conditions are

$$p_{ave} := \frac{1}{l} \sum_{q=1}^{l} p_q \leq \delta \text{ or } \|p\|_\infty := \max_{q \in \underline{l}} \{p_q\} \leq \delta,$$

where δ is a pre-specified tolerance.

For the same reason as the maximal margin classifier, the feasibility gap cannot be used as an indicator of the stopping criterion.

3.10 Illustrative Examples

In this section, we provide two numerical examples to illustrate the design of linear classifiers. The Sequential Minimal Optimization (SMO) algorithms for maximal margin classifier, 1-norm soft margin classifier, and 2-norm soft margin classifier are provided in Section 7.1 to Section 7.3.

Example 3.10.1:

Suppose that the true discriminant function is given by

$$g(x_1, x_2) = x_1 + x_2 - 1, \quad x_1 \in [-2, 2], \quad x_2 \in [-3, 3].$$

The training data set consists of 50 correct examples, 24 examples with positive label (+1) and 26 examples with negative label (-1). The training set is linearly separable.

The discriminant functions determined by the true function (TF), nearest mean classifier (NMC), Rosenblatt's algorithm (RA) with learning rate $\eta = 1.0$, and maximal margin classifier (MMC) are given by

TF: $\quad y = x_1 + x_2 - 1$;

NMC: $\quad y = 1.2965x_1 + 2.9812x_2 - 1.5120$;

RA: $\quad y = 2.2065x_1 + 2.6734x_2$;

MMC: $\quad y = 1.0189x_1 + 1.2997x_2 - 0.7448$.

Hence, the decision boundaries are given by

TF: $\quad x_2 = -x_1 + 1$;

NMC: $\quad x_2 = -0.4349x_1 + 0.5072$;

RA: $\quad x_2 = -0.8253x_1$;

MMC: $\quad x_2 = -0.7839x_1 + 0.5730$,

with the geometric margins given by

NMC: $\quad$ 0.1564

RA: $\quad$ 0.1094

MMC: $\quad$ 0.6055.

See Figure 3.10.1. It is clear that the maximal margin classifier provides the maximal geometric margin.

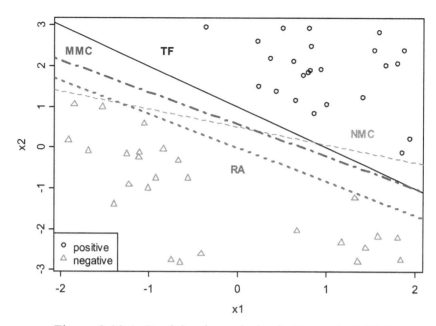

Figure 3.10.1: Decision boundaries in Example 3.10.1.

Example 3.10.2:

For the data set of Example 3.10.1, suppose we randomly choose 10 examples and change the corresponding labels to the opposite ones, i.e., we change the label +1 to -1 or -1 to +1. That is, these chosen corrupted examples actually become wrong examples. The training set is obviously not linearly separable.

The discriminant functions determined by the true function (TF), nearest mean classifier (NMC), 1-norm soft margin classifier with $C = 1$ (SVC1), and 2-norm soft margin classifier with $C = 1$ (SVC2) are given by

$$\begin{aligned}
\text{TF:} &\quad y = x_1 + x_2 - 1; \\
\text{NMC:} &\quad y = 1.2057x_1 + 1.8832x_2 - 1.0324; \\
\text{SVC1:} &\quad y = 0.6354x_1 + 0.5284x_2 - 0.3860; \\
\text{SVC2:} &\quad y = 0.3897x_1 + 0.2603x_2 - 0.2423.
\end{aligned}$$

Hence, the decision boundaries are given by

TF: $\quad x_2 = -x_1 + 1;$

NMC: $\quad x_2 = -0.6402 x_1 + 0.5482;$

SVC1: $\quad x_2 = -1.2026 x_1 + 0.7305;$

SVC2: $\quad x_2 = -1.4974 x_1 + 0.9312,$

with the geometric margins given by

NMC: $\quad$ -1.7937

SVC1: $\quad$ 1.2101

SVC2: $\quad$ 2.1340.

See Figure 3.10.2.

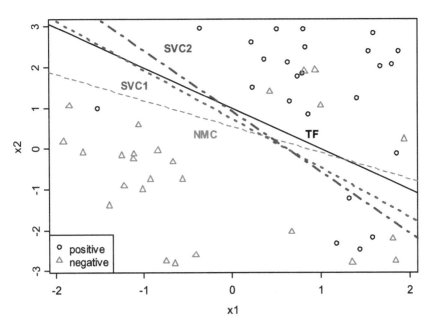

Figure 3.10.2: Decision boundaries in Example 3.10.2.

3.11 Exercises

Exercise 3.11.1: Let $X \subseteq \mathfrak{R}^n$ and $Y := \{1, -1\}$. Suppose the nontrivial training set $S := \{(x_q, d_q)\}_{q=1}^{\mathscr{U}} \subseteq X \times Y$ is linearly separable, then there exist a vector $w* \in \mathfrak{R}^n$, $\|w*\| = 1$, a number $b* \in \mathfrak{R}$, and a positive number $\gamma > 0$ such that

$$d_q \cdot \left[\langle w*, x_q \rangle + b* \right] \geq \gamma > 0 \quad \text{for all} \quad q \in \underline{l}.$$

Define

$$I_S^+ := \{ q \in \underline{l} : d_q = 1 \}, \quad I_S^- := \{ j \in \underline{l} : d_j = -1 \},$$

$$V := \max \left(\min_{q \in I_S^+} \|x_q\|, \min_{j \in I_S^-} \|x_j\| \right), \quad U := \max_{q=1}^{l} \|x_q\|.$$

Prove that $|b*| < V \leq U$.

Exercise 3.11.2: The modified Rosenblatt algorithm is shown below.

Data: training set $S := \{ (x_q, d_q) \}_{q=1}^{l} \subseteq X \times Y$ and a learning rate $\eta > 0$

Goal: (w, b) defining a linear discriminant function that correctly classifies the training set

Step 1: $w_0 \leftarrow 0$; $b_0 \leftarrow 0$; $k \leftarrow 0$;
$I_S^+ := \{ q \in \underline{l} : d_q = 1 \}$; $I_S^- := \{ j \in \underline{l} : d_j = -1 \}$;

Step 2:   Choose $Q \geq V := \max \left(\min_{q \in I_S^+} \|x_q\|, \min_{j \in I_S^-} \|x_j\| \right)$;

Step 3:   repeat
　　　　　for $q = 1$ to l
　　　　　　　if $d_k \cdot \left[\langle w_k, x_q \rangle + b_k \right] \leq 0$, then
　　　　　　　　　$w_{k+1} \leftarrow w_k + \eta d_q x_q$;
　　　　　　　　　$b_{k+1} \leftarrow b_k + \eta d_q Q^2$;
　　　　　　　　　$k \leftarrow k + 1$;
　　　　　　　end if
　　　　　end for
　　　　until no misclassification within the *for* loop
　　　　return k, (w_k, b_k), where k is the number of mistakes

(a) Use Exercise 3.11.1 to prove the following modified Novikoff's Theorem. Suppose S is a nontrivial training set and there exist a vector $w* \in \Re^n$, $\|w*\| = 1$, a number $b* \in \Re$, and a positive number $\gamma > 0$ such that

$$d_q \cdot \left(\langle w*, x_q \rangle + b* \right) \geq \gamma > 0 \quad \text{for all} \quad q \in \underline{l}.$$

Then, the number of mistakes made by the modified on-line perceptron algorithm on the training set S is at most $\gamma^{-2} \left[2 \left(R^2 + Q^2 \right) \right]$, where $R \geq U := \max_{q=1}^{l} \| x_q \|$.

(b) Prove that the modified Novikoff's Theorem gives a better estimate of the number of mistakes than the original Novikoff's Theorem.

(c) Prove that any positive scaling of the training examples will not affect the number of iterations taken by the modified perceptron algorithm. Furthermore, it will not change the estimate of the number of mistakes provided by the modified Novikoff's Theorem.

(d) Provide other modified Rosenblatt algorithms, one in primal form and the other two in dual form.

Exercise 3.11.3: Suppose that the true discriminant function is given by

$$g(x_1, x_2) = 2x_1 + x_2 - 1, \quad x_1 \in [-2, 2], \quad x_2 \in [-5, 5].$$

The training data set consists of 50 randomly selected correct examples, 24 examples with positive label (+1) and 26 examples with negative label (-1). The training set is linearly separable. Draw the decision boundaries determined by the nearest mean classifier, linear classifier using Rosenblatt's algorithm with learning rate $\eta = 0.1$, and maximal margin classifier.

Exercise 3.11.4: For the data set of Exercise 3.11.3, suppose we randomly choose 10 examples and change the corresponding labels to the opposite ones, i.e., we change the label +1 to -1 or -1 to +1. That is, these chosen corrupted examples actually become wrong examples. The training set is obviously not linearly separable. Draw the decision boundaries determined by the nearest mean classifier, 1-norm soft margin classifier with $C = 1$ and 2-norm soft margin classifier with $C = 1$.

Exercise 3.11.5: Consider the following training sample $S := \{(x_q, d_q)\}_{q=1}^{20}$, where $x_q \in \mathfrak{R}^4$ is the input pattern for the qth example and $d_q \in \{1, -1\}$ is the corresponding label:

q	x_q	d_q	q	x_q	d_q
1	$(-1.0 \quad 4.1 \quad 4.2 \quad 7.8)$	1	11	$(0.9 \quad 1.9 \quad 3.8 \quad -4.0)$	-1
2	$(8.5 \quad 12.1 \quad 6.8 \quad 11.4)$	1	12	$(5.1 \quad -8.2 \quad 6.0 \quad -2.3)$	-1
3	$(7.1 \quad 11.2 \quad 2.9 \quad 8.8)$	1	13	$(14.0 \quad 2.9 \quad 8.1 \quad -11.0)$	-1
4	$(2.2 \quad 9.1 \quad 10.2 \quad 20.0)$	1	14	$(3.0 \quad -9.2 \quad 2.9 \quad 7.0)$	-1
5	$(6.0 \quad 5.0 \quad 8.0 \quad 7.2)$	1	15	$(-9.2 \quad -8.2 \quad -7.1 \quad 2.0)$	-1
6	$(7.5 \quad 5.4 \quad 3.3 \quad 7.2)$	1	16	$(-4.8 \quad 6.0 \quad 7.0 \quad -4.2)$	-1
7	$(7.0 \quad 2.2 \quad 7.8 \quad 4.3)$	1	17	$(4.1 \quad -6.9 \quad 8.0 \quad 2.9)$	-1
8	$(3.2 \quad 9.1 \quad 3.8 \quad 7.5)$	1	18	$(6.0 \quad 0.0 \quad 11.2 \quad 7.8)$	-1
9	$(1.2 \quad 4.2 \quad 7.3 \quad 6.1)$	1	19	$(5.0 \quad -5.0 \quad 4.8 \quad 4.9)$	-1
10	$(6.2 \quad 8.1 \quad 9.2 \quad 1.1)$	1	20	$(3.1 \quad 1.2 \quad 12.0 \quad 7.2)$	-1

(a) Find a discriminant function by using the primal form of Rosenblatt's algorithm with learning rate $\eta = 0.5$ and test if the training set is indeed linearly separable.

(b) Find a discriminant function by using the dual form of Rosenblatt's algorithm with learning rate $\eta = 0.5$ and test if the training set is indeed linearly separable.

Exercise 3.11.6: Suppose we are given a two-dimensional NXOR problem with the training examples given as

pattern	label
$(x_1 \quad x_2)$	d
$(0 \quad 0)$	1
$(0 \quad 1)$	-1
$(1 \quad 0)$	-1
$(1 \quad 1)$	1

The polynomial kernel is given by

$$K(x, z) := \left(1 + x^T z\right)^2, \quad x := \begin{bmatrix} x_1 \\ x_2 \end{bmatrix}, z := \begin{bmatrix} z_1 \\ z_2 \end{bmatrix} \in \mathfrak{R}^2.$$

(a) Find a feature map corresponding to this kernel.
(b) Find the transformed training patterns, i.e., the features, in the feature space.
(c) Construct a nonlinear classifier by using the Rosenblatt's algorithm with learning rate $\eta = 0.01$.
(d) Design a support vector classifier. Draw the decision boundary clearly. (You can solve this problem solely by hand. No computer is needed!)

Exercise 3.11.7: In this exercise, we investigate the 1-norm υ-soft margin classifier. Let $X \subseteq \mathfrak{R}^n$ and $Y := \{1, -1\}$. Suppose we are given a non-trivial (possibly not linearly separable) training set $S := \{(x_q, d_q)\}_{q=1}^{\text{l}} \subseteq X \times Y$. It is desired to find a soft discriminant function $f(x) = \langle w, x \rangle + b$ that correctly classifies "most" training examples. Consider the following primal optimization problem, with $C > 0$, $D \geq 0$, and $0 \leq \upsilon \leq 1$:

(MUP1) minimize $\dfrac{1}{2} w^T w - D\upsilon\rho + C \displaystyle\sum_{q=1}^{l} \xi_q$

subject to $d_q \cdot \left[\langle w, x_q \rangle + b\right] \geq \rho - \xi_q$,

$\xi_q \geq 0$ for all $q \in \underline{l}$, and $\rho \geq 0$.

(a) Prove that the dual maximization problem of (MUP1) is given by

(MUD1) maximize $-\dfrac{1}{2} \displaystyle\sum_{q=1}^{l} \sum_{j=1}^{l} \alpha_q \alpha_j d_q d_j \langle x_q, x_j \rangle$

subject to $\displaystyle\sum_{q=1}^{l} \alpha_q d_q = 0, \quad \sum_{q=1}^{l} \alpha_q \geq D\upsilon$, and $0 \leq \alpha_q \leq C$

for all $q \in \underline{l}$.

(b) State the KKT conditions.

(c) Find the optimal discriminant function in terms of the dual variables.
(d) Find a stopping criterion based on KKT conditions.
(e) Find a stopping criterion based on percentage feasibility gap.

Exercise 3.11.8: In this exercise, we investigate the 2-norm υ-soft margin classifier. Let $X \subseteq \mathfrak{R}^n$ and $Y := \{1, -1\}$. Suppose we are given a non-trivial (possibly not linearly separable) training set $S := \{(x_q, d_q)\}_{q=1}^{\ell} \subseteq X \times Y$. It is desired to find a soft discriminant function $f(x) = \langle w, x \rangle + b$ that correctly classifies "most" training examples. Consider the following primal optimization problem, with $C > 0$, $D \geq 0$, and $0 \leq \upsilon \leq 1$:

(MUP20) minimize $\quad \dfrac{1}{2} w^T w - D\upsilon\rho + \dfrac{C}{2} \displaystyle\sum_{q=1}^{\ell} \xi_q^2$

subject to $\quad d_q \cdot [\langle w, x_q \rangle + b] \geq \rho - \xi_q, \ \xi_q \geq 0$

for all $q \in \underline{l}$, and $\rho \geq 0$.

(a) Show that the preceding optimization problem can be reduced to

(MUP2) minimize $\quad \dfrac{1}{2} w^T w - D\upsilon\rho + \dfrac{C}{2} \displaystyle\sum_{q=1}^{\ell} \xi_q^2$

subject to $\quad d_q \cdot [\langle w, x_q \rangle + b] \geq \rho - \xi_q,$

for all $q \in \underline{l}$, and $\rho \geq 0$.

(b) Prove that the dual maximization problem of (MUP1) is given by

(MUD2) maximize $\quad -\dfrac{1}{2} \displaystyle\sum_{q=1}^{\ell}\sum_{j=1}^{\ell} \alpha_q \alpha_j d_q d_j x_q^T x_j - \dfrac{1}{2C} \displaystyle\sum_{q=1}^{\ell} \alpha_q^2$

subject to $\quad \displaystyle\sum_{q=1}^{\ell} \alpha_q d_q = 0, \ \sum_{q=1}^{\ell} \alpha_q \geq D\upsilon,$ and $\alpha_q \geq 0$

for all $q \in \underline{l}$.

(c) State the KKT conditions.
(d) Find the optimal discriminant function in terms of the dual variables.
(e) Find a stopping criterion based on KKT conditions.

3.12 Notes and References

The nearest mean classifier can be found in Alpaydin (2010), Herbrich (2002), Kecman (2001), and Schölkopf and Smola (2002). The Rosenblatt's Algorithms can be found in Rosenblatt (1958), Rosenblatt (1962), Cristianini and Shawe-Taylor (2000), and Herbrich (2002). For Novikoff's Theorem, see Novikoff (1962). Our proof of Novikoff's Theorem follows from Cristianini and Shawe-Taylor (2000). Our development of maximal margin classifiers, slack variables, and soft margin classifiers were based on Cristianini and Shawe-Taylor (2000). The 1-norm υ-soft margin classifier in Exercise 3.11.7 can be found in Schölkopf and Smola (2002), Herbrich (2002), and Cristianini and Shawe-Taylor (2000). For the application of maximum margin classification in cellular neural networks (CNN), see Lin, Hsieh, and Jeng (2008).

Alpaydin, E. (2010). Introduction to Machine Learning. Second Edition. MIT Press, Cambridge, Massachusetts.

Cristianini, N. and J. Shawe-Taylor (2000). An Introduction to Support Vector Machines. Cambridge University Press, Cambridge, United Kingdom.

Herbrich, R. (2002). Learning Kernel Classifiers: Theory and Algorithms. MIT Press, Cambridge, Massachusetts.

Kecman, V. (2001). Learning and Soft Computing. MIT Press, Cambridge, Massachusetts.

Lin, Y.L., J.G. Hsieh, and J.H. Jeng (2008). Robust decomposition with restricted weights for cellular neural networks implementing an arbitrary Boolean function. International Journal of Bifurcation & Chaos, Vol. 17, No. 9, pp. 3151-3169.

Novikoff, A.B. (1962). On convergence proofs on perceptrons. Symposium on the Mathematical Theory of Automata, Polytechnic Institute of Brooklyn, New York, Vol. 12, pp. 615-622.

Rosenblatt, F. (1958). The perceptron: A probabilistic model for information storage and organization in the brain. Psychological Review, Vol. 65, No. 6, pp. 386-408.

Rosenblatt, F. (1962). Principles of Neurodynamics: Perceptron and Theory of Brain Mechanisms. Spartan-Books, Washington D.C.

Schölkopf, B. and A.J. Smola (2002). Learning with Kernels: Support Vector Machines, Regularization, and Beyond. MIT Press, Cambridge, Massachusetts.

Chapter 4   Linear Regression

In this chapter, we will discuss the linear regression problems. A linear regressor can be represented as a single-layer neural network with a linear output activation function. The Widrow-Hoff algorithms, in both primal form and dual form, are derived for finding the least squares solutions. It is also called the delta learning rule, which is an on-line (or pattern-based) gradient descent strategy for adaptive linear neurons (also called Adalines). In particular, the dual form of the Widrow-Hoff algorithm provides us a hint to construct kernel-based nonlinear regressors. A more powerful recursive least squares algorithm is also derived. Three natural strategies will be proposed when the linear squares regressor under consideration does not fit the data well. To tolerate the errors in corrupted data, we will consider the ridge regression and linear support vector regression. So, the ridge regression problem, stemmed from the regularization approach to learning problems, and recursive algorithms are introduced next. In the ridge regression problem, the objective function to be minimized includes a smoothing functional or stabilizer intended to assure that the approximating function is smooth. To prepare for the linear support vector regression problems, we will introduce slack variables for regression problems. Based on the concepts of regularization in ridge regression and slack variables for regression, soft regressors (or linear support vector regressors) are studied in detail.

4.1 Linear Least Squares Regressor

In a regression problem, the outputs assume continuous values, while those of a classification problem assume only discrete values, i.e., the labels.

A linear function $f(x)$ is given by

$$f(x) = w_1 x_1 + w_2 x_2 + \dots + w_n x_n + b = \langle x, w \rangle + b,$$

where

$$x = \begin{bmatrix} x_1 \\ \vdots \\ x_n \end{bmatrix} \in \mathfrak{R}^n, \quad w = \begin{bmatrix} w_1 \\ \vdots \\ w_n \end{bmatrix} \in \mathfrak{R}^n.$$

It can also be written as

$$f(z) = z^T \beta = \langle z, \beta \rangle$$

where

$$z = \begin{bmatrix} z_1 \\ \vdots \\ z_n \\ z_{n+1} \end{bmatrix} = \begin{bmatrix} x_1 \\ \vdots \\ x_n \\ 1 \end{bmatrix} = \begin{bmatrix} x \\ 1 \end{bmatrix} \in \mathfrak{R}^{n+1},$$

$$\beta = \begin{bmatrix} \beta_1 \\ \vdots \\ \beta_n \\ \beta_{n+1} \end{bmatrix} = \begin{bmatrix} w_1 \\ \vdots \\ w_n \\ b \end{bmatrix} = \begin{bmatrix} w \\ b \end{bmatrix} \in \mathfrak{R}^{n+1}.$$

Let $X \subseteq \mathfrak{R}^n$ and $Y \subseteq \mathfrak{R}$. Suppose we are given the training set

$$S := \left\{ \left(x_q, d_q \right) \right\}_{q=1}^{\forall} \subseteq X \times Y,$$

where

$$x_q := \begin{bmatrix} x_{q1} & \cdots & x_{qn} \end{bmatrix}^T \in \mathfrak{R}^n, \quad q \in \underline{l}.$$

The problem of linear regression is to find a linear function $f(x)$ that fits the data. This is illustrated schematically in Figure 4.1.1.

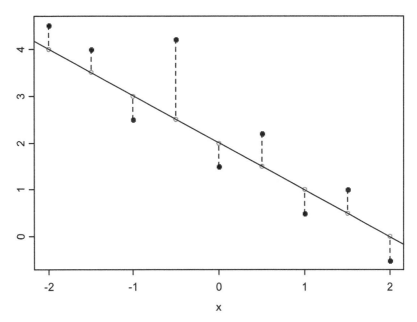

Figure 4.1.1: Linear regression.

The predictive function can be represented as a single-layer neural network as shown in Figure 4.1.2.

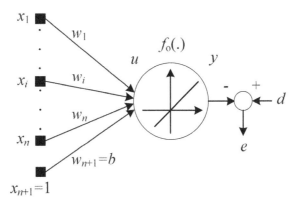

Figure 4.1.2: Single-layer neural network representation of a linear regressor.

In this network, x is the input of the network, d is the desired output of the network, u is the input of the neuron, y is the output of the neuron,

$f_o(\cdot)$ is the activation function of the neuron defined as the identity function, and e is the error (or residual). From the network, we have

$$u = \langle x, w \rangle + b = \langle z, \beta \rangle, \quad y = f_o(u) = u, \quad e = d - y.$$

The least squares approach is to choose a (w, b) that minimizes the sum of squared errors

$$E(\beta) := \frac{1}{2} \sum_{q=1}^{l} e_q^2 = \frac{1}{2} \sum_{q=1}^{l} (d_q - y_q)^2$$

$$= \frac{1}{2} \sum_{q=1}^{l} \left[d_q - \langle x_q, w \rangle - b \right]^2 = \frac{1}{2} \sum_{q=1}^{l} \left[d_q - \langle z_q, \beta \rangle \right]^2.$$

The problem is best cast to its matrix form. Define

$$d = \begin{bmatrix} d_1 \\ \vdots \\ d_l \end{bmatrix} \in \mathfrak{R}^l,$$

$$Z = \begin{bmatrix} x_{11} & x_{12} & \cdots & x_{1n} & 1 \\ x_{21} & x_{22} & \cdots & x_{2n} & 1 \\ \vdots & \vdots & \ddots & \vdots & \vdots \\ x_{l1} & x_{l2} & \cdots & x_{ln} & 1 \end{bmatrix} \in \mathfrak{R}^{l \times (n+1)} \quad \text{(model matrix)}.$$

Then, we have

$$E(\beta) = \frac{1}{2} \| d - Z\beta \|^2 = \frac{1}{2} \langle d - Z\beta, d - Z\beta \rangle$$

$$= \frac{1}{2} (d - Z\beta)^T (d - Z\beta)$$

$$= \frac{1}{2} \left(d^T d - 2\beta^T Z^T d + \beta^T Z^T Z\beta \right)$$

$$= \frac{1}{2} d^T d - \beta^T Z^T d + \frac{1}{2} \beta^T Z^T Z\beta.$$

Taking the derivative of E with respect to β and setting it to zero, we have

$$0 = \frac{\partial E}{\partial \beta} = -Z^T d + Z^T Z \beta *,$$

or

$$Z^T Z \beta * = Z^T d,$$

which is called the **normal equation** for the least squares regression. Since $Z^T d \in R(Z^T) = R(Z^T Z)$, the normal equation has a solution. If the column vectors of Z are linearly independent, then $Z^T Z$ is a real symmetric nonsingular matrix. In this case, $(Z^T Z)^{-1}$ exists and the (unique) solution of the normal equation is given by

$$\beta * = (Z^T Z)^{-1} Z^T d.$$

Note that in fact we are finding the least squares solution of the equation $Z\beta = d$. Define $\beta^+ := Z^+ d$, where Z^+ is the pseudo inverse of Z. Then, from the results of linear algebra, β^+ is a least squares solution of minimal length, i.e., $Z^T Z \beta^+ = Z^T d$ and if $\tilde{\beta}$ is any other least squares solution, then $\|\beta^+\| \le \|\tilde{\beta}\|$. If $(Z^T Z)^{-1}$ exists, then $Z^+ = (Z^T Z)^{-1} Z^T$, and so $\beta^+ := Z^+ d = (Z^T Z)^{-1} Z^T d = \beta *$.

4.2 Widrow-Hoff Algorithm for Least Squares Regressor

In this section, we derive the Widrow-Hoff algorithms, in both primal form and dual form, for finding the least squares solutions. It is also called the delta learning rule, which is an on-line (or pattern-based) incremental gradient descent strategy for adaptive linear neurons (also called Adalines). See Kecman (2001).

If x_q is the qth training pattern to the network with desired output d_q, then the squared error for this example is given by

$$E_q(w,b) := \frac{1}{2} e_q^2 = \frac{1}{2}(d_q - y_q)^2 = \frac{1}{2}[d_q - \langle x_q, w \rangle - b]^2.$$

Notice that we have

$$E(w, b) = \sum_{q=1}^{l} E_q(w, b).$$

The delta learning rule is given by

$$w \leftarrow w - \eta \frac{\partial E_q}{\partial w}(w, b), \quad b \leftarrow b - \eta \frac{\partial E_q}{\partial b}(w, b),$$

where $\eta > 0$ denotes the learning rate. By chain rule, we have

$$\frac{\partial E_q}{\partial w} = \frac{\partial E_q}{\partial u}\frac{\partial u}{\partial w} = \frac{\partial E_q}{\partial u}x_q = -\left(-\frac{\partial E_q}{\partial u}\right)x_q.$$

Define the δ-signal as

$$\delta_o := -\frac{\partial E_q}{\partial u} = -\frac{\partial E_q}{\partial y}\frac{\partial y}{\partial u} = -(d_q - y_q)(-1)f_o'(u) = d_q - y_q = e_q,$$

which is exactly the error signal in this case. Again by chain rule, we have

$$\frac{\partial E_q}{\partial b} = \frac{\partial E_q}{\partial u}\frac{\partial u}{\partial b} = \frac{\partial E_q}{\partial u} = -\delta_o.$$

Hence, the updating rules are given by

$$w \leftarrow w + \eta\delta_o x_q = w + \eta e_q x_q, \quad b \leftarrow b + \eta\delta_o = b + \eta e_q.$$

Based on the preceding analysis, we have the following primal form of the Widrow-Hoff algorithm. See Cristianini and Shawe-Taylor (2000).

Algorithm 4.2.1: (primal form)

Data: training set $S := \{(x_q, d_q)\}_{q=1}^{l} \subseteq X \times Y$ and a learning rate $\eta > 0$

Goal: (w, b) defining a linear predictive function minimizing the sum of squared errors

Step 1: $w \leftarrow 0$; $b \leftarrow 0$;
Step 2:   repeat
      for $q = 1$ to l

$$e \leftarrow d_q - \langle x_q, w \rangle - b; \quad w \leftarrow w + \eta e x_q; \quad b \leftarrow b + \eta e;$$

      end for
    until convergence criterion satisfied
    return (w, b)

In the preceding algorithm, when using (x_q, d_q) as the qth training example, after updating we can only change the value of the predictive function $f(x)$ by $\eta e \langle x_q, x \rangle + \eta e$, which requires just one evaluation of f with all training examples.   Thus, we have the following alternative learning algorithm.

Algorithm 4.2.2: (primal form)

Data: training set $S := \{(x_q, d_q)\}_{q=1}^{l} \subseteq X \times Y$ and a learning rate $\eta > 0$

Goal: (w, b) defining a linear predictive function minimizing the sum of squared errors

Step 1: $w \leftarrow 0$; $b \leftarrow 0$; $y_q \leftarrow 0$ for all $q \in \underline{l}$;
Step 2:   repeat
      for $q = 1$ to l

$$e \leftarrow d_q - y_q; \quad w \leftarrow w + \eta e x_q; \quad b \leftarrow b + \eta e;$$

      for $j = 1$ to l

$$y_j \leftarrow y_j + \eta e \langle x_q, x_j \rangle + \eta e;$$

      end for
    end for
    until convergence criterion satisfied
    return (w, b)

In the primal form of Algorithm 4.2.1, starting from $w_0 = 0$, the final weight is of the form

$$w = \sum_{q=1}^{l} \eta \alpha_q x_q, \quad q \in \underline{l},$$

and α_q, $q \in \underline{l}$, is the prediction error when using (x_q, d_q) as training example. Then, we have

$$f_{w,b}(x) := \langle w, x \rangle + b = \left\langle \sum_{j=1}^{l} \eta \alpha_j x_j, x \right\rangle + b = \sum_{j=1}^{l} \eta \alpha_j \langle x_j, x \rangle + b,$$

$$e_q := d_q - f_{w,b}(x_q) = d_q - \sum_{j=1}^{l} \eta \alpha_j \langle x_j, x_q \rangle - b.$$

This yields the dual form of the Widrow-Hoff algorithm.

Algorithm 4.2.3: (dual form)

Data: training set $S := \{(x_q, d_q)\}_{q=1}^{l} \subseteq X \times Y$ and a learning rate $\eta > 0$

Goal: (α, b) defining a linear predictive function minimizing the sum of squared errors

Step 1: $\alpha \leftarrow 0$; $b \leftarrow 0$;
Step 2:   repeat
            for $q = 1$ to l

$$e \leftarrow d_q - \sum_{j=1}^{l} \eta \alpha_j \langle x_j, x_q \rangle - b;$$

$$\alpha_q \leftarrow \alpha_q + e;$$
$$b \leftarrow b + \eta e;$$

            end for
         until convergence criterion satisfied
         return (α, b)

In the dual form of Algorithm 4.2.3, when using (x_q, d_q) as the qth training example, we only increase the α_q by e and bias b by ηe with other α_j, $j \neq q$, unaffected. This can only change the value of the predictive function $f(x)$ by $\eta e \langle x_q, x \rangle + \eta e$, which requires just one evaluation of f with all training examples. Thus, we have the following alternative learning algorithm.

Algorithm 4.2.4: (dual form)

Data: training set $S := \left\{ \left(x_q, d_q \right) \right\}_{q=1}^{l} \subseteq X \times Y$ and a learning rate $\eta > 0$

Goal: (α, b) defining a linear predictive function minimizing the sum of squared errors

Step 1: $\alpha \leftarrow 0$; $b \leftarrow 0$; $y_q \leftarrow 0$ for all $q \in \underline{l}$;

Step 2:   repeat

            for $q = 1$ to l

                $e \leftarrow d_q - y_q$; $\alpha_q \leftarrow \alpha_q + e$; $b \leftarrow b + \eta e$;

                for $j = 1$ to l

                    $y_j \leftarrow y_j + \eta e \left\langle x_q, x_j \right\rangle + \eta e$;

                end for

            end for

        until convergence criterion satisfied

        return (α, b)

Note that the training data only enters the algorithms through the entries of the Grammian matrix $G := \left[\left\langle x_q, x_j \right\rangle \right] \in \Re^{l \times l}$.

4.3 Recursive Algorithm for Linear Least Squares Regressor

The Widrow-Hoff algorithms introduced in the last section minimize the squared error of only one training example at a time. The recursive least squares (RLS) algorithm to be studied in this section is a recursive algorithm that minimizes the summation of squared errors for all training examples up to the present iteration k. It might well be the best on-line weight-adapting alternative for linear least squares regression. See Kecman (2001).

Suppose $k \in \underline{l}$ is given, then the least squares solution for k training data (x_1, d_1), ..., (x_k, d_k) is given by

$$\beta_{(k)} = \left(Z_{(k)}^T Z_{(k)}\right)^{-1} Z_{(k)}^T d_{(k)},$$

$$\beta_{(k)} := \begin{bmatrix} w_{(k)} \\ b_{(k)} \end{bmatrix} \in \Re^{n+1}, \quad d_{(k)} := \begin{bmatrix} d_1 \\ \vdots \\ d_k \end{bmatrix} \in \Re^k,$$

$$Z_{(k)} = \begin{bmatrix} x_{11} & x_{12} & \cdots & x_{1n} & 1 \\ x_{21} & x_{22} & \cdots & x_{2n} & 1 \\ \vdots & \vdots & \ddots & \vdots & \vdots \\ x_{k1} & x_{k2} & \cdots & x_{kn} & 1 \end{bmatrix} \in \Re^{k \times (n+1)},$$

where we have assumed that $Z_{(k)}^T Z_{(k)}$ is nonsingular. It can also be written as

$$\beta_{(k)} = H_k F_k, \quad H_k = \left(Z_{(k)}^T Z_{(k)}\right)^{-1}, \quad F_k = Z_{(k)}^T d_{(k)}.$$

Define

$$z_j := \begin{bmatrix} x_j \\ 1 \end{bmatrix} \in \Re^{n+1}, \quad j \in \underline{l},$$

then the prediction error of the next example $\left(x_{k+1}, d_{k+1}\right)$ becomes

$$e_{k+1} := d_{k+1} - \left\langle x_{k+1}, w_{(k)} \right\rangle - b_{(k)} = d_{k+1} - z_{k+1}^T \beta_{(k)}.$$

By the definition above, the least squares solution for $k+1$ training data $\left(x_1, d_1\right), \ldots, \left(x_k, d_k\right), \left(x_{k+1}, d_{k+1}\right)$ is given by

$$\beta_{(k+1)} = \left(Z_{(k+1)}^T Z_{(k+1)}\right)^{-1} Z_{(k+1)}^T d_{(k+1)} = H_{k+1} F_{k+1},$$

where

$$\beta_{(k+1)} := \begin{bmatrix} w_{(k+1)} \\ b_{(k+1)} \end{bmatrix}, \quad d_{(k+1)} := \begin{bmatrix} d_1 \\ \vdots \\ d_{k+1} \end{bmatrix} = \begin{bmatrix} d_{(k)} \\ d_{k+1} \end{bmatrix},$$

$$Z_{(k+1)} = \begin{bmatrix} x_{11} & x_{12} & \cdots & x_{1n} & 1 \\ x_{21} & x_{22} & \cdots & x_{2n} & 1 \\ \vdots & \vdots & \ddots & \vdots & \vdots \\ x_{(k+1),1} & x_{(k+1),2} & \cdots & x_{(k+1),n} & 1 \end{bmatrix} = \begin{bmatrix} Z_{(k)} \\ z_{k+1}^T \end{bmatrix},$$

$$H_{k+1} = \left(Z_{(k+1)}^T Z_{(k+1)} \right)^{-1}, \quad F_{k+1} = Z_{(k+1)}^T d_{(k+1)}.$$

From the definitions stated above, we have

$$H_{k+1}^{-1} = Z_{(k+1)}^T Z_{(k+1)} = \begin{bmatrix} Z_{(k)}^T & z_{k+1} \end{bmatrix} \begin{bmatrix} Z_{(k)} \\ z_{k+1}^T \end{bmatrix}$$

$$= Z_{(k)}^T Z_{(k)} + z_{k+1} z_{k+1}^T = H_k^{-1} + z_{k+1} z_{k+1}^T.$$

By using the famous Woodbury inversion formula:

$$(A + BCD)^{-1} = A^{-1} - A^{-1} B \left(DA^{-1}B + C^{-1} \right)^{-1} DA^{-1},$$

we have

$$H_{k+1} = \left(H_{k+1}^{-1} \right)^{-1} = \left(H_k^{-1} + z_{k+1} z_{k+1}^T \right)^{-1} = \left(H_k^{-1} + z_{k+1} \cdot 1 \cdot z_{k+1}^T \right)^{-1}$$

$$= H_k - H_k z_{k+1} \left(z_{k+1}^T H_k z_{k+1} + 1 \right)^{-1} z_{k+1}^T H_k$$

$$= H_k - \left(1 + z_{k+1}^T H_k z_{k+1} \right)^{-1} H_k z_{k+1} z_{k+1}^T H_k$$

$$= H_k - \left(1 + z_{k+1}^T H_k z_{k+1} \right)^{-1} H_k z_{k+1} \left(H_k z_{k+1} \right)^T,$$

where $\left(1 + z_{k+1}^T H_k z_{k+1} \right)$ is a scalar and $H_k z_{k+1} \left(H_k z_{k+1} \right)^T$ is a rank-one matrix. Moreover, we have

$$F_{k+1} = Z_{(k+1)}^T d_{(k+1)} = \begin{bmatrix} Z_{(k)}^T & z_{k+1} \end{bmatrix} \begin{bmatrix} d_{(k)} \\ d_{k+1} \end{bmatrix} = Z_{(k)}^T d_{(k)} + z_{k+1} d_{k+1}$$

$$= F_k + z_{k+1} \left(e_{k+1} + z_{k+1}^T \beta_{(k)} \right)$$

$$= H_k^{-1} \beta_{(k)} + z_{k+1} z_{k+1}^T \beta_{(k)} + z_{k+1} e_{k+1}$$

$$= \left(H_k^{-1} + z_{k+1} z_{k+1}^T \right) \beta_{(k)} + z_{k+1} e_{k+1}$$

$$= H_{k+1}^{-1} \beta_{(k)} + z_{k+1} e_{k+1}.$$

Hence, the updating law becomes

$$\beta_{(k+1)} = H_{k+1}F_{k+1} = H_{k+1}\left(H_{k+1}^{-1}\beta_{(k)} + z_{k+1}e_{k+1}\right) = \beta_{(k)} + H_{k+1}z_{k+1}e_{k+1}.$$

Let $G_k := \lambda H_k$, where $\lambda > 0$ is a scaling factor. It is easy to derive that

$$G_{k+1} = G_k - \left(\lambda + z_{k+1}^T G_k z_{k+1}\right)^{-1} G_k z_{k+1}\left(G_k z_{k+1}\right)^T,$$
$$\beta_{(k+1)} = \beta_{(k)} + \lambda^{-1} G_{k+1} z_{k+1} e_{k+1}.$$

Define $r_{k+1} := G_k z_{k+1}$ and $s_{k+1} := \left(\lambda + z_{k+1}^T r_{k+1}\right)^{-1}$. Then, we have

$$G_{k+1} = G_k - s_{k+1} r_{k+1} r_{k+1}^T, \quad \beta_{(k+1)} = \beta_{(k)} + \left(\lambda^{-1} e_{k+1}\right) G_{k+1} z_{k+1}.$$

Thus, we have the following algorithm.

Algorithm 4.3.1

Data: training set $S := \left\{\left(x_q, d_q\right)\right\}_{q=1}^{V} \subseteq X \times Y$

Goal: (w, b) defining a linear predictive function minimizing the sum
of squared errors

Step 1: $\beta = \begin{bmatrix} w \\ b \end{bmatrix} \leftarrow \begin{bmatrix} 0 \\ 0 \end{bmatrix}$ and $G \leftarrow \alpha I_{n+1}$, where α should be a large
number;

Step 2:   repeat
   for $q = 1$ to l
   $$z_q := \begin{bmatrix} x_q \\ 1 \end{bmatrix};$$
   $$e \leftarrow d_q - z_q^T \beta;$$
   $$r \leftarrow G z_q;$$
   $$s \leftarrow \left(\lambda + z_q^T r\right)^{-1};$$
   $$G \leftarrow G - srr^T;$$
   $$s \leftarrow \lambda^{-1} e;$$
   $$r \leftarrow G z_q;$$

$$\beta \leftarrow \beta + sr;$$
        end for
      until convergence criterion satisfied
      return $\beta = \begin{bmatrix} w \\ b \end{bmatrix}$

Note that in the preceding algorithm, since rr^T is a rank-one matrix, the statement $G \leftarrow G - srr^T$ can be implemented as

      for $j = 1$ to $n+1$
         for $k = 1$ to $n+1$
$$G_{jk} \leftarrow G_{jk} - s * r_j * r_k;$$
         end for
      end for

4.4 Widrow-Hoff Algorithm for Nonlinear Regressor

Let $X \subseteq \mathfrak{R}^n$ and $Y \subseteq \mathfrak{R}$. Suppose we are given the training set

$$S := \left\{ \left(x_q, d_q \right) \right\}_{q=1}^{Y} \subseteq X \times Y.$$

What if the linear least squares regressor does not fit the data well? There are three natural strategies:

(a) The first strategy is to nonlinearly transform the data to another space with the hope that better linear regressor can be found in the new space for the transformed data. This results in a linear regressor in the new space but a nonlinear regressor in the original space. See Figure 4.4.1 for illustration.

(b) In the second strategy, we still perform linear regression in the original space but with some robust cost function instead of the usual least squares criterion. The rationale behind this approach is that the lack of fit is often due to undesirable outliers in the data. Robust regression dampens the effect of outliers. In this direction, we will consider the ridge regression and linear support vector regression.

(c) The third strategy is to combine the previous two. First, nonlinearly transform the data to another feature space. Then, perform linear regression but with a robust cost function. This results in a linear regressor in the new space but a nonlinear regressor in the original space. The third strategy will be discussed when we discuss the nonlinear regressors.

In this section, we consider the first strategy.

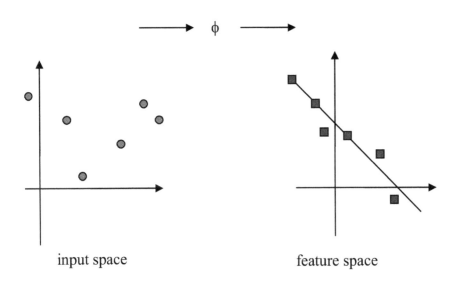

Figure 4.4.1: Nonlinear transformation of data.

As was done in Section 3.5, nonlinear regression can be achieved easily by use of kernels. Let $K(x, z)$ be a given kernel on $X \times X$ such that

$$K(x, z) := \langle \phi(x), \phi(z) \rangle, \quad x, z \in X,$$

where ϕ is the feature map from the input space X to the feature space F.

In the dual form of the Widrow-Hoff algorithms for the linear regressor, the training data only enters the algorithms through the inner product $\langle x_j, x_q \rangle$ and the final predictive function depends only upon the inner product $\langle x_j, x \rangle$. This motivates us to consider the mapping of x in the input space into $\phi(x)$ in the feature space. Thus, we have

$$\langle \phi(x_j), \phi(x_q) \rangle = K(x_j, x_q) \quad \text{and} \quad \langle \phi(x_j), \phi(x) \rangle = K(x_j, x).$$

Hence, the nonlinear predictive function becomes

$$f_{w,b}(x) = \sum_{j=1}^{l} \eta \alpha_j \langle \phi(x_j), \phi(x) \rangle + b = \sum_{j=1}^{l} \eta \alpha_j K(x_j, x) + b,$$

and the qth error becomes

$$e_q := d_q - f_{w,b}(x_q) = d_q - \sum_{j=1}^{l} \eta \alpha_j \langle \phi(x_j), \phi(x_q) \rangle - b$$

$$= d_q - \sum_{j=1}^{l} \eta \alpha_j K(x_j, x_q) - b.$$

We have the following algorithm.

Algorithm 4.4.1

Data: training set $S := \{(x_q, d_q)\}_{q=1}^{l} \subseteq X \times Y$ and a learning rate $\eta > 0$

Goal: (α, b) defining a nonlinear predictive function minimizing the sum of squared errors

Step 1: $\alpha \leftarrow 0$; $b \leftarrow 0$;

Step 2:   repeat

            for $q = 1$ to l

$$e \leftarrow d_q - \sum_{j=1}^{l} \eta \alpha_j K(x_j, x_q) - b;$$

$$\alpha_q \leftarrow \alpha_q + e;$$

$$b \leftarrow b + \eta e;$$

            end for

            until convergence criterion satisfied

            return (α, b)

In the preceding algorithm, when using (x_q, d_q) as the qth training example, we only increase the α_q by e and bias b by ηe with other α_j, $j \neq q$, unaffected. This can only change the value of the predictive function $f(x)$ by $\eta e K(x_q, x) + \eta e$, which requires just one evaluation of f with all training examples. Thus, we have the following alternative learning algorithm.

Algorithm 4.4.2

Data: training set $S := \{(x_q, d_q)\}_{q=1}^{l} \subseteq X \times Y$ and a learning rate $\eta > 0$

Goal: (α, b) defining a nonlinear predictive function minimizing the sum of squared errors

Step 1: $\alpha \leftarrow 0$; $b \leftarrow 0$; $y_q \leftarrow 0$ for all $q \in l$;

Step 2:   repeat

             for $q = 1$ to l

$$e \leftarrow d_q - y_q;$$
$$\alpha_q \leftarrow \alpha_q + e;$$
$$b \leftarrow b + \eta e;$$

                 for $j = 1$ to l

$$y_j \leftarrow y_j + \eta e K(x_q, x_j) + \eta e;$$

                 end for

             end for

         until convergence criterion satisfied

         return (α, b)

4.5   Ridge Regressor

Based on the second strategy presented in Section 4.4, we study in this section the ridge regressors, which some researchers call them least squares support vector machines (LS-SVMs).

Let $X \subseteq \mathfrak{R}^n$ and $Y \subseteq \mathfrak{R}$. Suppose we are given the training set

$$S := \{(x_q, d_q)\}_{q=1}^{l} \subseteq X \times Y.$$

The ridge regression is to choose a (w, b) that minimizes

$$E(w, b) := \frac{1}{2}\langle w, w \rangle + \frac{C}{2}\sum_{q=1}^{l}\left[d_q - \langle w, x_q \rangle - b\right]^2,$$

where $C > 0$ is the regularization parameter (or smoothing parameter) that controls a trade-off between low square loss and low norm of the solution. Note that for the linear function f, we have

$$\|\partial f / \partial x\|^2 = \|w\|^2.$$

In regularization theory, the term

$$\frac{1}{2C}\langle w, w \rangle = \frac{1}{2C}w^T w = \frac{1}{2C}\|w\|^2$$

is called the smoothing functional, stabilizer, or roughness penalty, which is used to assure that the approximating function is smooth.

Define

$$z := \begin{bmatrix} x \\ 1 \end{bmatrix} \in \mathfrak{R}^{n+1}, \quad x_{n+1} = 1, \quad \beta := \begin{bmatrix} w \\ b \end{bmatrix} \in \mathfrak{R}^{n+1}, \quad w_{n+1} = b,$$

$$d = \begin{bmatrix} d_1 \\ \vdots \\ d_l \end{bmatrix} \in \mathfrak{R}^l, \quad Z = \begin{bmatrix} x_{11} & x_{12} & \cdots & x_{1n} & 1 \\ x_{21} & x_{22} & \cdots & x_{2n} & 1 \\ \vdots & \vdots & \ddots & \vdots & \vdots \\ x_{l1} & x_{l2} & \cdots & x_{ln} & 1 \end{bmatrix} \in \mathfrak{R}^{l \times (n+1)},$$

$$J := \begin{bmatrix} I_n & 0 \\ 0 & 0 \end{bmatrix} \in \mathfrak{R}^{(n+1) \times (n+1)}.$$

Then, we have

$$E(\beta) = \frac{1}{2}\beta^T J\beta + \frac{C}{2}\|d - Z\beta\|^2$$

$$= \frac{1}{2}\beta^T J\beta + \frac{C}{2}\langle d - Z\beta, d - Z\beta \rangle$$

$$= \frac{1}{2}\beta^T J\beta + \frac{C}{2}\left(d^T d - 2\beta^T Z^T d + \beta^T Z^T Z\beta\right)$$

$$= \frac{1}{2}\beta^T J\beta + \frac{C}{2}d^T d - C\beta^T Z^T d + \frac{C}{2}\beta^T Z^T Z\beta.$$

Taking the derivative of E with respect to β and setting it to zero, we have

$$0 = \frac{\partial E}{\partial \beta} = J\beta* - CZ^T d + CZ^T Z\beta*,$$

or

$$\left(J + CZ^T Z\right)\beta* = CZ^T d.$$

This is the **normal equation** for the ridge regression. Since $J + CZ^T Z$ is nonsingular for any $C > 0$ (Exercise 4.12.8), the unique solution of the ridge normal equation is given by

$$\beta* = \left(J + CZ^T Z\right)^{-1}CZ^T d.$$

Now, we derive a delta learning rule, which is an on-line (or pattern-based) incremental gradient descent strategy, for finding the ridge regressor.

Define

$$E_q(w, b) := \frac{1}{2l}w^T w + \frac{C}{2}\left(d_q - x_q^T w - b\right)^2, \quad q \in \underline{l}$$

$$\Rightarrow \quad E(w, b) = \sum_{q=1}^{l} E_q(w, b).$$

The delta learning rule is given by

$$w \leftarrow w - \eta\frac{\partial E_q}{\partial w}(w, b), \quad b \leftarrow b - \eta\frac{\partial E_q}{\partial b}(w, b).$$

Since

$$\frac{\partial E_q}{\partial w} = \frac{1}{l}w - C\left(d_q - x_q^T w - b\right)x_q, \quad \frac{\partial E_q}{\partial b} = -C\left(d_q - x_q^T w - b\right),$$

if we define $e_q := d_q - x_q^T w - b$, then updating rule becomes

$$w \leftarrow \left(1 - l^{-1}\eta\right)w + \eta C e_q x_q, \quad b \leftarrow b + \eta C e_q.$$

Thus, we have the following primal form of the ridge regression algorithm.

Algorithm 4.5.1: (primal form)

Data: training set $S := \{(x_q, d_q)\}_{q=1}^{l} \subseteq X \times Y$ and a learning rate $0 < \eta < 2l$

Goal: (w, b) defining a linear predictive function based on ridge regression

Step 1: $w \leftarrow 0; \ b \leftarrow 0;$
Step 2:   repeat
            for $q = 1$ to l
                $e \leftarrow d_q - \langle x_q, w \rangle - b;$
                $w \leftarrow \left(1 - l^{-1}\eta\right)w + \eta Cex_q;$
                $b \leftarrow b + \eta Ce;$
            end for
            until convergence criterion satisfied
            return (w, b)

In the primal form of ridge regression algorithm starting from $w_0 = 0$, the final weight is of the form

$$w = \sum_{j=1}^{l} \eta \alpha_j x_j,$$

and α_j, $j \in \underline{l}$, are some scalars. Then, we have

$$f_{w,b}(x) := \langle x, w \rangle + b = \left\langle x, \sum_{j=1}^{l} \eta \alpha_j x_j \right\rangle + b = \sum_{j=1}^{l} \eta \alpha_j \langle x, x_j \rangle + b,$$

$$e_q := d_q - f_{w,b}(x_q) = d_q - \sum_{j=1}^{l} \eta \alpha_j \langle x_q, x_j \rangle - b.$$

In the preceding algorithm, we then have

$$w \leftarrow (1 - l^{-1}\eta)w + \eta C e x_q$$

$$= (1 - l^{-1}\eta) \sum_{j=1}^{l} \eta \alpha_j x_j + \eta C e x_q$$

$$= \sum_{j=1}^{l} \eta (1 - l^{-1}\eta) \alpha_j x_j + \eta C e x_q.$$

Hence we have the dual form of the ridge regression algorithm.

Algorithm 4.5.2: (dual form)

Data: training set $S := \{(x_q, d_q)\}_{q=1}^{l} \subseteq X \times Y$ and a learning rate $0 < \eta < 2l$

Goal: (α, b) defining a linear predictive function based on ridge regression

Step 1: $\alpha \leftarrow 0$; $b \leftarrow 0$; $scalar = 1 - l^{-1}\eta$;

Step 2:   repeat
         for $q = 1$ to l

$$e \leftarrow d_q - \sum_{j=1}^{l} \eta \alpha_j \langle x_q, x_j \rangle - b;$$

         for $j = 1$ to l
             if $(j = q)$ $\alpha_j \leftarrow scalar * \alpha_j + Ce$;
             else $\alpha_j \leftarrow scalar * \alpha_j$;
         end for
             $b \leftarrow b + \eta Ce$;
         end for
         until convergence criterion satisfied
         return (α, b)

4.6 Recursive Algorithm for Ridge Regressor

In this section, we present a recursive ridge algorithm that finds the best ridge regressor for all training examples up to the present iteration k.

Suppose $k \in \underline{l}$ is given, then the solution for k training data $(x_1, d_1), \ldots, (x_k, d_k)$ is given by

$$\beta_{(k)} = \left(J + CZ_{(k)}^T Z_{(k)} \right)^{-1} CZ_{(k)}^T d_{(k)},$$

where

$$\beta_{(k)} := \begin{bmatrix} w_{(k)} \\ b_{(k)} \end{bmatrix} \in \mathfrak{R}^{n+1}, \quad d_{(k)} := \begin{bmatrix} d_1 \\ \vdots \\ d_k \end{bmatrix} \in \mathfrak{R}^k,$$

$$Z_{(k)} = \begin{bmatrix} x_{11} & x_{12} & \cdots & x_{1n} & 1 \\ x_{21} & x_{22} & \cdots & x_{2n} & 1 \\ \vdots & \vdots & \ddots & \vdots & \vdots \\ x_{k1} & x_{k2} & \cdots & x_{kn} & 1 \end{bmatrix} \in \mathfrak{R}^{k \times (n+1)}.$$

It can also be written as

$$\beta_{(k)} = H_k F_k, \quad H_k = \left(J + CZ_{(k)}^T Z_{(k)} \right)^{-1}, \quad F_k = CZ_{(k)}^T d_{(k)}.$$

Define

$$z_j := \begin{bmatrix} x_j \\ 1 \end{bmatrix} \in \mathfrak{R}^{n+1}, \quad j \in \underline{l},$$

then the prediction error of the next example (x_{k+1}, d_{k+1}) becomes

$$e_{k+1} := d_{k+1} - \langle x_{k+1}, w_{(k)} \rangle - b_{(k)} = d_{k+1} - z_{k+1}^T \beta_{(k)}.$$

By the definition above, the least squares solution for $k+1$ training data $(x_1, d_1), \ldots, (x_k, d_k), (x_{k+1}, d_{k+1})$ is given by

$$\beta_{(k+1)} = \left(J + CZ_{(k+1)}^T Z_{(k+1)}\right)^{-1} CZ_{(k+1)}^T d_{(k+1)} = H_{k+1} F_{k+1},$$

where

$$\beta_{(k+1)} := \begin{bmatrix} w_{(k+1)} \\ b_{(k+1)} \end{bmatrix}, \quad d_{(k+1)} := \begin{bmatrix} d_1 \\ \vdots \\ d_{k+1} \end{bmatrix} = \begin{bmatrix} d_{(k)} \\ d_{k+1} \end{bmatrix},$$

$$Z_{(k+1)} = \begin{bmatrix} x_{11} & x_{12} & \cdots & x_{1n} & 1 \\ x_{21} & x_{22} & \cdots & x_{2n} & 1 \\ \vdots & \vdots & \ddots & \vdots & \vdots \\ x_{(k+1),1} & x_{(k+1),2} & \cdots & x_{(k+1),n} & 1 \end{bmatrix} = \begin{bmatrix} Z_{(k)} \\ z_{k+1}^T \end{bmatrix},$$

$$H_{k+1} = \left(J + CZ_{(k+1)}^T Z_{(k+1)}\right)^{-1}, \quad F_{k+1} = CZ_{(k+1)}^T d_{(k+1)}.$$

From the definitions stated above, we have

$$H_{k+1}^{-1} = J + CZ_{(k+1)}^T Z_{(k+1)} = J + C \begin{bmatrix} Z_{(k)}^T & z_{k+1} \end{bmatrix} \begin{bmatrix} Z_{(k)} \\ z_{k+1}^T \end{bmatrix}$$

$$= J + CZ_{(k)}^T Z_{(k)} + Cz_{k+1} z_{k+1}^T = H_k^{-1} + Cz_{k+1} z_{k+1}^T.$$

By using the famous Woodbury inversion formula:

$$\left(A + BCD\right)^{-1} = A^{-1} - A^{-1} B \left(DA^{-1} B + C^{-1}\right)^{-1} DA^{-1},$$

we have

$$H_{k+1} = \left(H_{k+1}^{-1}\right)^{-1} = \left(H_k^{-1} + Cz_{k+1} z_{k+1}^T\right)^{-1} = \left(H_k^{-1} + z_{k+1} \cdot C \cdot z_{k+1}^T\right)^{-1}$$

$$= H_k - H_k z_{k+1} \left(z_{k+1}^T H_k z_{k+1} + C^{-1}\right)^{-1} z_{k+1}^T H_k$$

$$= H_k - \left(C^{-1} + z_{k+1}^T H_k z_{k+1}\right)^{-1} H_k z_{k+1} z_{k+1}^T H_k$$

$$= H_k - \left(C^{-1} + z_{k+1}^T H_k z_{k+1}\right)^{-1} H_k z_{k+1} \left(H_k z_{k+1}\right)^T,$$

where $\left(C^{-1} + z_{k+1}^T H_k z_{k+1}\right)$ is a scalar and $H_k z_{k+1} \left(H_k z_{k+1}\right)^T$ is a rank-one matrix. Moreover, we have

$$F_{k+1} = CZ_{(k+1)}^T d_{(k+1)} = C\begin{bmatrix} Z_{(k)}^T & z_{k+1} \end{bmatrix}\begin{bmatrix} d_{(k)} \\ d_{k+1} \end{bmatrix} = CZ_{(k)}^T d_{(k)} + Cz_{k+1}d_{k+1}$$

$$= F_k + Cz_{k+1}\left(e_{k+1} + z_{k+1}^T \beta_{(k)}\right)$$

$$= H_k^{-1}\beta_{(k)} + Cz_{k+1}z_{k+1}^T \beta_{(k)} + Cz_{k+1}e_{k+1}$$

$$= \left(H_k^{-1} + Cz_{k+1}z_{k+1}^T\right)\beta_{(k)} + Cz_{k+1}e_{k+1}$$

$$= H_{k+1}^{-1}\beta_{(k)} + Cz_{k+1}e_{k+1}.$$

Hence, the updating law becomes

$$\beta_{(k+1)} = H_{k+1}F_{k+1} = H_{k+1}\left(H_{k+1}^{-1}\beta_{(k)} + Cz_{k+1}e_{k+1}\right)$$

$$= \beta_{(k)} + CH_{k+1}z_{k+1}e_{k+1}.$$

Define $r_{k+1} := H_k z_{k+1}$ and $s_{k+1} := \left(C^{-1} + z_{k+1}^T r_{k+1}\right)^{-1}$. Then, we have

$$H_{k+1} = H_k - s_{k+1}r_{k+1}r_{k+1}^T, \quad \beta_{(k+1)} = \beta_{(k)} + Ce_{k+1}H_{k+1}z_{k+1}.$$

To obtain a good initial guess of w and b, we solve the ridge regression problem when only the first example (x_1, d_1) is available. The solution is given by

$$\beta_{(1)} = \left(J + CZ_{(1)}^T Z_{(1)}\right)^{-1} CZ_{(1)}^T d_{(1)} = H_1 F_1.$$

By definition we have

$$J + CZ_{(1)}^T Z_{(1)} = \begin{bmatrix} I_n & 0 \\ 0 & 0 \end{bmatrix} + C\begin{bmatrix} x_1 \\ 1 \end{bmatrix}\begin{bmatrix} x_1^T & 1 \end{bmatrix} = \begin{bmatrix} I_n + Cx_1x_1^T & Cx_1 \\ Cx_1^T & C \end{bmatrix}$$

$$\Rightarrow H_1 = \left(J + CZ_{(1)}^T Z_{(1)}\right)^{-1} = \begin{bmatrix} I_n + Cx_1x_1^T & Cx_1 \\ Cx_1^T & C \end{bmatrix}^{-1}$$

$$= \begin{bmatrix} I_n & -x_1 \\ -x_1^T & C^{-1} + x_1^T x_1 \end{bmatrix},$$

$$F_1 = CZ_{(1)}^T d_{(1)} = C\begin{bmatrix} x_1 \\ 1 \end{bmatrix} d_1 = \begin{bmatrix} Cd_1 x_1 \\ Cd_1 \end{bmatrix}$$

$$\Rightarrow \begin{bmatrix} w \\ b \end{bmatrix} = \beta_{(1)} = H_1 F_1 = \begin{bmatrix} 0 \\ d_1 \end{bmatrix}.$$

Thus, we have the following algorithm.

Algorithm 4.6.1

Data: training set $S := \{(x_q, d_q)\}_{q=1}^l \subseteq X \times Y$

Goal: (w, b) defining a linear predictive function based on ridge regression

Step 1: $\beta = \begin{bmatrix} w \\ b \end{bmatrix} \leftarrow \begin{bmatrix} 0 \\ d_1 \end{bmatrix}$ and $H = \begin{bmatrix} I_n & -x_1 \\ -x_1^T & C^{-1} + x_1^T x_1 \end{bmatrix}$;

Step 2: //first epoch

for $q = 2$ to l

$$z_q := \begin{bmatrix} x_q \\ 1 \end{bmatrix};$$

$e \leftarrow d_q - z_q^T \beta$;

$r \leftarrow Hz_q$;

$s \leftarrow \left(C^{-1} + z_q^T r\right)^{-1}$;

$H \leftarrow H - srr^T$;

$r \leftarrow Hz_q$;

$\beta \leftarrow \beta + Cer$;

end for

//following epochs if necessary

repeat

for $q = 1$ to l

$$z_q := \begin{bmatrix} x_q \\ 1 \end{bmatrix};$$

$$e \leftarrow d_q - z_q^T \beta;$$

$$r \leftarrow Hz_q;$$

$$s \leftarrow \left(C^{-1} + z_q^T r\right)^{-1};$$

$$H \leftarrow H - srr^T;$$

$$r \leftarrow Hz_q;$$

$$\beta \leftarrow \beta + Cer;$$

      end for
    until convergence criterion satisfied

    return $\beta = \begin{bmatrix} w \\ b \end{bmatrix}$

Note that in the preceding algorithm, since rr^T is a rank-one matrix, the statement $H \leftarrow H - srr^T$ can be implemented as

    for $j = 1$ to $n+1$
      for $k = 1$ to $n+1$
        $H_{jk} \leftarrow H_{jk} - s * r_j * r_k;$
      end for
    end for

4.7 Dual Problem of Ridge Regression

The ridge regression problem can also be solved by using the Lagrange optimization technique. The ridge regression problem can be written as the following primal optimization problem:

(P0)   minimize $\dfrac{1}{2} w^T w + \dfrac{C}{2} \sum_{q=1}^{l} \xi_q^2$

          subject to $d_q - w^T x_q - b = \xi_q$ for all $q \in \underline{l}$.

This is a constrained minimization with l equality constraints. Now, we consider its dual problem. The Lagrangian is given by

$$L_p(w, b, \xi, \alpha) := \frac{1}{2}w^T w + \frac{C}{2}\sum_{q=1}^{l}\xi_q^2 - \sum_{q=1}^{l}\alpha_q(\xi_q - d_q + w^T x_q + b).$$

The dual function is defined by

$$J_d(\alpha) := \min_{w,b,\xi} L_p(w, b, \xi, \alpha).$$

Clearly, we have

$$0 = \frac{\partial L_p}{\partial w} = w - \sum_{q=1}^{l}\alpha_q x_q,$$

$$0 = \frac{\partial L_p}{\partial b} = -\sum_{q=1}^{l}\alpha_q,$$

$$0 = \frac{\partial L_p}{\partial \xi_q} = C\xi_q - \alpha_q, \quad q \in \underline{l}$$

$$\Rightarrow \quad w = \sum_{q=1}^{l}\alpha_q x_q, \quad \sum_{q=1}^{l}\alpha_q = 0, \quad \xi_q = C^{-1}\alpha_q, \quad q \in \underline{l}$$

$$\Rightarrow \quad J_d(\alpha) = \sum_{q=1}^{l}\alpha_q d_q - \frac{1}{2}\sum_{q=1}^{l}\sum_{j=1}^{l}\alpha_q \alpha_j x_q^T x_j - \frac{1}{2C}\sum_{q=1}^{l}\alpha_q^2.$$

Hence, the dual optimization problem can be stated as follows:

(D0)   maximize $\sum_{q=1}^{l}\alpha_q d_q - \frac{1}{2}\sum_{q=1}^{l}\sum_{j=1}^{l}\alpha_q \alpha_j \langle x_q, x_j \rangle - \frac{1}{2C}\sum_{q=1}^{l}\alpha_q^2$

subject to $\sum_{q=1}^{l}\alpha_q = 0.$

This is a constrained maximization with a single equality constraint. Suppose $\alpha*$ solves the problem (D0). Define $I_{sv} := \{q \in \underline{l} : \alpha_q^* \neq 0\}$. Then, we have

$$w* = \sum_{q=1}^{l}\alpha_q^* x_q = \sum_{q \in I_{sv}}\alpha_q^* x_q, \quad \xi_q^* = C^{-1}\alpha_q^*, \quad q \in \underline{l}.$$

Given any $k \in \underline{l}$, from

$$d_k - \left(w*\right)^T x_k - b* = \xi_k^* = C^{-1}\alpha_k^*,$$

we have

$$b* = d_k - C^{-1}\alpha_k^* - \left(w*\right)^T x_k = d_k - C^{-1}\alpha_k^* - \sum_{q \in I_{sv}} \alpha_q^* \langle x_q, x_k \rangle.$$

The optimal predictive function is thus given by

$$f*(x) = \langle w*, x \rangle + b* = \sum_{q \in I_{sv}} \alpha_q^* \langle x_q, x \rangle + b*.$$

Let α_q, $q \in \underline{l}$, be the current value of the dual variable. Then, the current primal variables, i.e., weight, bias, and slack variables, are calculated as

$$w = \sum_{q=1}^{l} \alpha_q x_q,$$

$$b = d_k - C^{-1}\alpha_k - \sum_{q=1}^{l} \alpha_q \langle x_q, x_k \rangle,$$

$$\xi_q = C^{-1}\alpha_q,$$

for any α_k. There is no guarantee that these primal variables are feasible, i.e., for all $q \in \underline{l}$,

$$d_q - w^T x_q - b$$

$$= \left(d_q - d_k\right) + C^{-1}\alpha_k - \left[\sum_{j=1}^{l}\alpha_j \langle x_j, x_q \rangle - \sum_{j=1}^{l}\alpha_j \langle x_j, x_k \rangle\right]$$

$$= \xi_q = C^{-1}\alpha_q.$$

Hence, it may not always be possible to use the feasibility gap or the percentage duality gap, as an indicator of the stopping criterion.

Note that (P0) and (D0) are quadratic programs. In fact, we can solve (P0) and (D0) simultaneously via a linear equation. Using the KKT conditions, we have

$$w = \sum_{j=1}^{l} \alpha_j x_j, \quad \sum_{q=1}^{l} \alpha_q = 0,$$

$$\xi_q = C^{-1}\alpha_q, \quad d_q - w^T x_q - b = \xi_q, \quad q \in \underline{l}$$

$$\Rightarrow \sum_{q=1}^{l} \alpha_q = 0, \quad d_q - \sum_{j=1}^{l} \alpha_j x_j^T x_q - b = C^{-1}\alpha_q, \quad q \in \underline{l}$$

$$\Rightarrow \sum_{q=1}^{l} \alpha_q = 0, \quad b + C^{-1}\alpha_q + \sum_{j=1}^{l} \alpha_j x_j^T x_q = d_q, \quad q \in \underline{l}.$$

In matrix form, this becomes

$$\left[\begin{array}{c|c} 0 & \mathbf{1}^T \\ \hline \mathbf{1} & \Omega + C^{-1}I_l \end{array} \right] \left[\begin{array}{c} b \\ \hline \alpha \end{array} \right] = \left[\begin{array}{c} 0 \\ d \end{array} \right],$$

where

$$\alpha = \begin{bmatrix} \alpha_1 \\ \vdots \\ \alpha_l \end{bmatrix}, \quad \mathbf{1} = \begin{bmatrix} 1 \\ \vdots \\ 1 \end{bmatrix}, \quad d = \begin{bmatrix} d_1 \\ \vdots \\ d_l \end{bmatrix} \in \mathfrak{R}^l,$$

$$\Omega = \begin{bmatrix} \langle x_1, x_1 \rangle & \langle x_1, x_2 \rangle & \cdots & \langle x_1, x_l \rangle \\ \langle x_2, x_1 \rangle & \langle x_2, x_2 \rangle & \cdots & \langle x_2, x_l \rangle \\ \cdots & \cdots & \cdots & \cdots \\ \langle x_l, x_1 \rangle & \langle x_l, x_2 \rangle & \cdots & \langle x_l, x_l \rangle \end{bmatrix}.$$

Thus we need only solve the preceding matrix equation. If the kernel is used to replace the inner product, Ω becomes

$$\Omega = \begin{bmatrix} K(x_1, x_1) & K(x_1, x_2) & \cdots & K(x_1, x_l) \\ K(x_2, x_1) & K(x_2, x_2) & \cdots & K(x_2, x_l) \\ \cdots & \cdots & \cdots & \cdots \\ K(x_l, x_1) & K(x_l, x_2) & \cdots & K(x_l, x_l) \end{bmatrix}.$$

4.8 Slack Variable for Regression

In this section, we introduce the slack variables for regression problems. This will be useful when we consider the soft regressors in later sections.

Let $\varepsilon > 0$ be given. The **(margin) slack variable** s_q of an example (x_q, d_q) with respect to the hyperplane $H_{w,b}$ and target margin ε is defined via the following ε-insensitive loss function by

$$s_q := \max\left(0, |d_q - [\langle w, x_q \rangle + b]| - \varepsilon\right).$$

From the definition, we have

$$s_q \geq 0 \quad \text{and} \quad |d_q - [\langle w, x_q \rangle + b]| \leq s_q + \varepsilon.$$

See Figure 4.8.1 for illustration. Clearly, ξ_q measures the amount by which the example (x_q, d_q) fails to fall in the ε-band of the hyperplane $H_{w,b}$.

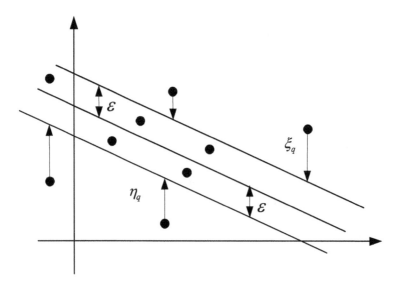

Figure 4.8.1: Slack variables for regression problems.

Let us analyze the slack variable more closely.

Case 1: If $d_q - \left[\langle w, x_q \rangle + b \right] > \varepsilon > 0$, then

$$\left| d_q - \left[\langle w, x_q \rangle + b \right] \right| - \varepsilon = d_q - \left[\langle w, x_q \rangle + b \right] - \varepsilon > 0,$$
$$s_q = d_q - \left[\langle w, x_q \rangle + b \right] - \varepsilon > 0,$$
$$d_q - \left[\langle w, x_q \rangle + b \right] = \varepsilon + s_q, \quad s_q > 0.$$

Case 2: If $0 \leq d_q - \left[\langle w, x_q \rangle + b \right] \leq \varepsilon$, then

$$\left| d_q - \left[\langle w, x_q \rangle + b \right] \right| - \varepsilon = d_q - \left[\langle w, x_q \rangle + b \right] - \varepsilon \leq 0, \quad s_q = 0,$$
$$d_q - \left[\langle w, x_q \rangle + b \right] \leq \varepsilon + s_q, \quad s_q = 0.$$

Case 3: If $-\varepsilon \leq d_q - \left[\langle w, x_q \rangle + b \right] \leq 0$, then

$$\left| d_q - \left[\langle w, x_q \rangle + b \right] \right| - \varepsilon = \left[\langle w, x_q \rangle + b \right] - d_q - \varepsilon \leq 0, \quad s_q = 0,$$

$$\left[\langle w, x_q \rangle + b\right] - d_q \leq \varepsilon + s_q, \quad s_q = 0.$$

Case 4: If $d_q - \left[\langle w, x_q \rangle + b\right] < -\varepsilon < 0$, then

$$\left|d_q - \left[\langle w, x_q \rangle + b\right]\right| - \varepsilon = \left[\langle w, x_q \rangle + b\right] - d_q - \varepsilon > 0,$$
$$s_q = \left[\langle w, x_q \rangle + b\right] - d_q - \varepsilon > 0,$$
$$\left[\langle w, x_q \rangle + b\right] - d_q = \varepsilon + s_q, \quad s_q > 0.$$

From the preceding analysis, the quantity defined by

$$\|s\|_1 := \sum_{q=1}^{l} s_q \quad \text{or} \quad \|s\|_2^2 := \sum_{q=1}^{l} s_q^2$$

measures the amount by which the training set fails to fall in the ε-band of the hyperplane.

It is convenient to introduce two slack variables, one for exceeding the target value by more than ε, and the other for being more than ε below the target. Let us define the slack variables as

$$\xi_q := \max\left(0, d_q - \left[\langle w, x_q \rangle + b\right] - \varepsilon\right),$$
$$\eta_q := \max\left(0, \left[\langle w, x_q \rangle + b\right] - d_q - \varepsilon\right).$$

Thus, we have

$$d_q - \left[\langle w, x_q \rangle + b\right] \leq \varepsilon + \xi_q, \quad \xi_q \geq 0,$$
$$\left[\langle w, x_q \rangle + b\right] - d_q \leq \varepsilon + \eta_q, \quad \eta_q \geq 0.$$

Let us analyze these slack variables more closely.

Case 1': If $d_q - \left[\langle w, x_q \rangle + b\right] > \varepsilon > 0$, then

$$d_q - \left[\langle w, x_q \rangle + b\right] - \varepsilon > 0, \quad \xi_q = d_q - \left[\langle w, x_q \rangle + b\right] - \varepsilon > 0,$$

$$d_q - \left[\langle w, x_q \rangle + b\right] = \varepsilon + \xi_q, \quad \xi_q > 0,$$
$$\left[\langle w, x_q \rangle + b\right] - d_q - \varepsilon < -\varepsilon - \varepsilon = -2\varepsilon < 0, \quad \eta_q = 0,$$
$$\left[\langle w, x_q \rangle + b\right] - d_q < \varepsilon + \eta_q, \quad \eta_q = 0.$$

Case 2': If $d_q - \left[\langle w, x_q \rangle + b\right] = \varepsilon > 0$, then

$$d_q - \left[\langle w, x_q \rangle + b\right] - \varepsilon = 0, \quad \xi_q = d_q - \left[\langle w, x_q \rangle + b\right] - \varepsilon = 0,$$
$$d_q - \left[\langle w, x_q \rangle + b\right] = \varepsilon + \xi_q, \quad \xi_q = 0,$$
$$\left[\langle w, x_q \rangle + b\right] - d_q - \varepsilon = -\varepsilon - \varepsilon = -2\varepsilon < 0, \quad \eta_q = 0,$$
$$\left[\langle w, x_q \rangle + b\right] - d_q < \varepsilon + \eta_q, \quad \eta_q = 0.$$

Case 3': If $-\varepsilon < d_q - \left[\langle w, x_q \rangle + b\right] < \varepsilon$, then

$$d_q - \left[\langle w, x_q \rangle + b\right] - \varepsilon < 0, \quad \xi_q = 0,$$
$$d_q - \left[\langle w, x_q \rangle + b\right] < \varepsilon + \xi_q, \quad \xi_q = 0,$$
$$\left[\langle w, x_q \rangle + b\right] - d_q - \varepsilon < 0, \quad \eta_q = 0,$$
$$\left[\langle w, x_q \rangle + b\right] - d_q < \varepsilon + \eta_q, \quad \eta_q = 0.$$

Case 4': If $-\varepsilon = d_q - \left[\langle w, x_q \rangle + b\right] < 0$, then

$$d_q - \left[\langle w, x_q \rangle + b\right] - \varepsilon = -\varepsilon - \varepsilon = -2\varepsilon < 0, \quad \xi_q = 0,$$
$$d_q - \left[\langle w, x_q \rangle + b\right] < \varepsilon + \xi_q, \quad \xi_q = 0,$$
$$\left[\langle w, x_q \rangle + b\right] - d_q - \varepsilon = \varepsilon - \varepsilon = 0,$$
$$\eta_q = \left[\langle w, x_q \rangle + b\right] - d_q - \varepsilon = 0,$$
$$\left[\langle w, x_q \rangle + b\right] - d_q = \varepsilon + \eta_q, \quad \eta_q = 0.$$

Case 5': If $d_q - \left[\langle w, x_q \rangle + b\right] < -\varepsilon < 0$, then

$$d_q - \left[\langle w, x_q \rangle + b\right] - \varepsilon < -\varepsilon - \varepsilon = -2\varepsilon < 0, \quad \xi_q = 0,$$

$$d_q - \left[\langle w, x_q \rangle + b\right] < \varepsilon + \xi_q, \quad \xi_q = 0,$$
$$\left[\langle w, x_q \rangle + b\right] - d_q - \varepsilon > 0, \quad \eta_q = \left[\langle w, x_q \rangle + b\right] - d_q - \varepsilon > 0,$$
$$\left[\langle w, x_q \rangle + b\right] - d_q = \varepsilon + \eta_q, \quad \eta_q > 0.$$

From the preceding analysis, it is clear that $\xi_q \eta_q = 0$. Hence, we have

$$\xi_q + \eta_q = s_q := \max\left(0, \left|d_q - \left[\langle w, x_q \rangle + b\right] - \varepsilon\right|\right),$$

which is exactly the slack variable we defined at the beginning. Likewise, the quantity defined by

$$\sum_{q=1}^{l} \left(\xi_q + \eta_q\right) \text{ or } \sum_{q=1}^{l} \left(\xi_q^2 + \eta_q^2\right)$$

measures the total amount by which the training set fails to fall in the ε-band of the hyperplane $H_{w,b}$.

4.9 1-norm Soft Regressor

Recall the second strategy presented in Section 4.4. Based on the concepts of regularization in ridge regression and slack variables for regression, in this and the next sections, we present the soft regressors. First, we consider the 1-norm soft regressors.

Let $X \subseteq \mathfrak{R}^n$ and $Y \subseteq \mathfrak{R}$. Suppose we are given the training set

$$S := \left\{\left(x_q, d_q\right)\right\}_{q=1}^{l} \subseteq X \times Y.$$

The problem of linear regression is to find a linear function f that fits the data:

$$f(x) = \langle w, x \rangle + b.$$

Now we use $\sum_{q=1}^{l}\left(\xi_q + \eta_q\right)$ to measure the amount by which the training set fails to fall in the ε-band of the hyperplane.

Consider the following primal optimization problem (with $C > 0$):

(P1) minimize $\dfrac{1}{2}w^T w + C\sum_{q=1}^{l}\left(\xi_q + \eta_q\right)$

    subject to $d_q - \left[\langle w, x_q\rangle + b\right] \leq \varepsilon + \xi_q, \ \ \xi_q \geq 0,$

         $\left[\langle w, x_q\rangle + b\right] - d_q \leq \varepsilon + \eta_q, \ \ \eta_q \geq 0,$ for all $q \in l.$

The problem (P1) is a standard quadratic convex program. Note that we have introduced two slack variables, one for exceeding the target value by more than ε, and the other for being more than ε below the target.

Suppose $\left(w^*, b^*, \xi^*, \eta^*\right)$ solves the preceding primal optimization problem. Then the optimal predictive function is given by $f^*(x) = \langle w^*, x\rangle + b^*.$

Now, we consider its dual problem. The Lagrangian is given by

$$L\left(w, b, \xi, \eta, \alpha, \beta, \mu, \rho\right) := \frac{1}{2}w^T w + C\sum_{q=1}^{l}\left(\xi_q + \eta_q\right)$$

$$-\sum_{q=1}^{l}\alpha_q\left(\varepsilon + \xi_q - d_q + w^T x_q + b\right)$$

$$-\sum_{q=1}^{l}\beta_q\left(\varepsilon + \eta_q - w^T x_q - b + d_q\right)$$

$$-\sum_{q=1}^{l}\mu_q\xi_q - \sum_{q=1}^{l}\rho_q\eta_q .$$

The dual function is given by

$$J_d\left(\alpha, \beta, \mu, \rho\right) := \min_{w,b,\xi,\eta} L\left(w, b, \xi, \eta, \alpha, \beta, \mu, \rho\right).$$

Clearly, we have

$$0 = \frac{\partial L}{\partial w} = w - \sum_{q=1}^{l} \alpha_q x_q + \sum_{q=1}^{l} \beta_q x_q, \quad 0 = \frac{\partial L}{\partial b} = -\sum_{q=1}^{l} \alpha_q + \sum_{q=1}^{l} \beta_q,$$

$$0 = \frac{\partial L}{\partial \xi_q} = C - \alpha_q - \mu_q, \quad 0 = \frac{\partial L}{\partial \eta_q} = C - \beta_q - \rho_q, \quad q \in \underline{l}$$

$$\Rightarrow \quad w = \sum_{q=1}^{l}(\alpha_q - \beta_q)x_q, \quad \sum_{q=1}^{l}(\alpha_q - \beta_q) = 0,$$

$$\alpha_q + \mu_q = C, \quad \beta_q + \rho_q = C, \quad q \in \underline{l}$$

$$\Rightarrow \quad 2^{-1} w^T w = 2^{-1} \sum_{i=1}^{l} \sum_{j=1}^{l} (\alpha_i - \beta_i)(\alpha_j - \beta_j) x_i^T x_j,$$

$$-\sum_{q=1}^{l} \alpha_q w^T x_q + \sum_{q=1}^{l} \beta_q w^T x_q = -\sum_{q=1}^{l} (\alpha_q - \beta_q)\left[\sum_{j=1}^{l}(\alpha_j - \beta_j) x_j^T\right] x_q$$

$$= -\sum_{q=1}^{l} \sum_{j=1}^{l} (\alpha_q - \beta_q)(\alpha_j - \beta_j) x_q^T x_j,$$

$$-b\sum_{q=1}^{l} \alpha_q + b\sum_{q=1}^{l} \beta_q = -b\sum_{q=1}^{l}(\alpha_q - \beta_q) = 0,$$

$$C\sum_{q=1}^{l} \xi_q - \sum_{q=1}^{l} \alpha_q \xi_q - \sum_{q=1}^{l} \mu_q \xi_q = 0,$$

$$C\sum_{q=1}^{l} \eta_q - \sum_{q=1}^{l} \beta_q \eta_q - \sum_{q=1}^{l} \rho_q \eta_q = 0$$

$$\Rightarrow \quad J_d(\alpha, \beta) = J_d(\alpha, \beta, \mu, \rho)$$

$$= \sum_{q=1}^{l}(\alpha_q - \beta_q)d_q - \varepsilon \sum_{q=1}^{l}(\alpha_q + \beta_q)$$

$$- 2^{-1} \sum_{q=1}^{l} \sum_{j=1}^{l}(\alpha_q - \beta_q)(\alpha_j - \beta_j) x_q^T x_j.$$

Since, for all $q \in \underline{l}$,

$$\alpha_q \geq 0, \quad \mu_q \geq 0, \quad \alpha_q + \mu_q = C, \quad \beta_q \geq 0, \quad \rho_q \geq 0, \quad \beta_q + \rho_q = C$$

$$\Rightarrow \quad 0 \le \alpha_q \le C, \quad 0 \le \beta_q \le C,$$

which are often called the **box constraints**. Hence, the dual optimization problem can be stated as follows:

(D1)   maximize

$$\sum_{q=1}^{l} \left(\alpha_q - \beta_q \right) d_q - \varepsilon \sum_{q=1}^{l} \left(\alpha_q + \beta_q \right)$$

$$-\frac{1}{2} \sum_{q=1}^{l} \sum_{j=1}^{l} \left(\alpha_q - \beta_q \right)\left(\alpha_j - \beta_j \right)\left\langle x_q, x_j \right\rangle$$

subject to

$$\sum_{q=1}^{l} \left(\alpha_q - \beta_q \right) = 0, \quad 0 \le \alpha_q \le C, \quad 0 \le \beta_q \le C, \quad q \in \underline{l}.$$

The KKT conditions become, for all $q \in \underline{l}$,

$$\alpha_q^* \left[\varepsilon + \xi_q^* - d_q + \left\langle w^*, x_q \right\rangle + b^* \right] = 0,$$

$$\varepsilon + \xi_q^* - d_q + \left\langle w^*, x_q \right\rangle + b^* \ge 0, \quad \alpha_q^* \ge 0,$$

$$\beta_q^* \left[\varepsilon + \eta_q^* - \left\langle w^*, x_q \right\rangle - b^* + d_q \right] = 0,$$

$$\varepsilon + \eta_q^* - \left\langle w^*, x_q \right\rangle - b^* + d_q \ge 0, \quad \beta_q^* \ge 0,$$

$$\mu_q^* \xi_q^* = 0, \quad \xi_q^* \ge 0, \quad \mu_q^* \ge 0, \quad \rho_q^* \eta_q^* = 0, \quad \eta_q^* \ge 0, \quad \rho_q^* \ge 0.$$

For data points strictly outside the ε-band, either α_q^* or β_q^* will be nonzero. For data points strictly inside (inclusive of) the ε-band, both multipliers will be equal to zero. These facts may be displayed via the following new KKT conditions.

Now, we derive a new set of KKT conditions. First, we prove that, for all $q \in \underline{l}$,

$$\alpha_q^* \beta_q^* = 0, \quad \xi_q^* \eta_q^* = 0, \quad \left(\alpha_i^* - C \right)\xi_q^* = 0, \text{ and } \left(\beta_q^* - C \right)\eta_q^* = 0.$$

Suppose $\alpha_q^* > 0$, then $d_q - \langle w*, x_q \rangle - b* = \varepsilon + \xi_q^*$. In this case, we have

$$\langle w*, x_q \rangle + b* - d_q - \varepsilon - \eta_q^* = -2\varepsilon - \xi_q^* - \eta_q^* < 0.$$

This implies that $\beta_q^* = 0$. Similarly, if $\beta_q^* > 0$, then $\alpha_q^* = 0$. Suppose $\xi_q^* > 0$, then we have

$$\mu_q^* = 0 \;\Rightarrow\; \alpha_q^* = C > 0 \;\Rightarrow\; \beta_q^* = 0$$
$$\Rightarrow\; \rho_q^* = C > 0 \;\Rightarrow\; \eta_q^* = 0.$$

Similarly, if $\eta_q^* > 0$, then $\xi_q^* > 0$. From $\alpha_q^* + \mu_q^* = C$ and $\mu_q^* \xi_q^* = 0$, we have $(\alpha_i^* - C)\xi_q^* = 0$. Similarly, from $\beta_q^* + \rho_q^* = C$ and $\rho_q^* \eta_q^* = 0$, we have $(\beta_q^* - C)\eta_q^* = 0$.

The new KKT conditions become, for all $q \in l$,

$$\alpha_q^* \left[\varepsilon + \xi_q^* - d_q + \langle w*, x_q \rangle + b* \right] = 0,$$
$$\varepsilon + \xi_q^* - d_q + \langle w*, x_q \rangle + b* \geq 0,$$
$$\beta_q^* \left[\varepsilon + \eta_q^* - \langle w*, x_q \rangle - b* + d_q \right] = 0,$$
$$\varepsilon + \eta_q^* - \langle w*, x_q \rangle - b* + d_q \geq 0,$$
$$\xi_q^* \eta_q^* = 0, \; \alpha_q^* \beta_q^* = 0, \; (\alpha_q^* - C)\xi_q^* = 0, \; (\beta_q^* - C)\eta_q^* = 0,$$
$$\xi_q^* \geq 0, \; \eta_q^* \geq 0, \; \alpha_q^* \geq 0, \; \beta_q^* \geq 0.$$

Suppose $(\alpha*, \beta*)$ solves the dual problem (D1). Then, we have

$$w* = \sum_{q=1}^{l} (\alpha_q^* - \beta_q^*) x_q.$$

Choose any $0 < \alpha_k^* < C$. From the KKT conditions, we have $\xi_k^* = 0$ and

$$0 = \varepsilon + \xi_k^* - d_k + \langle w*, x_k \rangle + b* = \varepsilon - d_k + \langle w*, x_k \rangle + b*$$

$$\Rightarrow \quad b* = d_k - \varepsilon - \langle w*, x_k \rangle = d_k - \varepsilon - \sum_{q \in I_{sv}} \left(\alpha_q^* - \beta_q^* \right)\langle x_q, x_k \rangle .$$

Suppose we choose $0 < \beta_k^* < C$. From the KKT conditions, we have $\eta_k^* = 0$ and

$$0 = \varepsilon + \eta_k^* - \langle w*, x_k \rangle - b* + d_k = \varepsilon - \langle w*, x_k \rangle - b* + d_k$$

$$\Rightarrow \quad b* = d_k + \varepsilon - \langle w*, x_k \rangle = d_k + \varepsilon - \sum_{q \in I_{sv}} \left(\alpha_q^* - \beta_q^* \right)\langle x_q, x_k \rangle .$$

The optimal predictive function is thus given by

$$f*(x) = \langle w*, x \rangle + b* = \sum_{q=1}^{l} \left(\alpha_q^* - \beta_q^* \right)\langle x_q, x \rangle + b* .$$

Now, we discuss the stopping criteria for any algorithm of finding the 1-norm soft regressor. First we present a stopping criterion based on the KKT conditions. Keep in mind that $\alpha_q^* \beta_q^* = 0$ in the following derivation.

Suppose $\alpha_q^* - \beta_q^* = -C$. Then we have $\alpha_q^* = 0$ and $\beta_q^* = C$. In this case, we have

$$\varepsilon + \eta_q^* - \langle w*, x_q \rangle - b* + d_q = 0$$
$$\Rightarrow \quad f*(x_q) = \langle w*, x_q \rangle + b* = d_q + \varepsilon + \eta_q^* \geq d_q + \varepsilon .$$

Suppose $-C < \alpha_q^* - \beta_q^* < 0$. Then we have $\alpha_q^* = 0$ and $0 < \beta_q^* < C$. Hence, we have $\eta_q^* = 0$ and

$$\varepsilon + \eta_q^* - \langle w*, x_q \rangle - b* + d_q = 0$$
$$\Rightarrow \quad f*(x_q) = \langle w*, x_q \rangle + b* = d_q + \varepsilon + \eta_q^* = d_q + \varepsilon .$$

Suppose $\alpha_q^* - \beta_q^* = 0$. Then we have $\alpha_q^* = 0$ and $\beta_q^* = 0$, which imply that $\xi_q^* = 0$ and $\eta_q^* = 0$. In this case, we have

$$\varepsilon + \xi_q^* - d_q + \langle w^*, x_q \rangle + b^* \geq 0$$
$$\Rightarrow \quad f^*(x_q) = \langle w^*, x_q \rangle + b^* \geq d_q - \varepsilon - \xi_q^* = d_q - \varepsilon,$$

and

$$\varepsilon + \eta_q^* - \langle w^*, x_q \rangle - b^* + d_q \geq 0$$
$$\Rightarrow \quad f^*(x_q) = \langle w^*, x_q \rangle + b^* \leq d_q + \varepsilon + \eta_q^* = d_q + \varepsilon,$$

so $d_q - \varepsilon \leq f^*(x_q) \leq d_q + \varepsilon$. Suppose $0 < \alpha_q^* - \beta_q^* < C$. Then, we have $0 < \alpha_q^* < C$ and $\beta_q^* = 0$. Hence we have $\xi_q^* = 0$ and

$$\varepsilon + \xi_q^* - d_q + \langle w^*, x_q \rangle + b^* = 0$$
$$\Rightarrow \quad f^*(x_q) = \langle w^*, x_q \rangle + b^* = d_q - \varepsilon - \xi_q^* = d_q - \varepsilon.$$

Suppose $\alpha_q^* - \beta_q^* = C$. Then we have $\alpha_q^* = C$ and $\beta_q^* = 0$. In this case, we have

$$\varepsilon + \xi_q^* - d_q + \langle w^*, x_q \rangle + b^* = 0$$
$$\Rightarrow \quad f^*(x_q) = \langle w^*, x_q \rangle + b^* = d_q - \varepsilon - \xi_q^* \leq d_q - \varepsilon.$$

Suppose α_q, β_q, $q \in \underline{l}$, are the current values of the dual variables. The current primal variables and predictive function can thus be calculated. Then, reasonable KKT stopping conditions are given by, for $q \in \underline{l}$,

$$0 \leq \alpha_q \leq C, \ 0 \leq \beta_q \leq C,$$
$$f(x_q) \geq d_q + \varepsilon \quad \text{if} \quad \alpha_q - \beta_q = -C,$$
$$f(x_q) = d_q + \varepsilon \quad \text{if} \quad -C < \alpha_q - \beta_q < 0,$$
$$d_q - \varepsilon \leq f(x_q) \leq d_q + \varepsilon \quad \text{if} \quad \alpha_q - \beta_q = 0,$$
$$f(x_q) = d_q + \varepsilon \quad \text{if} \quad 0 < \alpha_q - \beta_q < C,$$
$$f(x_q) \leq d_q - \varepsilon \quad \text{if} \quad \alpha_q - \beta_q = C.$$

We may define p_q, $q \in \underline{l}$, to be the measure of dissatisfaction of the KKT stopping conditions for the qth example as

$$p_q := \max\left[0, d_q - f(x_q) + \varepsilon\right] \text{ if } \alpha_q - \beta_q = -C,$$
$$p_q := \left| d_q - f(x_q) + \varepsilon \right| \text{ if } -C < \alpha_q - \beta_q < 0,$$
$$p_q := \max\left[0, \left| d_q - f(x_q) \right| - \varepsilon\right] \text{ if } \alpha_q - \beta_q = 0,$$
$$p_q := \left| d_q - f(x_q) - \varepsilon \right| \text{ if } 0 < \alpha_q - \beta_q < C,$$
$$p_q := \max\left[0, f(x_q) - d_q + \varepsilon\right] \text{ if } \alpha_q - \beta_q = C.$$

Then, reasonable stopping criteria based on KKT stopping conditions are

$$p_{ave} := \frac{1}{l}\sum_{q=1}^{l} p_q \leq \delta \text{ or } \|p\|_{\infty} := \max_{q \in \underline{l}}\{p_q\} \leq \delta,$$

where δ is a pre-specified tolerance.

Next, we present another stopping criterion based on the feasibility gap. Let α_q, β_q, $q \in \underline{l}$, be the current values of the dual variables. The current weight, bias, and predictive function can thus be calculated. However, note that the slack variables ξ_q and η_q are not specified when moving from the primal to the dual. We may choose the current slack variables to ensure that the primal variables are all feasible. Hence, we define the current slack variables as, $q \in \underline{l}$,

$$\xi_q := \max\left(0, d_q - \left[\langle w, x_q \rangle + b\right] - \varepsilon\right)$$
$$= \max\left(0, d_q - \left[\sum_{j=1}^{l}(\alpha_j - \beta_j)\langle x_j, x_q \rangle + b\right] - \varepsilon\right)$$
$$= \max\left[0, d_q - f(x_q) - \varepsilon\right],$$

$$\eta_q := \max\left(0, \left[\langle w, x_q \rangle + b\right] - d_q - \varepsilon\right)$$
$$= \max\left(0, \left[\sum_{j=1}^{l}(\alpha_j - \beta_j)\langle x_j, x_q \rangle + b\right] - d_q - \varepsilon\right)$$

$$= \max\left[0, f(x_q) - d_q - \varepsilon\right].$$

Then, we have

$$J_p(w, \xi, \eta) - J_d(\alpha, \beta)$$

$$= 2^{-1} w^T w + C \sum_{q=1}^{l} (\xi_q + \eta_q) - J_d(\alpha, \beta)$$

$$= 2^{-1} \sum_{q=1}^{l} \sum_{j=1}^{l} (\alpha_q - \beta_q)(\alpha_j - \beta_j)\langle x_q, x_j \rangle + C \sum_{q=1}^{l} (\xi_q + \eta_q) - J_d(\alpha, \beta)$$

$$= -J_d(\alpha, \beta) + \sum_{q=1}^{l} (\alpha_q - \beta_q) d_q - \varepsilon \sum_{q=1}^{l} (\alpha_q + \beta_q)$$

$$\quad + C \sum_{q=1}^{l} (\xi_q + \eta_q) - J_d(\alpha, \beta)$$

$$= \sum_{q=1}^{l} (\alpha_q - \beta_q) d_q - \varepsilon \sum_{q=1}^{l} (\alpha_q + \beta_q) - 2J_d(\alpha, \beta) + C \sum_{q=1}^{l} (\xi_q + \eta_q),$$

$$J_p(w, \xi, \eta) + 1$$

$$= J_d(\alpha, \beta) + \sum_{q=1}^{l} (\alpha_q - \beta_q) d_q - \varepsilon \sum_{q=1}^{l} (\alpha_q + \beta_q) - 2J_d(\alpha, \beta)$$

$$\quad + C \sum_{q=1}^{l} (\xi_q + \eta_q) + 1$$

$$= \sum_{q=1}^{l} (\alpha_q - \beta_q) d_q - \varepsilon \sum_{q=1}^{l} (\alpha_q + \beta_q) - J_d(\alpha, \beta) + C \sum_{q=1}^{l} (\xi_q + \eta_q) + 1.$$

A reasonable stopping criterion is given by

$$\frac{J_p - J_d}{J_p + 1}$$

$$= \frac{\sum_{q=1}^{l} (\alpha_q - \beta_q) d_q - \varepsilon \sum_{q=1}^{l} (\alpha_q + \beta_q) - 2J_d(\alpha, \beta) + C \sum_{q=1}^{l} (\xi_q + \eta_q)}{\sum_{q=1}^{l} (\alpha_q - \beta_q) d_q - \varepsilon \sum_{q=1}^{l} (\alpha_q + \beta_q) - J_d(\alpha, \beta) + C \sum_{q=1}^{l} (\xi_q + \eta_q) + 1} \leq \delta,$$

where δ is a pre-specified tolerance.

Suppose we let $\theta_q^* := \alpha_q^* - \beta_q^*$, $q \in \underline{l}$. Then, in view of $\alpha_q^* \beta_q^* = 0$, we have $|\theta_q^*| = \alpha_q^* + \beta_q^*$. Thus, the problem (D1) can be rewritten in a simpler form as

(D1')   maximize $\sum_{q=1}^{l} \theta_q d_q - \varepsilon \sum_{q=1}^{l} |\theta_q| - \frac{1}{2} \sum_{q=1}^{l} \sum_{j=1}^{l} \theta_q \theta_j \langle x_q, x_j \rangle$

     subject to $\sum_{q=1}^{l} \theta_q = 0$, $-C \le \theta_q \le C$, $q \in \underline{l}$.

Suppose $\theta *$ solves the problem (D1'). Define $I_{sv} := \{ q \in \underline{l} : \theta_q^* \ne 0 \}$. Then, we have

$$w^* = \sum_{q=1}^{l} \theta_q^* x_q = \sum_{q \in I_{sv}} \theta_q^* x_q .$$

Because of the box constraints, the influence of the individual pattern gets limited.

Choose any $0 < \theta_k^* < C$. Since $\alpha_q^* \beta_q^* = 0$, we have $0 < \alpha_k^* = \theta_k^* < C$ and $\beta_k^* = 0$. From the KKT conditions, we have $\xi_k^* = 0$ and

$$0 = \varepsilon + \xi_k^* - d_k + \langle w^*, x_k \rangle + b^* = \varepsilon - d_k + \langle w^*, x_k \rangle + b *$$

$$\Rightarrow \quad b^* = d_k - \varepsilon - \langle w^*, x_k \rangle = d_k - \varepsilon - \sum_{q \in I_{sv}} \theta_q^* \langle x_q, x_k \rangle .$$

Suppose we choose any $-C < \theta_k^* < 0$. Then we have $\alpha_k^* = 0$ and $0 < \beta_k^* = -\theta_k^* < C$. From the KKT conditions, we have $\eta_k^* = 0$ and

$$0 = \varepsilon + \eta_k^* - \langle w^*, x_k \rangle - b * + d_k = \varepsilon - \langle w^*, x_k \rangle - b * + d_k$$

$$\Rightarrow \quad b^* = d_k + \varepsilon - \langle w^*, x_k \rangle = d_k + \varepsilon - \sum_{q \in I_{sv}} \theta_q^* \langle x_q, x_k \rangle.$$

The optimal predictive function is thus given by

$$f^*(x) = \langle w^*, x \rangle + b^* = \sum_{q \in I_{sv}} \theta_q^* \langle x_q, x \rangle + b^*.$$

Now, we discuss the stopping criteria for any algorithm of finding the 1-norm soft regressor. First we present a stopping criterion based on the KKT conditions. Keep in mind that $\alpha_q^* \beta_q^* = 0$ in the following derivation.

Suppose $\theta_q^* = -C$, then we have $\beta_q^* = -\theta_q^* = C$. In this case, we have

$$\varepsilon + \eta_q^* - \langle w^*, x_q \rangle - b^* + d_q = 0$$
$$\Rightarrow \quad f^*(x_q) = \langle w^*, x_q \rangle + b^* = d_q + \varepsilon + \eta_q^* \geq d_q + \varepsilon.$$

Suppose $-C < \theta_q^* < 0$, then we have $0 < \beta_q^* = -\theta_q^* < C$. Hence, we have $\eta_q^* = 0$ and

$$\varepsilon + \eta_q^* - \langle w^*, x_q \rangle - b^* + d_q = 0$$
$$\Rightarrow \quad f^*(x_q) = \langle w^*, x_q \rangle + b^* = d_q + \varepsilon + \eta_q^* = d_q + \varepsilon.$$

Suppose $\theta_q^* = 0$, then we have $\alpha_q^* = \beta_q^* = 0$. Hence, we have $\xi_q^* = 0$ and $\eta_q^* = 0$. In this case, we have

$$\varepsilon + \xi_q^* - d_q + \langle w^*, x_q \rangle + b^* \geq 0$$
$$\Rightarrow \quad f^*(x_q) = \langle w^*, x_q \rangle + b^* \geq d_q - \varepsilon - \xi_q^* = d_q - \varepsilon,$$

and

$$\varepsilon + \eta_q^* - \langle w^*, x_q \rangle - b^* + d_q \geq 0$$

$$\Rightarrow \quad f*\left(x_q\right)=\left\langle w^*, x_q\right\rangle + b^* \le d_q + \varepsilon + \eta_q^* = d_q + \varepsilon ,$$

so $d_q - \varepsilon \le f*\left(x_q\right) \le d_q + \varepsilon$. Suppose $0 < \theta_q^* < C$, then we have $0 < \alpha_q^* = \theta_q^* < C$. Hence, we have $\xi_q^* = 0$ and

$$\varepsilon + \xi_q^* - d_q + \left\langle w^*, x_q\right\rangle + b^* = 0$$
$$\Rightarrow \quad f*\left(x_q\right)=\left\langle w^*, x_q\right\rangle + b^* = d_q - \varepsilon - \xi_q^* = d_q - \varepsilon .$$

Suppose $\theta_q^* = C$, then we have $\alpha_q^* = \theta_q^* = C$. In this case, we have

$$\varepsilon + \xi_q^* - d_q + \left\langle w^*, x_q\right\rangle + b^* = 0$$
$$\Rightarrow \quad f*\left(x_q\right)=\left\langle w^*, x_q\right\rangle + b^* = d_q - \varepsilon - \xi_q^* \le d_q - \varepsilon .$$

Suppose θ_q, $q \in \underline{l}$, is the current value of the dual variable. The current primal variables and predictive function can thus be calculated. Then, reasonable KKT stopping conditions are given by, for $q \in \underline{l}$,

$$C \le \theta_q \le C ,$$
$$f\left(x_q\right) \ge d_q + \varepsilon \quad \text{if} \quad \theta_q = -C ,$$
$$f\left(x_q\right) = d_q + \varepsilon \quad \text{if} \quad -C < \theta_q < 0 ,$$
$$d_q - \varepsilon \le f\left(x_q\right) \le d_q + \varepsilon \quad \text{if} \quad \theta_q = 0 ,$$
$$f\left(x_q\right) = d_q + \varepsilon \quad \text{if} \quad 0 < \theta_q < C ,$$
$$f\left(x_q\right) \le d_q - \varepsilon \quad \text{if} \quad \theta_q = C .$$

We may define p_q, $q \in \underline{l}$, to be the measure of dissatisfaction of the KKT stopping conditions for the qth example as

$$p_q := \max\left[0, d_q - f\left(x_q\right) + \varepsilon\right] \quad \text{if} \quad \theta_q = -C ,$$
$$p_q := \left| d_q - f\left(x_q\right) + \varepsilon\right| \quad \text{if} \quad -C < \theta_q < 0 ,$$
$$p_q := \max\left[0, \left| d_q - f\left(x_q\right) \right| - \varepsilon\right] \quad \text{if} \quad \theta_q = 0 ,$$
$$p_q := \left| d_q - f\left(x_q\right) - \varepsilon\right| \quad \text{if} \quad 0 < \theta_q < C ,$$

$$p_q := \max\left[0, f(x_q) - d_q + \varepsilon\right] \text{ if } \theta_q = C.$$

Then, reasonable stopping criteria based on KKT stopping conditions are

$$p_{ave} := \frac{1}{l}\sum_{q=1}^{l} p_q \le \delta \text{ or } \|p\|_\infty := \max_{q \in \underline{l}}\{p_q\} \le \delta,$$

where δ is a pre-specified tolerance.

Next, we present a stopping criterion based on the feasibility gap. Let θ_q, $q \in \underline{l}$, be the current value of the dual variable. The current weight, bias, and predictive function can thus be calculated. However, note that the slack variables ξ_q and η_q are not specified when moving to the dual. We may choose the current slack variables to ensure that the primal variables are all feasible. Hence, we define the current slack variables as, $q \in \underline{l}$,

$$\xi_q := \max\left(0, d_q - \left[\langle w, x_q \rangle + b\right] - \varepsilon\right)$$
$$= \max\left(0, d_q - \left[\sum_{j=1}^{l} \theta_j \langle x_j, x_q \rangle + b\right] - \varepsilon\right)$$
$$= \max\left[0, d_q - f(x_q) - \varepsilon\right],$$

$$\eta_q := \max\left(0, \left[\langle w, x_q \rangle + b\right] - d_q - \varepsilon\right)$$
$$= \max\left(0, \left[\sum_{j=1}^{l} \theta_j \langle x_j, x_q \rangle + b\right] - d_q - \varepsilon\right)$$
$$= \max\left[0, f(x_q) - d_q - \varepsilon\right].$$

Then, we have

$$J_p(w, \xi, \eta) - J_d(\theta)$$
$$= 2^{-1} w^T w + C\sum_{q=1}^{l}(\xi_q + \eta_q) - J_d(\theta)$$
$$= 2^{-1}\sum_{q=1}^{l}\sum_{j=1}^{l} \theta_q \theta_j \langle x_q, x_j \rangle + C\sum_{q=1}^{l}(\xi_q + \eta_q) - J_d(\theta)$$

$$= -J_d(\theta) + \sum_{q=1}^{l} \theta_q d_q - \varepsilon \sum_{q=1}^{l} |\theta_q| + C \sum_{q=1}^{l} (\xi_q + \eta_q) - J_d(\theta)$$

$$= \sum_{q=1}^{l} \theta_q d_q - \varepsilon \sum_{q=1}^{l} |\theta_q| - 2J_d(\theta) + C \sum_{q=1}^{l} (\xi_q + \eta_q),$$

$$J_p(w, \xi, \eta) + 1$$

$$= J_d(\theta) + \sum_{q=1}^{l} \theta_q d_q - \varepsilon \sum_{q=1}^{l} |\theta_q| - 2J_d(\theta) + C \sum_{q=1}^{l} (\xi_q + \eta_q) + 1$$

$$= \sum_{q=1}^{l} \theta_q d_q - \varepsilon \sum_{q=1}^{l} |\theta_q| - J_d(\theta) + C \sum_{q=1}^{l} (\xi_q + \eta_q) + 1.$$

A reasonable stopping criterion is given by

$$\frac{J_p - J_d}{J_p + 1} = \frac{\displaystyle\sum_{q=1}^{l} \theta_q d_q - \varepsilon \sum_{q=1}^{l} |\theta_q| - 2J_d(\theta) + C \sum_{q=1}^{l} (\xi_q + \eta_q)}{\displaystyle\sum_{q=1}^{l} \theta_q d_q - \varepsilon \sum_{q=1}^{l} |\theta_q| - J_d(\theta) + C \sum_{q=1}^{l} (\xi_q + \eta_q) + 1} \leq \delta,$$

where δ is a pre-specified tolerance.

4.10 2-norm Soft Regressor

In this section, we continue the study on soft regressors. Specifically, we study the 2-norm soft regressors.

Let $X \subseteq \mathfrak{R}^n$ and $Y \subseteq \mathfrak{R}$. Suppose we are given the training set

$$S := \{(x_q, d_q)\}_{q=1}^{l} \subseteq X \times Y.$$

The problem of linear regression is to find a linear function f that fits the data:

$$f(x) = \langle w, x \rangle + b.$$

Now, we use $\sum_{q=1}^{l} \left(\xi_q^2 + \eta_q^2 \right)$ to measure the amount by which the training set fails to fall in the ε-band of the hyperplane.

Consider the following primal optimization problem (with $C > 0$):

(P20)   minimize $\dfrac{1}{2} w^T w + \dfrac{C}{2} \sum_{q=1}^{l} \left(\xi_q^2 + \eta_q^2 \right)$

subject to $d_q - \left[\langle w, x_q \rangle + b \right] \leq \varepsilon + \xi_q, \quad \xi_q \geq 0,$

$\left[\langle w, x_q \rangle + b \right] - d_q \leq \varepsilon + \eta_q, \quad \eta_q \geq 0$, for all $q \in \underline{l}.$

Suppose ξ_q and η_q, $q \in \underline{l}$, in problem (P20) are unconstrained and we have, for some fixed w and b,

$$d_q - \left[\langle w, x_q \rangle + b \right] \leq \varepsilon + \xi_q, \quad \xi_q < 0, \text{ for some } q \in \underline{l},$$
$$\left[\langle w, x_j \rangle + b \right] - d_j \leq \varepsilon + \eta_j, \quad \eta_j < 0, \text{ for some } j \in \underline{l}.$$

By setting $\varsigma_q = 0 \geq 0$, $\kappa_j = 0 \geq 0$, then, for the same w and b,

$$d_q - \left[\langle w, x_q \rangle + b \right] \leq \varepsilon + \xi_q \leq \varepsilon + \varsigma_q,$$
$$\left[\langle w, x_j \rangle + b \right] - d_j \leq \varepsilon + \eta_j \leq \varepsilon + \kappa_j.$$

However, the new choices would lower the cost functional. Hence the positivity constraints on ξ_q and η_j can be removed. Thus, we consider the following simpler primal optimization problem:

(P2)   minimize $\dfrac{1}{2} w^T w + \dfrac{C}{2} \sum_{q=1}^{l} \left(\xi_q^2 + \eta_q^2 \right)$

subject to $d_q - \left[\langle w, x_q \rangle + b \right] \leq \varepsilon + \xi_q,$

$\left[\langle w, x_q \rangle + b \right] - d_q \leq \varepsilon + \eta_q$, for all $q \in \underline{l}.$

Suppose $(w*, b*, \xi*, \eta*)$ solves the preceding primal optimization problem. Then the optimal predictive function is given by $f*(x) = \langle w*, x \rangle + b*$.

Now, we consider its dual problem. The Lagrangian is given by

$$L(w, b, \xi, \eta, \alpha, \beta) := \frac{1}{2} w^T w + \frac{1}{2} C \sum_{q=1}^{l} (\xi_q^2 + \eta_q^2)$$

$$- \sum_{q=1}^{l} \alpha_q (\varepsilon + \xi_q - d_q + w^T x_q + b)$$

$$- \sum_{q=1}^{l} \beta_q (\varepsilon + \eta_q - w^T x_q - b + d_q).$$

The dual function is defined by

$$J_d(\alpha, \beta) := \min_{w, b, \xi, \eta} L(w, b, \xi, \eta, \alpha, \beta).$$

Clearly, we have

$$0 = \frac{\partial L}{\partial w} = w - \sum_{q=1}^{l} \alpha_q x_q + \sum_{q=1}^{l} \beta_q x_q, \quad 0 = \frac{\partial L}{\partial b} = -\sum_{q=1}^{l} \alpha_q + \sum_{q=1}^{l} \beta_q,$$

$$0 = \frac{\partial L}{\partial \xi_q} = C\xi_q - \alpha_q, \quad 0 = \frac{\partial L}{\partial \eta_q} = C\eta_q - \beta_q, \quad q \in \underline{l}$$

$$\Rightarrow \quad w = \sum_{q=1}^{l} (\alpha_q - \beta_q) x_q, \quad \sum_{q=1}^{l} (\alpha_q - \beta_q) = 0,$$

$$\xi_q = C^{-1} \alpha_q, \quad \eta_q = C^{-1} \beta_q, \quad q \in \underline{l}$$

$$\Rightarrow \quad 2^{-1} w^T w = 2^{-1} \sum_{q=1}^{l} \sum_{j=1}^{l} (\alpha_q - \beta_q)(\alpha_j - \beta_j) x_q^T x_j,$$

$$- \sum_{q=1}^{l} \alpha_q w^T x_q + \sum_{q=1}^{l} \beta_q w^T x_q = -\sum_{q=1}^{l} (\alpha_q - \beta_q) \left[\sum_{j=1}^{l} (\alpha_j - \beta_j) x_j^T \right] x_q$$

$$= -\sum_{q=1}^{l} \sum_{j=1}^{l} (\alpha_q - \beta_q)(\alpha_j - \beta_j) x_q^T x_j,$$

$$-b\sum_{q=1}^{l}\alpha_q + b\sum_{q=1}^{l}\beta_q = -b\sum_{q=1}^{l}(\alpha_i - \beta_i) = 0,$$

$$2^{-1}C\sum_{q=1}^{l}\xi_q^2 - \sum_{q=1}^{l}\alpha_q\xi_q = -(2C)^{-1}\sum_{q=1}^{l}\alpha_q^2,$$

$$2^{-1}C\sum_{q=1}^{l}\eta_q^2 - \sum_{q=1}^{l}\beta_q\eta_q = -(2C)^{-1}\sum_{i=1}^{l}\beta_q^2$$

$$\Rightarrow \quad J_d(\alpha,\beta) := \min_{w,b,\xi,\eta} L(w,b,\xi,\eta,\alpha,\beta)$$

$$= \sum_{q=1}^{l}(\alpha_q - \beta_q)d_q - \varepsilon\sum_{q=1}^{l}(\alpha_q + \beta_q)$$

$$-\frac{1}{2}\sum_{q=1}^{l}\sum_{j=1}^{l}(\alpha_q - \beta_q)(\alpha_j - \beta_j)x_q^T x_j$$

$$-\frac{1}{2C}\sum_{q=1}^{l}(\alpha_i^2 + \beta_i^2).$$

Hence, the dual optimization problem can be stated as follows:

(D2)   maximize

$$\sum_{q=1}^{l}(\alpha_q - \beta_q)d_q - \varepsilon\sum_{q=1}^{l}(\alpha_q + \beta_q)$$

$$-\frac{1}{2}\sum_{q=1}^{l}\sum_{j=1}^{l}(\alpha_q - \beta_q)(\alpha_j - \beta_j)\langle x_q, x_j\rangle$$

$$-\frac{1}{2C}\sum_{q=1}^{l}(\alpha_i^2 + \beta_i^2)$$

subject to

$$\sum_{q=1}^{l}(\alpha_q - \beta_q) = 0,\quad \alpha_q \geq 0,\quad \beta_q \geq 0,\text{ for all }q \in \underline{l}.$$

The KKT conditions become, for all $q \in \underline{l}$,

$$\alpha_q^*\left[\varepsilon + \xi_q^* - d_q + \langle w^*, x_q\rangle + b^*\right] = 0,$$

$$\varepsilon + \xi_q^* - d_q + \langle w^*, x_q\rangle + b^* \geq 0,\quad \alpha_q^* \geq 0,$$

$$\beta_q^*\left[\varepsilon + \eta_q^* - \left\langle w^*, x_q \right\rangle - b^* + d_q\right] = 0,$$

$$\varepsilon + \eta_q^* - \left\langle w^*, x_q \right\rangle - b^* + d_q \geq 0, \quad \beta_q^* \geq 0.$$

Now, we derive a new set of KKT conditions. First, we prove that $\alpha_q^* \beta_q^* = 0$ and then prove that $\xi_q^* \eta_q^* = 0$ for all $q \in \underline{l}$. Suppose $\alpha_q^* > 0$, then $d_q - \left\langle w^*, x_q \right\rangle - b^* = \varepsilon + \xi_q^*$. In this case, we have

$$\varepsilon + \eta_q^* - \left\langle w^*, x_q \right\rangle - b^* + d_q$$
$$= 2\varepsilon + \xi_q^* + \eta_q^* = 2\varepsilon + C^{-1}\alpha_q^* + C^{-1}\beta_q^* > 0.$$

This implies that $\beta_q^* = 0$. Similarly, if $\beta_q^* > 0$, then $\alpha_q^* = 0$. Suppose $\xi_q^* > 0$, then we have

$$\alpha_q^* = C\xi_q^* > 0 \implies \beta_q^* = 0 \implies \eta_q^* = C^{-1}\beta_q^* = 0.$$

Similarly, if $\eta_q^* > 0$, then $\xi_q^* > 0$. Thus, the new KKT conditions become, for all $q \in \underline{l}$,

$$\alpha_q^*\left[\varepsilon + \xi_q^* - d_q + \left\langle w^*, x_q \right\rangle + b^*\right] = 0,$$

$$\varepsilon + \xi_q^* - d_q + \left\langle w^*, x_q \right\rangle + b^* \geq 0,$$

$$\beta_q^*\left[\varepsilon + \eta_q^* - \left\langle w^*, x_q \right\rangle - b^* + d_q\right] = 0,$$

$$\varepsilon + \eta_q^* - \left\langle w^*, x_q \right\rangle - b^* + d_q \geq 0,$$

$$\xi_q^* \eta_q^* = 0, \quad \xi_q^* \geq 0, \quad \eta_q^* \geq 0, \quad \alpha_q^* \beta_q^* = 0, \quad \alpha_q^* \geq 0, \quad \beta_q^* \geq 0.$$

Suppose (α^*, β^*) solves the dual problem (D2). Then, we have

$$w^* = \sum_{q=1}^{l}\left(\alpha_q^* - \beta_q^*\right)x_q.$$

Choose any $\alpha_k^* > 0$. From the KKT conditions, we have

$$0 = \varepsilon + \xi_k^* - d_k + \left\langle w^*, x_k \right\rangle + b^* = \varepsilon + C^{-1}\alpha_k^* - d_k + \left\langle w^*, x_k \right\rangle + b^*$$

$$\Rightarrow \quad b* = d_k - \varepsilon - C^{-1}\alpha_k^* - \langle w*, x_k \rangle$$
$$= d_k - \varepsilon - C^{-1}\alpha_k^* - \sum_{q \in I_{sv}} \left(\alpha_q^* - \beta_q^* \right) \langle x_q, x_k \rangle.$$

Or one may choose any $\beta_k^* > 0$. From the KKT conditions, we have

$$0 = \varepsilon + \eta_k^* - \langle w*, x_k \rangle - b* + d_k = \varepsilon + C^{-1}\beta_k^* - \langle w*, x_k \rangle - b* + d_k$$

$$\Rightarrow \quad b* = b_k + \varepsilon + C^{-1}\beta_k^* - \langle w*, x_k \rangle$$
$$= b_k + \varepsilon + C^{-1}\beta_k^* - \sum_{q \in I_{sv}} \left(\alpha_q^* - \beta_q^* \right) \langle x_q, x_k \rangle.$$

The optimal predictive function is thus given by

$$f*(x) = \langle w*, x \rangle + b* = \sum_{q \in I_{sv}} \left(\alpha_q^* - \beta_q^* \right) \langle x_q, x \rangle + b*.$$

Now, we discuss a stopping criterion, based on KKT conditions, for any algorithm of finding the 2-norm soft regressor. Keep in mind that $\alpha_q^* \beta_q^* = 0$ in the following derivation.

Suppose $\alpha_q^* - \beta_q^* = 0$. Then, we have $\alpha_q^* = \beta_q^* = 0$. Hence, we have $\xi_q^* = C^{-1}\alpha_q^* = 0$ and $\eta_q^* = C^{-1}\beta_q^* = 0$. In this case, we have

$$\varepsilon + \xi_q^* - d_q + \langle w*, x_q \rangle + b* \geq 0$$
$$\Rightarrow \quad f*(x_q) = \langle w*, x_q \rangle + b* \geq d_q - \varepsilon - \xi_q^* = d_q - \varepsilon,$$

and

$$\varepsilon + \eta_q^* - \langle w*, x_q \rangle - b* + d_q \geq 0$$
$$\Rightarrow \quad f*(x_q) = \langle w*, x_q \rangle + b* \leq d_q + \varepsilon + \eta_q^* = d_q + \varepsilon,$$

so $d_q - \varepsilon \leq f*(x_q) \leq d_q + \varepsilon$. Suppose $\alpha_q^* - \beta_q^* > 0$. Then, we have $\alpha_q^* > 0$ and $\beta_q^* = 0$. Hence, we have $\xi_q^* = C^{-1}\alpha_q^*$ and

$$\varepsilon + \xi_q^* - d_q + \langle w^*, x_q \rangle + b^* = 0$$
$$\Rightarrow \quad f^*(x_q) = \langle w^*, x_q \rangle + b^* = d_q - \varepsilon - \xi_q^* = d_q - \varepsilon - C^{-1}\alpha_q^*$$
$$= d_q - \varepsilon - C^{-1}(\alpha_q^* - \beta_q^*).$$

Suppose $\alpha_q^* - \beta_q^* < 0$. Then, we have $\alpha_q^* = 0$ and $\beta_q^* > 0$. Hence, we have $\eta_q^* = C^{-1}\beta_q^*$ and

$$\varepsilon + \eta_q^* - \langle w^*, x_q \rangle - b^* + d_q = 0$$
$$\Rightarrow \quad f^*(x_q) = \langle w^*, x_q \rangle + b^* = d_q + \varepsilon + \eta_q^* = d_q + \varepsilon + C^{-1}\beta_q^*$$
$$= d_q + \varepsilon - C^{-1}(\alpha_q^* - \beta_q^*).$$

Suppose α_q, β_q, $q \in \underline{l}$, are the current values of the dual variables. The primal variables and predictive function can thus be calculated. Then, reasonable KKT stopping conditions are given by, for $q \in \underline{l}$,

$$\alpha_q \geq 0, \quad \beta_q \geq 0,$$
$$d_q - \varepsilon \leq f(x_q) \leq d_q + \varepsilon \quad \text{if} \quad \alpha_q - \beta_q = 0,$$
$$f(x_q) = d_q - \varepsilon - C^{-1}(\alpha_q - \beta_q) \quad \text{if} \quad \alpha_q - \beta_q > 0,$$
$$f(x_q) = d_q + \varepsilon - C^{-1}(\alpha_q - \beta_q) \quad \text{if} \quad \alpha_q - \beta_q < 0.$$

We may define p_q, $q \in \underline{l}$, to be the measure of dissatisfaction of the KKT stopping conditions for the qth example as

$$p_q := \max\left[0, |f(x_q) - d_q| - \varepsilon\right] \quad \text{if} \quad \alpha_q - \beta_q = 0,$$
$$p_q := |f(x_q) - d_q + \varepsilon + C^{-1}(\alpha_q - \beta_q)| \quad \text{if} \quad \alpha_q - \beta_q > 0,$$
$$p_q := |f(x_q) - d_q - \varepsilon + C^{-1}(\alpha_q - \beta_q)| \quad \text{if} \quad \alpha_q - \beta_q < 0.$$

Then, reasonable stopping criteria based on KKT stopping conditions are

$$p_{ave} := \frac{1}{l}\sum_{q=1}^{l} p_q \leq \delta \quad \text{or} \quad \|p\|_\infty := \max_{q \in \underline{l}}\{p_q\} \leq \delta,$$

where δ is a pre-specified tolerance.

For the same reason as the ridge regression, the feasibility gap cannot be used as an indicator of the stopping criterion.

Suppose we let $\theta_q^* := \alpha_q^* - \beta_q^*$, $q \in \underline{l}$. Then, in view of $\alpha_q^* \beta_q^* = 0$, we have $\left| \theta_q^* \right| = \alpha_q^* + \beta_q^*$. Thus, the problem can be rewritten in a simpler form as

(D2')   maximize

$$\sum_{q=1}^{l} \theta_q d_q - \varepsilon \sum_{q=1}^{l} \left| \theta_q \right| - \frac{1}{2} \sum_{q=1}^{l} \sum_{j=1}^{l} \theta_q \theta_j \langle x_q, x_j \rangle$$
$$- \frac{1}{2C} \sum_{q=1}^{l} \theta_q^2$$

subject to

$$\sum_{q=1}^{l} \theta_q = 0.$$

Suppose θ^* solves the problem (D2'). Define $I_{sv} := \{ q \in \underline{l} : \theta_q^* \neq 0 \}$. Then, we have

$$w^* = \sum_{q=1}^{l} \theta_q^* x_q = \sum_{q \in I_{sv}} \theta_q^* x_q.$$

Choose any $\theta_k^* > 0$. Then we have $\alpha_k^* = \theta_k^* > 0$ and $\beta_k^* = 0$. From the KKT conditions, we have

$$0 = \varepsilon + \xi_k^* - d_k + \langle w^*, x_k \rangle + b *$$
$$= \varepsilon + C^{-1} \alpha_k^* - d_k + \langle w^*, x_k \rangle + b *$$
$$= \varepsilon + C^{-1} \theta_k^* - d_k + \langle w^*, x_k \rangle + b *$$

$$\Rightarrow \quad b* = b_k - \varepsilon - C^{-1} \theta_k^* - \langle w^*, x_k \rangle$$

$$= b_k - \varepsilon - C^{-1}\theta_k^* - \sum_{q \in I_{sv}} \theta_q^* \langle x_q, x_k \rangle .$$

Or we may also choose $\theta_k^* < 0$. Then, we have $\alpha_k^* = 0$ and $\beta_k^* = -\theta_k^* > 0$. From the KKT conditions, we have

$$0 = \varepsilon + \eta_k^* - \langle w^*, x_k \rangle - b^* + d_k$$
$$= \varepsilon + C^{-1}\beta_k^* - \langle w^*, x_k \rangle - b^* + d_k$$
$$= \varepsilon - C^{-1}\theta_k^* - \langle w^*, x_k \rangle - b^* + d_k$$

$$\Rightarrow \quad b^* = d_k + \varepsilon - C^{-1}\theta_k^* - \langle w^*, x_k \rangle$$
$$= d_k + \varepsilon - C^{-1}\theta_k^* - \sum_{q \in I_{sv}} \theta_q^* \langle x_q, x_k \rangle .$$

The optimal predictive function is thus given by

$$f^*(x) = \langle w^*, x \rangle + b^* = \sum_{q \in I_{sv}} \theta_q^* \langle x_q, x \rangle + b^* .$$

Now, we discuss a stopping criterion, based on KKT conditions, for any algorithm of finding the 2-norm soft regressor. Keep in mind that $\alpha_q^* \beta_q^* = 0$ in the following derivation.

Suppose $\theta_q^* = 0$, then we have $\alpha_q^* = \beta_q^* = 0$. Hence, we have $\xi_q^* = C^{-1}\alpha_q^* = 0$ and $\eta_q^* = C^{-1}\beta_q^* = 0$. In this case, we have

$$\varepsilon + \xi_q^* - d_q + \langle w^*, x_q \rangle + b^* \geq 0$$
$$\Rightarrow \quad f^*(x_q) = \langle w^*, x_q \rangle + b^* \geq d_q - \varepsilon - \xi_q^* = d_q - \varepsilon ,$$

and

$$\varepsilon + \eta_q^* - \langle w^*, x_q \rangle - b^* + d_q \geq 0$$
$$\Rightarrow \quad f^*(x_q) = \langle w^*, x_q \rangle + b^* \leq d_q + \varepsilon + \eta_q^* = d_q + \varepsilon ,$$

so $d_q - \varepsilon \leq f^*(x_q) \leq d_q + \varepsilon$. Suppose $\theta_q^* > 0$, then we have $\alpha_q^* = \theta_q^* > 0$. Hence, we have $\xi_q^* = C^{-1}\alpha_q^* = C^{-1}\theta_q^*$ and

$$\varepsilon + \xi_q^* - d_q + \langle w^*, x_q \rangle + b^* = 0$$
$$\Rightarrow \quad f^*(x_q) = \langle w^*, x_q \rangle + b^* = d_q - \varepsilon - \xi_q^* = d_q - \varepsilon - C^{-1}\theta_q^*.$$

Suppose $\theta_q^* < 0$, then we have $\beta_q^* = -\theta_q^* > 0$. Hence, we have $\eta_q^* = C^{-1}\beta_q^* = -C^{-1}\theta_q^*$ and

$$\varepsilon + \eta_q^* - \langle w^*, x_q \rangle - b^* + d_q = 0$$
$$\Rightarrow \quad f^*(x_q) = \langle w^*, x_q \rangle + b^* = d_q + \varepsilon + \eta_q^* = d_q + \varepsilon - C^{-1}\theta_q^*.$$

Suppose θ_q, $q \in \underline{l}$, is the current value of the dual variable. The primal variables and predictive function can thus be calculated. Then, reasonable KKT stopping conditions are given by, for $q \in \underline{l}$,

$$d_q - \varepsilon \le f(x_q) \le d_q + \varepsilon \quad \text{if } \theta_q = 0,$$
$$f(x_q) = d_q - \varepsilon - C^{-1}\theta_q \quad \text{if } \theta_q > 0,$$
$$f(x_q) = d_q + \varepsilon - C^{-1}\theta_q \quad \text{if } \theta_q < 0.$$

We may define p_q, $q \in \underline{l}$, to be the measure of dissatisfaction of the KKT stopping conditions for the qth example as

$$p_q := \max\left[0, \left|f(x_q) - d_q\right| - \varepsilon\right] \quad \text{if } \theta_q = 0,$$
$$p_q := \left|f(x_q) - d_q + \varepsilon + C^{-1}\theta_q\right| \quad \text{if } \theta_q > 0,$$
$$p_q := \left|f(x_q) - d_q - \varepsilon + C^{-1}\theta_q\right| \quad \text{if } \theta_q < 0.$$

Then, reasonable stopping criteria based on KKT stopping conditions are

$$p_{ave} := \frac{1}{l}\sum_{q=1}^{l} p_q \le \delta \quad \text{or} \quad \|p\|_\infty := \max_{q \in \underline{l}}\{p_q\} \le \delta,$$

where δ is a pre-specified tolerance.

For the same reason as the ridge regression, the feasibility gap cannot be used as an indicator of the stopping criterion.

4.11 Illustrative Example

In this section, we provide a numerical example to illustrate the design of linear regressors. The Sequential Minimal Optimization (SMO) algorithms for ridge regressor, 1-norm soft regressor, and 2-norm soft regressor are provided in Section 7.4 to Section 7.6.

Example 4.11.1:

Suppose the true regression function is given by

$$y = x + 1, \quad x \in [-2, 2].$$

To form the training data set, we first randomly choose 20 x-points with the corresponding y-values evaluated from the underlying true function. Then, 10 randomly chosen y-values will be corrupted by adding random values from a uniform distribution defined on $[0, 2]$.

Together with the true function (TF), the predictive functions determined by the least squares regressor (LSR), ridge regressor with $C = 0.1$ (RR), 1-norm soft regressor with $C = 1$, $\varepsilon = 0.01$ (SVR1), and 2-norm soft regressor with $C = 1$, $\varepsilon = 0.01$ (SVR2) are given by

$$
\begin{array}{ll}
\text{TF:} & y = x + 1 \\
\text{LSR:} & y = 1.0952x + 1.6176 \\
\text{RR:} & y = 0.8151x + 1.7247 \\
\text{SVR1:} & y = 0.9257x + 1.1575 \\
\text{SVR2:} & y = 1.0582x + 1.6327
\end{array}
$$

See Figure 4.11.1.

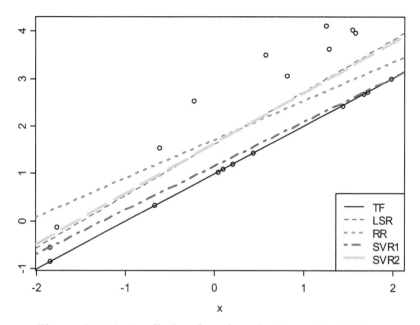

Figure 4.11.1: Predictive functions in Example 4.11.1.

4.12 Exercises

Exercise 4.12.1: Let $X \subseteq \mathfrak{R}^n$ and $Y \subseteq \mathfrak{R}$. Suppose we are given the training set

$$S := \left\{ \left(x_q, d_q \right) \right\}_{q=1}^{l} \subseteq X \times Y.$$

The problem of linear regression is to find a linear function $f(x) = \langle w, x \rangle + b$ that models the data. Consider the following primal optimization problem:

(PL)   minimize $\dfrac{1}{2} \displaystyle\sum_{q=1}^{l} \xi_q^2$

            subject to $d_q - w^T x_q - b = \xi_q$ for all $q \in \underline{l}$.

(a) Derive the normal equation by using the Lagrange optimization technique.
(b) Derive the dual problem for (PL).

Exercise 4.12.2: Suppose the true regression function is given by

$$y = 2x + 1, \quad x \in [-2, 2].$$

To form the training data set, we first randomly choose 20 x-points with the corresponding y-values evaluated from the underlying true function. Then, 10 randomly chosen y-values will be corrupted by adding random values from a uniform distribution defined on $[0, 2]$. Draw the predictive functions determined by the least squares regressor, ridge regressor (with $C = 1$), 1-norm soft regressor (with $C = 1$, $\varepsilon = 0.01$), and 2-norm soft regressor (with $C = 1$, $\varepsilon = 0.01$).

Exercise 4.12.3: Consider the training set $S := \{(x_q, d_q)\}_{q=1}^{20}$ in the following table, where $x_q \in \Re^4$ is the input pattern for the qth example and $d_q \in \Re$ is the corresponding target.

(a) Find a predictive function by using the primal form of Widrow-Hoff algorithm with learning rate $\eta = 0.001$ and calculate the average sum of squared errors.

(b) Find a predictive function by using the dual form of Widrow-Hoff algorithm with learning rate $\eta = 0.001$ and calculate the average sum of squared errors.

(c) Find a predictive function by using the recursive least squares algorithm and calculate the average sum of squared errors.

q	x_q	d_q	q	x_q	d_q
1	$(-1.0 \quad 4.1 \quad 4.2 \quad 7.8)$	1.7	11	$(0.9 \quad 1.9 \quad 3.8 \quad -4.0)$	-1.8
2	$(8.5 \quad 12.1 \quad 6.8 \quad 11.4)$	-2.0	12	$(5.1 \quad -8.2 \quad 6.0 \quad -2.3)$	-1.0
3	$(7.1 \quad 11.2 \quad 2.9 \quad 8.8)$	1.0	13	$(14.0 \quad 2.9 \quad 8.1 \quad -11.0)$	3.6
4	$(2.2 \quad 9.1 \quad 10.2 \quad 20.0)$	0.8	14	$(3.0 \quad -9.2 \quad 2.9 \quad 7.0)$	-2.5
5	$(6.0 \quad 5.0 \quad 8.0 \quad 7.2)$	1.2	15	$(-9.2 \quad -8.2 \quad -7.1 \quad 2.0)$	-1.3
6	$(7.5 \quad 5.4 \quad 3.3 \quad 7.2)$	-3.0	16	$(-4.8 \quad 6.0 \quad 7.0 \quad -4.2)$	3.2
7	$(7.0 \quad 2.2 \quad 7.8 \quad 4.3)$	4.7	17	$(4.1 \quad -6.9 \quad 8.0 \quad 2.9)$	-4.0
8	$(3.2 \quad 9.1 \quad 3.8 \quad 7.5)$	1.5	18	$(6.0 \quad 0.0 \quad 11.2 \quad 7.8)$	-5.5
9	$(1.2 \quad 4.2 \quad 7.3 \quad 6.1)$	-1.2	19	$(5.0 \quad -5.0 \quad 4.8 \quad 4.9)$	-1.0
10	$(6.2 \quad 8.1 \quad 9.2 \quad 1.1)$	1.0	20	$(3.1 \quad 1.2 \quad 12.0 \quad 7.2)$	-1.2

In the following two exercises, we investigate the effect of scaling the input data.

Exercise 4.12.4: Consider Exercise 4.12.3. Suppose we normalize each of the four input variables and the output variable to the interval $[0, 1]$ as

$$z_j = \frac{x_j - x_j^{(m)}}{x_j^{(M)} - x_j^{(m)}}, \quad j \in \underline{4}, \quad \tilde{d} = \frac{d - d^{(m)}}{d^{(M)} - d^{(m)}},$$

where $x_j^{(m)}$ and $x_j^{(M)}$ are the minimum and maximum of the values of the jth input variable in the training set, respectively. Similarly, $d^{(m)}$ and $d^{(M)}$ are the minimum and maximum of the values of the output variable in the training set, respectively. Note that all scaled variables become dimensionless.

(a) Obtain the new set of training set.
(b) Fit the plain (original) data and normalized data using 1-norm soft regressor with $C = 1$, $\varepsilon = 0.01$ (SVR1). Discuss if there are any advantages of performing the normalization?

(c) Fit the plain (original) data and normalized data using 2-norm soft regressor with $C = 1$, $\varepsilon = 0.01$ (SVR2). Discuss if there are any advantages of performing the normalization?

Exercise 4.12.5: Consider Exercise 4.12.3. It is found that the sample means and sample standard deviations of the four input variables and the output variable are

$$\begin{pmatrix} \bar{x}_1 & \bar{x}_2 & \bar{x}_3 & \bar{x}_4 \end{pmatrix} = \begin{pmatrix} 3.755 & 2.250 & 6.010 & 4.585 \end{pmatrix},$$
$$\begin{pmatrix} s_1 & s_2 & s_3 & s_4 \end{pmatrix} = \begin{pmatrix} 4.946 & 6.635 & 4.119 & 6.580 \end{pmatrix},$$
$$\bar{d} = -0.290, \ s_d = 2.597.$$

Suppose we standardize each of the four input variables and the output variable as

$$z_j := \left(x_j - \bar{x}_j \right) / s_j, \ j \in \underline{4}, \ \tilde{d} = \left(d - \bar{d} \right) / s_d.$$

In statistical regression theory, this is called the unit normal scaling. Note that all scaled variables become dimensionless.

(a) Obtain the new set of training set.
(b) Fit the plain (original) data and normalized data using 1-norm soft regressor with $C = 1$, $\varepsilon = 0.01$ (SVR1). Discuss if there are any advantages of performing the normalization?
(c) Fit the plain (original) data and normalized data using 2-norm soft regressor with $C = 1$, $\varepsilon = 0.01$ (SVR2). Discuss if there are any advantages of performing the normalization?

Exercise 4.12.6: Solve the primal problem (P) and dual problem (D) of Section 4.7 by using the Lagrange theory of Chapter 2. Check if your results are the same as the result of Section 4.5.

Exercise 4.12.7: Consider the data set of Exercise 4.12.3.

(a) Find a predictive function by using the primal form of ridge regression algorithm with $C = 1$ and learning rate $\eta = 0.001$, and calculate the cost of the ridge regression problem.

(b) Find a predictive function by using the dual form of ridge regression algorithm with $C = 1$ and learning rate $\eta = 0.001$, and calculate the cost of the ridge regression problem.

(c) Find a predictive function by using the recursive ridge regression algorithm with $C = 1$ and calculate the cost of the ridge regression problem.

Exercise 4.12.8: For the ridge regression problem of Section 4.5, prove that $J + CZ^T Z$ is nonsingular for any $C > 0$.

Exercise 4.12.9: In this exercise, we investigate the 1-norm υ-soft regressor. Let $X \subseteq \Re^n$ and $Y \subseteq \Re$. Suppose we are given the training set $S := \{(x_q, d_q)\}_{q=1}^{y} \subseteq X \times Y$. It is desired to find a soft predictive function $f(x) = \langle w, x \rangle + b$ that automatically computes the error tolerance band size ε. Consider the following primal optimization problem (with $C > 0$, $D > 0$, and $\upsilon \geq 0$):

(MUP1)   minimize $\dfrac{1}{2} w^T w + D\upsilon\varepsilon + C\sum_{q=1}^{l}\left(\xi_q + \eta_q\right)$

subject to $d_q - \left(\langle w, x_q \rangle + b\right) \leq \varepsilon + \xi_q$,

$\left(\langle w, x_q \rangle + b\right) - d_q \leq \varepsilon + \eta_q$,

$\varepsilon \geq 0$, $\xi_q \geq 0$, $\eta_q \geq 0$, for all $q \in \underline{l}$.

(a) Prove that the dual maximization problem of (MUP1) is given by

(MUD1)   maximize $\displaystyle\sum_{q=1}^{l}\left(\alpha_q - \beta_q\right)d_q - \frac{1}{2}\sum_{q=1}^{l}\sum_{j=1}^{l}\left(\alpha_q - \beta_q\right)\left(\alpha_j - \beta_j\right)x_q^T x_j$

subject to $\displaystyle\sum_{q=1}^{l}\left(\alpha_q - \beta_q\right) = 0$, $\displaystyle\sum_{q=1}^{l}\left(\alpha_q + \beta_q\right) \leq D\upsilon$,

$0 \leq \alpha_q \leq C$, $0 \leq \beta_q \leq C$, $q \in \underline{l}$.

(b) State the KKT conditions.
(c) Find the optimal predictive function in terms of the dual variables.
(d) Find a stopping criterion based on KKT conditions.
(e) Find a stopping criterion based on percentage feasibility gap.

Exercise 4.12.10: In this exercise, we investigate the 2-norm υ-soft regressor. Let $X \subseteq \mathfrak{R}^n$ and $Y \subseteq \mathfrak{R}$. Suppose we are given the training set $S := \{(x_q, d_q)\}_{q=1}^l \subseteq X \times Y$. It is desired to find a soft predictive function $f(x) = \langle w, x \rangle + b$ that automatically computes the error tolerance band size ε. Consider the following primal optimization problem (with $C > 0$, $D > 0$, and $\upsilon \geq 0$):

(MUP20) minimize $\quad \dfrac{1}{2} w^T w + D \upsilon \varepsilon + \dfrac{C}{2} \sum_{q=1}^l \left(\xi_q^2 + \eta_q^2 \right)$

subject to $\quad d_q - \left(\langle w, x_q \rangle + b \right) \leq \varepsilon + \xi_q$,

$\quad\quad\quad\quad \left(\langle w, x_q \rangle + b \right) - d_q \leq \varepsilon + \eta_q$,

$\quad\quad\quad\quad \varepsilon \geq 0$, $\xi_q \geq 0$, $\eta_q \geq 0$, for all $q \in \underline{l}$.

(a) Show that the preceding optimization problem can be reduced to

(MUP2) minimize $\quad \dfrac{1}{2} w^T w + D \upsilon \varepsilon + \dfrac{C}{2} \sum_{q=1}^l \left(\xi_q^2 + \eta_q^2 \right)$

subject to $\quad d_q - \left(\langle w, x_q \rangle + b \right) \leq \varepsilon + \xi_q$,

$\quad\quad\quad\quad \left(\langle w, x_q \rangle + b \right) - d_q \leq \varepsilon + \eta_q$, for all $q \in \underline{l}$,

$\quad\quad\quad\quad \varepsilon \geq 0$.

(b) Prove that the dual maximization problem of (MUP2) is given by

(MUD2) maximize $\quad \sum_{q=1}^l (\alpha_q - \beta_q) d_q - \dfrac{1}{2} \sum_{q=1}^l \sum_{j=1}^l (\alpha_q - \beta_q)(\alpha_j - \beta_j) x_q^T x_j$

$\quad\quad\quad\quad\quad\quad\quad - \dfrac{1}{2C} \sum_{q=1}^l \left(\alpha_q^2 + \beta_q^2 \right)$

subject to $\quad \sum_{q=1}^l (\alpha_q - \beta_q) = 0$, $\sum_{q=1}^l (\alpha_q + \beta_q) \leq D\upsilon$,

$\quad\quad\quad\quad \alpha_q \geq 0$, $\beta_q \geq 0$, for all $q \in \underline{l}$.

(c) State the KKT conditions.
(d) Find the optimal predictive function in terms of the dual variables.
(e) Find a stopping criterion based on KKT conditions.

Exercise 4.12.11: In this exercise, we consider the weighted least squares (WLS) problem. Let $X \subseteq \mathfrak{R}^n$ and $Y \subseteq \mathfrak{R}$. Suppose we are given the training set

$$S := \left\{ \left(x_q, d_q \right) \right\}_{q=1}^{Y} \subseteq X \times Y.$$

The problem of WLS regression is to find a linear function $f(x) = \langle w, x \rangle + b$, $w \in \mathfrak{R}^n$, $b \in \mathfrak{R}$, that minimize the weighted sum of squared errors

$$E(w, b) := \frac{1}{2} \sum_{q=1}^{l} \xi_q e_q^2,$$

where

$$e_q := d_q - \langle w, x_q \rangle - b, \quad q \in \underline{l},$$

is the error due to the qth example and ξ_q, $q \in \underline{l}$, is a given positive constant.

(a) Derive the normal equation or the WLS problem.
(b) Develop the recursive weighted least squares (RWLS) algorithm which minimizes the summation of weighted squared errors for all training examples up to the present iteration k.

Exercise 4.12.12: Consider the data set of Exercise 4.12.3. Suppose the weights of the data are given by the following table. Apply the algorithm developed in Exercise 4.12.11 to find the solution of the weighted least squares (WLS) problem.

q	ξ_q	q	ξ_q
1	1.7	11	1.8
2	0.5	12	1.0
3	1.0	13	2.4
4	0.8	14	1.5
5	1.2	15	1.3
6	2.8	16	0.3
7	0.7	17	2.0
8	1.5	18	0.5
9	1.2	19	1.0
10	1.0	20	1.2

4.13 Notes and References

For the original paper of Widrow-Hoff algorithm, see Widrow and Hoff (1960). The Widrow-Hoff algorithms can also be found in Cristianini and Shawe-Taylor (2000) and Kecman (2001). The recursive least squares algorithm for linear regressors can be found in Kecman (2001). Our development of slack variables and soft regressors were based on Cristianini and Shawe-Taylor (2000). The 1-norm υ-soft regressor in Exercise 4.12.9 can be found in Schölkopf and Smola (2002). For least squares support vector machines, see Suykens etc. (2002).

Cristianini, N. and J. Shawe-Taylor (2000). An Introduction to Support Vector Machines. Cambridge University Press, Cambridge, United Kingdom.

Kecman, V. (2001). Learning and Soft Computing. MIT Press, Cambridge, Massachusetts.

Schölkopf, B. and A.J. Smola (2002). Learning with Kernels: Support Vector Machines, Regularization, and Beyond. MIT Press, Cambridge, Massachusetts.

Suykens, J.A.K, T. Van Gestel, J. De Brabanter, and B. De Moor (2002). Least Squares Support Vector Machines. World Scientific Publishing, Singapore.

Widrow, B. and M.E. Hoff (1960). Adaptive switching circuits. IRE Western Electric Show and Connection Record. Part 4, pp. 96-104. Reprinted in Anderson and Rosenfield (1998).

Chapter 5   Multi-layer Neural Networks

In this chapter, we will introduce three popular and powerful learning machines, i.e., artificial neural networks, generalized radial basis function networks, and fuzzy neural networks.   All three learning machines can be represented as multi-layer neural networks with hidden layers, and the activation functions of the hidden nodes are nonlinear and continuously differentiable.   All learning algorithms presented for the three learning machines are based on a simple back propagation algorithm, which is a direct generalization of the delta learning rule used in Widrow-Hoff algorithm for Adalines.   The invention of the back propagation learning rules is a major breakthrough in machine learning theory.   It will be seen that the nonlinearity of the activation functions of hidden nodes solves the problem of representation, while the differentiability of the activations functions of both hidden nodes and output nodes solves the problem of learning.   Furthermore, each learning machine nonlinearly transform in a peculiar way the input vectors to a feature space and perform (generalized) linear regression in feature space to produce the output vectors.   This is consistent with the strategies mentioned in Section 3.5 for nonlinear classification and Section 4.4 for nonlinear regression.   The ridge version of the artificial neural network is discussed in Exercise 5.7.5.   A simplified version of the generalized radial basis function network is discussed in Exercise 5.7.6.   The ridge version of the generalized radial basis function network is discussed in Exercise 5.7.7.

5.1   Cover's Theorem

For a linearly inseparable training data set, the first strategy proposed in Section 3.5 was to nonlinearly transform the data to another space.   If the transformed data is linearly separable in the new space, called the feature space, then we may apply the techniques for linearly separable data. This results in a linear classifier in the new space but a nonlinear classifier in the original space.   See Figure 5.1.1 for illustration.   Are we too optimistic?   The following theorem due to Cover provides a theoretical answer to this problem.

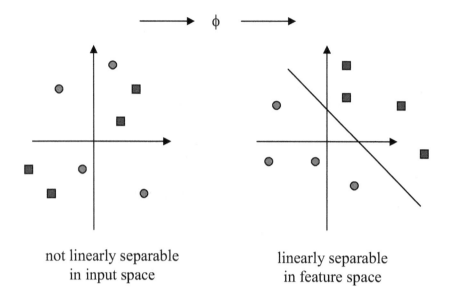

not linearly separable   linearly separable
in input space   in feature space

Figure 5.1.1: Nonlinear transformation of data.

Before presenting the Cover's Theorem, let us first note that every training set is nonlinearly separable in the sense that there exists a nonlinear map such that the transformed data is linearly separable in the new space. To show this, let $X \subseteq \Re^n$ and $Y := \{1, -1\}$. For the simplicity of notation, suppose the training set is given by $S = S_1 \cup S_2$, where

$$S_1 := \left\{(x_i, d_i)\right\}_{i=1}^{l_1} \neq \varnothing,$$
$$d_i = 1 \quad \text{for all} \quad i = 1, 2, ..., l_1,$$
$$S_2 = \left\{(x_i, d_i)\right\}_{i=l_1+1}^{l_1+l_2} \neq \varnothing,$$
$$d_i = -1 \quad \text{for all} \quad i = l_1 + 1, l_1 + 2, ..., l_1 + l_2,$$
$$x_i \neq x_j \quad \text{for all} \quad i \neq j.$$

Define $l := l_1 + l_2$, $d := 2 \cdot \min(l_1, l_2) \leq l$, and

$$\varepsilon_M := \min_{i \neq j, i, j \in \underline{l}} \left\| x_i - x_j \right\|.$$

Choose an ε, $0 < \varepsilon < \varepsilon_M$, and define a function $\phi(x): \Re^n \to \Re$ as

$$\phi(x) := \begin{cases} -\prod_{i=1}^{l_1}\left[\|x - x_i\|^2 - \varepsilon^2\right], & \text{if } l_1 \le l_2, \\ \prod_{i=l_1+1}^{l_1+l_2}\left[\|x - x_i\|^2 - \varepsilon^2\right], & \text{if } l_1 > l_2. \end{cases}$$

Clearly, $\phi(x)$ is a monomial function with $\deg[\phi(x)] = d$. Furthermore, we have

$$\phi(x_i) > 0 \quad \text{for all} \quad i = 1, 2, ..., l_1,$$
$$\phi(x_i) < 0 \quad \text{for all} \quad i = l_1 + 1, l_1 + 2, ..., l_1 + l_2.$$

This shows that the nonlinear map $\phi(\cdot)$ defined above is a desired map for nonlinear classification. Consequently, any training set is nonlinearly separable in the one-dimensional real space $\Re$. The nearest-neighboring approach used above can indeed "memorize" all training data. However, there are two drawbacks. First, we are faced with the curse of dimensionality. That is, as the number of training data becomes large, the degree of the nonlinear map $\phi(\cdot)$ also becomes large. This causes great numerical difficulty. Second, correct classification of all training data does not imply correct classification of all previously unseen data.

Proposition 5.1.1: (Cover's Theorem)

A complex pattern-classification problem cast in a high-dimensional space nonlinearly is more likely to be linearly separable than a low-dimensional space.

Cover's Theorem states that the training set may be transformed into a new feature space where the patterns are linearly separable with high probability, provided two conditions are satisfied. First, the transformation is nonlinear. Second, the dimensionality of the feature space is high enough. What is meant by Cover's Theorem is, given a set of patterns and "unknown" labeling, if we nonlinearly transform the pattern into some feature space with dimension higher than the original input space, then the transformation to be done by a hyperplane becomes more likely.

5.2 Artificial Neural Network

Recall Example 3.5.1 for NXOR problem. There, we transformed the training data to a higher-dimensional space and performed linear classification for the transformed data. The resulting nonlinear classifier can be represented as a two-layer network with a hidden layer. One of the activation functions of the hidden neuron is nonlinear. The strategies mentioned in Section 3.5 and Section 4.4 motivate us to consider a more general network for nonlinear classification and regression.

Artificial neural network (ANN) is a biologically motivated learning machine mimicking lightly the structure and behavior of biological neurons and the nervous system. There are variants of ANNs. In this book, we only consider the most popular feed-forward ANN as shown in Figure 5.2.1. There is a single input layer with $n+1$ nodes, a single hidden layer with $m+1$ nodes, and a single output layer with p nodes.

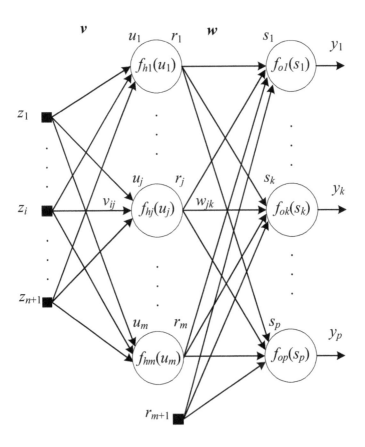

Figure 5.2.1: Feed-forward artificial neural network.

Let the input vector be

$$x := [x_1 \quad \cdots \quad x_n]^T \in \mathfrak{R}^n$$

or

$$z := [z_1 \quad \cdots \quad z_n \quad z_{n+1}]^T = [x_1 \quad \cdots \quad x_n \quad 1]^T \in \mathfrak{R}^{n+1},$$

i.e.,

$$z_i := x_i, \quad i \in \underline{n}, \quad z_{n+1} := 1.$$

Let v_{ij} denote the connection weight from the ith input node to the input of the jth hidden node. Then, the input u_j and output r_j of the jth hidden node are given by, respectively,

$$u_j = \sum_{i=1}^{n+1} v_{ij} z_i, \quad r_j = f_{hj}(u_j), \quad z_{n+1} := 1, \quad j \in \underline{m},$$

where f_{hj} is the activation function of the jth hidden node. Any monotonically increasing or decreasing function can be used as an activation function. Some commonly used activation functions are sigmoidal functions, i.e., monotonically increasing S-shaped functions as follows:

$$\text{unipolar logistic function:} \quad r_j = f_{hj}(u_j) = \frac{1}{1 + e^{-u_j}};$$

$$\text{bipolar sigmoidal function:} \quad r_j = f_{hj}(u_j) = \frac{2}{1 + e^{-u_j}} - 1 = \frac{1 - e^{-u_j}}{1 + e^{-u_j}};$$

$$\text{hyperbolic tangent function:} \quad r_j = f_{hj}(u_j) = \frac{e^{u_j} - e^{-u_j}}{e^{u_j} + e^{-u_j}}.$$

See Figure 5.2.2 for illustration. Note that the hyperbolic tangent function can be obtained from the bipolar sigmoidal function by replacing u_j by $2u_j$. The inverse of an activation function is often called the link function in the terminology of generalized linear regression theory. The inverses of the sigmoidal functions are shown in Figure 5.2.3.

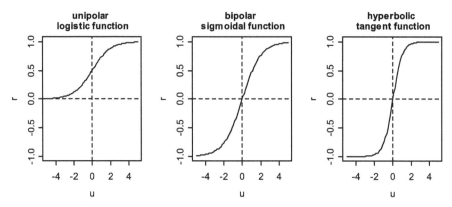

Figure 5.2.2: Sigmoidal functions.

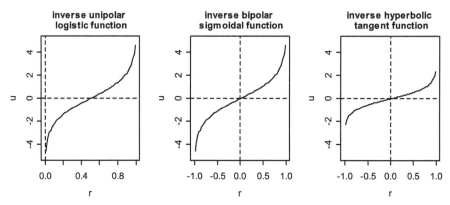

Figure 5.2.3: Inverse sigmoidal functions.

These activation functions are continuously differentiable with derivatives given by, respectively,

unipolar logistic function: $\quad f'_{hj}\left(u_j\right) = r_j\left(1 - r_j\right);$

bipolar sigmoidal function: $\quad f'_{hj}\left(u_j\right) = 2^{-1}\left(1 - r_j^2\right);$

hyperbolic tangent function: $\quad f'_{hj}\left(u_j\right) = 1 - r_j^2\,.$

See Figure 5.2.4 for illustration.

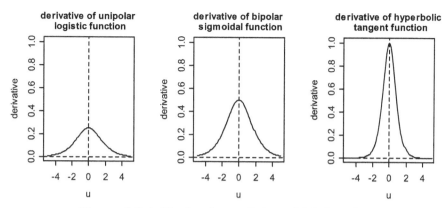

Figure 5.2.4: Derivatives of sigmoidal functions.

Recently, especially in deep learning, a very simple function defined by

rectified linear unit (ReLU): $r_j = f_{hj}(u_j) = \max(0, u_j)$

is frequently used. It is zero for negative values and has unit slope for positive values.

Let w_{jk} denote the connection weight from the output of the jth hidden node to the input of the kth output node. Then, the input s_k and output y_k of the kth output node are given by, respectively,

$$s_k = \sum_{j=1}^{m+1} w_{jk} r_j, \quad y_k = f_{ok}(s_k), \quad r_{m+1} := 1, \quad k \in \underline{p},$$

where f_{ok} is the activation function of the kth output node. For binary classification problems, if the output labels were coded as 0 or 1, the output activation functions can be chosen as unipolar logistic function, and if the output labels were coded as -1 or 1, the output activation functions can be chosen as bipolar sigmoidal function or hyperbolic tangent function. For regression (or function learning) problems, the standard choice of the output activation function is the identity function (i.e., the linear function with unit slope). However, if the response data have been scaled to $[0, 1]$ or $[-1, 1]$, then the unipolar logistic function, bipolar sigmoidal function, or hyperbolic tangent function may be used as the output activation function.

The class of approximating functions represented as artificial neural networks, with m unfixed, possesses the **universal approximation property**, i.e., they are **universal approximators**, in the sense that given any continuous function $g(x)$ defined on a compact set $U \subseteq \mathfrak{R}^n$ and any positive constant $\varepsilon > 0$, no matter how small, there is an artificial neural network f_ε belonging to this class of functions such that

$$\sup_{x \in U} \| f_\varepsilon(x) - g(x) \| \leq \varepsilon.$$

See Cybenko (1989), Funahashi (1989), and Hornik, Stinchcombe, and White (1989). The universal approximation property is crucial for the success of a learning machine in a variety of applications. It will be seen that the nonlinearity of the activation functions of hidden nodes solves the problem of representation, while the differentiability of the activations functions of both hidden nodes and output nodes solves the problem of learning.

Let $X \subseteq \mathfrak{R}^n$ and $Y \subseteq \mathfrak{R}^p$. Suppose we are given the training set

$$S := \left\{ \left(x_q, d_q \right) \right\}_{q=1}^{l} \subseteq X \times Y \quad \text{or} \quad S := \left\{ \left(z_q, d_q \right) \right\}_{q=1}^{l} \subseteq \mathfrak{R}^{n+1} \times \mathfrak{R}^p.$$

In the following, we will use the subscript q to denote the qth example. For instance, x_{qi} denotes the ith component of the qth pattern $x_q \in \mathfrak{R}^n$, $q \in \underline{l}$, $i \in \underline{n}$. By this convention, we have

$$u_{qj} = \sum_{i=1}^{n+1} v_{ij} z_{qi}, \quad r_{qj} = f_{hj}\left(u_{qj} \right), \quad z_{q,n+1} := 1, \quad q \in \underline{l}, \quad j \in \underline{m},$$

$$s_{qk} = \sum_{j=1}^{m+1} w_{jk} r_{qj}, \quad y_{qk} = f_{ok}\left(s_{qk} \right), \quad r_{q,m+1} := 1, \quad q \in \underline{l}, \quad k \in \underline{p}.$$

The error (or residual) e_{qk} at the kth output node due to the qth example is defined by

$$e_{qk} := d_{qk} - y_{qk}, \quad q \in \underline{l}, \quad k \in \underline{p}.$$

Consider a regression (or function learning) problem, where the outputs (i.e., targets or responses) assume continuous values instead of discrete labels. The usual least squares approach is to choose weights that minimize the total sum of squared errors given by

$$E_{total} := \frac{1}{2} \sum_{q=1}^{l} \sum_{k=1}^{p} e_{qk}^2 \ .$$

Define the sum of squared errors due to the qth example as

$$E_q := \frac{1}{2} \sum_{k=1}^{p} e_{qk}^2 \ , \quad q \in \underline{l}.$$

Then, we have

$$E_{total} = \sum_{q=1}^{l} E_q \ .$$

Now, we introduce the error **back propagation (BP) algorithm**, also called the generalized delta learning rule, which is an on-line (or pattern-based) incremental gradient descent algorithm. See Rumelhart, Hinton, and Williams (1986) and Le Cun (1986). In this algorithm, E_q's are minimized in sequence.

First, we propose an updating rule for w_{jk}, which is given by

$$w_{jk} \leftarrow w_{jk} - \eta_w \frac{\partial E_q}{\partial w_{jk}}, \quad j \in \underline{m+1}, \ k \in \underline{p},$$

where $\eta_w > 0$ is a learning rate. By chain rule, we have

$$\frac{\partial E_q}{\partial w_{jk}} = \frac{\partial E_q}{\partial s_{qk}} \frac{\partial s_{qk}}{\partial w_{jk}} = \frac{\partial E_q}{\partial s_{qk}} r_{qj} = - \left(- \frac{\partial E_q}{\partial s_{qk}} \right) r_{qj} \ .$$

Define

$$\delta_{qk}^{(o)} = -\frac{\partial E_q}{\partial s_{qk}} = -\frac{\partial E_q}{\partial e_{qk}}\frac{\partial e_{qk}}{\partial y_{qk}}\frac{\partial y_{qk}}{\partial s_{qk}} = -e_{qk}(-1)f'_{ok}(s_{qk}) = e_{qk}f'_{ok}(s_{qk}).$$

Hence, the updating rule becomes

$$w_{jk} \leftarrow w_{jk} - \eta_w \frac{\partial E_q}{\partial w_{jk}}$$

$$= w_{jk} + \eta_w \cdot \delta_{qk}^{(o)} r_{qj}$$

$$= w_{jk} + \eta_w \cdot e_{qk} f'_{ok}(s_{qk}) r_{qj}.$$

Next, we propose an updating rule for v_{ij}, which is given by

$$v_{ij} \leftarrow v_{ij} - \eta_v \frac{\partial E_q}{\partial v_{ij}}, \quad i \in \underline{n+1}, \quad j \in \underline{m},$$

where $\eta_v > 0$ is a learning rate. By chain rule, we have

$$\frac{\partial E_q}{\partial v_{ij}} = \frac{\partial E_q}{\partial u_{qj}}\frac{\partial u_{qj}}{\partial v_{ij}} = \frac{\partial E_q}{\partial u_{qj}} z_{qi} = -\left(-\frac{\partial E_q}{\partial u_{qj}}\right) z_{qi}.$$

Define

$$\delta_{qj}^{(h)} = -\frac{\partial E_q}{\partial u_{qj}} = -\frac{\partial E_q}{\partial r_{qj}}\frac{\partial r_{qj}}{\partial u_{qj}} = -\frac{\partial E_q}{\partial r_{qj}}f'_{hj}(u_{qj})$$

$$= -\left[\sum_{k=1}^{p}\frac{\partial E_q}{\partial s_{qk}}\frac{\partial s_{qk}}{\partial r_{qj}}\right]f'_{hj}(u_{qj})$$

$$= \left[\sum_{k=1}^{p}\delta_{qk}^{(o)}w_{jk}\right]f'_{hj}(u_{qj}).$$

Hence, the updating rule becomes

$$v_{ij} \leftarrow v_{ij} - \eta_v \frac{\partial E_q}{\partial v_{ij}}$$

$$= v_{ij} + \eta_v \cdot \delta_{qj}^{(h)} z_{qi}$$

$$= v_{ij} + \eta_v \cdot \left\{ \sum_{k=1}^{p} e_{qk} f'_{ok}\left(s_{qk}\right) w_{jk} \right\} f'_{hj}\left(u_{qj}\right) z_{qi}.$$

The on-line (or sequential) version of BP algorithm is summarized as follows.

Algorithm 5.2.1: (on-line version)

Step 1: Choose the learning rates η_w, η_v, and tolerance ε.

Step 2: Initialize v_{ij}, $i \in \underline{n+1}$, $j \in \underline{m}$; w_{jk}, $j \in \underline{m+1}$, $k \in \underline{p}$.

Step 3: //one epoch

      for $q = 1$ to l

Step (3a):   //feed-forward part

      for $j = 1$ to m
         $u_{qj} \leftarrow 0$;
         for $i = 1$ to $n+1$ $\{ u_{qj} \leftarrow u_{qj} + v_{ij} z_{qi} ; \}$
         $r_{qj} \leftarrow f_{hj}\left(u_{qj}\right)$;
      end for
      for $k = 1$ to p
         $s_{qk} \leftarrow 0$;
         for $j = 1$ to $m+1$ $\{ s_{qk} \leftarrow s_{qk} + w_{jk} r_{qj} ; \}$
         $y_{qk} \leftarrow f_{ok}\left(s_{qk}\right)$;
         $e_{qk} \leftarrow d_{qk} - y_{qk}$;
      end for

Step (3b):   //back-propagation part

      for $k = 1$ to p $\{ \delta_{qk}^{(o)} \leftarrow e_{qk} f'_{ok}\left(s_{qk}\right) ; \}$
      for $k = 1$ to p
         for $j = 1$ to $m+1$
             $w_{jk} \leftarrow w_{jk} + \eta_w \delta_{qk}^{(o)} r_{qj}$;
         end for
      end for

$$\text{for} \quad j = 1 \quad \text{to } m$$

$$\delta_{qj}^{(h)} \leftarrow 0;$$

$$\text{for} \quad k = 1 \quad \text{to } p \; \{ \delta_{qj}^{(h)} \leftarrow \delta_{qj}^{(h)} + \delta_{qk}^{(o)} w_{jk} \; ; \}$$

$$\delta_{qj}^{(h)} \leftarrow \delta_{qj}^{(h)} f_{hj}' \left(u_{qj} \right);$$

end for

$$\text{for} \quad j = 1 \quad \text{to } m$$

$$\text{for} \quad i = 1 \quad \text{to} \quad n+1$$

$$v_{ij} \leftarrow v_{ij} + \eta_v \delta_{qj}^{(h)} z_{qi} \; ;$$

end for

end for

end for

Step 4:   //calculating the mean squared error after one epoch

Repeat Step 3(a) to obtain the new e_{qk} .

$$MSE \leftarrow 0;$$

$$\text{for} \quad q = 1 \quad \text{to } l$$

$$\text{for} \quad k = 1 \quad \text{to } p$$

$$MSE \leftarrow MSE + e_{qk}^2 \; ;$$

end for

end for

$$MSE \leftarrow MSE / (l \cdot p)$$

Step 5:   If $\left| MSE - MSE_{old} \right| \leq \varepsilon$ over some consecutive epoches, then Stop; otherwise go to Step 3.

Artificial neural network training problems can be quite challenging. The cost surface (or landscape) is typically nonconvex and is riddled with multiple local minima and saddle points.   See Figure 5.2.5 for illustration of the cost surface of a simple artificial neural network with a single hidden node and a single input variable.

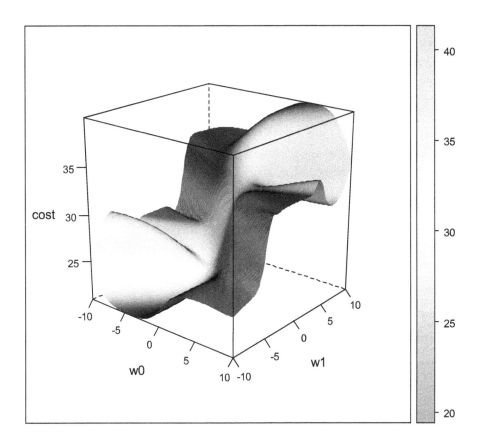

Figure 5.2.5: Cost surface of an artificial network with a single hidden node.

It is important to note that different numbers of hidden nodes correspond to different learning problems. The number of parameters of an ANN to be optimized is given by

$$(n+1)\times m + (m+1)\times p = m \times (n+1+p) + p \,.$$

Increasing one hidden node, i.e., from m to $m+1$, increase $(n+1+p)$ parameters, which could be large for problems of high input and/or output dimensions. Consequently, increasing the number of hidden nodes further complicates the accuracy and stability of the numerical optimization. Further, it raises the risk of overfitting.

For a given data set, the number of hidden nodes m (or $m+1$) is possibly the most important factor for successful learning. Unfortunately, there is no universally accepted method to determine m. Experimentally, our old friend, the method of cross validation (specifically, the k-fold method), may help determine this important number. First, we divide the given experimental data randomly into two parts, one part for training and the other for validating or testing. In the pruning method, or top-down method, we start with a big m, possibly the number of training data. Then, we start to decrease m. In the process, we record the training errors and testing errors. Usually, the training error is low but the testing error is high when m is big. Decreasing m has the effect of decreasing the testing error but increasing the training error. The pruning process is stopped when the training and testing errors are both tolerable. In the growing method, or bottom-up method, we start with a small m. Then, we start to increase m. In the process, we record the training errors and testing errors. Similarly, the growing process is stopped when the training and testing errors are both tolerable.

Some modifications of the standard BP algorithm can be made to overcome the numerical difficulty and/or to speed up the convergence. First, it should be cautioned that the standard BP algorithm is quite sensitive to initial settings including the choices of initial output weights, initial input weights, and learning rates. It is our experience that the choice of the activation functions doesn't make too much difference.

There is no universal method of setting the initial output and input weights. Different initial weights may lead to different local solutions, or may even diverge. One possibility is to assign those weights with random numbers in pre-specified regions. Very often, one must try many different sets of initial weights to ensure that the final weights produce fitted output values which are close to the observed values. Our experience shows that it is also advisable to perform the data pre-processing before using the BP algorithm. For instance, we may normalize the input and/or output data to $[-1, 1]$ or $[0, 1]$. Or one may standardize the data by subtracting the sample mean from each datum and dividing the resulting quantity by the sample standard deviation.

There are three variants of gradient descent, namely batch gradient descent, stochastic gradient descent (SGD), and mini-batch gradient descent. They differ in how much data we use to compute the gradient of the objective function. Depending on the amount of data, a trade-off between the accuracy of the parameter update and the time it takes to perform an update must be made; see Ruder (2016) and the references therein.

The batch gradient descent algorithm for updating connection weights is discussed in Exercise 5.7.1. The updating rules are given by

$$w_{jk} \leftarrow w_{jk} - \eta_w \frac{\partial E_{total}}{\partial w_{jk}}, \quad v_{ij} \leftarrow v_{ij} - \eta_v \frac{\partial E_{total}}{\partial v_{ij}},$$

where

$$E_{total} := \frac{1}{2} \sum_{q=1}^{l} \sum_{k=1}^{p} e_{qk}^2 .$$

Since we have to use the whole dataset to calculate the gradients in order to perform just one update, the batch gradient descent can be very slow and is intractable for big datasets. Furthermore, batch gradient descent does not allow us to update our model online, i.e., for new examples on-the-fly (Ruder, 2016).

The convergence of the batch gradient descent algorithm can be speeded up by making the learning rate adaptive via some step size selection rules, e.g., line minimization, limited line minimization, Armijo, Goldstein, Wolfe, or diminishing step size rules. See Bertsekas (1999). In the following, we briefly sketch the commonly used Armijo rule, which is a successive step size reduction method. Recall that our goal here is to choose weights that minimize the total sum of squared errors given by

$$E(w,v) := \frac{1}{2} \sum_{q=1}^{l} \sum_{k=1}^{p} e_{qk}^2 .$$

Let $\nabla_w E$ and $\nabla_v E$ be the gradient vectors of E with respect to weight vectors w and v, respectively. The batch-type updating rules are given by

$$w \leftarrow w - \eta_w \nabla_w E(w,v), \quad v \leftarrow v - \eta_v \nabla_v E(w,v),$$

where η_w and η_v are learning rates to be determined. To determine an appropriate learning rate η_w^*, we first fix positive scalars ξ, β, and σ, with $0 < \beta < 1$ and $0 < \sigma < 1$. Then, set $\eta_w^* = \beta^{\lambda *}\xi$, where $\lambda *$ is the first nonnegative integer λ for which

$$E(w, v) - E\left(w - \beta^\lambda \xi \nabla_w E(w,v), v\right) \geq \sigma\left(\beta^\lambda \xi\right)\left\|\nabla_w E(w,v)\right\|^2,$$

where $\|\cdot\|$ denotes the norm of a vector. In other words, the learning rate $\eta_w = \beta^\lambda \xi$, $\lambda = 0, 1, \ldots$, are tried successively until the above inequality is satisfied for $\lambda = \lambda *$. Thus, the cost improvement must not be just positive; it must be sufficiently large. Usually, we have

$$\sigma \sim \left[10^{-5}, 10^{-1}\right], \quad \beta \sim [0.1, 0.5], \quad \xi \sim 1.$$

The learning rate η_v is determined similarly.

Stochastic gradient descent (SGD) performs a parameter update for each training example, just as we did previously, i.e.,

$$w_{jk} \leftarrow w_{jk} - \eta_w \frac{\partial E_q}{\partial w_{jk}}, \quad v_{ij} \leftarrow v_{ij} - \eta_v \frac{\partial E_q}{\partial v_{ij}},$$

where

$$E_q := \frac{1}{2}\sum_{k=1}^p e_{qk}^2.$$

Note that since the batch gradient descent recomputes gradients for similar examples before each parameter update, it performs redundant computations for large datasets. SGD does away with this redundancy by performing one update at a time. It is therefore usually much faster and can also be used to learn online. However, SGD performs frequent updates with a high variance that cause the objective function to fluctuate heavily (Ruder, 2016).

Mini-batch gradient descent takes the best of both worlds and performs an update for every mini-batch of $\tilde{l}$ training examples (Ruder, 2016). Suppose we randomly select $\tilde{l}$ indices from $\{1, 2, \ldots, l\}$ to form the index set IS. Then the updating rules become

$$w_{jk} \leftarrow w_{jk} - \eta_w \sum_{q \in IS} \frac{\partial E_q}{\partial w_{jk}}, \quad v_{ij} \leftarrow v_{ij} - \eta_v \sum_{q \in IS} \frac{\partial E_q}{\partial v_{ij}}.$$

Mini-batch gradient descent reduces the variance of the parameter updates, which can lead to more stable convergence. Moreover, it can make use of highly optimized matrix optimizations common to state-of-the-art deep learning libraries that make computing the gradient with respect to a mini-batch very efficient. Mini-batch gradient descent is typically the algorithm of choice when training a neural network and the term SGD usually is employed also when mini-batches are used (Ruder, 2016).

Very often, the convergence can be speeded up by using the heavy ball method. That is, we add momentum terms to the updating laws, i.e., a fraction of the update vector of the past time step. Specifically, the updating rules for output and input weights are modified as

$$w_{jk} \leftarrow w_{jk} - \eta_w \sum_{q \in IS} \frac{\partial E_q}{\partial w_{jk}} + \tilde{\eta}_w \tilde{w}_{jk}, \quad v_{ij} \leftarrow v_{ij} - \eta_v \sum_{q \in IS} \frac{\partial E_q}{\partial v_{ij}} + \tilde{\eta}_v \tilde{v}_{ij},$$

where $\tilde{w}_{jk}$, $\tilde{v}_{ij}$ are the output and input weights from the previous iteration, and $\tilde{\eta}_w$, $\tilde{\eta}_v$ are the pre-specified momentum learning rates, usually set to be 0.9 or similar values.

There are some popular algorithms modifying momentum terms and/or learning rates, e.g., NAG (Nesterov accelerated gradient), Adagrad, Adadelta, RMSprop, and Adam (Adaptive Moment Estimation). See Ruder (2016) and the references therein.

In the following, we briefly sketch the popular Adam algorithm; see Kingma and Lei Ba (2015) and Ruder (2016). For simplicity, we consider only the updating of the output weights w_{jk}. The updating of the input weights v_{ij} can be performed similarly. Adam first computes estimates $M_{jk}^{(w)}$ and $V_{jk}^{(w)}$ of the first moment (i.e., the mean) and the second (raw) moment of the gradients with respect to w_{jk}, respectively, hence the name of the method:

$$M_{jk}^{(w)} = \beta_1 \tilde{M}_{jk}^{(w)} + \left(1 - \beta_1\right) \sum_{q \in IS} \frac{\partial E_q}{\partial w_{jk}},$$

$$V_{jk}^{(w)} = \beta_2 \tilde{V}_{jk}^{(w)} + \left(1 - \beta_2\right) \sum_{q \in IS} \left(\frac{\partial E_q}{\partial w_{jk}}\right)^2,$$

where $\tilde{M}_{jk}^{(w)}$ and $\tilde{V}_{jk}^{(w)}$ are the corresponding estimates from the previous iteration, and β_1, β_2 are two pre-specified constants. The terms $M_{jk}^{(w)}$ and $V_{jk}^{(w)}$ are usually initialized as 0's. Then we compute the bias-corrected first and second moment estimates:

$$\hat{M}_{jk}^{(w)} = \frac{M_{jk}^{(w)}}{1 - \left(\beta_1\right)^t}, \quad \hat{V}_{jk}^{(w)} = \frac{V_{jk}^{(w)}}{1 - \left(\beta_2\right)^t},$$

where t is the index (or number) of iteration. Then the updating rule for w_{jk} is given by

$$w_{jk} \leftarrow w_{jk} - \frac{\eta_w}{\sqrt{\hat{V}_{jk}^{(w)}} + \varepsilon} \hat{M}_{jk}^{(w)}.$$

The authors proposed default values: $\beta_1 = 0.9$, $\beta_2 = 0.999$, and $\varepsilon = 10^{-8}$. Note that Adam computes adaptive learning rates for each parameter.

An artificial neural network can be viewed in another way. In the previous chapter, we were concerned mainly on the design of a linear regressor $f(x) = w^T x + b$, which is a linear model. It can be extended to a generalized linear model (GLM) of the form

$$f(x) = G\left(w^T x + b\right),$$

where G denotes a known function, called the inverse link function in generalized linear regression theory. That is, the link function is $g = G^{-1}$. By treating the activation functions of an artificial neural network as the inverse link functions, we see that an artificial neural network is the cascade of two layers of interconnected GLMs. This will motivate the consideration of response distribution other than the usual normal distribution and the choice of appropriate output activation functions. Moreover, the computational techniques from the GLM theory can be employed to update the network weights. For instance, the Fisher scoring algorithm, which is a (second-order) Newton-like algorithm, can be used to update the output weights for any given output activation function.

In our view, the operational tasks of these two layers of GLMs are different in essence. First, in a peculiar way, the input vector $z \in \Re^{n+1}$ is transformed nonlinearly to the feature vector $r \in \Re^m$ via the first layer of GLMs, with $\Re^m$ treated as the feature space. Then, perform the generalized linear regression in feature space via the second layer of GLMs to produce the output vector $y \in \Re^p$ of the network. This is consistent with the third strategies mentioned in Section 3.5 for nonlinear classification and Section 4.4 for nonlinear regression, respectively.

For binary classification problems, the binary cross-entropy (a binary logarithmic loss) is a suitable objective function to be minimized. If the output labels were coded as 0 or 1, then the binary cross-entropy function (with $p = 1$) is given by

$$ J_{bce} := -\sum_{q=1}^{l} \left[d_q \log(y_q) + (1 - d_q) \log(1 - y_q) \right], $$

where y_q, $0 < y_q < 1$, $q \in \underline{l}$, is deemed the estimated probability of x_q belonging to the class labeled as 1. Note that

$$ d_q \log(y_q) + (1 - d_q) \log(1 - y_q) $$

$$ = \begin{cases} \log(1 - y_q), & d_q = 0, \\ \log(y_q), & d_q = 1. \end{cases} $$

If $y_q \approx d_q$ for all q, then $J_{bce} \approx 0$.

If the output labels were coded as -1 or 1, then the binary cross-entropy function (with $p = 1$) is given by, using the linear transformation $z_2 = 0.5 + 0.5z_1$,

$$J_{bce} := -\sum_{q=1}^{l}\left[\begin{array}{l}(0.5 + 0.5d_q)\log(0.5 + 0.5y_q)\\ +(0.5 - 0.5d_q)\log(0.5 - 0.5y_q)\end{array}\right],$$

where $0.5 + 0.5y_q$, $-1 < y_q < 1$, $q \in \underline{l}$, is deemed the estimated probability of x_q belonging to the class labeled as 1. Note that

$$(0.5 + 0.5d_q)\log(0.5 + 0.5y_q) + (0.5 - 0.5d_q)\log(0.5 - 0.5y_q)$$

$$= \begin{cases} \log(0.5 - 0.5y_q), & d_q = -1, \\ \log(0.5 + 0.5y_q), & d_q = 1. \end{cases}$$

We wish to point out that regularized cost functions to be minimized for binary classification problems (with $p = 1$) may also be used:

$$J = \frac{1}{2}\sum_{j=1}^{m}\sum_{k=1}^{p}w_{jk}^2 + C \cdot \frac{1}{l \cdot p}\sum_{k=1}^{p}\sum_{q=1}^{l}I(y_{qk} \cdot d_{qk} \le 0)$$

or

$$J = \frac{1}{2}\sum_{i=1}^{n}\sum_{j=1}^{m}v_{ij}^2 + \frac{1}{2}\sum_{j=1}^{m}\sum_{k=1}^{p}w_{jk}^2 + C \cdot \frac{1}{l \cdot p}\sum_{k=1}^{p}\sum_{q=1}^{l}I(y_{qk} \cdot d_{qk} \le 0),$$

where $I(condition)$ is the indicator function with value 1 if the "condition" is true and 0 otherwise, and the positive constant C is a smoothing parameter. Thus

$$\sum_{k=1}^{p}\sum_{q=1}^{l}I(y_{qk} \cdot d_{qk} \le 0)$$

is the number of misclassifications for the training data, and

$$\frac{1}{l \cdot p}\sum_{k=1}^{p}\sum_{q=1}^{l}I(y_{qk} \cdot d_{qk} \le 0)$$

is the misclassification rate for the training data.

We may also use the following robust cost functions to be minimized for binary classification problems (with $p = 1$):

$$J = \frac{1}{2} \sum_{j=1}^{m} \sum_{k=1}^{p} w_{jk}^2 + C \sum_{k=1}^{p} \sum_{q=1}^{l} \xi_{qk}$$

or

$$J = \frac{1}{2} \sum_{i=1}^{n} \sum_{j=1}^{m} v_{ij}^2 + \frac{1}{2} \sum_{j=1}^{m} \sum_{k=1}^{p} w_{jk}^2 + C \sum_{k=1}^{p} \sum_{q=1}^{l} \xi_{qk} ,$$

where ξ_{qk}'s are the slack variables for binary classification problems introduced in Section 3.7.

Regularized cost functions to be minimized for regression problems may also be used:

$$J = \frac{1}{2} \sum_{j=1}^{m} \sum_{k=1}^{p} w_{jk}^2 + \frac{C}{2} \sum_{q=1}^{l} \sum_{k=1}^{p} e_{qk}^2$$

or

$$J = \frac{1}{2} \sum_{i=1}^{n} \sum_{j=1}^{m} v_{ij}^2 + \frac{1}{2} \sum_{j=1}^{m} \sum_{k=1}^{p} w_{jk}^2 + \frac{C}{2} \sum_{q=1}^{l} \sum_{k=1}^{p} e_{qk}^2 .$$

See Exercise 5.7.5.

We may also use the following robust cost functions to be minimized for regression problems:

$$J = \frac{1}{2} \sum_{j=1}^{m} \sum_{k=1}^{p} w_{jk}^2 + C \sum_{k=1}^{p} \sum_{q=1}^{l} \left(\xi_{qk} + \eta_{qk} \right)$$

or

$$J = \frac{1}{2} \sum_{i=1}^{n} \sum_{j=1}^{m} v_{ij}^2 + \frac{1}{2} \sum_{j=1}^{m} \sum_{k=1}^{p} w_{jk}^2 + C \sum_{k=1}^{p} \sum_{q=1}^{l} \left(\xi_{qk} + \eta_{qk} \right),$$

where ξ_{qk}'s and η_{qk}'s are the slack variables for regression problems introduced in Section 4.8.

5.3 Generalized Radial Basis Function Network

In this section, we discuss the generalized radial basis function networks (GRBFNs). In particular, we will only consider a commonly used class of approximating functions $g : \mathfrak{R}^n \to \mathfrak{R}^p$ with Gaussian basis functions, which can be represented as a feed-forward network shown in Figure 5.3.1. In this network, there is a single input layer with n nodes, a single hidden layer with m nodes, and a single output layer with p nodes.

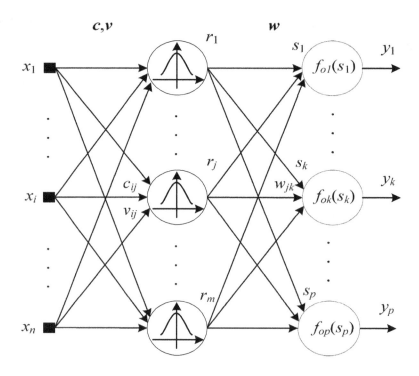

Figure 5.3.1: Generalized radial basis function network.

Let

$$x := \begin{bmatrix} x_1 & \cdots & x_n \end{bmatrix}^T \in \mathfrak{R}^n$$

be the input vector. Let $c_j := \begin{bmatrix} c_{1j} & c_{2j} & \dots & c_{nj} \end{bmatrix}^T$, $j \in \underline{m}$, be the center of the jth basis function and v_{ij} be the ith "precision" of the jth basis function, with $v_{ij} := 1/(2\sigma_{ij}^2) > 0$, $i \in \underline{n}$. Then, the output r_j of the jth hidden node is given by

$$u_j = \sum_{i=1}^{n} (x_i - c_{ij})^2 v_{ij}, \quad r_j = \exp(-u_j).$$

Let w_{jk} denote the connection weight from the output of the jth hidden node to the input of the kth output node. Then, the input s_k and output y_k of the kth output node are given by, respectively,

$$s_k = \sum_{j=1}^{m} w_{jk} r_j, \quad y_k = f_{ok}(s_k), \quad k \in \underline{p},$$

where f_{ok} is the activation function of the kth output node. For binary classification problems, if the output labels were coded as 0 or 1, the output activation functions can be chosen as unipolar logistic function, and if the output labels were coded as -1 or 1, the output activation functions can be chosen as bipolar sigmoidal function or hyperbolic tangent function. For regression problems, the standard choice of the output activation function is the identity function (i.e., the linear function with unit slope). However, if the response data have been scaled to $[0, 1]$ or $[-1, 1]$, then the unipolar logistic function, bipolar sigmoidal function, or hyperbolic tangent function may be used as the output activation function.

The predictive function $f_k(x)$ is a nonlinear map given by

$$y_k = f_k(x) = f_{ok}\left(\sum_{j=1}^{m} w_{jk} \exp\left[-\sum_{i=1}^{n} (x_i - c_{ij})^2 v_{ij} \right] \right), \quad k \in \underline{p}.$$

As in artificial neural networks, the operational tasks of a GRBFN can be described in two steps. First, in a peculiar way, the input vector $x \in \mathfrak{R}^n$ is transformed nonlinearly to the feature vector $r \in \mathfrak{R}^m$ via the first layer of generalized radial basis function models, with $\mathfrak{R}^m$ treated as the feature space. Then, perform the generalized linear regression in feature space via the second layer of generalized linear models to produce the output vector $y \in \mathfrak{R}^p$ of the network.

The class of approximating functions represented as generalized radial basis function networks, with m unfixed, possesses the **universal approximation property**, i.e., they are **universal approximators**. See Hartman, Keeler, and Kowalski (1990) and Park and Sandberg (1991).

Let $X \subseteq \mathfrak{R}^n$ and $Y \subseteq \mathfrak{R}^p$. Suppose we are given the training set

$$S := \left\{ \left(x_q, d_q \right) \right\}_{q=1}^{V} \subseteq X \times Y.$$

In the following, we will use the subscript q to denote the qth example. For instance, x_{qi} denotes the ith component of the qth pattern $x_q \in \mathfrak{R}^n$, $q \in \underline{l}$, $i \in \underline{n}$. By this convention, we have

$$u_{qj} = \sum_{i=1}^{n} \left(x_{qi} - c_{ij} \right)^2 v_{ij}, \quad r_{qj} = \exp\left(-u_{qj} \right), \quad q \in \underline{l}, \quad j \in \underline{m},$$

$$s_{qk} = \sum_{j=1}^{m} w_{jk} r_{qj}, \quad y_{qk} = f_{ok}\left(s_{qk} \right), \quad q \in \underline{l}, \quad k \in \underline{p}.$$

The error (or residual) e_{qk} at the kth output node due to the qth example is defined by

$$e_{qk} := d_{qk} - y_{qk}, \quad q \in \underline{l}, \quad k \in \underline{p}.$$

The usual least squares approach is to choose weights that minimize the total sum of squared errors given by

$$E_{total} := \frac{1}{2} \sum_{q=1}^{l} \sum_{k=1}^{p} e_{qk}^2.$$

Define the sum of squared errors due to the qth example as

$$E_q := \frac{1}{2} \sum_{k=1}^{p} e_{qk}^2, \quad q \in \underline{l}.$$

Then, we have

$$E_{total} = \sum_{q=1}^{l} E_q \;.$$

Now, we introduce the error **back propagation (BP) algorithm**, also called the generalized delta learning rule, which is an on-line (or pattern-based) incremental gradient descent algorithm. In this algorithm, E_q's are minimized in sequence.

First, we propose an updating rule for w_{jk}, which is given by

$$w_{jk} \leftarrow w_{jk} - \eta_w \frac{\partial E_q}{\partial w_{jk}}, \quad j \in \underline{m}, \; k \in \underline{p},$$

where $\eta_w > 0$ is a learning rate. By chain rule, we have

$$\frac{\partial E_q}{\partial w_{jk}} = \frac{\partial E_q}{\partial s_{qk}} \frac{\partial s_{qk}}{\partial w_{jk}} = \frac{\partial E_q}{\partial s_{qk}} r_{qj} = -\left(-\frac{\partial E_q}{\partial s_{qk}}\right) r_{qj} \;.$$

Define

$$\delta_{qk}^{(o)} = -\frac{\partial E_q}{\partial s_{qk}} = -\frac{\partial E_q}{\partial e_{qk}} \frac{\partial e_{qk}}{\partial y_{qk}} \frac{\partial y_{qk}}{\partial s_{qk}} = -e_{qk}(-1) f'_{ok}\left(s_{qk}\right) = e_{qk} f'_{ok}\left(s_{qk}\right).$$

Hence, the updating rule becomes

$$\begin{aligned}
w_{jk} &\leftarrow w_{jk} - \eta_w \frac{\partial E_q}{\partial w_{jk}} \\
&= w_{jk} + \eta_w \cdot \delta_{qk}^{(o)} r_{qj} \\
&= w_{jk} + \eta_w \cdot e_{qk} f'_{ok}\left(s_{qk}\right) r_{qj} \;.
\end{aligned}$$

Next, we propose an updating rule for c_{ij}, which is given by

$$c_{ij} \leftarrow c_{ij} - \eta_c \frac{\partial E_q}{\partial c_{ij}}, \quad i \in \underline{n}, \; j \in \underline{m},$$

where $\eta_c > 0$ is a learning rate. By chain rule, we have

$$\frac{\partial E_q}{\partial c_{ij}} = \frac{\partial E_q}{\partial u_{qj}} \frac{\partial u_{qj}}{\partial c_{ij}} = \frac{\partial E_q}{\partial u_{qj}} 2\left(x_{qi} - c_{ij}\right)\left(-1\right)v_{ij} = -\frac{\partial E_q}{\partial u_{qj}} 2\left(x_{qi} - c_{ij}\right)v_{ij}.$$

Define

$$\delta_{qj}^{(h)} = \frac{\partial E_q}{\partial u_{qj}} = \sum_{k=1}^{p} \frac{\partial E_q}{\partial s_{qk}} \frac{\partial s_{qk}}{\partial r_{qj}} \frac{\partial r_{qj}}{\partial u_{qj}} = -\sum_{k=1}^{p} \delta_{qk}^{(o)} w_{jk}\left(-r_{qj}\right)$$

$$= \left(\sum_{k=1}^{p} \delta_{qk}^{(o)} w_{jk}\right)r_{qj}.$$

Hence, the updating rule becomes

$$c_{ij} \leftarrow c_{ij} - \eta_c \frac{\partial E_q}{\partial c_{ij}}$$

$$= c_{ij} + \eta_c \cdot \delta_{qj}^{(h)} \cdot 2\left(x_{qi} - c_{ij}\right)v_{ij}$$

$$= c_{ij} + \eta_c \cdot \left\{\sum_{k=1}^{p} e_{qk} f_{ok}'\left(s_{qk}\right)w_{jk}\right\}r_{qj} \cdot 2\left(x_{qi} - c_{ij}\right)v_{ij}.$$

Finally, we propose an updating rule for v_{ij}, which is given by

$$v_{ij} \leftarrow v_{ij} - \eta_v \frac{\partial E_q}{\partial v_{ij}}, \quad i \in \underline{n}, \quad j \in \underline{m},$$

where $\eta_v > 0$ is a learning rate. By chain rule, we have

$$\frac{\partial E_q}{\partial v_{ij}} = \frac{\partial E_q}{\partial u_{qj}} \frac{\partial u_{qj}}{\partial v_{ij}} = \delta_{qj}^{(h)}\left(x_{qi} - c_{ij}\right)^2.$$

Hence, the updating rule becomes

$$v_{ij} \leftarrow v_{ij} - \eta_v \frac{\partial E_q}{\partial v_{ij}}$$

$$= v_{ij} - \eta_v \cdot \delta_{qj}^{(h)} \left(x_{qi} - c_{ij} \right)^2$$

$$= v_{ij} - \eta_v \cdot \left\{ \sum_{k=1}^{p} e_{qk} f_{ok}' \left(s_{qk} \right) w_{jk} \right\} r_{qj} \left(x_{qi} - c_{ij} \right)^2 .$$

The on-line version of BP algorithm is summarized as follows.

Algorithm 5.3.1: (on-line version)

Step 1:　Choose the learning rates η_w, η_c, and η_v, and tolerance ε.

Step 2:　Initialize c_{ij}, v_{ij}, $i \in \underline{n}$, $j \in \underline{m}$; w_{jk}, $j \in \underline{m}$, $k \in \underline{p}$.

Step 3:　//one epoch

　　　for $q = 1$ to l

Step (3a):　//feed-forward part

　　　　for $j = 1$ to m
　　　　　$u_{qj} \leftarrow 0$;
　　　　　for $i = 1$ to n $\{ u_{qj} \leftarrow u_{qj} + \left(x_{qi} - c_{ij} \right)^2 v_{ij} ;\}$
　　　　　$r_{qj} \leftarrow \exp\left(-u_{qj} \right)$;
　　　　end for
　　　　for $k = 1$ to p
　　　　　$s_{qk} \leftarrow 0$;
　　　　　for $j = 1$ to m $\{ s_{qk} \leftarrow s_{qk} + w_{jk} r_{qj} ;\}$
　　　　　$y_{qk} \leftarrow f_{ok}\left(s_{qk} \right)$;
　　　　　$e_{qk} \leftarrow d_{qk} - y_{qk}$;
　　　　end for

Step 3(b):　//back-propagation part

　　　　for $k = 1$ to p $\{ \delta_{qk}^{(o)} \leftarrow e_{qk} f_{ok}'\left(s_{qk} \right) ;\}$
　　　　for $k = 1$ to p
　　　　　for $j = 1$ to m
　　　　　　$w_{jk} \leftarrow w_{jk} + \eta_w \delta_{qk}^{(o)} r_{qj}$;
　　　　end for

end for

for $j = 1$ to m

$$\delta_{qj}^{(h)} \leftarrow 0;$$

for $k = 1$ to p $\{\delta_{qj}^{(h)} \leftarrow \delta_{qj}^{(h)} + \delta_{qk}^{(o)} w_{jk} ;\}$

$$\delta_{qj}^{(h)} \leftarrow \delta_{qj}^{(h)} r_{qj} ;$$

end for

for $j = 1$ to m

for $i = 1$ to n

$$value \leftarrow x_{qi} - c_{ij} ;$$

$$c_{ij} \leftarrow c_{ij} + \eta_c \delta_{qj}^{(h)} \big(2 * value * v_{ij} \big);$$

$$v_{ij} \leftarrow v_{ij} - \eta_v \delta_{qj}^{(h)} * value * value ;$$

end for

end for

end for

Step 4:   //calculating the mean squared error after one epoch

Repeat Step 3(a) to obtain the new e_{qk} .

$$MSE \leftarrow 0;$$

for $q = 1$ to l

for $k = 1$ to p

$$MSE \leftarrow MSE + e_{qk}^2 ;$$

end for

end for

$$MSE \leftarrow MSE/(l \cdot p)$$

Step 5:   If $|MSE - MSE_{old}| \le \varepsilon$ over some consecutive epoches, then Stop; otherwise go to Step 3.

It is important to put a safeguard in the algorithm to avoid $v_{ij} \le 0$. Moreover, the techniques of mini-batch, momentum, and Adam can equally be applied here to update the weights w_{jk}, c_{ij}, and v_{ij}.

In (Gaussian) regression problem, the output activation functions can be chosen as linear functions with unit slope so that $f_{ok}'(s_k) = 1$ for all

$k \in \underline{p}$. Then, the updating of the output weights w_{jk} can also be done by using the recursive least squares (RLS) algorithm.

Let $x := [x_1 \quad \cdots \quad x_n]^T$ be the test input to the system with the desired output $d := [d_1 \quad \cdots \quad d_p]^T$. For each y_k, $k \in \underline{p}$, we have

$$y_k = \sum_{j=1}^{m} w_{jk} r_j .$$

Define

$$w_k := [w_{1k} \quad w_{2k} \quad \cdots \quad w_{mk}]^T, \quad r := [r_1 \quad r_2 \quad \cdots \quad r_m]^T ,$$

then $y_k = r^T w_k$. Now, r becomes the input to the output neurons. Initially, we set $G_k \leftarrow \alpha I_m$, $k \in \underline{p}$, where α should be a large number and set $\lambda > 0$ be a scaling factor. For each $k \in \underline{p}$, we have the following steps:

$$e \leftarrow d_k - r^T w_k ;$$
$$h \leftarrow G_k r ;$$
$$scalar \leftarrow (\lambda + r^T h)^{-1} ;$$
$$G_k \leftarrow G_k - (scalar) * hh^T ;$$
$$scalar \leftarrow \lambda^{-1} e ;$$
$$h \leftarrow G_k r ;$$
$$w_k \leftarrow w_k + (scalar) * h .$$

Note that in the preceding algorithm, since hh^T is a rank-one matrix, the statement $G_k \leftarrow G_k - (scalar) * hh^T$ can be implemented easily. By combining the RLS method for the updating of output weights w_{jk} with the BP algorithm for updating the c_{ij} and v_{ij}, one usually obtains faster convergence.

Many training algorithms for GRBFNs separate the training into two distinct phases. In the first phase, we choose the centers and variances in a non-supervised fashion. In the second phase, the output weights are updated in a supervised fashion. The algorithm originally developed for training RBF networks requires the number of hidden nodes being equal to that of the training examples. However, in the situation when there are many training examples, the network becomes very large which makes the network structure excessively complex and the computation expensive. We face the same problem when we use the artificial neural networks for learning. From the viewpoints of computational load and generalization capability, it is necessary to restrict the number of hidden nodes. This is the problem of subset selection. In the following, we provide a popular k-means subset selection algorithm, which is a simple clustering algorithm capable of yielding good results. Suppose the basis function of each hidden node is a Gaussian function.

Algorithm 5.3.2: (k-means)

Step 1:   Initialization of the first m centers:

$$c_j := \begin{bmatrix} c_{1j} & c_{2j} & \cdots & c_{nj} \end{bmatrix}^T, \quad j \in \underline{m};$$

Usually one may choose the first m training patterns as these initial centers:

$$x_q := \begin{bmatrix} x_{q1} & x_{q2} & \cdots & x_{qn} \end{bmatrix}^T, \quad q \in \underline{m};$$

Step 2:   Clustering of all training patterns around the nearest center: For all training patterns x_q, $q \in \underline{l}$, find

$$j^* := \arg\min_{j \in \underline{m}} \left\| x_q - c_j \right\|^2,$$

and assign x_q to the cluster j^*.

Step 3:   Calculation of new centers: For $j \in \underline{m}$, calculate

$$c_j = \frac{1}{M_j} \sum_{x_q \in I_j} x_q,$$

where I_j is the set of all patterns x_q belonging to the cluster j and M_j is the number of such patterns.

Step 4: If there is no change in the clustering of patterns from one iteration to another, then Stop; otherwise, go to Step 2.

Once the centers have been calculated, the variances, which represent measures of the data dispersion around the centers, are calculated as

$$\sigma_{ij}^2 = \frac{1}{M_j} \sum_{x_q \in I_j} \left(x_{qi} - c_{ij} \right)^2, \quad j \in \underline{m}.$$

One must be cautious that it may happen that $\sigma_{ij}^2 = 0$ for some j when $c_j = x_q$ for some q and there is only a single member in I_j, i.e., x_q. In which case, we may just assign some appropriate positive number to such a σ_{ij}^2. Finally, we set

$$v_{ij} = \frac{1}{2\sigma_{ij}^2}.$$

5.4 Fuzzy System as a Nonlinear Map

Suppose we let A denote the set of all tall persons in a city. Somebody, probably your classmates, may not agree that this is a precisely defined set. To remedy this, we define a person to be tall if his height is equal or greater than 170 cm. Now we let again A denote the set of all tall persons in a city. This time, A is a precisely defined set. However, a person with height 170.1 cm would be high, but a person with height 169.9 cm would be short. This is not consistent with our every-day experience. In fact, belonging is actually a matter of degree. The fuzzy theory is the theory to treat such fuzziness. See Wang (1997).

A fuzzy system is a system to be precisely defined. Though the phenomena that the fuzzy system theory characterizes may be fuzzy, the fuzzy theory itself is precise. In fact, it defuzzifies the world. Hence, the fuzzy theory is non-fuzzy at all.

According to Wang (1997), there are two good reasons for the justification of fuzzy system theory:

(a) As a system becomes increasingly complex, the possibility of obtaining a precise description of it in quantitative terms decreases. What we desire in practice is a reasonable yet tractable model.

(b) Human reasoning is set up on imprecise logic rather than on binary logic. A theory is needed to systematically transform structured human knowledge into workable algorithms.

Thus, the fuzzy system is a knowledge-based or rule-based system. As we shall see that an important contribution of the fuzzy system theory is that it provides a systematic procedure for transforming a set of linguistic rules into a nonlinear mapping.

Consider a standard fuzzy system as shown in Figure 5.4.1, where U is the input space and V is the output space. It consists of four principal components, namely fuzzy rule base, fuzzy inference engine, fuzzifier, and defuzzifier. The most important one is the fuzzy rule base, which consists of a family of IF-THEN rules reflecting human knowledge of the system. The main task of the fuzzy inference engine is to combine those IF-THEN rules in order to map a fuzzy set in U to a fuzzy set in V. To provide the interface with the crisp environment, the fuzzifier transforms a crisp point in U to a fuzzy set in U, whilst the defuzzifier specifies a fuzzy set in V to a crisp point in V. Hence the fuzzy system is in fact a crisp nonlinear map from the input space U to the output space V. The goal is to understand how the fuzzy system works.

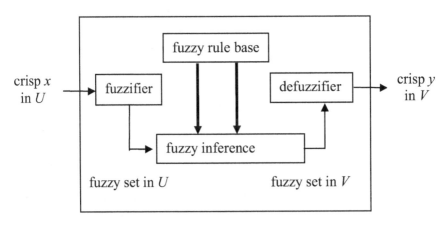

Crisp nonlinear map from U to V

Figure 5.4.1: Standard fuzzy system.

To get some flavor of the fuzzy rules, consider a fuzzy system with n inputs and p outputs. The fuzzy rule base is usually composed of m fuzzy rules in canonical form:

$$R_j: \text{ IF } x_1 \text{ is } A_{1j} \text{ and } x_2 \text{ is } A_{2j} \text{ and } \ldots \text{ and } x_n \text{ is } A_{nj},$$
$$\text{THEN } y_1 \text{ is } B_{j1} \text{ and } y_2 \text{ is } B_{j2} \text{ and } \ldots \text{ and } y_p \text{ is } B_{jp},$$

where $j \in \underline{m}$. Define

$$x := \begin{bmatrix} x_1 & \cdots & x_n \end{bmatrix}^T \in \mathfrak{R}^n, \quad y := \begin{bmatrix} y_1 & \cdots & y_p \end{bmatrix}^T \in \mathfrak{R}^p.$$

Let $\mu_{ij}(x_i)$, $i \in \underline{n}$, $j \in \underline{m}$, be the membership function of the fuzzy set A_{ij} and w_{jk}, $j \in \underline{m}$, $k \in \underline{p}$, be the center of the normal fuzzy set B_{jk}. Then, the fuzzy system with singleton fuzzifier, product inference engine, and center-average defuzzifier is given by the following map:

$$y_k = f_k(x) = \frac{\sum_{j=1}^{m} w_{jk} \left[\prod_{i=1}^{n} \mu_{ij}(x_i) \right]}{\sum_{j=1}^{m} \left[\prod_{i=1}^{n} \mu_{ij}(x_i) \right]}, \quad k \in \underline{p}.$$

This fuzzy system is called a SUM-PROD model by some authors. As in the artificial neural network and generalized radial basis function network, this class of functions, with m unfixed, possesses the **universal approximation property**, i.e., they are **universal approximators**. This fact is usually proved via the famous Stone-Weierstrass Theorem from mathematical analysis [Wang, p. 127].

Consider a fuzzy system with singleton fuzzifier, product inference engine, center-average defuzzifier, and Gaussian membership functions. Then, the fuzzy system f is a nonlinear map given by

$$y_k = f_k(x) = \frac{\sum_{j=1}^{m} w_{jk} \prod_{i=1}^{n} a_{ij} \exp\left[-(x_i - c_{ij})^2 / v_{ij} \right]}{\sum_{j=1}^{m} \prod_{i=1}^{n} a_{ij} \exp\left[-(x_i - c_{ij})^2 / v_{ij} \right]}, \quad k \in \underline{p},$$

where w_{jk} is the center of the kth normal fuzzy set B_{jk} of THEN part in the jth rule, and c_{ij}, v_{ij}, with $v_{ij} := 2\sigma_{ij}^2 > 0$, $i \in \underline{n}$, $j \in \underline{m}$, are the center and "variance" of the ith Gaussian fuzzy set A_{ij} of IF part in the jth rule, respectively.

With normal Gaussian membership functions, i.e., $a_{ij} = 1$ for all $i \in \underline{n}$ and $j \in \underline{m}$, the preceding nonlinear map is simplified as

$$y_k = f_k(x) = \frac{\sum\limits_{j=1}^{m} w_{jk} \prod\limits_{i=1}^{n} \exp\left[-\left(x_i - c_{ij}\right)^2 / v_{ij}\right]}{\sum\limits_{j=1}^{m} \prod\limits_{i=1}^{n} \exp\left[-\left(x_i - c_{ij}\right)^2 / v_{ij}\right]}, \quad k \in \underline{p},$$

which is equivalent to

$$y_k = f_k(x) = \frac{\sum\limits_{j=1}^{m} w_{jk} \exp\left[-\sum\limits_{i=1}^{n}\left(x_i - c_{ij}\right)^2 / v_{ij}\right]}{\sum\limits_{j=1}^{m} \exp\left[-\sum\limits_{i=1}^{n}\left(x_i - c_{ij}\right)^2 / v_{ij}\right]}, \quad k \in \underline{p}.$$

Similarly, the fuzzy system with singleton fuzzifier, minimum inference engine, and center-average defuzzifier is given by the following map:

$$y_k = f_k(x) = \frac{\sum\limits_{j=1}^{m} w_{jk} \left[\min\limits_{i=1}^{n} \mu_{ij}(x_i)\right]}{\sum\limits_{j=1}^{m} \left[\min\limits_{i=1}^{n} \mu_{ij}(x_i)\right]}, \quad k \in \underline{p}.$$

The class of these functions with pseudo-trapezoid membership functions also has the universal approximation property. The preceding fuzzy system is called a SUM-MIN model by some authors. Some authors call the SUM-PROD model and SUM-MIN model presented above the Fuzzy Additive Models (FAMs) or Standard Additive Models (SAMs).

Consider a fuzzy system with singleton fuzzifier, minimum inference engine, center-average defuzzifier, and Gaussian membership functions. Then the fuzzy system f is a nonlinear map given by

$$y_k = f_k(x) = \frac{\sum\limits_{j=1}^{m} w_{jk}\left[\min\limits_{i=1}^{n} a_{ij}\exp\left[-\left(x_i - c_{ij}\right)^2/v_{ij}\right]\right]}{\sum\limits_{j=1}^{m}\left[\min\limits_{i=1}^{n} a_{ij}\exp\left[-\left(x_i - c_{ij}\right)^2/v_{ij}\right]\right]}, \quad k \in \underline{p}.$$

Next, consider a fuzzy system with Gaussian fuzzifier with *=product, product inference engine, center-average defuzzifier, and normal Gaussian membership functions with $a_{ij} = 1$ for all $i \in \underline{n}$ and $j \in \underline{m}$. Then, the fuzzy system f is a nonlinear map given by

$$y_k = f_k(x) = \frac{\sum\limits_{j=1}^{m} w_{jk}\prod\limits_{i=1}^{n}\exp\left[-\left(x_i - c_{ij}\right)^2/\left(a_i^2 + v_{ij}\right)\right]}{\sum\limits_{j=1}^{m}\prod\limits_{i=1}^{n}\exp\left[-\left(x_i - c_{ij}\right)^2/\left(a_i^2 + v_{ij}\right)\right]}, \quad k \in \underline{p},$$

which is equivalent to

$$y_k = f_k(x) = \frac{\sum\limits_{j=1}^{m} w_{jk}\exp\left[-\sum\limits_{i=1}^{n}\left(x_i - c_{ij}\right)^2/\left(a_i^2 + v_{ij}\right)\right]}{\sum\limits_{j=1}^{m}\exp\left[-\sum\limits_{i=1}^{n}\left(x_i - c_{ij}\right)^2/\left(a_i^2 + v_{ij}\right)\right]}, \quad k \in \underline{p}.$$

Finally, consider a fuzzy system with Gaussian fuzzifier with *=min, minimum inference engine, center-average defuzzifier, and normal Gaussian membership functions with $a_{ij} = 1$ for all $i \in \underline{n}$ and $j \in \underline{m}$. Then, the fuzzy system f is a nonlinear map given by

$$y_k = f_k(x) = \frac{\sum\limits_{j=1}^{m} w_{jk}\left\{\min\limits_{i=1}^{n}\exp\left[-\left(x_i - c_{ij}\right)^2/\left(a_i + \sqrt{v_{ij}}\right)^2\right]\right\}}{\sum\limits_{j=1}^{m}\left\{\min\limits_{i=1}^{n}\exp\left[-\left(x_i - c_{ij}\right)^2/\left(a_i + \sqrt{v_{ij}}\right)^2\right]\right\}}, \quad k \in \underline{p}.$$

It is clear from the preceding expressions that the output y_k of the fuzzy system is a convex combination of w_{jk}, the center of the kth fuzzy set B_{jk} of the THEN part in the jth rule, with weighting equal to membership value, or "intensity", of the corresponding IF part. Consequently, the more the input point agrees with the IF part of a rule, the larger weight this rule is given; this makes sense intuitively.

In the preceding expressions, the only restriction put on the output fuzzy sets in the THEN part is that they should be normal. The output fuzzy sets can be fuzzy singletons and fuzzy sets with triangular, trapezoid, or Gaussian membership functions.

Fuzzy systems with singleton fuzzifier, product inference engine, and maximum defuzzifier are also universal approximators.

5.5 Fuzzy Neural Network

Motivated by the fuzzy system with singleton fuzzifier, product inference engine, center-average defuzzifier, and normal Gaussian membership functions, we consider in this section the fuzzy neural network (FNN) as shown in Figure 5.5.1.

Let c_{ij} and v_{ij}, with $v_{ij} := 1/(2\sigma_{ij}^2) > 0$, $i \in \underline{n}$, $j \in \underline{m}$, be the center and "precision" of the ith normal Gaussian fuzzy set A_{ij} of IF part in the jth rule, respectively. Further, let w_{jk} be the center of the kth normal fuzzy set B_{jk} of THEN part in the jth rule.

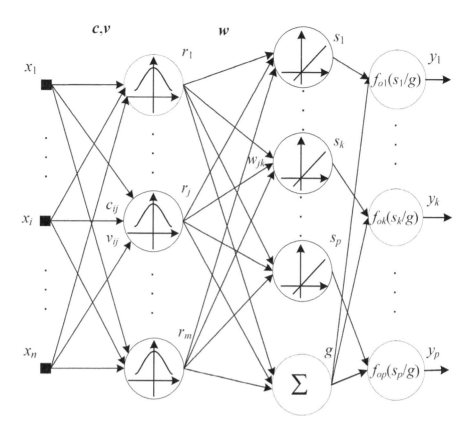

Figure 5.5.1: Fuzzy neural network.

Define, for $i \in \underline{n}$, $j \in \underline{m}$, and $k \in \underline{p}$,

$$x := \begin{bmatrix} x_1 & \cdots & x_n \end{bmatrix}^T \in \mathfrak{R}^n,$$

$$u_j = \sum_{i=1}^{n} (x_i - c_{ij})^2 v_{ij},$$

$$r_j = \exp(-u_j), \quad s_k = \sum_{j=1}^{m} w_{jk} r_j, \quad g = \sum_{j=1}^{m} r_j,$$

then

$$y_k = f_{ok}(s_k / g).$$

Here, f_{ok} is the activation function of the kth output node. For binary classification problems, if the output labels were coded as 0 or 1, the output activation functions can be chosen as unipolar logistic function, and if the output labels were coded as -1 or 1, the output activation functions can be chosen as bipolar sigmoidal function or hyperbolic tangent function. For regression problems, the standard choice of the output activation function is the identity function (i.e., the linear function with unit slope). However, if the response data have been scaled to $[0,1]$ or $[-1,1]$, then the unipolar logistic function, bipolar sigmoidal function, or hyperbolic tangent function may be used as the output activation function.

The predictive function $f_k(x)$ is a nonlinear map given by

$$y_k = f_k(x) = f_{ok}\left(\frac{\sum_{j=1}^{m} w_{jk} \exp\left[-\sum_{i=1}^{n}(x_i - c_{ij})^2 v_{ij}\right]}{\sum_{j=1}^{m} \exp\left[-\sum_{i=1}^{n}(x_i - c_{ij})^2 v_{ij}\right]}\right), \quad k \in \underline{p}.$$

The advantage of using fuzzy neural network for machine learning is that the parameters w_{jk}, c_{ij}, and v_{ij} usually have clear physical meanings and we have some intuitive methods to choose good initial values for them.

As in artificial neural networks and generalized radial basis function networks, the operational tasks of an FNN can be described in two steps. First, in a peculiar way, the input vector $x \in \Re^n$ is transformed nonlinearly to the feature vector $r \in \Re^m$ via the first layer, with $\Re^m$ treated as the feature space. Then, perform the generalized linear regression in feature space via the second layer to produce the output vector $y \in \Re^p$ of the network.

Let $X \subseteq \Re^n$ and $Y \subseteq \Re^p$. Suppose we are given the training set

$$S := \left\{(x_q, d_q)\right\}_{q=1}^{N} \subseteq X \times Y.$$

In the following, we will use the subscript q to denote the qth example. For instance, x_{qi} denotes the ith component of the qth pattern $x_q \in \Re^n$, $q \in \underline{l}$, $i \in \underline{n}$. By this convention, we have

$$u_{qj} = \sum_{i=1}^{n} (x_{qi} - c_{ij})^2 v_{ij}, \quad r_{qj} = \exp(-u_{qj}), \quad q \in \underline{l}, \quad j \in \underline{m},$$

$$s_{qk} = \sum_{j=1}^{m} w_{jk} r_{qj}, \quad g_q = \sum_{j=1}^{m} r_{qj}, \quad y_{qk} = f_{ok}(s_{qk}/g_q), \quad q \in \underline{l}, \quad k \in \underline{p}.$$

The error (or residual) e_{qk} at the kth output node due to the qth example is defined by

$$e_{qk} := d_{qk} - y_{qk}, \quad q \in \underline{l}, \quad k \in \underline{p}.$$

The usual least squares approach is to choose weights that minimize the total sum of squared errors given by

$$E_{total} := \frac{1}{2} \sum_{q=1}^{l} \sum_{k=1}^{p} e_{qk}^2.$$

Define the sum of squared errors due to the qth example as

$$E_q := \frac{1}{2} \sum_{k=1}^{p} e_{qk}^2, \quad q \in \underline{l}.$$

Then, we have

$$E_{total} = \sum_{q=1}^{l} E_q.$$

Now, we introduce the error **back propagation (BP) algorithm**, also called the generalized delta learning rule, which is an on-line (or pattern-based) incremental gradient descent algorithm. In this algorithm, E_q's are minimized in sequence.

First, we propose an updating rule for w_{jk}, which is given by

$$w_{jk} \leftarrow w_{jk} - \eta_w \frac{\partial E_q}{\partial w_{jk}}, \quad j \in \underline{m}, \quad k \in \underline{p},$$

where $\eta_w > 0$ is a learning rate. By chain rule, we have

$$\frac{\partial E_q}{\partial w_{jk}} = \frac{\partial E_q}{\partial s_{qk}} \frac{\partial s_{qk}}{\partial w_{jk}} = \frac{\partial E_q}{\partial s_{qk}} r_{qj} = -\left(-\frac{\partial E_q}{\partial s_{qk}}\right) r_{qj}.$$

Define

$$\delta_{qk}^{(o)} = -\frac{\partial E_q}{\partial s_{qk}} = -\frac{\partial E_q}{\partial e_{qk}} \frac{\partial e_{qk}}{\partial y_{qk}} \frac{\partial y_{qk}}{\partial s_{qk}}$$

$$= -e_{qk}(-1) f'_{ok}\left(\frac{s_{qk}}{g_q}\right) \frac{1}{g_q} = e_{qk} f'_{ok}\left(\frac{s_{qk}}{g_q}\right) \frac{1}{g_q}.$$

Hence, the updating rule becomes

$$w_{jk} \leftarrow w_{jk} - \eta_w \frac{\partial E_q}{\partial w_{jk}}$$

$$= w_{jk} + \eta_w \cdot \delta_{qk}^{(o)} r_{qj}$$

$$= w_{jk} + \eta_w \cdot e_{qk} f'_{ok}\left(\frac{s_{qk}}{g_q}\right) \frac{r_{qj}}{g_q}.$$

Next, we propose an updating rule for c_{ij}, which is given by

$$c_{ij} \leftarrow c_{ij} - \eta_c \frac{\partial E_q}{\partial c_{ij}}, \quad i \in \underline{n}, \quad j \in \underline{m},$$

where $\eta_c > 0$ is a learning rate. By chain rule, we have

$$\frac{\partial E_q}{\partial c_{ij}} = \frac{\partial E_q}{\partial u_{qj}} \frac{\partial u_{qj}}{\partial c_{ij}} = \frac{\partial E_q}{\partial u_{qj}} 2(x_{qi} - c_{ij})(-1) v_{ij} = -\frac{\partial E_q}{\partial u_{qj}} 2(x_{qi} - c_{ij}) v_{ij}.$$

Define

$$\delta_{qj}^{(h)} = \frac{\partial E_q}{\partial u_{qj}} = \sum_{k=1}^{p} \frac{\partial E_q}{\partial e_{qk}} \frac{\partial e_{qk}}{\partial y_{qk}} \frac{\partial y_{qk}}{\partial u_{qj}}$$

$$= -\sum_{k=1}^{p} e_{qk} \left[\frac{\partial y_{qk}}{\partial s_{qk}} \frac{\partial s_{qk}}{\partial r_{qj}} \frac{\partial r_{qj}}{\partial u_{qj}} + \frac{\partial y_{qk}}{\partial g_q} \frac{\partial g_q}{\partial r_{qj}} \frac{\partial r_{qj}}{\partial u_{qj}} \right]$$

$$= -\sum_{k=1}^{p} e_{qk} \left[\begin{array}{c} f'_{ok}\left(\dfrac{s_{qk}}{g_q}\right) \dfrac{1}{g_q} w_{jk} \left(-r_{qj}\right) \\[3mm] + f'_{ok}\left(\dfrac{s_{qk}}{g_q}\right) \cdot \left(\dfrac{-s_{qk}}{g_q^2}\right) \cdot 1 \cdot \left(-r_{qj}\right) \end{array} \right]$$

$$= -\sum_{k=1}^{p} e_{qk} f'_{ok}\left(\frac{s_{qk}}{g_q}\right) \frac{1}{g_q} \left(\frac{s_{qk}}{g_q} - w_{jk}\right) r_{qj}$$

$$= \sum_{k=1}^{p} \delta_{qk}^{(o)} \left(w_{jk} - \frac{s_{qk}}{g_q}\right) r_{qj}.$$

Hence, the updating rule becomes

$$c_{ij} \leftarrow c_{ij} - \eta_c \frac{\partial E_q}{\partial c_{ij}}$$

$$= c_{ij} + \eta_c \cdot \delta_{qj}^{(h)} \cdot 2\left(x_{qi} - c_{ij}\right) v_{ij}$$

$$= c_{ij} + \eta_c \cdot \left\{ \sum_{k=1}^{p} e_{qk} f'_{ok}\left(\frac{s_{qk}}{g_q}\right) \left(w_{jk} - \frac{s_{qk}}{g_q}\right) \right\} \frac{r_{qj}}{g_q} \cdot 2\left(x_{qi} - c_{ij}\right) v_{ij}.$$

Finally, we propose an updating rule for v_{ij}, which is given by

$$v_{ij} \leftarrow v_{ij} - \eta_v \frac{\partial E_q}{\partial v_{ij}}, \quad i \in \underline{n}, \quad j \in \underline{m},$$

where $\eta_v > 0$ is a learning rate. By chain rule, we have

$$\frac{\partial E_q}{\partial v_{ij}} = \frac{\partial E_q}{\partial u_{qj}} \frac{\partial u_{qj}}{\partial v_{ij}} = \delta_{qj}^{(h)} \left(x_{qi} - c_{ij}\right)^2.$$

Thus, the updating rule becomes

$$v_{ij} \leftarrow v_{ij} - \eta_v \frac{\partial E_q}{\partial v_{ij}}$$

$$= v_{ij} - \eta_v \cdot \delta_{qj}^{(h)} \left(x_{qi} - c_{ij} \right)^2$$

$$= v_{ij} - \eta_v \cdot \left\{ \sum_{k=1}^{p} e_{qk} f'_{ok} \left(\frac{s_{qk}}{g_q} \right) \left(w_{jk} - \frac{s_{qk}}{g_q} \right) \right\} \frac{r_{qj}}{g_q} \left(x_{qi} - c_{ij} \right)^2.$$

The on-line version of BP algorithm is summarized as follows.

Algorithm 5.5.1: (on-line version)

Step 1: Choose the learning rates η_w, η_c, and η_v, and tolerance ε.

Step 2: Initialize c_{ij}, v_{ij}, $i \in \underline{n}$, $j \in \underline{m}$; w_{jk}, $j \in \underline{m}$, $k \in \underline{p}$.

Step 3: //one epoch

      for $q = 1$ to l

Step (3a): //feed-forward part

      for $j = 1$ to m
         $u_{qj} \leftarrow 0;$
         for $i = 1$ to n $\{ u_{qj} \leftarrow u_{qj} + \left(x_{qi} - c_{ij} \right)^2 v_{ij} ;\}$
         $r_{qj} \leftarrow \exp\left(-u_{qj} \right);$
      end for
      $g_q \leftarrow 0;$
      for $j = 1$ to m $\{ g_q \leftarrow g_q + r_{qj} ;\}$
      for $k = 1$ to p
         $s_{qk} \leftarrow 0;$
         for $j = 1$ to m $\{ s_{qk} \leftarrow s_{qk} + w_{jk} r_{qj} ;\}$
         $y_{qk} \leftarrow f_{ok}\left(s_{qk} / g_q \right);$
         $e_{qk} \leftarrow d_{qk} - y_{qk} ;$
      end for

Step 3(b): //back-propagation part

for $k = 1$ to p $\{ \delta_{qk}^{(o)} \leftarrow e_{qk} f_{ok}'\left(s_{qk}/g_q\right)/g_q \;\}$

for $k = 1$ to p

    for $j = 1$ to m

$$w_{jk} \leftarrow w_{jk} + \eta_w \delta_{qk}^{(o)} r_{qj} \;$$

    end for

end for

for $j = 1$ to m

$$\delta_{qj}^{(h)} \leftarrow 0 \;$$

    for $k = 1$ to p $\left\{ \delta_{qj}^{(h)} \leftarrow \delta_{qj}^{(h)} + \delta_{qk}^{(o)}\left(w_{jk} - \dfrac{s_{qk}}{g_q} \right) \;\right\}$

$$\delta_{qj}^{(h)} \leftarrow \delta_{qj}^{(h)} r_{qj} \;$$

end for

for $j = 1$ to m

    for $i = 1$ to n

$$value \leftarrow x_{qi} - c_{ij} \;$$
$$c_{ij} \leftarrow c_{ij} + \eta_c \delta_{qj}^{(h)}\left(2 * value * v_{ij}\right) ;$$
$$v_{ij} \leftarrow v_{ij} - \eta_v \delta_{qj}^{(h)} * value * value \;$$

    end for

end for

end for

Step 4: //calculating the mean squared error after one epoch

Repeat Step 3(a) to obtain the new e_{qk}.

$MSE \leftarrow 0 \;$

for $q = 1$ to l

    for $k = 1$ to p

$$MSE \leftarrow MSE + e_{qk}^2 \;$$

    end for

end for

$MSE \leftarrow MSE/(l \cdot p)$

Step 5: If $\left| MSE - MSE_{old} \right| \leq \varepsilon$ over some consecutive epoches, then Stop; otherwise go to Step 3.

It is important to put a safeguard in the algorithm to avoid $v_{ij} \leq 0$. Moreover, the techniques of mini-batch, momentum, and Adam can equally be applied here to update the weights w_{jk}, c_{ij}, and v_{ij}.

In (Gaussian) regression problem, the output activation functions can be chosen as linear functions with unit slope so that $f'_{ok}(s_k) = 1$ for all $k \in \underline{p}$. Then, the updating of the output weights w_{jk} can also be done by using the recursive least squares (RLS) algorithm.

Let $x := [x_1 \quad \cdots \quad x_n]^T$ be the test input to the system with the desired output $d := [d_1 \quad \cdots \quad d_p]^T$. For each y_k, $k \in \underline{p}$, we have

$$y_k = \sum_{j=1}^{m} w_{jk} \frac{r_j}{g} := \sum_{j=1}^{m} w_{jk} \theta_j, \quad \theta_j := g^{-1} r_j, \quad j \in \underline{m}.$$

Define

$$w_k := [w_{1k} \quad w_{2k} \quad \cdots \quad w_{mk}]^T,$$
$$\theta := [\theta_1 \quad \theta_2 \quad \cdots \quad \theta_m]^T = [g^{-1} r_1 \quad g^{-1} r_2 \quad \cdots \quad g^{-1} r_m]^T,$$

then $y_k = \theta^T w_k$. Now, θ becomes the input to the output neurons. Initially, we set $G_k \leftarrow \alpha I_m$, $k \in \underline{p}$, where α should be a large number and set $\lambda > 0$ be a scaling factor. For each $k \in \underline{p}$, we have the following steps:

$$e \leftarrow d_k - \theta^T w_k;$$
$$h \leftarrow G_k \theta;$$
$$scalar \leftarrow (\lambda + \theta^T h)^{-1};$$
$$G_k \leftarrow G_k - (scalar) * hh^T;$$
$$scalar \leftarrow \lambda^{-1} e;$$
$$h \leftarrow G_k \theta;$$
$$w_k \leftarrow w_k + (scalar) * h.$$

Note that in the preceding algorithm, since hh^T is a rank-one matrix, the statement $G_k \leftarrow G_k - (scalar) * hh^T$ can be implemented easily. By combining the RLS method for the updating of output weights w_{jk} with the BP algorithm for updating the c_{ij} and v_{ij}, one usually obtains faster convergence.

For the fuzzy system with singleton fuzzifier, product inference engine, and center-average defuzzifier, if $\prod_{i=1}^{n} \mu_{ij}(x_i)$ is not differentiable, then only output weightings w_{jk} can be updated on-line by back propagation algorithm.

For the fuzzy system with singleton fuzzifier, minimum inference engine, and center-average defuzzifier, only output weightings w_{jk} can be updated on-line by back propagation algorithm since $\min_{i=1}^{n} \mu_{ij}(x_i)$ is usually not differentiable.

5.6 Illustrative Examples

In this section, we compare the performances of ANNs, GRBFNs, and FNNs introduced in this chapter for several illustrative nonlinear classification and regression problems. Emphasis is put particularly on the robustness against outliers. The model selection problem, i.e., choosing optimal parameters for a given learning problem at hand, will be bypassed.

Our first example is a nonlinear classification problem. In the following simulation of Example 5.6.1, the uncorrupted training data set consists of 50 randomly chosen x-points (training patterns) with the corresponding y-labels (target values) determined from the underlying true discriminant function. To investigate the robustness of the classifiers against outliers (or wrong examples), we will create corrupted training data sets. This is done by randomly choosing some x-points from the uncorrupted training data set and changing the corresponding labels to the opposite ones, i.e., we change the label +1 to 0 or 0 to +1. That is, these chosen corrupted examples actually become wrong examples. In the simulation, 30% randomly chosen y-labels of the training data points will be changed. As will be clear from the following figures, this indeed means that the training data are highly corrupted. The advantage of using simulated data is that we can see how close our models come to the truth.

In the following simulations, the initial weights are randomly generated 100 times, each resulting in a trained learning machine. We then choose the best learning machine according to the cost value.

In the simulation of Example 5.6.1, the binary cross-entropy is used as the objective function. The activation functions of the output nodes for ANN, GRBFN, and FNN are all unipolar logistic functions. For ANN, the activation functions of the hidden nodes are bipolar sigmoidal functions.

Example 5.6.1: Suppose the true discriminant function is given by the fractional power function

$$g(x_1, x_2) = x_2 - x_1^{2/3}, \quad x_1 \in [-2, 2], \quad x_2 \in [0, 2].$$

The parameter settings and simulation results for ANN, GRBFN, and FNN are shown in Table 5.6.1. Together with the true decision boundary, the decision boundaries determined by ANN, GRBFN, and FNN for corrupted data are shown in Figure 5.6.1. With such highly corrupted training data, it is not expected that these decision boundaries are close to the true decision boundary.

Table 5.6.1: Parameter settings and simulation results in Example 5.6.1.

	ANN	GRBFN	FNN
No. of hidden nodes	4	4	4
No. of weights	17	20	20
Hidden activation function	bipolar	RBF	RBF
Output activation function	unipolar	unipolar	unipolar
Scaling on x_1, x_2	none	none	none
Initialization	$v_{ij} \in [-1, 1]$ $w_{jk} \in [-1, 1]$	$c_{ij} \in [-2, 2]$ $v_{ij} \in [0.01, 4]$ $w_{jk} \in [-1, 1]$	$c_{ij} \in [-2, 2]$ $v_{ij} \in [0.01, 4]$ $w_{jk} \in [-1, 1]$
Estimated minimal cost	10.9259	11.4502	9.8443
Number of misclassifications	5	4	8

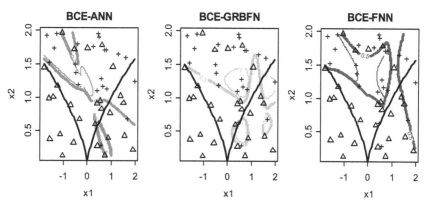

Figure 5.6.1: Decision boundaries in Example 5.6.1.

Our next two examples are nonlinear regression problems. In the following simulations of Example 5.6.2 and Example 5.6.3, the uncorrupted training data set consists of 50 randomly chosen x-points (training patterns) with the corresponding y-values (target values) evaluated from the underlying true regression function. The corrupted training data set is composed of the same x-points as the corresponding uncorrupted one but with randomly chosen y-values corrupted by adding random values from a uniform distribution defined on $[-1, 1]$. In the following simulations, 30% randomly chosen y-values of the training data points will be corrupted. As will be clear from the following figures, this indeed means that the target values are highly corrupted.

In the next two simulations, half of the total sum of squared errors E_{total} is used as the objective function. The activation functions of the output nodes for ANNs, GRBFNs, and FNNs are all linear functions with unit slope. For ANNs, the activation functions of the hidden nodes are bipolar sigmoidal functions.

Example 5.6.2: Suppose the true regression function is given by the sinc function

$$g(x) = \begin{cases} 1, & x = 0, \\ \sin(x)/x, & x \neq 0, \end{cases} \quad x \in [-10, 10].$$

The parameter settings and simulation results for ANN, GRBFN, and FNN are shown in Table 5.6.2. Together with the true regression function, the predictive functions determined by ANN, GRBFN, and FNN for corrupted data are shown in Figure 5.6.2.

It is observed that all three learning machines fit reasonably well in the middle part of the data, but not on both ends. Also notice that the fitted curves are sensitive to outliers. Furthermore, note that a small cost value does not guarantee good generalization capability of the trained learning machine. That is, a small training error does not imply that the predictive function will be close to the underlying true regression function.

It is important to note that, even with the same machine parameter settings, different initial weights might lead to different local minima. Further, if the weights are initialized randomly, as is usually done, one may get different result for each execution of the same algorithm. Consequently, your simulation results may be different from those reported in Table 5.6.2 and Figure 5.6.2.

Table 5.6.2: Parameter settings and simulation results in Example 5.6.2.

	ANN	GRBFN	FNN
No. of hidden nodes	4	4	4
No. of weights	13	12	12
Hidden activation function	bipolar	RBF	RBF
Output activation function	identity	identity	identity
Scaling on x	none	none	none
Scaling on y	none	none	none
Initialization	$v_{ij} \in [-1, 1]$ $w_{jk} \in [-1, 1]$	$c_{ij} \in [-5, 5]$ $v_{ij} \in [0.01, 4]$ $w_{jk} \in [-2, 2]$	$c_{ij} \in [-5, 5]$ $v_{ij} \in [0.01, 4]$ $w_{jk} \in [-2, 2]$
Estimated minimal cost	2.1115	1.6991	2.0371
Mean squared error (MSE)	0.0845	0.0680	0.0815
Mean absolute deviation (MAD)	0.2025	0.1812	0.2065

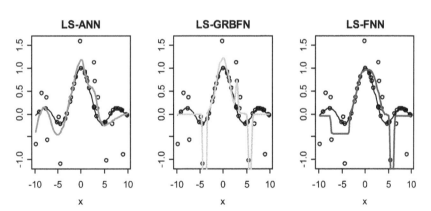

Figure 5.6.2: Predictive functions in Example 5.6.2.

Example 5.6.3: Suppose the true regression function is given by the Hermite function

$$g(x) = 1.1 \cdot \left(1 - x + 2x^2\right) \cdot e^{-x^2/2}, \quad x \in [-5, 5].$$

The parameter settings and simulation results for ANN, GRBFN, and FNN are shown in Table 5.6.3. Together with the true regression function, the predictive functions determined by ANN, GRBFN, and FNN for corrupted data are shown in Figure 5.6.3.

Again, it can be observed that some outliers pull the (least-squares) fitted curves too much in their direction, making the trained learning machines not robust against outliers.

Table 5.6.3: Parameter settings and simulation results in Example 5.6.3.

	ANN	GRBFN	FNN
No. of hidden nodes	4	4	4
No. of weights	13	12	12
Hidden activation function	bipolar	RBF	RBF
Output activation function	identity	identity	identity
Scaling on x	none	none	none
Scaling on y	none	none	none
Initialization	$v_{ij} \in [-1, 1]$ $w_{jk} \in [-1, 1]$	$c_{ij} \in [-5, 5]$ $v_{ij} \in [0.01, 4]$ $w_{jk} \in [-2, 2]$	$c_{ij} \in [-5, 5]$ $v_{ij} \in [0.01, 4]$ $w_{jk} \in [-2, 2]$
Estimated minimal cost	1.5273	1.7247	1.5103
Mean squared error (MSE)	0.0611	0.0690	0.0604
Mean absolute deviation (MAD)	0.1840	0.1694	0.1909

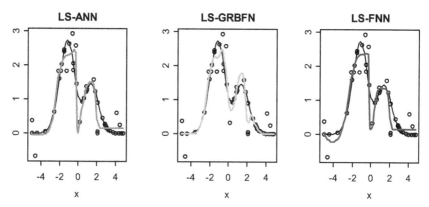

Figure 5.6.3: Predictive functions in Example 5.6.3.

5.7 Exercises

Exercise 5.7.1: Consider the artificial neural network shown in Figure 5.2.1.

(a) The updating for the weights w_{jk} and v_{ij} can also be performed by another incremental gradient descent algorithm. The total sum of squared errors can also be written as

$$\Psi_{total} := \frac{1}{2}\sum_{q=1}^{l}\sum_{k=1}^{p}e_{qk}^2 = \frac{1}{2}\sum_{k=1}^{p}\sum_{q=1}^{l}e_{qk}^2 .$$

Define the sum of squared error at the output node k as

$$\Psi_k := \frac{1}{2}\sum_{q=1}^{l}e_{qk}^2 , \quad k \in \underline{p} .$$

Then we have

$$\Psi_{total} = \sum_{k=1}^{p}\Psi_k .$$

In this alternative algorithm, Ψ_k's are minimized in sequence. Derive the details of the updating rules

$$w_{jk} \leftarrow w_{jk} - \eta_w \frac{\partial \Psi_k}{\partial w_{jk}}, \quad v_{ij} \leftarrow v_{ij} - \eta_v \frac{\partial \Psi_k}{\partial v_{ij}}.$$

(b)   We may also use usual batch-type steepest descent method for the updating of the weights w_{jk} and v_{ij}.   Derive the details of the updating rules

$$w_{jk} \leftarrow w_{jk} - \eta_w \frac{\partial E_{total}}{\partial w_{jk}}, \quad v_{ij} \leftarrow v_{ij} - \eta_v \frac{\partial E_{total}}{\partial v_{ij}},$$

where

$$E_{total} := \frac{1}{2} \sum_{q=1}^{l} \sum_{k=1}^{p} e_{qk}^2 .$$

Exercise 5.7.2:   Repeat Exercise 5.7.1 for the generalized radial basis function network shown in Figure 5.3.1.

Exercise 5.7.3:   Repeat Exercise 5.7.1 for the fuzzy neural network shown in Figure 5.5.1.

Exercise 5.7.4:   Let $X \subseteq \mathfrak{R}^n$ and $Y := \{1, -1\}$.   Suppose we are given the training set $S := \{(x_q, d_q)\}_{q=1}^{l} \subseteq X \times Y$.   Define a nonlinear map

$$\phi(x) = \sum_{q=1}^{l} d_q \cdot \exp\left(\frac{-\|x - x_q\|^2}{\sigma^2} \right), \quad x \in \mathfrak{R}^n .$$

Under what condition on σ^2, can this map be used for correct nonlinear classification of all training data?

Exercise 5.7.5: Consider the artificial neural network as shown in Figure 5.2.1.   Suppose the goal is to choose weights that minimize the cost given by

$$E := \sum_{q=1}^{l} E_q^{reg} ,$$

where

$$E_q^{reg} = 2^{-1} \sum_{k=1}^{p} \sum_{j=1}^{m} w_{jk}^2 + C \cdot E_q, \quad E_q := 2^{-1} \sum_{k=1}^{p} e_{qk}^2, \quad q \in \underline{l},$$

and $C > 0$ is the regularization parameter (or smoothing parameter). Develop a back propagation algorithm for updating w_{jk} and v_{ij}.

Exercise 5.7.6: Consider the generalized radial basis function network as shown in Figure 5.3.1. Suppose $v_{ij} = v_j$ for all $i \in \underline{n}$. Develop a back propagation algorithm for updating w_{jk}, c_{ij}, and v_j.

Exercise 5.7.7: Consider the generalized radial basis function network as shown in Figure 5.3.1. Suppose the goal is to choose weights that minimize the cost given by

$$E := \sum_{q=1}^{l} E_q^{reg},$$

where

$$E_q^{reg} = 2^{-1} \sum_{k=1}^{p} \sum_{j=1}^{m} w_{jk}^2 + C \cdot E_q, \quad E_q := 2^{-1} \sum_{k=1}^{p} e_{qk}^2, \quad q \in \underline{l},$$

and $C > 0$ is the regularization parameter (or smoothing parameter). Develop a back propagation algorithm for updating w_{jk}, c_{ij}, and v_{ij}.

In the next two exercises, the activation functions of the output nodes for ANNs, GRBFNs, and FNNs are all bipolar sigmoidal functions. For ANNs, the activation functions of the hidden nodes are bipolar sigmoidal functions.

Exercise 5.7.8: Suppose the true discriminant function is given by the Hermite function

$$g(x_1, x_2) = x_2 - 1.1 \cdot \left(1 - x_1 + 2x_1^2\right) \cdot e^{-x_1^2/2},$$
$$x_1 \in [-5, 5], \quad x_2 \in [-1, 3].$$

The number of hidden nodes for each learning machine is 4. The binary cross-entropy is used as the objective function. Draw the decision boundaries thus determined for 30% corrupted training data. Discuss whether these machine parameter settings are reasonable.

Exercise 5.7.9: Suppose the true discriminant function is given by the sinc function

$$g(x_1, x_2) = \begin{cases} x_2 - 1, & x_1 = 0, \\ x_2 - [\sin(x_1)/x_1], & x_1 \neq 0, \end{cases}$$
$$x_1 \in [-10, 10], \quad x_2 \in [-2, 2].$$

The number of hidden nodes for each learning machine is 4. The binary cross-entropy is used as the objective function. Draw the decision boundaries thus determined for 30% corrupted training data. Discuss whether these machine parameter settings are reasonable.

In the next two exercises, the activation functions of the output nodes for ANNs, GRBFNs, and FNNs are all linear functions with unit slope. For ANNs, the activation functions of the hidden nodes are bipolar sigmoidal functions.

Exercise 5.7.10: Suppose the true regression function is given by the fractional power function

$$g(x) = x^{2/3}, \quad x \in [-2, 2].$$

The number of hidden nodes for each learning machine is 4. Half of the total sum of squared errors E_{total} is used as the objective function. Draw the predictive functions thus determined for 30% corrupted training data. Discuss whether these machine parameter settings are reasonable.

Exercise 5.7.11: Consider a system with 4 input variables and 3 output variables. Suppose that 200 training examples are generated from a simple function with 5% corruption as follows:

$$g_1(x_1, x_2, x_3, x_4) = 0.2 \times [x_1 \sin(4x_1) + x_2 \sin(2x_2) + x_3 \cos(2x_4)]$$
$$+ 5\% \text{ corruption,}$$
$$g_2(x_1, x_2, x_3, x_4) = 0.5 \times [x_2 \cos(x_1) + x_3 \sin(3x_4)]$$
$$+ 5\% \text{ corruption,}$$
$$g_3(x_1, x_2, x_3, x_4) = 0.5 \times [x_1 \sin(x_1) + \cos(x_2) + \cos(x_3 x_4)]$$
$$+ 5\% \text{ corruption,}$$

$-2 \le x_i \le 2$, $i \in \underline{4}$.

The 40 testing examples are corruption-free. Half of the total sum of squared errors E_{total} is used as the objective function. Apply the BP algorithm with the following parameter settings:

Table 5.7.11: Simulation results in Exercise 5.7.11.

	ANN	GRBFN	FNN
No. of hidden nodes	4	3	3
No. of weights	35	33	33

For each learning machine, calculate the mean squared errors (MSEs) and the mean absolute deviations (MADs) for the training data and testing data. Discuss whether these machine parameter settings are reasonable.

Exercise 5.7.12: Consider a binary classification problem with the objective function given by binary cross-entropy.

(a) Derive the updating formulas for the weights w_{jk} and v_{ij} in an artificial neural network if the output labels were coded as 0 or 1.

(b) Derive the updating formulas for the weights w_{jk} and v_{ij} in an artificial neural network if the output labels were coded as -1 or 1.

Exercise 5.7.13: Consider a binary classification problem with the objective function given by binary cross-entropy.

(a) Derive the updating formulas for the weights w_{jk}, c_{ij}, and v_{ij} in a generalized radial basis function network if the output labels were coded as 0 or 1.

(b) Derive the updating formulas for the weights w_{jk}, c_{ij}, and v_{ij} in a generalized radial basis function network if the output labels were coded as -1 or 1.

Exercise 5.7.14: Consider a binary classification problem with the objective function given by binary cross-entropy.

(a) Derive the updating formulas for the weights w_{jk}, c_{ij}, and v_{ij} in a fuzzy neural network if the output labels were coded as 0 or 1.

(b) Derive the updating formulas for the weights w_{jk}, c_{ij}, and v_{ij} in a fuzzy neural network if the output labels were coded as -1 or 1.

5.8 Notes and References

For the original paper of Cover's Theorem, see Cover (1965). The statement of Cover's Theorem in Theorem 5.1.1 was quoted from Haykin (1999). The nonlinear map constructed for correct classification of all training data was made by Professor Yeong-Jeu Sun of I-Shou University, a former PhD student of the first author.

Our development of artificial neural networks and generalized radial basis function networks follows the same line as Kecman (2001). More topics on artificial neural networks can be found in Anthony and Bartlett (1999), Golden (1996), and Haykin (1999). Important references on radial basis function networks are Tikhonov (1963), Poggio and Girosi (1989a), and Poggio and Girosi (1989b).

For the original paper of fuzzy theory, see Zadeh (1965). The materials on standard fuzzy systems were based entirely on Wang (1997). More topics on fuzzy theory can be found in Klir and Yuan (1995), Kosko (1994), Yen and Langari (1999), Wang (1992), Wang and Mendel (1992), and Zimmermann (1991).

Back propagation algorithm is not the only algorithm for updating the connection weights in a neural network. In fact, the candidate solution of the connection weights is easily trapped into the local optima or saddle points of the cost function (or cost landscape) using the back propagation algorithm. It is desirable to have algorithms which yield higher possibilities for the candidate solution to escape from the local optima (or leapfrog over the sticking points) of the cost landscape. To this end, the evolutionary computation algorithms such as genetic algorithm (GA) and particle swarm optimization (PSO), to be introduced in Chapter 8, may be good choices.

For the original paper on generalized linear models (GLMs), see Nelder and Wedderburn (1972). For introductory texts on GLMs, see Dobson and Barnett (2008) and Hardin and Hilbe (2007).

Many real world data sets may be found in Blake and Merz (1998) and Chang and Lin (2001).

From the simulation results of Section 5.6, it is clear that the discriminant or predictive functions determined by ANN, GRBFN, and FNN with least squares criterion are much influenced by outliers. To avoid this, robust regression techniques, e.g., *M*-estimation or least trimmed squares (LTS), may be applied; see Rousseeuw and Leroy (2003), Hampel, Ronchetti, Rousseeuw, and Stahel (2005), Maronna, Martin, and Yohai (2006), Huber and Ronchetti (2009), Wu etc. (2010), and Lin etc. (2015).

Apart from the feed-forward neural networks considered in this chapter, there are some powerful neural networks currently in use, for instance convolutional neural networks and recurrent neural networks used especially in deep learning.

Anthony, M. and P.L. Bartlett (1999). Neural Network Learning: Theoretical Foundation. Cambridge University Press, Cambridge, United Kingdom.

Bertsekas, D.P. (1999). Nonlinear Programming. Second Edition. Athena Scientific, Massachusetts.

Blake, C. and C. Merz (1998). UCI machine learning repository [online]. Available: http://www.ics.uci.edu/~mlearn/MLRepository.html.

Chang, C.C. and C. J. Lin (2001). LIMSVM: A library for support vector machines [online]. Available: http://www.csie.ntu.edu.tw/~cjlin/libsvm.

Cover, T.M. (1965). Geometrical and statistical properties of systems of linear inequalities with applications in pattern recognition. IEEE Transactions on Electronic Computers, Vol. EC-14, pp. 326-334.

Cybenko, G. (1989). Approximation by superposition of a sigmoidal functions. Mathematics of Control, Signals, and Systems, Vol. 2, pp. 304-314.

Dobson, A. J. and A. G. Barnett (2008). An Introduction to Generalized Linear Models. Chapman & Hall/CRC, Florida.

Funahashi, K. (1989). On the approximate realization of continuous mappings by neural networks. Neural Networks, Vol. 2, No. 3, pp. 183-192.

Golden, R.M. (1996). Mathematical Methods for Neural Network Analysis and Design. MIT Press, Cambridge, Massachusetts.

Hampel, F. R., E. M. Ronchetti, P. J. Rousseeuw, and W. A. Stahel (2005). Robust Statistics: The Approach Based on Influence Functions. Wiley, New York.

Hardin, J. W. and J. M. Hilbe (2007). Generalized Linear Models and Extensions. Stata Press, Texas.

Hartman, E.J., J.D. Keeler, and J.M. Kowalski (1990). Layered neural networks with Gaussian hidden units as universal approximations. Neural Computation, Vol. 2, No. 2, pp. 210-215.

Haykin, S. (1999). Neural Networks. Second Edition. Prentice-Hall, New Jersey.

Hornik, K., M. Stinchcombe, and H. White (1989). Multilayer feedforward networks are universal approximators. Neural Networks, Vol. 2, No. 5, pp. 359-366.

Huber, P. J. and E. M. Ronchetti (2009). Robust Statistics. Second Edition. Wiley, Hoboken, New Jersey.

Kecman, V. (2001). Learning and Soft Computing. MIT Press, Cambridge, Massachusetts.

Kingma, D.P. and J. Lei Ba (2015). Adam: A method for stochastic optimization. Proceeding of the Third International Conference on Learning Representations, San Diego, pp. 1-13.

Klir, G.J. and B. Yuan (1995). Fuzzy Sets and Fuzzy Logic. Prentice-Hall, New Jersey.

Kosko, B. (1994). Fuzzy systems as universal approximators. IEEE Transactions on Computers, Vol. 43, No. 11, pp. 1329-1333.

Le Cun, Y. (1986). Learning processes in an asymmetric threshold network. Distributed Systems and Biological Organization, Springer, Les Houches, France, pp. 233-240.

Lin, Y.L., J.G. Hsieh, J.H. Jeng, and W.C. Cheng (2015). On least trimmed squares neural networks. Neurocomputing, vol. 161, pp. 107-112.

Maronna, R. A., R. D. Martin, and V. J. Yohai (2006). Robust Statistics: Theory and Methods. Wiley, Chichester, United Kingdom.

Nelder, J. A. and R. W. M. Wedderburn (1972). Generalized linear models. Journal of the Royal Statistical Society Series A, vol. 135, pp. 370-384.

Park, J. and I.W. Sandberg (1991). Universal approximation using radial basis function networks. Neural Computation, Vol. 3, No. 2, pp. 246-257.

Poggio, T. and F. Girosi (1989a). A theory of networks for approximation and learning. A.I. Memo No. 1140, MIT, Cambridge, Massachusetts.

Poggio, T. and F. Girosi (1989b). Networks and the best approximation property. A.I. Memo No. 1164, MIT, Cambridge, Massachusetts.

Rousseeuw, P. J. and A. M. Leroy (2003). Robust Regression and Outlier Detection. Wiley, New York.

Ruder, S. (2016). An overview of gradient descent optimization algorithms. Website: http://ruder.io/optimizing-gradient-descent/index.html.

Rumelhart, D.E., G.E. Hinton, and R.J. Williams (1986). Learning internal representations by error propagation. In D.E. Rumelhart, J.L. McClelland, and the PDP Research Group (Eds.), Parallel Distributed Processing: Explorations in the Microstructure of Cognition, MIT Press, Cambridge, Massachusetts, Vol. 1, Foundations, pp. 318-362. Reprinted in Anderson and Rosenfield (1988).

Tikhonov, A.N. (1963). On solving incorrectly posed problems and method of regularization. Doklady Akademii Nauk USSR, Vol. 151, pp. 501-504 (in Russian).

Wang, L.X. (1992). Fuzzy systems are universal approximators. Proceeding of IEEE International Conference on Fuzzy Systems, San Diego, pp. 1163-1170.

Wang, L.X. and J.M. Mendel (1992). Fuzzy basis functions, universal approximation, and orthogonal least squares learning. IEEE Transactions on Neural Networks, Vol. 3, No. 5, pp. 807-814.

Wang, L.X. (1997). A Course in Fuzzy Systems and Control. Prentice-Hall, New Jersey.

Wu, H.K., J.G. Hsieh, Y.L. Lin, and J.H. Jeng (2010). On maximum likelihood fuzzy neural networks. Fuzzy Sets and Systems, Vol. 161, No. 21, pp. 2795-2807.

Yen, J. and R. Langari (1999). Fuzzy Logic. Prentice-Hall, New Jersey.

Zadeh, L.A. (1965). Fuzzy sets. Information and Control, Vol. 8, pp. 338-353.

Zimmermann, H.J. (1991). Fuzzy Set Theory and Its Applications. Second Edition. Kluwer Academic, Boston.

Chapter 6   Kernel-based Support Vector Classification and Regression

The concept of kernel was introduced early in Section 3.5, which was applied there for nonlinear classification, and later for nonlinear regression in Section 4.4.   In this chapter, we study the kernels in more detail.   The idea of a kernel generalizes the standard inner product in $\Re^n$ by making the feature map the identity map.   The Mercer's Theorem characterizing the kernels will be introduced.   Some commonly used kernels are presented.

It is almost without effort to transform the linear classifiers and regressors to kernel-based nonlinear classifiers and regressors.   Simply replace the inner product by the kernel.   Some researchers call this the kernel trick.   It should be noted that, in playing the kernel trick, we don't even compute the nonlinear feature maps.   Furthermore, the curse of dimensionality for nonlinear classifiers and regressors is bypassed because the computation of kernel values is done on the original space but not on the high-dimensional (even infinite-dimensional) feature space.   Such kernel-based approach results in the invention of kernel-based support vector machines.   The support vector machine, abbreviated as SVM, was invented by Boser, Guyon and Vapnik, and first introduced in 1992 at the Computational Learning Theory conference where they presented their paper.   This learning method is based on the structural risk minimization principle rooted in statistical learning theory and is a powerful technique for nonlinear regression or pattern recognition.   We summarize the results on kernel-based classifiers in Section 6.3 and kernel-based regressors in Section 6.4.   The multi-class classification problems are discussed next.   Very often, a multi-class classification problem can be reduced to several binary classification problems.

6.1 Kernel and Mercer's Theorem

Let $\left(F, \langle .,. \rangle\right)$, called the **feature space**, be a real inner product space and $X \subseteq \Re^n$.   A **kernel** is a real-valued function on $X \times X$ such that

$$K(x, z) := \langle \phi(x), \phi(z) \rangle, \quad x, z \in X,$$

where ϕ, called the **feature map**, is a mapping from X to F. The idea of a kernel generalizes the standard inner product in $\mathfrak{R}^n$ by making the feature map the identity map, i.e.,

$$K(x, z) := \langle \phi(x), \phi(z) \rangle = \langle x, z \rangle := x^T z.$$

Very often, it is more practical and easier to define the kernel function directly, serving as a similarity measure between objects, and then specify the corresponding feature map if necessary.

Example 6.1.1: Suppose we first specify the kernel as

$$K(x, z) := \left(\langle x, z \rangle + c \right)^2 = \left(x^T z + c \right)^2,$$
$$x = [x_1 \quad \cdots \quad x_n]^T, \quad z = [z_1 \quad \cdots \quad z_n]^T \in \mathfrak{R}^n, \quad c \geq 0.$$

Then we have

$$K(x, z) = \left(x^T z + c \right)^2 = \left(\sum_{i=1}^{n} x_i z_i + c \right)^2$$

$$= \left(\sum_{i=1}^{n} x_i z_i + c \right) \cdot \left(\sum_{j=1}^{n} x_j z_j + c \right)$$

$$= \sum_{i=1}^{n} \sum_{j=1}^{n} x_i x_j z_i z_j + 2c \sum_{i=1}^{n} x_i z_i + c^2$$

$$= \sum_{(i,j)=(1,1)}^{(n,n)} \left(x_i x_j \right) \left(z_i z_j \right) + \sum_{i=1}^{n} \left(\sqrt{2c} x_i \right) \left(\sqrt{2c} z_i \right) + (c)(c).$$

This shows that the feature map is given by

$$\phi(x) = \left(c, \left(\sqrt{2c} x_i \right)_{i=1}^{n}, \left(x_i x_j \right)_{(i,j)=(1,1)}^{(n,n)} \right), \quad x = [x_1 \quad \cdots \quad x_n]^T \in \mathfrak{R}^n.$$

Similarly, we may consider the kernel of the form

$$K(x, z) := (\langle x, z \rangle + c)^d = (x^T z + c)^d, \quad c \geq 0, \quad d \geq 2.$$

In these cases, the decision boundary in the input space corresponding to a hyperplane in these feature spaces is a polynomial curve of degree d, so these kernels are frequently called **polynomial kernels**.

What types of functions on $X \times X$ are qualified as kernels? The following theorem provides a necessary and sufficient condition.

Proposition 6.1.1: Suppose $X \subseteq \mathfrak{R}^n$ and $K(x, z)$ is a symmetric function on $X \times X$, i.e., $K(x, z) = K(z, x)$ for all $x, z \in X$. Then $K(x, z)$ is a kernel on $X \times X$ if and only if the Gram matrix with respect to any points $x_1, \ldots, x_m \in X$, where m is any positive integer, defined by

$$\left[K(x_i, x_j) \right]_{i,j=1}^m$$

is positive semi-definite, i.e.,

$$\sum_{i=1}^m \sum_{j=1}^m c_i c_j K(x_i, x_j) \geq 0 \quad \text{for all} \quad c_i, \ c_j \in \mathfrak{R}, \ i, j \in \underline{m}.$$

In fact, the qualification of a symmetric function as a kernel was solved over a hundred years ago, i.e., the Mercer's Theorem. In the following, we introduce this theorem.

Suppose X is a compact subset of $\mathfrak{R}^n$. Define

$$L_2(X) := \left\{ f : X \to \mathfrak{R} : \int_X f^2(x) dx < \infty \right\}$$

and an inner product

$$\langle f, g \rangle := \int_X f(x) g(x) dx, \quad f, g \in L_2(X).$$

Note that $L_2(X)$ is a real Hilbert space. Suppose $K : X \times X \to \mathfrak{R}$ is a bounded symmetric function, i.e.,

$$K(x, z) = K(z, x) \quad \text{for all} \quad x, z \in X,$$

and there is a constant $M_0 > 0$ such that

$$|K(x, z)| \le M_0 \quad \text{for all} \quad x, z \in X.$$

Define a function T_K on $L_2(X)$ as

$$(T_K f)(x) := \int_X K(x, z) f(z) dz = \langle K(x, \cdot), f \rangle, \quad f \in L_2(X), \quad x \in X.$$

Then, $T_K f$ is a function defined on X. Set

$$g(x) := (T_K f)(x) := \int_X K(x, z) f(z) dz, \quad f \in L_2(X), \quad x \in X.$$

In view of the Jensen's inequality (Royden (1989)), we have

$$
\begin{aligned}
\|g\|^2 &:= \langle g, g \rangle = \int_X g^2(x) dx = \int_X \left[\int_X K(x, z) f(z) dz \right]^2 dx \\
&\le \int_X \left[\int_X K^2(x, z) f^2(z) dz \right] dx \le M_0^2 \int_X \left[\int_X f^2(z) dz \right] dx \\
&= M_0^2 \int_X \|f\|^2 dx = M_0^2 m(X) \|f\|^2 < \infty,
\end{aligned}
$$

where $m(X)$ is the measure of X, which is finite by the compactness of X. This shows that T_K is a bounded linear function from $L_2(X)$ to $L_2(X)$.

Next, we assert that T_K is self-adjoint. Indeed, for any given $f, g \in L_2(X)$, we have

$$
\begin{aligned}
\langle T_K f, g \rangle &:= \int_X \left[\int_X K(x, z) f(z) dz \right] g(x) dx \\
&= \int_X \int_X K(x, z) f(z) g(x) dz dx \\
&= \int_X \int_X K(z, x) f(x) g(z) dz dx \\
&= \int_X \int_X K(x, z) f(x) g(z) dz dx \\
&= \int_X \left[\int_X K(x, z) g(z) dz \right] f(x) dx := \langle f, T_K g \rangle.
\end{aligned}
$$

Hence, all eigenvalues of T_K are real. Indeed, suppose $T_K f = \lambda f$, $f \neq 0$, $f \in L_2(X)$, then we have

$$\langle f, T_K f \rangle = \langle f, \lambda f \rangle = \lambda \langle f, f \rangle = \lambda \| f \|^2.$$

This implies that $\lambda \in \Re$. Moreover, eigen-functions corresponding to different eigenvalues are orthogonal. Indeed, suppose

$$T_K f_1 = \lambda_1 f_1, \ T_K f_2 = \lambda_2 f_2, \ \lambda_1 \neq \lambda_2, \ \lambda_1, \lambda_2 \in \Re,$$
$$f_1 \neq 0, \ f_2 \neq 0, \ f_1, f_2 \in L_2(X).$$

Then, we have

$$\lambda_1 \langle f_2, f_1 \rangle = \langle f_2, \lambda_1 f_1 \rangle = \langle f_2, T_K f_1 \rangle,$$
$$\lambda_2 \langle f_2, f_1 \rangle = \langle \lambda_2 f_2, f_1 \rangle = \langle T_K f_2, f_1 \rangle.$$

Subtracting both sides, we have

$$(\lambda_1 - \lambda_2)\langle f_2, f_1 \rangle = \langle f_2, T_K f_1 \rangle - \langle T_K f_2, f_1 \rangle = 0.$$

Since $\lambda_1 \neq \lambda_2$, we have $\langle f_1, f_2 \rangle = 0$, i.e., f_1 and f_2 are orthogonal. Note that the compactness of the input space X is required to ensure that the (point) spectrum is a countable set.

Now, suppose T_K is positive semi-definite, i.e.,

$$\langle f, T_K f \rangle \geq 0 \ \text{ for all } \ f \in L_2(X).$$

Note that this means, for all $f \in L_2(X)$,

$$0 \leq \langle f, T_K f \rangle = \int_X \left[\int_X K(x, z) f(z) dz \right] f(x) dx$$
$$= \int_X \int_X K(x, z) f(x) f(z) dx dz.$$

In this case, all eigenvalues of T_K are non-negative. Indeed, suppose $T_K f = \lambda f$, $f \neq 0$, $f \in L_2(X)$, then we have

$$0 \le \langle f, T_K f \rangle = \langle f, \lambda f \rangle = \lambda \langle f, f \rangle = \lambda \|f\|^2.$$

This shows that $\lambda \ge 0$.

Now, we are ready to state the Mercer's Theorem.

Proposition 6.1.2: (Mercer's Theorem)

Let X be a compact subset of $\mathfrak{R}^n$. Suppose $K : X \times X \to \mathfrak{R}$ is a bounded symmetric function. Define a function $T_K : L_2(X) \to L_2(X)$ as

$$(T_K f)(x) := \int_X K(x, z) f(z) dz = \langle K(x, \cdot), f \rangle, \quad f \in L_2(X), \quad x \in X.$$

If T_K is positive semi-definite, i.e.,

$$0 \le \langle f, T_K f \rangle = \int_X \int_X K(x, z) f(x) f(z) dx dz \quad \text{for all} \quad f \in L_2(X),$$

then $K(x, z)$ can be expanded as a (possibly terminating) uniformly convergent series on $X \times X$ in terms of T_K's (normalized) eigen-functions $\phi_j \in L_2(X)$, $\|\phi_j\| = 1$, corresponding to the (non-negative) eigenvalues λ_j as

$$K(x, z) = \sum_{j=1}^{\infty} \lambda_j \phi_j(x) \phi_j(z), \quad x, z \in X.$$

Moreover, we have $(\lambda_1 \ \lambda_2 \ \lambda_3 \ \dots) \in l_1$ and $\phi_j \in L_\infty(X)$.

Proposition 6.1.3: In Mercer's theorem, T_K is positive semi-definite if and only if for any finite set $M := \{x_1, \dots, x_m\} \subseteq X$, $m < \infty$, the corresponding matrix $A := [K(x_i, x_j)]_{i,j=1}^m$ is positive semi-definite.

A kernel satisfying the assumptions of the Mercer's theorem is often called a **Mercer kernel**. Suppose $K(x, z)$ is a Mercer kernel. The Mercer's theorem suggests that we consider the feature map

$$x := \begin{bmatrix} x_1 & \cdots & x_n \end{bmatrix}^T \in X \mapsto \phi(x) := \begin{bmatrix} \sqrt{\lambda_1}\phi_1(x) & \cdots & \sqrt{\lambda_j}\phi_j(x) & \cdots \end{bmatrix}$$

in a feature space l_2, which is a Hilbert space,

$$l_2 := \left\{ \begin{bmatrix} \xi_1 & \cdots & \xi_j & \cdots \end{bmatrix} : \sum_{j=1}^{\infty} \xi_j^2 < \infty \right\}$$

with the inner product

$$\langle \xi, \eta \rangle_2 := \sum_{j=1}^{\infty} \xi_j \eta_j, \quad \xi, \eta \in l_2.$$

In this case, we have

$$\langle \phi(x), \phi(z) \rangle_2 := \sum_{j=1}^{\infty} \sqrt{\lambda_j}\phi_j(x)\sqrt{\lambda_j}\phi_j(z) = \sum_{j=1}^{\infty} \lambda_j \phi_j(x)\phi_j(z) = K(x, z).$$

Note that we have mapped a finite-dimensional vector $x \in X \subseteq \mathfrak{R}^n$ to a possibly infinite-dimensional feature $\phi(x) \in l_2$.

6.2 Commonly Used Kernels

In this section, we present some commonly used kernels. The propositions of this section are quoted from Cristianini and Shawe-Taylor (2000) and Herbrich (2002).

Proposition 6.2.1: Let K_1 and K_2 be kernels on $X \times X$, $X \subseteq \mathfrak{R}^n$, K_3 a kernel on $\mathfrak{R}^m \times \mathfrak{R}^m$, $a > 0$, $f : X \to \mathfrak{R}$, $g : X \to \mathfrak{R}^m$, and $B \in \mathfrak{R}^{n \times n}$ a symmetric and positive semi-definite matrix. Then the following functions are kernels ($x, z \in X$):

(a) $K(x, z) := K_1(x, z) + K_2(x, z)$;
(b) $K(x, z) := K_1(x, z) + a$;
(c) $K(x, z) := a \cdot K_1(x, z)$;

(d) $K(x, z) := K_1(x, z) \cdot K_2(x, z)$;

(e) $K(x, z) := f(x) \cdot f(z)$;

(f) $K(x, z) := K_3(g(x), g(z))$;

(g) $K(x, z) := x^T Bz$.

Proof: Let $\{x_1, ..., x_l\} \subseteq X$ be any given finite subset.   Let

$$A_1 := \left[K_1(x_i, x_j) \right]_{i,j=1}^l, \quad A_2 := \left[K_2(x_i, x_j) \right]_{i,j=1}^l, \quad A := \left[K(x_i, x_j) \right]_{i,j=1}^l.$$

Let $q := [q_1 \quad \cdots \quad q_l] \in \Re^l$.   The results of (a), (b), and (c) are obvious from the following inequalities, respectively,

$$q^T Aq = q^T (A_1 + A_2)q = q^T A_1 q + q^T A_2 q \geq 0,$$

$$q^T Aq = q^T A_1 q + a \cdot \left| \sum_{j=1}^l q_j \right|^2 \geq 0,$$

$$q^T Aq = q^T (aA_1)q = aq^T A_1 q \geq 0.$$

(d) Let $P := A_1 \otimes A_2$ be the tensor (or Kronecker) product of the matrices A_1 and A_2.   See Kailath (1980).   Since the eigenvalues of P are all pairs of products of the eigenvalues of A_1 and A_2, P is also positive semi-definite.   Moreover, the matrix

$$A := \left[K(x_i, x_j) \right]_{i,j=1}^l = \left[K_1(x_i, x_j) \cdot K_2(x_i, x_j) \right]_{i,j=1}^l$$

is the Schur product of A_1 and A_2.   The matrix A is a principal submatrix of P defined by a set of columns and the same set of rows. Hence for any $q \in \Re^l$, there is a corresponding $q_1 \in \Re^{l^2}$ such that

$$q^T Aq = q_1^T Pq_1 \geq 0.$$

This   shows   that A is   positive   semi-definite.   Hence $K(x, z) := K_1(x, z) \cdot K_2(x, z)$ is a kernel.

(e) For any $q := [q_1 \quad \cdots \quad q_l] \in \Re^l$, we have

$$q^T Aq = \sum_{i=1}^{l}\sum_{j=1}^{l} q_i q_j f(x_i) f(x_j)$$

$$= \left[\sum_{i=1}^{l} q_i f(x_i)\right] \cdot \left[\sum_{j=1}^{l} q_j f(x_j)\right] = \left[\sum_{i=1}^{l} q_i f(x_i)\right]^2 \geq 0 .$$

This shows that A is positive semi-definite. Hence $K(x, z):= f(x) \cdot f(z)$ is a kernel.

(f) Set $z_i := g(x_i) \in \Re^m$, $i \in \underline{l}$, we have

$$A := \left[K(x_i, x_j)\right]_{i,j=1}^{l} = \left[K_3(g(x_i), g(x_j))\right]_{i,j=1}^{l} = \left[K_3(z_i, z_j)\right]_{i,j=1}^{l} \geq 0 .$$

Hence $K(x, z):= K_3(g(x), g(z))$ is a kernel.

(g) Since B is symmetric and positive semi-definite, there is an orthonormal matrix P such that $P^T BP = D$, where D is a diagonal matrix with eigenvalues $\lambda_i \geq 0$ on its diagonal, and each column p_i of P is an eigenvector of B corresponding to the eigenvalue λ_i. Let $Q := P^T$. Then Q is also an orthonormal matrix and $B = Q^T DQ$. Set $A := \sqrt{D}Q$, then we have

$$K(x, z):= x^T Bz = x^T Q^T DQz = x^T Q^T \sqrt{D}\sqrt{D}Qz$$

$$= \left(\sqrt{D}Qx\right)^T \left(\sqrt{D}Qz\right) = (Ax)^T (Az) = \langle Ax, Az \rangle .$$

This shows that $K(x, z):= x^T Bz$ is a kernel.

Proposition 6.2.2: Let K_1 be a kernel on $X \times X$, $X \subseteq \Re^n$, $x, z \in X$, and $p(\cdot)$ is a polynomial with positive coefficients. Then the following functions are kernels:

(a) $K(x, z):= p(K_1(x, z))$; e.g., $K(x, z):= [K_1(x, z) + c]^d$, $c \geq 0$, $d = 1, 2,...$;

(b) $\quad K(x, z) := \dfrac{K_1(x, z)}{\sqrt{K_1(x, x) \cdot K_1(z, z)}}$;

(c) $\quad K(x, z) := \exp[K_1(x, z)]$; or more generally,

$\quad K(x, z) := \exp[K_1(x, z)/\sigma^2]$;

(d) $\quad K(x, z) := \exp(-\sigma^{-2}\|x - z\|^2)$; or more generally,

$\quad K(x, z) := \exp[-\sigma^{-2}(K_1(x, x) - 2K_1(x, z) + K_1(z, z))]$;

(e) $\quad K(x, z) := \exp[-\sigma_1^{-2}(x_1 - z_1)^2 - \ldots - \sigma_n^{-2}(x_n - z_n)^2]$.

Proof: (a) First note that the positive constant function is a kernel by part (e) of the preceding proposition. Suppose

$$p(s) = a_m s^m + \ldots + a_1 s + a_0, \quad a_i > 0, \quad i \in \overline{m}.$$

Then we have

$$p(K_1(x, z)) = a_m K_1(x, z)^m + \ldots + a_1 K_1(x, z) + a_0.$$

By (a), (b), (c), and (d) of the preceding proposition, this is indeed a kernel.

(b) Clearly, we have

$$K(x, z) := \dfrac{K_1(x, z)}{\sqrt{K_1(x, x) \cdot K_1(z, z)}} = \dfrac{1}{\sqrt{K_1(x, x)}} \dfrac{1}{\sqrt{K_1(z, z)}} \cdot K_1(x, z)$$

$$:= [f(x) \cdot f(z)] \cdot K_1(x, z).$$

Thus the result follows by (e) and (d) of the preceding proposition.

(c) The exponential function can be arbitrarily approximated by polynomials with positive coefficients and hence is a limit of kernels. Since kernels are clearly closed under taking pointwise limits, the result follows.

(d) By definition, we have

$$K(x, z) := \exp(-\sigma^{-2}\|x - z\|^2) = \exp(-\sigma^{-2}\langle x - z, x - z\rangle)$$

$$= [\exp(-\sigma^{-2}\|x\|^2) \cdot \exp(-\sigma^{-2}\|z\|^2)]\exp(2\sigma^{-2}\langle x, z\rangle).$$

The first two terms together form a kernel by part (e) of the preceding proposition, while the third term is a kernel by part (c) of this proposition. This shows that $K(x, z) := \exp\left(-\sigma^{-2}\|x - z\|^2\right)$ is a kernel.

Let ϕ be a feature map corresponding to the kernel K_1. Then we have

$$\|\phi(x) - \phi(z)\|^2 = \langle\phi(x) - \phi(z), \phi(x) - \phi(z)\rangle$$
$$= \langle\phi(x), \phi(x)\rangle - 2\langle\phi(x), \phi(z)\rangle + \langle\phi(z), \phi(z)\rangle$$
$$= K_1(x, x) - 2K_1(x, z) + K_1(z, z).$$

Hence $K(x, z) := \exp\left[-\sigma^{-2}\left(K_1(x, x) - 2K_1(x, z) + K_1(z, z)\right)\right]$ is a kernel by part (f) of the preceding proposition.

(e) The proof of (e) is similar to (d).

Now, we discuss some interesting properties of the kernels of the preceding proposition. By using the second kernel, it is possible to normalize data in feature space without performing the explicit mapping, since

$$K(x, z) := \frac{K_1(x, z)}{\sqrt{K_1(x, x) \cdot K_1(z, z)}}$$

$$= \frac{1}{\sqrt{\|\phi(x)\|^2 \cdot \|\phi(z)\|^2}} \langle\phi(x), \phi(z)\rangle = \left\langle \frac{\phi(x)}{\|\phi(x)\|}, \frac{\phi(z)}{\|\phi(z)\|}\right\rangle.$$

The fourth kernel is known as the **Radial Basis Function kernel** (RBF kernel) or **Gaussian kernel**. It forms the core of a radial basis function network and hence, using this kernel will mean the hypotheses are radial basis function networks. The parameter σ controls the amount of smoothing, i.e., big values of σ lead to very flat and smooth functions f—hence it defines the unit on which $\|x - x_i\|$ are measured. The RBF kernel maps the input space onto the surface of an infinite-dimensional unit hyperspace, since

$$\|\phi(x)\|^2 = \langle \phi(x), \phi(x) \rangle = K(x, x) = \exp\left(-\sigma^{-2}\|x - x\|^2\right) = 1.$$

Moreover, by using RBF kernel, we have automatically chosen a model which is shift-invariant, i.e., translating the whole input space by some fixed vector x_0 does not change anything because

$$\|(x + x_0) - (z + x_0)\| = \|x - z\|.$$

The last kernel of the preceding proposition is known as the **Mahalanobis kernel**. It differs from the standard RBF kernel insofar as each axis of the input space has a separate smoothing parameter, i.e., a separate scale on which differences on this axis are viewed.

6.3 Kernel-based Support Vector Classifier

Let $X \subseteq \Re^n$ and $Y := \{1, -1\}$. Suppose we are given a non-trivial training set

$$S := \left\{(x_q, d_q)\right\}_{q=1}^{\prime\prime} \subseteq X \times Y.$$

Let $K(x, z)$ be a given kernel on $X \times X$ such that

$$K(x, z) := \langle \phi(x), \phi(z) \rangle, \quad x, z \in X,$$

where ϕ is the feature map from the input space X to the feature space F.

First, we consider the construction of the maximal margin classifier in the feature space when the transformed training set $S_\phi := \left\{(\phi(x_q), d_q)\right\}_{q=1}^{\prime\prime} \subseteq F \times Y$ is linearly separable in the feature space. Consider the following quadratic optimization problem:

(D0)   maximize $\displaystyle\sum_{q=1}^{l} \alpha_q - \frac{1}{2}\sum_{q=1}^{l}\sum_{j=1}^{l} \alpha_q \alpha_j d_q d_j \langle \phi(x_q), \phi(x_j) \rangle$

$$= \sum_{q=1}^{l} \alpha_q - \frac{1}{2}\sum_{q=1}^{l}\sum_{j=1}^{l} \alpha_q \alpha_j d_q d_j K(x_q, x_j)$$

subject to $\sum_{q=1}^{l} \alpha_q d_q = 0$ and $\alpha_q \geq 0$ for all $q \in \underline{l}$.

Suppose $\alpha *$ solves the problem (D0). Define $I_{sv} := \{q \in \underline{l} : \alpha_q^* > 0\}$. Then we have

$$w* = \sum_{q=1}^{l} \alpha_q^* d_q \phi(x_q) = \sum_{q \in I_{sv}} \alpha_q^* d_q \phi(x_q).$$

Choose any $\alpha_k^* > 0$, then we have

$$b* = d_k - \sum_{q \in I_{sv}} \alpha_q^* d_q \langle \phi(x_q), \phi(x_k) \rangle = d_k - \sum_{q \in I_{sv}} \alpha_q^* d_q K(x_q, x_k).$$

The optimal discriminant function is thus given by

$$f*(x) = \sum_{q \in I_{sv}} \alpha_q^* d_q \langle \phi(x_q), \phi(x) \rangle + b* = \sum_{q \in I_{sv}} \alpha_q^* d_q K(x_q, x) + b*.$$

It is interesting to note that it is not necessary to calculate any features to form the final discriminant function. Kernel is just good enough. Moreover, the margin (in the feature space) is given by

$$\gamma_S = \|w*\|^{-1} = \left(\sum_{q \in I_{sv}} \alpha_q^* \right)^{-1/2},$$

and the value of the problem (D0) is given by

$$J_d(\alpha*) = \frac{1}{2} \sum_{q \in I_{sv}} \alpha_q^*.$$

It is interesting to note that if one uses Gaussian kernels, there is no need for equality constraint $\sum_{q=1}^{l} \alpha_q d_q = 0$ because Gaussian basis functions do not necessarily require bias term.

Now, we discuss the stopping criteria for any algorithm of finding the maximal margin classifier. Suppose α_q, $q \in \underline{l}$, is the current value of the dual variable. The current primal variables and discriminant function can thus be calculated. We may define p_q, $q \in \underline{l}$, to be the measure of dissatisfaction of the KKT stopping conditions for the qth example as

$$p_q := \max\left[0, 1 - d_q f(x_q)\right] \text{ if } \alpha_q = 0,$$
$$p_q := \left|d_q f(x_q) - 1\right| \text{ if } \alpha_q > 0.$$

Then, reasonable stopping criteria based on KKT stopping conditions are

$$P_{ave} := \frac{1}{l}\sum_{q=1}^{l} p_q \leq \delta \text{ or } \|p\|_\infty := \max_{q \in \underline{l}}\{p_q\} \leq \delta,$$

where δ is a pre-specified tolerance.

As has been pointed out that it may not be possible to calculate the feasibility gap as an indicator of the stopping criterion, since the corresponding primal variables may not be feasible.

Next, we consider the construction of the 1-norm soft margin classifier in the feature space. Consider the following quadratic optimization problem:

(D1)   maximize $\sum_{q=1}^{l}\alpha_q - \frac{1}{2}\sum_{q=1}^{l}\sum_{j=1}^{l}\alpha_q\alpha_j d_q d_j \langle \phi(x_q), \phi(x_j)\rangle$

$$= \sum_{q=1}^{l}\alpha_q - \frac{1}{2}\sum_{q=1}^{l}\sum_{j=1}^{l}\alpha_q\alpha_j d_q d_j K(x_q, x_j)$$

subject to $\sum_{q=1}^{l}\alpha_q d_q = 0 \text{ and } 0 \leq \alpha_q \leq C \text{ for all } q \in \underline{l}.$

Notice that as C becomes large, problem (D1) is close to problem (D0).

Suppose α^* solves   the   problem   (D1).   Define $I_{sv} := \{q \in \underline{l} : \alpha_q^* > 0\}$. Then we have

$$w^* = \sum_{q=1}^{l} \alpha_q^* d_q \phi(x_q) = \sum_{q \in I_{sv}} \alpha_q^* d_q \phi(x_q).$$

Choose any $k \in I_{sv}$ such that $0 < \alpha_k^* < C$. Then we have

$$b^* = d_k - \sum_{q \in I_{sv}} \alpha_q^* d_q \langle \phi(x_q), \phi(x_k) \rangle = d_k - \sum_{q \in I_{sv}} \alpha_q^* d_q K(x_q, x_k).$$

The optimal discriminant function is thus given by

$$f^*(x) = \sum_{q \in I_{sv}} \alpha_q^* d_q \langle \phi(x_q), \phi(x) \rangle + b^* = \sum_{q \in I_{sv}} \alpha_q^* d_q K(x_q, x) + b^*.$$

Moreover, the margin (in the feature space) is given by

$$\gamma_S = \|w^*\|^{-1} = \left[\sum_{q,j \in I_{sv}} \alpha_q^* \alpha_j^* d_q d_j K(x_q, x_j) \right]^{-1/2}$$

$$= \left[2 \sum_{q \in I_{sv}} \alpha_q^* - 2 J_d(\alpha^*) \right]^{-1/2}.$$

Note that the curse of dimensionality for the nonlinear classification problem is bypassed by focusing on the dual problem for performing the constrained optimization problem.

Now, we discuss the stopping criteria for any algorithm of finding the 1-norm soft margin classifier. Suppose α_q, $q \in \underline{l}$, is the current value of the dual variable. The current primal variables and discriminant function can thus be calculated. We may define p_q, $q \in \underline{l}$, to be the measure of dissatisfaction of the KKT stopping conditions for the qth example as

$$p_q := \max\left[0, 1 - d_q f(x_q)\right] \text{ if } \alpha_q = 0,$$
$$p_q := \left| d_q f(x_q) - 1 \right| \text{ if } 0 < \alpha_q < C,$$
$$p_q := \max\left[0, d_q f(x_q) - 1\right] \text{ if } \alpha_q = C.$$

Then, reasonable stopping criteria based on KKT stopping conditions are

$$P_{ave} := \frac{1}{l}\sum_{q=1}^{l} p_q \leq \delta \quad \text{or} \quad \|p\|_{\infty} := \max_{q \in \underline{l}}\{p_q\} \leq \delta,$$

where δ is a pre-specified tolerance.

Let α_q, $q \in \underline{l}$, be the current value of the dual variable. Define the current slack variable as

$$\xi_q := \max\left(0, 1 - d_q \cdot \left[\sum_{j=1}^{l} d_j \alpha_j \langle \phi(x_j), \phi(x_q)\rangle + b\right]\right)$$

$$= \max\left(0, 1 - d_q \cdot \left[\sum_{j=1}^{l} d_j \alpha_j K(x_j, x_q) + b\right]\right)$$

$$= \max\left[0, 1 - d_q \cdot f(x_q)\right].$$

Then a reasonable stopping criterion based on feasibility gap is given by

$$\frac{J_p - J_d}{J_p + 1} = \frac{\sum_{q=1}^{l}\alpha_q - 2J_d(\alpha) + C\sum_{q=1}^{l}\xi_q}{\sum_{q=1}^{l}\alpha_q - J_d(\alpha) + C\sum_{q=1}^{l}\xi_q + 1} \leq \delta,$$

where δ is a pre-specified tolerance.

Finally, we consider the construction of the 2-norm soft margin classifier in the feature space. Consider the following quadratic optimization problem:

(D2)   maximize

$$\sum_{q=1}^{l}\alpha_q - \frac{1}{2}\sum_{q=1}^{l}\sum_{j=1}^{l}\alpha_q \alpha_j d_q d_j \langle \phi(x_q), \phi(x_j)\rangle$$

$$- \frac{1}{2C}\sum_{q=1}^{l}\alpha_q^2$$

$$= \sum_{q=1}^{l} \alpha_q - \frac{1}{2} \sum_{q=1}^{l} \sum_{j=1}^{l} \alpha_q \alpha_j d_q d_j K(x_q, x_j) - \frac{1}{2C} \sum_{q=1}^{l} \alpha_q^2$$

subject to

$$\sum_{q=1}^{l} \alpha_q d_q = 0 \quad \text{and} \quad \alpha_q \geq 0 \quad \text{for all} \quad q \in \underline{l}.$$

Notice that as C becomes large, problem (D2) is close to problem (D0).

Suppose $\alpha *$ solves the problem (D2). Define $I_{sv} := \{q \in \underline{l} : \alpha_q^* > 0\}.$ Then we have

$$w* = \sum_{q=1}^{l} \alpha_q^* d_q \phi(x_q) = \sum_{q \in I_{sv}} \alpha_q^* d_q \phi(x_q).$$

Choose any $\alpha_k^* > 0$, then we have

$$b* = d_k \left(1 - C^{-1} \alpha_k^*\right) - \sum_{q \in I_{sv}} \alpha_q^* d_q \left\langle \phi(x_q), \phi(x_k) \right\rangle$$
$$= d_k \left(1 - C^{-1} \alpha_k^*\right) - \sum_{q \in I_{sv}} \alpha_q^* d_q K(x_q, x_k).$$

The optimal discriminant function is thus given by

$$f*(x) = \sum_{q \in I_{sv}} \alpha_q^* d_q \left\langle \phi(x_q), \phi(x) \right\rangle + b* = \sum_{q \in I_{sv}} \alpha_q^* d_q K(x_q, x) + b*.$$

Moreover, the margin (in the feature space) is given by

$$\gamma_S = \|w*\|^{-1} = \left[\sum_{q \in I_{sv}} \alpha_q^* - C^{-1} \sum_{q \in I_{sv}} (\alpha_q^*)^2 \right]^{-1/2},$$

and the value of the problem (D2) is given by

$$J_d(\alpha^*) = \frac{1}{2}\sum_{q \in I_{sv}} \alpha_q^* .$$

Now we discuss the stopping criteria for any algorithm of finding the 2-norm soft margin classifier. Suppose α_q, $q \in \underline{l}$, is the current value of the dual variable. The current primal variables and discriminant function can thus be calculated. We may define p_q, $q \in \underline{l}$, to be the measure of dissatisfaction of the KKT stopping conditions for the qth example as

$$p_q := \max[0, 1 - d_q f(x_q)] \text{ if } \alpha_q = 0,$$
$$p_q := |1 - d_q f(x_q) - C^{-1}\alpha_q| \text{ if } \alpha_q > 0.$$

Then, reasonable stopping criteria based on KKT stopping conditions are

$$p_{ave} := \frac{1}{l}\sum_{q=1}^{l} p_q \le \delta \text{ or } \|p\|_\infty := \max_{q \in \underline{l}}\{p_q\} \le \delta,$$

where δ is a pre-specified tolerance.

As has been pointed out that it may not be possible to calculate the feasibility gap as an indicator of the stopping criterion, since the corresponding primal variables may not be feasible.

The kernel-based support vector classifier (SVC) can be represented as a multi-layer feed-forward network with a single hidden layer and with nonlinear activation functions as shown in Figure 6.3.1. The number of hidden neurons is equal to the number of support vectors, which is automatically determined by the support vector machine under consideration. From Figure 6.3.1, it is clear that the SVM, just like other learning machines, nonlinearly transform in a peculiar way the input vectors to a feature space and perform the linear classification or regression in the feature space to produce the output vectors. This is consistent with the third strategy mentioned in Section 3.5 for nonlinear classification.

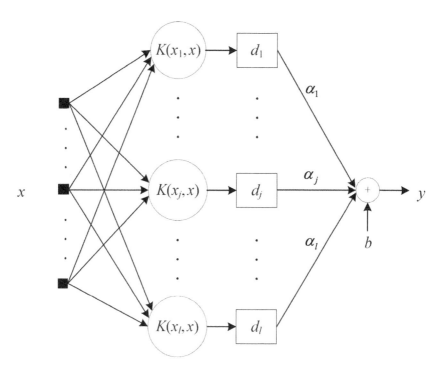

Figure 6.3.1: SVC represented as a multi-layer feed-forward network.

6.4 Kernel-based Support Vector Regressor

Let $X \subseteq \mathfrak{R}^n$ and $Y \subseteq \mathfrak{R}$. Suppose we are given the training set

$$S := \left\{ (x_q, d_q) \right\}_{q=1}^l \subseteq X \times Y.$$

Let $K(x, z)$ be a given kernel on $X \times X$ such that

$$K(x, z) := \langle \phi(x), \phi(z) \rangle, \quad x, z \in X,$$

where ϕ is the feature map from the input space X to the feature space F.

First, we consider the construction of the ridge regressor in the feature space. Consider the following quadratic optimization problem:

(D0)   maximize $\displaystyle \sum_{q=1}^l \alpha_q d_q - \frac{1}{2} \sum_{q=1}^l \sum_{j=1}^l \alpha_q \alpha_j K(x_q, x_j) - \frac{1}{2C} \sum_{q=1}^l \alpha_q^2$

subject to $\displaystyle\sum_{q=1}^{l}\alpha_q = 0$.

Suppose $\alpha *$ solves the problem (D0). Define $I_{sv} := \{q \in \underline{l} : \alpha_q^* \neq 0\}$. Then we have

$$w^* = \sum_{q=1}^{l}\alpha_q^*\phi(x_q) = \sum_{q \in I_{sv}}\alpha_q^*\phi(x_q).$$

Given any $k \in \underline{l}$, we have

$$b^* = d_k - C^{-1}\alpha_k^* - \sum_{q \in I_{sv}}\alpha_q^*\langle\phi(x_q), \phi(x_k)\rangle$$

$$= d_k - C^{-1}\alpha_k^* - \sum_{q \in I_{sv}}\alpha_q^*K(x_q, x_k).$$

The optimal predictive function is thus given by

$$f*(x) = \sum_{q \in I_{sv}}\alpha_q^*\langle\phi(x_q), \phi(x)\rangle + b^* = \sum_{q \in I_{sv}}\alpha_q^*K(x_q, x) + b*.$$

The stopping criterion is met if there are no significant improvements in consecutive values of the payoff over some pre-specified iterations.

It is interesting to note that it is not necessary to calculate any features to form the final predictive function. Kernel is just good enough.

As has been pointed out that it may not be possible to calculate the feasibility gap as an indicator of the stopping criterion, since the corresponding primal variables may not be feasible.

Next, we consider the construction of the 1-norm soft regressor in the feature space. Consider the following quadratic optimization problem:

(D1)   maximize

$$\sum_{q=1}^{l}(\alpha_q - \beta_q)d_q - \varepsilon\sum_{q=1}^{l}(\alpha_q + \beta_q)$$

$$-\frac{1}{2}\sum_{q=1}^{l}\sum_{j=1}^{l}(\alpha_q - \beta_q)(\alpha_j - \beta_j)K(x_q, x_j)$$

subject to

$$\sum_{q=1}^{l}(\alpha_q - \beta_q) = 0, \ \ 0 \le \alpha_q \le C, \ \ 0 \le \beta_q \le C, \ \ q \in \underline{l}.$$

Suppose $(\alpha*, \beta*)$ solves the dual problem (D1). Then we have

$$w* = \sum_{q=1}^{l}(\alpha_q^* - \beta_q^*)\phi(x_q).$$

Choose any $0 < \alpha_k^* < C$. Then we have

$$b* = d_k - \varepsilon - \sum_{q=1}^{l}(\alpha_q^* - \beta_q^*)\langle\phi(x_q), \phi(x_k)\rangle$$

$$= d_k - \varepsilon - \sum_{q=1}^{l}(\alpha_q^* - \beta_q^*)K(x_q, x_k).$$

Or, one may choose $0 < \beta_k^* < C$. Then we have

$$b* = d_k + \varepsilon - \sum_{q=1}^{l}(\alpha_q^* - \beta_q^*)\langle\phi(x_q), \phi(x_k)\rangle$$

$$= d_k + \varepsilon - \sum_{q=1}^{l}(\alpha_q^* - \beta_q^*)K(x_q, x_k).$$

Then, the optimal predictive function is given by

$$f*(x) = \sum_{q=1}^{l}(\alpha_q^* - \beta_q^*)\langle\phi(x_q), \phi(x)\rangle + b*$$

$$= \sum_{q=1}^{l}(\alpha_q^* - \beta_q^*)K(x_q, x) + b*.$$

Now, we discuss the stopping criteria for any algorithm of finding the 1-norm soft regressor. Suppose α_q, β_q, $q \in \underline{l}$, are the current values of the dual variables. The current primal variables and predictive function can thus be calculated. We may define p_q, $q \in \underline{l}$, to be the measure of dissatisfaction of the KKT stopping conditions for the qth example as

$$p_q := \max\left[0, d_q - f(x_q) + \varepsilon\right] \text{ if } \alpha_q - \beta_q = -C,$$
$$p_q := \left|d_q - f(x_q) + \varepsilon\right| \text{ if } -C < \alpha_q - \beta_q < 0,$$
$$p_q := \max\left[0, \left|d_q - f(x_q)\right| - \varepsilon\right] \text{ if } \alpha_q - \beta_q = 0,$$
$$p_q := \left|d_q - f(x_q) - \varepsilon\right| \text{ if } 0 < \alpha_q - \beta_q < C,$$
$$p_q := \max\left[0, f(x_q) - d_q + \varepsilon\right] \text{ if } \alpha_q - \beta_q = C.$$

Then, reasonable stopping criteria based on KKT stopping conditions are

$$p_{ave} := \frac{1}{l}\sum_{q=1}^{l} p_q \leq \delta \text{ or } \|p\|_\infty := \max_{q \in \underline{l}}\{p_q\} \leq \delta,$$

where δ is a pre-specified tolerance.

Let α_q, β_q, $q \in \underline{l}$, be the current values of the dual variables. Define the slack variables as, $q \in \underline{l}$,

$$\xi_q := \max\left(0, d_q - \left[\sum_{j=1}^{l}(\alpha_j - \beta_j)K(x_j, x_q) + b\right] - \varepsilon\right)$$
$$= \max\left[0, d_q - f(x_q) - \varepsilon\right],$$

$$\eta_q := \max\left(0, \left[\sum_{j=1}^{l}(\alpha_j - \beta_j)K(x_j, x_q) + b\right] - d_q - \varepsilon\right)$$
$$= \max\left[0, f(x_q) - d_q - \varepsilon\right].$$

Then, a reasonable stopping criterion based on percentage feasibility gap is given by

$$\frac{J_p - J_d}{J_p + 1}$$

$$= \frac{\sum_{q=1}^{l}(\alpha_q - \beta_q)d_q - \varepsilon\sum_{q=1}^{l}(\alpha_q + \beta_q) - 2J_d(\alpha, \beta) + C\sum_{q=1}^{l}(\xi_q + \eta_q)}{\sum_{q=1}^{l}(\alpha_q - \beta_q)d_q - \varepsilon\sum_{q=1}^{l}(\alpha_q + \beta_q) - J_d(\alpha, \beta) + C\sum_{q=1}^{l}(\xi_q + \eta_q) + 1} \leq \delta,$$

where δ is a pre-specified tolerance.

We may also consider the following quadratic optimization problem:

(D1')   maximize $\displaystyle\sum_{q=1}^{l}\theta_q d_q - \varepsilon\sum_{q=1}^{l}|\theta_q| - \frac{1}{2}\sum_{q=1}^{l}\sum_{j=1}^{l}\theta_q\theta_j K(x_q, x_j)$

            subject to $\displaystyle\sum_{q=1}^{l}\theta_q = 0, \quad -C \leq \theta_q \leq C, \quad q \in \underline{l}.$

Suppose $\theta*$ solves the problem (D1'). Define $I_{sv} := \{q \in \underline{l} : \theta_q^* \neq 0\}$. Then we have

$$w* = \sum_{q=1}^{l}\theta_q^*\phi(x_q) = \sum_{q \in I_{sv}}\theta_q^*\phi(x_q).$$

Choose any $0 < \theta_k^* < C$. Then we have

$$b* = d_k - \varepsilon - \sum_{q \in I_{sv}}\theta_q^*\langle\phi(x_q), \phi(x_k)\rangle = d_k - \varepsilon - \sum_{q \in I_{sv}}\theta_q^* K(x_q, x_k).$$

Or, we may choose $-C < \theta_k^* < 0$. Then we have

$$b* = d_k + \varepsilon - \sum_{q \in I_{sv}}\theta_q^*\langle\phi(x_q), \phi(x_k)\rangle = d_k + \varepsilon - \sum_{q \in I_{sv}}\theta_q^* K(x_q, x_k).$$

The optimal predictive function is thus given by

$$f*(x) = \sum_{q \in I_{sv}}\theta_q^*\langle\phi(x_q), \phi(x)\rangle + b* = \sum_{q \in I_{sv}}\theta_q^* K(x_q, x) + b*.$$

Now, we discuss the stopping criteria for any algorithm of finding the 1-norm soft regressor. Suppose θ_q, $q \in \underline{l}$, is the current value of the dual variable. The current primal variables and predictive function can thus be calculated. We may define p_q, $q \in \underline{l}$, to be the measure of dissatisfaction of the KKT stopping conditions for the qth example as

$$p_q := \max\left[0, d_q - f(x_q) + \varepsilon\right] \text{ if } \theta_q = -C,$$
$$p_q := \left|d_q - f(x_q) + \varepsilon\right| \text{ if } -C < \theta_q < 0,$$
$$p_q := \max\left[0, \left|d_q - f(x_q)\right| - \varepsilon\right] \text{ if } \theta_q = 0,$$
$$p_q := \left|d_q - f(x_q) - \varepsilon\right| \text{ if } 0 < \theta_q < C,$$
$$p_q := \max\left[0, f(x_q) - d_q + \varepsilon\right] \text{ if } \theta_q = C.$$

Then, reasonable stopping criteria based on KKT stopping conditions are

$$p_{ave} := \frac{1}{l}\sum_{q=1}^{l} p_q \leq \delta \text{ or } \|p\|_{\infty} := \max_{q \in \underline{l}}\{p_q\} \leq \delta,$$

where δ is a pre-specified tolerance.

Let θ_q, $q \in \underline{l}$, be the current value of the dual variable. Define the slack variables as, $q \in \underline{l}$,

$$\xi_q := \max\left(0, d_q - \left[\sum_{j=1}^{l}\theta_j\langle\phi(x_j), \phi(x_q)\rangle + b\right] - \varepsilon\right)$$
$$= \max\left(0, d_q - \left[\sum_{j=1}^{l}\theta_j K(x_j, x_q) + b\right] - \varepsilon\right)$$
$$= \max\left[0, d_q - f(x_q) - \varepsilon\right],$$

$$\eta_q := \max\left(0, \left[\sum_{j=1}^{l}\theta_j\langle\phi(x_j), \phi(x_q)\rangle + b\right] - d_q - \varepsilon\right)$$
$$= \max\left(0, \left[\sum_{j=1}^{l}\theta_j K(x_j, x_q) + b\right] - d_q - \varepsilon\right)$$

$$= \max\left[0, \, f(x_q) - d_q - \varepsilon\right].$$

Then, a reasonable stopping criterion based on feasibility gap is given by

$$\frac{J_p - J_d}{J_p + 1} = \frac{\sum\limits_{q=1}^{l}\theta_q d_q - \varepsilon\sum\limits_{q=1}^{l}|\theta_q| - 2J_d(\theta) + C\sum\limits_{q=1}^{l}(\xi_q + \eta_q)}{\sum\limits_{q=1}^{l}\theta_q d_q - \varepsilon\sum\limits_{q=1}^{l}|\theta_q| - J_d(\theta) + C\sum\limits_{q=1}^{l}(\xi_q + \eta_q) + 1} \le \delta,$$

where δ is a pre-specified tolerance.

Finally, we consider the construction of the 2-norm soft regressor in the feature space. Consider the following quadratic optimization problem:

(D2)   maximize

$$\sum_{q=1}^{l}(\alpha_q - \beta_q)d_q - \varepsilon\sum_{q=1}^{l}(\alpha_q + \beta_q)$$

$$-\frac{1}{2}\sum_{q=1}^{l}\sum_{j=1}^{l}(\alpha_q - \beta_q)(\alpha_j - \beta_j)K(x_q, x_j)$$

$$-\frac{1}{2C}\sum_{q=1}^{l}(\alpha_q^2 + \beta_q^2)$$

subject to

$$\sum_{q=1}^{l}(\alpha_q - \beta_q) = 0, \quad \alpha_q \ge 0, \quad \beta_q \ge 0, \text{ for all } q \in \underline{l}.$$

Suppose $(\alpha*, \beta*)$ solves the dual problem (D2). Then we have

$$w* = \sum_{q=1}^{l}(\alpha_q^* - \beta_q^*)\phi(x_q).$$

Choose any $\alpha_k^* > 0$. Then we have

$$b* = d_k - \varepsilon - C^{-1}\alpha_k^* - \sum_{q=1}^{l}\left(\alpha_q^* - \beta_q^*\right)\!\left\langle\phi(x_q), \phi(x_k)\right\rangle$$

$$= d_k - \varepsilon - C^{-1}\alpha_k^* - \sum_{q=1}^{l}\left(\alpha_q^* - \beta_q^*\right)K\!\left(x_q, x_k\right).$$

Or, one may choose $\beta_k^* > 0$. Then we have

$$b* = d_k + \varepsilon + C^{-1}\beta_k^* - \sum_{q=1}^{l}\left(\alpha_q^* - \beta_q^*\right)\!\left\langle\phi(x_q), \phi(x_k)\right\rangle$$

$$= d_k + \varepsilon + C^{-1}\beta_k^* - \sum_{q=1}^{l}\left(\alpha_q^* - \beta_q^*\right)K\!\left(x_q, x_k\right).$$

Then, the optimal predictive function is given by

$$f*(x) = \sum_{q=1}^{l}\left(\alpha_q^* - \beta_q^*\right)\!\left\langle\phi(x_q), \phi(x)\right\rangle + b*$$

$$= \sum_{q=1}^{l}\left(\alpha_q^* - \beta_q^*\right)K\!\left(x_q, x\right) + b*.$$

Now, we discuss the stopping criteria for any algorithm of finding the 2-norm soft regressor. Suppose α_q, β_q, $q \in \underline{l}$, are the current values of the dual variables. The current primal variables and predictive function can thus be calculated. We may define p_q, $q \in \underline{l}$, to be the measure of dissatisfaction of the KKT stopping conditions for the qth example as

$$p_q := \max\!\left[0, \left|f(x_q) - d_q\right| - \varepsilon\right] \text{ if } \alpha_q - \beta_q = 0,$$
$$p_q := \left|f(x_q) - d_q + \varepsilon + C^{-1}\left(\alpha_q - \beta_q\right)\right| \text{ if } \alpha_q - \beta_q > 0,$$
$$p_q := \left|f(x_q) - d_q - \varepsilon + C^{-1}\left(\alpha_q - \beta_q\right)\right| \text{ if } \alpha_q - \beta_q < 0.$$

Then, reasonable stopping criteria based on KKT stopping conditions are

$$p_{ave} := \frac{1}{l}\sum_{q=1}^{l}p_q \leq \delta \text{ or } \|p\|_\infty := \max_{q \in \underline{l}}\{p_q\} \leq \delta,$$

where δ is a pre-specified tolerance.

As has been pointed out that it may not be possible to calculate the feasibility gap as an indicator of the stopping criterion, since the corresponding primal variables may not be feasible.

We may also consider the following quadratic optimization problem:

(D2')   maximize

$$\sum_{q=1}^{l} \theta_q d_q - \varepsilon \sum_{q=1}^{l} |\theta_q| - \frac{1}{2} \sum_{q=1}^{l} \sum_{j=1}^{l} \theta_q \theta_j K(x_q, x_j) - \frac{1}{2C} \sum_{q=1}^{l} \theta_q^2$$

subject to

$$\sum_{q=1}^{l} \theta_q = 0, \quad q \in \underline{l}.$$

Notice that as C becomes large, problem (D2') is close to problem (D1').

Suppose $\theta *$ solves the problem (D2'). Define $I_{sv} := \{q \in \underline{l} : \theta_q^* \neq 0\}$. Then we have

$$w* = \sum_{q=1}^{l} \theta_q^* \phi(x_q) = \sum_{q \in I_{sv}} \theta_q^* \phi(x_q).$$

Given any $\theta_k^* > 0$, we have

$$b* = d_k - \varepsilon - C^{-1}\theta_k^* - \sum_{q \in I_{sv}} \theta_q^* \langle \phi(x_q), \phi(x_k) \rangle$$

$$= d_k - \varepsilon - C^{-1}\theta_k^* - \sum_{q \in I_{sv}} \theta_q^* K(x_q, x_k).$$

Or, given any $\theta_k^* < 0$, we have

$$b* = d_k + \varepsilon - C^{-1}\theta_k^* - \sum_{q \in I_{sv}} \theta_q^* \langle \phi(x_q), \phi(x_k) \rangle$$

$$= d_k + \varepsilon - C^{-1}\theta_k^* - \sum_{q \in I_{sv}} \theta_q^* K\left(x_q, x_k\right).$$

The optimal predictive function is thus given by

$$f^*(x) = \sum_{q \in I_{sv}} \theta_q^* \left\langle \phi(x_q), \phi(x) \right\rangle + b^* = \sum_{q \in I_{sv}} \theta_q^* K\left(x_q, x\right) + b^*.$$

Now, we discuss the stopping criteria for any algorithm of finding the 2-norm soft regressor. Suppose θ_q, $q \in \underline{l}$, is the current value of the dual variable. The current primal variables and predictive function can thus be calculated. We may define p_q, $q \in \underline{l}$, to be the measure of dissatisfaction of the KKT stopping conditions for the qth example as

$$p_q := \max\left[0, \left|f(x_q) - d_q\right| - \varepsilon\right] \text{ if } \theta_q = 0,$$
$$p_q := \left|f(x_q) - d_q + \varepsilon + C^{-1}\theta_q\right| \text{ if } \theta_q > 0,$$
$$p_q := \left|f(x_q) - d_q - \varepsilon + C^{-1}\theta_q\right| \text{ if } \theta_q < 0.$$

Then, reasonable stopping criteria based on KKT stopping conditions are

$$p_{ave} := \frac{1}{l}\sum_{q=1}^{l} p_q \le \delta \text{ or } \|p\|_\infty := \max_{q \in \underline{l}}\{p_q\} \le \delta,$$

where δ is a pre-specified tolerance.

As has been pointed out that it may not be possible to calculate the feasibility gap as an indicator of the stopping criterion, since the corresponding primal variables may not be feasible.

The kernel-based support vector regressor (SVR) can be represented as a multi-layer feed-forward network with a single hidden layer and with nonlinear activation functions as shown in Figure 6.4.1. The number of hidden neurons is equal to the number of support vectors, which is automatically determined by the support vector machine under consideration. From Figure 6.4.1, it is clear that the SVM, just like other learning machines, nonlinearly transform in a peculiar way the input vector to a feature space and perform linear classification or regression in

the feature space to produce the output vector.   This is consistent with the
third strategy mentioned in Section 4.4 for nonlinear regression.

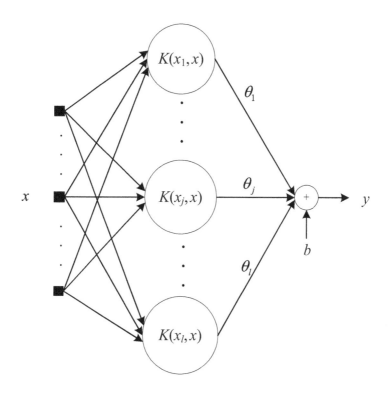

Figure 6.4.1: SVR represented as a multi-layer feed-forward network.

6.5 Multi-class Classification

A natural approach to a multi-class classification problem is to reduce
this *m*-class classification problem to several binary classification
problems.   Before doing this, let us reconsider the binary (i.e., two-class)
classification problems.

Let $X \subseteq \Re^n$ and $Y := \{1, -1\}$.   Suppose we are given the training
set

$$S := \{(x_q, d_q)\}_{q=1}^{l'} \subseteq X \times Y.$$

In the specification of the labels of the training data set, the labels of the examples in, say, class 1, have been chosen as 1, and those in class 2 as -1. Then we may obtain the following, say, 1-norm soft margin classifier

$$f_1(x) = \sum_{q=1}^{l} z_q^{(1)} d_q^{(1)} K(x_q, x) + b^{(1)},$$

where $K(x, x')$ is a given kernel on $X \times X$. If $x \in X$ is such that $f_1(x) > 0$, then it is assigned to class 1, otherwise to class 2. Usually, there is no ordering between the classes. Consequently, the same binary classification problem can also be approached by assigning 1 to the labels of examples in class 2 and -1 to those in class 1. Similarly, we may obtain the following 1-norm soft margin classifier

$$f_2(x) = \sum_{q=1}^{l} z_q^{(2)} d_q^{(2)} K(x_q, x) + b^{(2)}.$$

If $x \in X$ is such that $f_2(x) > 0$, then it is assigned to class 2, otherwise to class 1. Can the same binary classification problem be approached in a third way? To this end, we let

$$f_{dis}(x) := \max[f_1(x), f_2(x)], \quad x \in X.$$

If $x \in X$ belongs to class 1, then ideally $f_1(x) > 0$ but $f_2(x) < 0$. This implies that

$$f_{dis}(x) = \max[f_1(x), f_2(x)] = f_1(x).$$

Similarly, if $x \in X$ belongs to class 2, then ideally $f_1(x) < 0$ but $f_2(x) > 0$. This implies that

$$f_{dis}(x) = \max[f_1(x), f_2(x)] = f_2(x).$$

Naturally, we may assign x with the class j that has the maximum value between $f_1(x)$ and $f(x_2)$, i.e.,

$$j(x) = \arg\max\{f_1(x), f_2(x)\}.$$

It may seem redundant to the use of $f_{dis}(\cdot)$ in binary classification problems, but the approach can be generalized easily to multi-class classification problems.

Consider the multi-class classification problem where $Y := \underline{m} := \{1, 2, ..., m\}$. First, we introduce the **one-versus-rest (OVR)** method, which is a generalization of the procedure stated above for two-class classification problems. It is required to design m binary classifiers. For each $j \in \underline{m}$, we label all training examples having $d_q = j$ with 1 and $d_q \neq j$ with -1 during the training of the jth classifier. The final decision is to assign $x \in X$ with class j if

$$j(x) = \arg\max_{i=1}^{m} f_i(x).$$

Clearly, this method learns one classifier for each of the m classes against all the other cases and is hence known as the one-versus-rest method. It is a winner-takes-all approach. It is advisable to check whether the training data are on comparable scales or not. If not, some data pre-processing might be required. One drawback of this approach is that there might happen that several binary classifiers assign the pattern to their respective class.

Next, we introduce the **one-versus-one (OVO)** method for m-class classification problems. It is required to design $m(m-1)/2$ binary classifiers. If $1 \leq i < j \leq m$, the classifier f_{ij} is learned using only training samples from class i and class j, labeling them 1 and -1, respectively. Given a new point $x \in X$, the frequency n_i of "wins" (or "votes") for class i is computed by applying f_{ij} for all $j \neq i$. The final decision is to assign x with the most frequent class, i.e.,

$$j(x) = \arg\max_{i=1}^{m} n_i(x).$$

The multi-class classification problems can also be addressed without transforming them to a sequence of two-class classification problems. Suppose we have p classes. A pattern $x \in X \subseteq \mathfrak{R}^n$ will be assigned an output vector c_k if it belongs to class k, where c_k, $k \in \underline{p}$, are defined by

$$c_1 := \begin{bmatrix} 1 & 0 & \ldots & 0 & 0 \end{bmatrix}^T,$$
$$c_2 := \begin{bmatrix} 0 & 1 & 0 & \ldots & 0 \end{bmatrix}^T,$$
$$\ldots,$$
$$c_p := \begin{bmatrix} 0 & 0 & \ldots & 0 & 1 \end{bmatrix}^T,$$

or

$$c_1 := \begin{bmatrix} 1 & -1 & \ldots & -1 & -1 \end{bmatrix}^T,$$
$$c_2 := \begin{bmatrix} -1 & 1 & -1 & \ldots & -1 \end{bmatrix}^T,$$
$$\ldots,$$
$$c_p := \begin{bmatrix} -1 & -1 & \ldots & -1 & 1 \end{bmatrix}^T.$$

This is usually called the one-hot encoding.

For p-class classification problems, the categorical cross-entropy (a multi-class logarithmic loss) is a suitable objective function to be minimized. Consider the artificial neural network shown in Figure 5.2.1 with "softmax" activation function, then

$$y_{qk} = \frac{\exp(s_{qk})}{\sum_{b=1}^{p} \exp(s_{qb})}, \quad q \in \underline{l}, \ k \in \underline{p}.$$

Here, y_{qk}, $0 < y_{qk} < 1$, is the estimated probability of x_q belonging to the kth class.

If the output labels were coded as 0 or 1 (as in the one-hot encoding above), then the categorical cross-entropy is given by

$$J_{cce} := -\sum_{q=1}^{l} \sum_{k=1}^{p} \left[d_{qk} \log(y_{qk}) \right].$$

Note that if x_q belongs to the $\tilde{k}$ class, $\tilde{k} \in \underline{p}$, then $d_{q\tilde{k}} = 1$ and $d_{qk} = 0$ for all $k \neq \tilde{k}$. This implies that

$$\sum_{k=1}^{p}\left[d_{qk}\log\left(y_{qk}\right)\right]=\log\left(y_{q\tilde{k}}\right).$$

If $y_{qk}\approx d_{qk}$ for all q and k, then $J_{cce}\approx 0$.

Suppose in the binary classification problems, we use the "softmax" function as the output activation function. Then we have

$$y_1=\frac{\exp(s_1)}{\exp(s_1)+\exp(s_2)}, \quad y_2=\frac{\exp(s_2)}{\exp(s_1)+\exp(s_2)}.$$

Consequently, we have

$$y_1=\frac{1}{1+\exp(s_2-s_1)}=\frac{1}{1+\exp[-(s_1-s_2)]},$$

which is in the form of a unipolar logistic function and $y_2=1-y_1$. This says that in the binary classification problems, it is sufficient to use only the unipolar logistic function as the output activation function.

If the output labels were coded as -1 or 1 (as in the one-hot encoding above), then the categorical cross-entropy function is given by, using the linear transformation $z_2=0.5+0.5z_1$,

$$J_{cce}:=-\sum_{q=1}^{l}\sum_{k=1}^{p}\left[\left(0.5+0.5d_{qk}\right)\log\left(y_{qk}\right)\right].$$

Similarly, if x_q belongs to the $\tilde{k}$ class, $\tilde{k}\in \underline{p}$, then $d_{q\tilde{k}}=1$ and $d_{qk}=-1$ for all $k\neq \tilde{k}$. This implies that

$$\sum_{k=1}^{p}\left[\left(0.5+0.5d_{qk}\right)\log\left(y_{qk}\right)\right]=\log\left(y_{q\tilde{k}}\right).$$

Let $S:=\left\{\left(x_q,c_q\right)\right\}_{q=1}^{l}$ be the training set. The learning machine we choose is then trained by using this training set. For any $x\in X$, there are p output values $y_1(x)$, $y_2(x)$, ..., $y_p(x)$ generated by the trained learning machine. We then assign x with the class j that has the maximum value among those p output values, i.e.,

$$\tilde{k}(x) = \underset{k}{\text{argmax}}\{y_k(x)\}.$$

In terms of the multi-layer representation of a learning machine, this amounts to adding a maximum selector to the outputs of the network.

6.6 Exercises

Exercise 6.6.1: Suppose $X \subseteq \mathfrak{R}^n$ and $K(x, z)$ is a kernel on $X \times X$. Prove that

(a) $K(x, x) \geq 0$, $x \in X$;
(b) $K(x, z) = K(z, x)$ for all $x, z \in X$;
(c) $K(x, z)^2 \leq K(x, x)K(z, z)$ for all $x, z \in X$.

Exercise 6.6.2: Let $X \subseteq \mathfrak{R}^n$ and assume $K(x, z)$ is a symmetric function on $X \times X$ such that for any finite set $M := \{x_1, ..., x_m\} \subseteq X$, $m < \infty$, the corresponding matrix $A := \left[K(x_i, x_j)\right]_{i, j=1}^{m}$ is positive semi-definite. Prove that

(a) $K(x, x) \geq 0$, $x \in X$;
(b) $K(x, z) = K(z, x)$ for all $x, z \in X$;
(c) $K(x, z)^2 \leq K(x, x)K(z, z)$ for all $x, z \in X$.

Exercise 6.6.3: State the kernel-based 1-norm υ-soft margin classifier of Exercise 3.11.7.

Exercise 6.6.4: State the kernel-based 2-norm υ-soft margin classifier of Exercise 3.11.8.

Exercise 6.6.5: State the kernel-based 1-norm υ-soft regressor of Exercise 4.12.9.

Exercise 6.6.6: State the kernel-based 2-norm υ-soft regressor of Exercise 4.12.10.

Exercise 6.6.7: Consider the multi-class classification problem.

(a) Is it possible to propose a two-versus-rest method? If yes, how many binary classifiers are required?
(b) Is it possible to propose a two-versus-two method? If yes, how many binary classifiers are required?

Exercise 6.6.8: Let $S := \left\{ \left(x_q, d_q \right) \right\}_{q=1}^{\mathsf{y}} \subseteq X \times Y$, where $X \subseteq \mathfrak{R}^n$ and $Y \subseteq \mathfrak{R}$, be the training set and $K(x,z)$ be a given kernel on $X \times X$. Suppose the predictive function is given by

$$f(x) = \sum_{q=1}^{l} z_q K\left(x_q, x \right) + b.$$

Suppose we choose the kernel as the standard inner product in $\mathfrak{R}^n$, resulting a linear predictive function

$$f(x) = \langle w, x \rangle + b, \quad x_i, w_i, b \in \mathfrak{R},$$
$$x := \begin{bmatrix} x_1 & \cdots & x_n \end{bmatrix}^T, \quad w := \begin{bmatrix} w_1 & \cdots & w_n \end{bmatrix}^T \in \mathfrak{R}^n.$$

Find the relationship between z_q, $q \in \underline{l}$, and w_i, $i \in \underline{n}$.

Exercise 6.6.9: Consider a multi-class classification problem with the objective function given by categorical cross-entropy. Derive the updating formulas for w_{jk} and v_{ij} in an artificial neural network if the output labels were coded as 0 or 1.

(a) Derive the updating formulas for w_{jk} and v_{ij} in an artificial neural network if the output labels were coded as 0 or 1.

(b) Derive the updating formulas for w_{jk} and v_{ij} in an artificial neural network if the output labels were coded as -1 or 1.

6.7 Notes and References

For original paper of Mercer's theorem, see Mercer (1909). It can also be found in Cristianini and Shawe-Taylor (2000), Haykin (1999), Herbrich (2002), and Schölkopf and Smola (2002). Example 6.1.1 was quoted from Cristianini and Shawe-Taylor (2000). Proposition 6.1.1 was quoted from Schölkopf and Smola (2002). Proposition 6.1.3 was quoted from Herbrich (2002).

The support vector machine (SVM) was invented by Boser, Guyon and Vapnik, and first introduced in 1992 at the Computational Learning Theory conference where they presented their paper. For original papers, see Boser, Guyon and Vapnik (1992) and Cortes and Vapnik (1995). This learning method is based on the structural risk minimization principle rooted in statistical learning theory and is a powerful technique for nonlinear regression or pattern recognition. Other topics on support vector machines can be found in Vapnik and Chervonenkis (1971), Vapnik (1982), Vapnik (1998), and Vapnik (2000). Cristianini and Shawe-Taylor (2000), Herbrich (2002), and Schölkopf and Smola (2002) are pretty good textbooks for the study of support vector machines. Our development on kernel-based nonlinear classification and regression was based on Cristianini and Shawe-Taylor (2000), Haykin (1999), and Kecman (2001). The development of multi-class classification was based on Cristianini and Shawe-Taylor (2000), Herbrich (2002), and Schölkopf and Smola (2002).

Boser, B.E., I.M. Guyon, and V.N. Vapnik (1992). A training algorithm for optimal margin classifiers. In D. Haussler (Ed.), Proceedings of the Fifth Annual ACM Workshop on Computational Learning Theory. ACM Press, Pittsburgh, Pennsylvania, pp. 144-152.

Cortes, C. and V.N. Vapnik (1995). Support vector networks. Machine Learning, Vol. 20, pp. 273-297.

Cristianini, N. and J. Shawe-Taylor (2000). An Introduction to Support Vector Machines. Cambridge University Press, Cambridge, United Kingdom.

Haykin, S. (1999). Neural Networks. Second Edition. Prentice-Hall, New Jersey.

Herbrich, R. (2002). Learning Kernel Classifiers: Theory and Algorithms. MIT Press, Cambridge, Massachusetts.

Kailath, T. (1980). Linear Systems. Prentice-Hall, New Jersey.

Kecman, V. (2001). Learning and Soft Computing. MIT Press, Cambridge, Massachusetts.

Mercer, J. (1909). Functions of positive and negative type and their connection with the theory of integral equations. Philosophical Transactions of the Royal Society, London, A 209, pp. 415-446.

Royden, H. L. (1989). Real Analysis. Third Edition. Macmillan, New York.

Schölkopf, B. and A.J. Smola (2002). Learning with Kernels: Support Vector Machines, Regularization, and Beyond. MIT Press, Cambridge, Massachusetts.

Vapnik, V.N. and A.Y. Chervonenkis (1971). On the uniform convergence of relative frequencies of events to their probabilities. Theory of Probability and its Applications, Vol. 16, No. 2, pp. 264-281.

Vapnik, V.N. (1982). Estimation of Dependences Based on Empirical Data. Springer, Berlin, Germany.

Vapnik, V.N. (1998). Statistical Learning Theory. Wiley, New York.

Vapnik, V.N. (2000). The Nature of Statistical Learning Theory. Second Edition. Springer, New York.

Chapter 7   Sequential Minimal Optimization Techniques

In this chapter, we introduce an elegant and powerful method, i.e., the sequential minimal optimization (SMO) technique, for solving the kernel-based machine learning optimization problems presented in Section 6.3 and Section 6.4. At each iteration of the algorithm, SMO jointly optimizes only two chosen parameters. This optimization is performed analytically, i.e., it admits an analytical solution, thus eliminating the need to include an iterative quadratic program optimizer as part of the algorithm. It is fast and is easy to implement. The two parameters are selected either heuristically or randomly. SMO algorithms for maximal margin classifiers and ridge regressors are derived in detail. For soft margin classifiers and soft regressors, we simply state the SMO algorithms without proof. They are left as exercises.

7.1 SMO for Maximal Margin Classifier

Let $X \subseteq \mathfrak{R}^n$ and $Y := \{1, -1\}$. Suppose we are given a non-trivial training set

$$S := \{(x_q, d_q)\}_{q=1}^{l} \subseteq X \times Y .$$

Let $K(x, z)$ be a given kernel on $X \times X$. Consider the following optimization problem for maximal margin classifier in the feature space when the training set S is linearly separable in the feature space:

(D0)   maximize $\sum_{q=1}^{l} z_q - \frac{1}{2}\sum_{q=1}^{l}\sum_{j=1}^{l} z_q z_j d_q d_j K(x_q, x_j)$

   subject to $\sum_{q=1}^{l} z_q d_q = 0$ and $z_q \geq 0$ for all $q \in \underline{l}$.

Suppose z_q, $q \in \underline{l}$, is the current value of the dual variable. Then the current discriminant function is given by

$$f(x) = \sum_{q=1}^{l} z_q d_q K(x_q, x) + b,$$

where

$$b = d_k - \sum_{q=1}^{l} z_q d_q K(x_q, x_k) \quad \text{for any} \quad z_k > 0.$$

In the SMO algorithm, suppose we choose z_1 and z_2 for maximizatiom with other variables unchanged. In order to compute the new values for these two variables, one can observe that in order not to violate the constraints, we must have

$$z_1 d_1 + z_2 d_2 = r = const = z_1^{old} d_1 + z_2^{old} d_2, \quad z_1 \geq 0, \quad z_2 \geq 0.$$

Without loss of generality, the SMO algorithm first computes z_2^{new} and then obtains z_1^{new}. Let

$$W(z_1, z_2) := \sum_{q=1}^{l} z_q - \frac{1}{2} \sum_{q=1}^{l} \sum_{j=1}^{l} z_q z_j d_q d_j k_{qj},$$

$$k_{qj} = K(x_q, x_j) = K(x_j, x_q) = k_{jq}.$$

Since

$$\sum_{q=1}^{l} \sum_{j=1}^{l} z_q z_j d_q d_j k_{qj}$$

$$= z_1 z_1 d_1 d_1 k_{11} + z_1 z_2 d_1 d_2 k_{12} + z_1 z_3 d_1 d_3 k_{13} + \ldots + z_1 z_l d_1 d_l k_{1l}$$
$$+ z_2 z_1 d_2 d_1 k_{21} + z_2 z_2 d_2 d_2 k_{22} + z_2 z_3 d_2 d_3 k_{23} + \ldots + z_2 z_l d_2 d_l k_{2l}$$
$$+ z_3 z_1 d_3 d_1 k_{31} + z_3 z_2 d_3 d_2 k_{32} + z_3 z_3 d_3 d_3 k_{33} + \ldots + z_3 z_l d_3 d_l k_{3l}$$
$$+ \ldots$$
$$+ z_l z_1 d_l d_1 k_{l1} + z_l z_2 d_l d_2 k_{l2} + z_l z_3 d_l d_3 k_{l3} + \ldots + z_l z_l d_l d_l k_{ll},$$

we have

$$W(z_1, z_2) = z_1 + z_2 - 2^{-1} k_{11} z_1^2 - 2^{-1} k_{22} z_2^2 - k_{12} d_1 d_2 z_1 z_2$$

$$- d_1 z_1 \sum_{j=3}^{l} z_j d_j k_{1j} - d_2 z_2 \sum_{j=3}^{l} z_j d_j k_{2j} + const.$$

Define

$$v_1 := \sum_{j=3}^{l} z_j d_j k_{1j}, \quad v_2 := \sum_{j=3}^{l} z_j d_j k_{2j}$$

$$\Rightarrow \quad W(z_1, z_2) = z_1 + z_2 - 2^{-1} k_{11} z_1^2 - 2^{-1} k_{22} z_2^2 - k_{12} d_1 d_2 z_1 z_2$$
$$- d_1 v_1 z_1 - d_2 v_2 z_2 + const.$$

Since $z_1 d_1 + z_2 d_2 = r = const = z_1^{old} d_1 + z_2^{old} d_2$, we have

$$z_1 + z_2 d_1 d_2 = d_1 r := g = const = z_1^{old} + z_2^{old} d_1 d_2,$$

i.e., $z_1 + s z_2 = g$, where $s := d_1 d_2$. Hence we have

$$z_1 = g - s z_2, \quad d_2 = s d_1, \quad d_1 = s d_2.$$

This implies that

$$W(z_2) = (g - s z_2) + z_2 - d_1 v_1 (g - s z_2) - d_2 v_2 z_2$$
$$- 2^{-1} k_{11} (g - s z_2)^2 - 2^{-1} k_{22} z_2^2 - k_{12} d_1 d_2 (g - s z_2) z_2 + const$$
$$= -2^{-1} (k_{11} s^2 + k_{22} - 2 k_{12} d_1 d_2 s) z_2^2$$
$$+ (-s + 1 + k_{11} g s - k_{12} d_1 d_2 g + d_1 v_1 s - d_2 v_2) z_2 + const$$
$$= -2^{-1} (k_{11} + k_{22} - 2 k_{12}) z_2^2$$
$$+ (-s + 1 + k_{11} g s - k_{12} g s + d_2 v_1 - d_2 v_2) z_2 + const$$
$$= -2^{-1} k z_2^2 + \beta z_2 + const,$$

where

$$k := k_{11} + k_{22} - 2 k_{12}, \quad \beta = -s + 1 + k_{11} g s - k_{12} g s + d_2 v_1 - d_2 v_2.$$

Define the current prediction errors as (here z_1 and z_2 actually mean z_1^{old} and z_2^{old}, respectively)

$$e_1 := f(x_1) - d_1 = \sum_{j=1}^{l} z_j d_j k_{1j} + b - d_1$$

$$= d_1 z_1 k_{11} + d_2 z_2 k_{12} + \sum_{j=3}^{l} d_j z_j k_{1j} + b - d_1$$

$$= d_1 z_1 k_{11} + d_2 z_2 k_{12} + v_1 + b - d_1,$$

$$e_2 := f(x_2) - d_2 = \sum_{j=1}^{l} z_j d_j k_{2j} + b - d_2$$

$$= d_1 z_1 k_{12} + d_2 z_2 k_{22} + \sum_{j=3}^{l} d_j z_j k_{2j} + b - d_2$$

$$= d_1 z_1 k_{12} + d_2 z_2 k_{22} + v_2 + b - d_2$$

$$\Rightarrow \quad e_1 - e_2 = d_2 - d_1 + v_1 - v_2 + d_1 z_1 k_{11} + d_2 z_2 k_{12} - d_1 z_1 k_{12} - d_2 z_2 k_{22} .$$

Since

$$d_1 z_1 k_{11} + d_2 z_2 k_{12} - d_1 z_1 k_{12} - d_2 z_2 k_{22}$$
$$= d_1 (g - sz_2) k_{11} + d_2 z_2 k_{12} - d_1 (g - sz_2) k_{12} - d_2 z_2 k_{22}$$
$$= d_1 g k_{11} - d_2 k_{11} z_2 + d_2 k_{12} z_2 - d_1 g k_{12} + d_2 k_{12} z_2 - d_2 k_{22} z_2$$
$$= d_1 g (k_{11} - k_{12}) - d_2 (k_{11} + k_{22} - 2k_{12}) z_2^{old}$$
$$= r(k_{11} - k_{12}) - k d_2 z_2^{old}$$

$$\Rightarrow \quad e_1 - e_2 = d_2 - d_1 + v_1 - v_2 + r(k_{11} - k_{12}) - k d_2 z_2^{old} .$$

Setting $dW/dz_2 = 0$ yields $0 = -kz_2^{unc} + \beta$ or $kz_2^{unc} = \beta$. This implies that

$$kd_2 z_2^{unc} = d_2 \beta = d_2 - d_1 + v_1 - v_2 + r(k_{11} - k_{12}) = kd_2 z_2^{old} + e_1 - e_2$$

$$\Rightarrow \quad z_2^{unc} = z_2^{old} + k^{-1} d_2 (e_1 - e_2)$$

which is the desired result.   Now since

$$z_1^{new} d_1 + z_2^{new} d_2 = r = const = z_1^{old} d_1 + z_2^{old} d_2$$

$$\Rightarrow \quad z_1^{new} + z_2^{new} d_1 d_2 = d_1 r = z_1^{old} + z_2^{old} d_1 d_2$$

$$\Rightarrow \quad z_1^{new} = d_1 (r - d_2 z_2^{new}) \quad \text{or} \quad z_1^{new} = z_1^{old} + d_1 d_2 (z_2^{old} - z_2^{new}).$$

It is required to clip z_2^{unc} to an appropriate range.   See Figure 7.1.1 for illustration.   Let

$$z_1 d_1 + z_2 d_2 = r = const = z_1^{old} d_1 + z_2^{old} d_2, \quad z_1 \geq 0, \quad z_2 \geq 0.$$

Case 1: Suppose $d_1 = 1$, $d_2 = 1$. Then we have $z_1 d_1 + z_2 d_2 = z_1 + z_2 := r \geq 0$.

> Case 1a: Suppose $r = 0$, i.e., $z_1 = 0$ and $z_2 = 0$. Then no further search is possible and we may find another $z_1 > 0$ to continue the algorithm or simply ignore this case.
>
> Case 1b: Suppose $r > 0$, then $z_2 \in [0, r]$.

Case 2: Suppose $d_1 = -1$, $d_2 = 1$. Then we have $z_1 d_1 + z_2 d_2 = -z_1 + z_2 := r$.

> In this case, let $U = \max(0, r)$, then $z_2 \in [U, \infty)$.

Case 3: Suppose $d_1 = -1$, $d_2 = -1$. Then we have $z_1 d_1 + z_2 d_2 = -z_1 - z_2 := r \leq 0$.

> Case 3a: Suppose $r = 0$, i.e., $z_1 = 0$ and $z_2 = 0$. Then no further search is possible and we may find another $z_1 > 0$ to continue the algorithm or simply ignore this case.
>
> Case 3b: Suppose $r < 0$, then $z_2 \in [0, -r]$.

Case 4: Suppose $d_1 = 1$, $d_2 = -1$. Then we have $z_1 d_1 + z_2 d_2 = z_1 - z_2 := r$.

> In this case, let $U = \max(0, -r)$, then $z_2 \in [U, \infty)$.

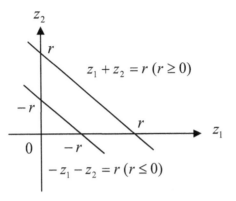

Case 1 and Case 3

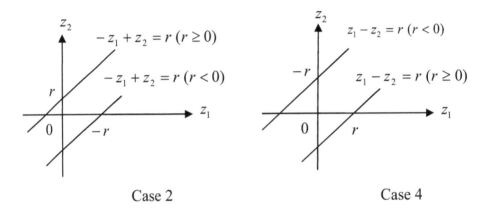

Case 2   Case 4

Figure 7.1.1: Illustration of four cases.

The main loop of the algorithm for updating z_1 and z_2 can be summarized as follows.

Step 1: $k \leftarrow k_{11} + k_{22} - 2k_{12}$.
Step 2:   Determine the current bias b.
Step 3:   Determine the current fitted values $f(x_1)$ and $f(x_2)$.
Step 4: $r \leftarrow z_1 d_1 + z_2 d_2$.
Step 5:   Determine an appropriate interval $[U, V]$ used for clipping z_2.
Step 6:   Calculate   the   current   errors $e_1 \leftarrow f(x_1) - d_1$ and
                $e_2 \leftarrow f(x_2) - d_2$.
Step 7: $z_2 \leftarrow z_2 + k^{-1} d_2 (e_1 - e_2)$.

Step 8: Clipping z_2 to $[U, V]$.

Step 9: $z_1 \leftarrow d_1(r - d_2 z_2)$.

7.2 SMO for 1-norm Soft Margin Classifier

Let $X \subseteq \mathfrak{R}^n$ and $Y := \{1, -1\}$. Suppose we are given a non-trivial training set

$$S := \{(x_q, d_q)\}_{q=1}^{l} \subseteq X \times Y.$$

Let $K(x, z)$ be a given kernel on $X \times X$. In the following, we will list an SMO algorithm for designing the 1-norm soft margin classifiers. The derivation is very similar to that of the previous section.

Consider the following dual optimization problem:

(D1)   maximize $\displaystyle\sum_{q=1}^{l} z_q - \frac{1}{2} \sum_{q=1}^{l} \sum_{j=1}^{l} z_q z_j d_q d_j K(x_q, x_j)$

subject to $\displaystyle\sum_{q=1}^{l} z_q d_q = 0$ and $0 \le z_q \le C$ for all $q \in \underline{l}$.

Suppose z_q, $q \in \underline{l}$, is the current value of the dual variable. Then the current discriminant function is given by

$$f(x) = \sum_{q=1}^{l} z_q d_q K(x_q, x) + b,$$

where

$$b = d_k - \sum_{i=1}^{l} z_q d_q K(x_q, x_k) \quad \text{for any } 0 < z_k < C.$$

In the SMO algorithm, suppose we choose z_1 and z_2 for maximizatiom with other variables unchanged. Then we must have

$$z_1 d_1 + z_2 d_2 = r = const = z_1^{old} d_1 + z_2^{old} d_2, \quad 0 \le z_1, z_2 \le C.$$

Without loss of generality, the SMO algorithm first computes z_2^{new} and then obtains z_1^{new}. It is required that the updated z_2 lies in the interval $[U,V]$ because of the box constraints.

Define the current prediction errors as

$$e_1 := f(x_1) - d_1 = \sum_{j=1}^{l} z_j d_j K(x_j, x_1) + b - d_1,$$

$$e_2 := f(x_2) - d_2 = \sum_{j=1}^{l} z_j d_j K(x_j, x_2) + b - d_2,$$

and

$$k := k_{11} + k_{22} - 2k_{12}, \quad k_{qj} = K(x_q, x_j) = K(x_j, x_q) = k_{jq}.$$

The main loop of the algorithm for updating z_1 and z_2 can be summarized as follows.

Step 1: $k \leftarrow k_{11} + k_{22} - 2k_{12}$.
Step 2: Determine the current bias b.
Step 3: Determine the current fitted values $f(x_1)$ and $f(x_2)$.
Step 4: $r \leftarrow z_1 d_1 + z_2 d_2$.
Step 5: Determine an appropriate interval $[U,V]$ used for clipping z_2.
Step 6: Calculate the current errors $e_1 \leftarrow f(x_1) - d_1$ and $e_2 \leftarrow f(x_2) - d_2$.
Step 7: $z_2 \leftarrow z_2 + k^{-1} d_2 (e_1 - e_2)$.
Step 8: Clipping z_2 to $[U,V]$.
Step 9: $z_1 \leftarrow d_1 (r - d_2 z_2)$.

The determination of the range $[U,V]$ is provided in the following. See Figure 7.2.1 for illustration.

Case 1: Suppose $d_1 = 1$, $d_2 = 1$. Then we have $z_1 d_1 + z_2 d_2 = z_1 + z_2 := r \geq 0$.

Case 1a: If $r = 2C$, no further search is possible. Then we may find another $0 < z_1 < C$ to continue the algorithm or simply ignore this case.

Case 1b: If $C < r < 2C$, then $z_2 \in [r - C, C]$.

Case 1c: If $0 < r \le C$, then $z_2 \in [0, r]$.

Case 1d: If $r = 0$, no further search is possible. Then we may find another $0 < z_1 < C$ to continue the algorithm or simply ignore this case.

Case 2: Suppose $d_1 = -1$, $d_2 = 1$. Then we have $z_1 d_1 + z_2 d_2 = -z_1 + z_2 := r$.

Case 2a: If $r = -C$, no further search is possible. Then we may find another $0 < z_1 < C$ to continue the algorithm or simply ignore this case.

Case 2b: If $-C < r < 0$, then $z_2 \in [0, r + C]$.

Case 2c: If $0 \le r < C$, then $z_2 \in [r, C]$.

Case 2d: If $r = C$, no further search is possible. Then we may find another $0 < z_1 < C$ to continue the algorithm or simply ignore this case.

Case 3: Suppose $d_1 = -1$, $d_2 = -1$. Then we have $z_1 d_1 + z_2 d_2 = -z_1 - z_2 := r \le 0$.

Case 3a: If $r = -2C$, no further search is possible. Then we may find another $0 < z_1 < C$ to continue the algorithm or simply ignore this case.

Case 3b: If $-2C < r < -C$, then $z_2 \in [-r - C, C]$.

Case 3c: If $-C \le r < 0$, then $z_2 \in [0, -r]$.

Case 3d: If $r = 0$, no further search is possible. Then we may find another $0 < z_1 < C$ to continue the algorithm or simply ignore this case.

Case 4: Suppose $d_1 = 1$, $d_2 = -1$. Then we have $z_1 d_1 + z_2 d_2 = z_1 - z_2 := r$.

Case 4a: If $r = C$, no further search is possible. Then we may find another $0 < z_1 < C$ to continue the algorithm or simply ignore this case.

Case 4b: If $0 \le r < C$, then $z_2 \in [0, C - r]$.
Case 4c: If $-C < r < 0$, then $z_2 \in [-r, C]$.

Case 4d: If $r = -C$, no further search is possible. Then we may find another $0 < z_1 < C$ to continue the algorithm or simply ignore this case.

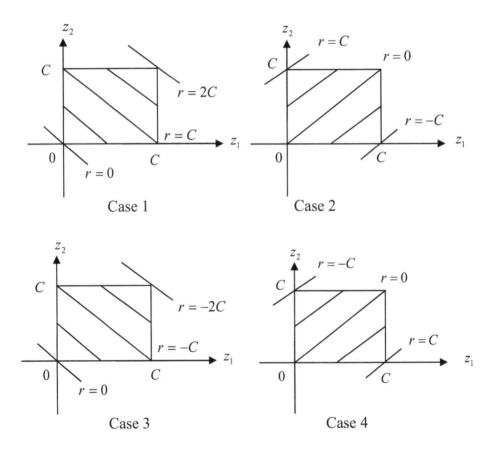

Figure 7.2.1: Illustration of four cases.

7.3 SMO for 2-norm Soft Margin Classifier

Let $X \subseteq \Re^n$ and $Y := \{1, -1\}$. Suppose we are given a non-trivial training set

$$S := \left\{ \left(x_q, d_q \right) \right\}_{q=1}^{l} \subseteq X \times Y.$$

Let $K(x, z)$ be a given kernel on $X \times X$. In the following, we will list an SMO algorithm for designing the 2-norm soft margin classifiers.

Consider the following dual optimization problem:

(D2)   maximize $\displaystyle\sum_{q=1}^{l} z_q - \frac{1}{2} \sum_{q=1}^{l} \sum_{j=1}^{l} z_q z_j d_q d_j K\left(x_q, x_j \right) - \frac{1}{2C} \sum_{q=1}^{l} z_q^2$

subject to $\displaystyle\sum_{q=1}^{l} z_q d_q = 0$ and $z_q \geq 0$ for all $q \in \underline{l}$.

Suppose z_q, $q \in \underline{l}$, is the current value of the dual variable. Then the current discriminant function is given by

$$f(x) = \sum_{q=1}^{l} z_q d_q K\left(x_q, x \right) + b,$$

where

$$b = d_k \left(1 - C^{-1} z_k \right) - \sum_{q=1}^{l} z_q d_q K\left(x_q, x_k \right) \text{ for any } z_k > 0.$$

In the SMO algorithm, suppose we choose z_1 and z_2 for maximizatiom with other variables unchanged. Then we must have

$$z_1 d_1 + z_2 d_2 = r = const = z_1^{old} d_1 + z_2^{old} d_2, \quad z_1, z_2 \geq 0.$$

Without loss of generality, the SMO algorithm first computes z_2^{new} and then obtains z_1^{new}. It is required that the updated z_2 lies in the interval $[U, V]$.

Define the current prediction errors as

$$e_1 := f(x_1) - d_1 = \sum_{j=1}^{l} z_j d_j K(x_j, x_1) + b - d_1,$$

$$e_2 := f(x_2) - d_2 = \sum_{j=1}^{l} z_j d_j K(x_j, x_2) + b - d_2,$$

and

$$k := k_{11} + k_{22} - 2k_{12}, \quad k_{qj} = K(x_q, x_j) = K(x_j, x_q) = k_{jq}.$$

The main loop of the algorithm for updating z_1 and z_2 can be summarized as follows.

Step 1: $k \leftarrow k_{11} + k_{22} - 2k_{12} + 2C^{-1}$.

Step 2:   Determine the current bias b.

Step 3:   Determine the current fitted values $f(x_1)$ and $f(x_2)$.

Step 4: $r \leftarrow z_1 d_1 + z_2 d_2$.

Step 5:   Determine an appropriate interval $[U, V]$ used for clipping z_2.

Step 6:   Calculate the current errors $e_1 \leftarrow f(x_1) - d_1$ and $e_2 \leftarrow f(x_2) - d_2$.

Step 7: $z_2 \leftarrow z_2 + k^{-1} d_2 [(e_1 - e_2) + C^{-1}(d_1 z_1 - d_2 z_2)]$.

Step 8:   Clipping z_2 to $[U, V]$.

Step 9: $z_1 \leftarrow d_1 (r - d_2 z_2)$.

The determination of the range $[U, V]$ is provided in the following. See Figure 7.3.1 for illustration.

Case 1: Suppose $d_1 = 1$, $d_2 = 1$. Then we have $z_1 d_1 + z_2 d_2 = z_1 + z_2 := r \geq 0$.

Case 1a: Suppose $r = 0$, i.e., $z_1 = 0$ and $z_2 = 0$. Then no further search is possible and we may find another $z_1 > 0$ to continue the algorithm or simply ignore this case.

Case 1b: Suppose $r > 0$, then $z_2 \in [0, r]$.

Case 2: Suppose $d_1 = -1$, $d_2 = 1$. Then we have $z_1 d_1 + z_2 d_2 = -z_1 + z_2 := r$.

In this case, let $U = \max(0, r)$, then $z_2 \in [U, \infty)$.

Case 3: Suppose $d_1 = -1$, $d_2 = -1$. Then we have $z_1 d_1 + z_2 d_2 = -z_1 - z_2 := r \leq 0$.

Case 3a: Suppose $r = 0$, i.e., $z_1 = 0$ and $z_2 = 0$. Then no further search is possible and we may find another $z_1 > 0$ to continue the algorithm or simply ignore this case.

Case 3b: Suppose $r < 0$, then $z_2 \in [0, -r]$.

Case 4: Suppose $d_1 = 1$, $d_2 = -1$. Then we have $z_1 d_1 + z_2 d_2 = z_1 - z_2 := r$.

In this case, let $U = \max(0, -r)$, then $z_2 \in [U, \infty)$.

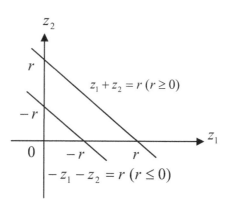

Case 1 and Case 3

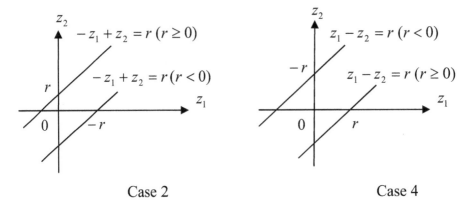

Case 2   Case 4

Figure 7.3.1: Illustration of four cases.

7.4 SMO for Ridge Regressor

Let $X \subseteq \mathfrak{R}^n$ and $Y \subseteq \mathfrak{R}$. Suppose we are given the training set

$$S := \left\{ (x_q, d_q) \right\}_{q=1}^{l} \subseteq X \times Y.$$

Let $K(x, z)$ be a given kernel on $X \times X$. Consider the following optimization problem for ridge regressor in the feature space:

(D0)   maximize $\displaystyle \sum_{q=1}^{l} z_q d_q - \frac{1}{2} \sum_{q=1}^{l} \sum_{j=1}^{l} z_q z_j K(x_q, x_j) - \frac{1}{2C} \sum_{q=1}^{l} z_q^2$

subject to $\displaystyle \sum_{q=1}^{l} z_q = 0.$

Suppose z_q, $q \in \underline{l}$, is the current value of the dual variable. Then the current predictive function is given by

$$f(x) = \sum_{q=1}^{l} z_q K(x_q, x) + b,$$

where

$$b = d_k - C^{-1} z_k - \sum_{q=1}^{l} z_q K(x_q, x_k) \text{ for any } k \in \underline{l}.$$

In the SMO algorithm for regression, suppose we choose z_1 and z_2 for maximization with other variables unchanged. In order to compute the new values of these two variables, one can observe that in order not to violate the equality constraint, we must have

$$z_1 + z_2 = r = const = z_1^{old} + z_2^{old}.$$

Without loss of generality, the SMO algorithm first computes z_2^{new} and then obtains z_1^{new}. Let

$$W(z) := \sum_{q=1}^{l} z_q d_q - \frac{1}{2} \sum_{q=1}^{l} \sum_{j=1}^{l} z_q z_j k_{qj} - \frac{1}{2C} \sum_{q=1}^{l} z_q^2,$$

where

$$k_{qj} = K(x_q, x_j) = K(x_j, x_q) = k_{jq}.$$

Since

$$\sum_{q=1}^{l} \sum_{j=1}^{l} z_q z_j k_{qj}$$

$$= z_1 z_1 k_{11} + z_1 z_2 k_{12} + z_1 z_3 k_{13} + \ldots + z_1 z_l k_{1l}$$
$$+ z_2 z_1 k_{21} + z_2 z_2 k_{22} + z_2 z_3 k_{23} + \ldots + z_2 z_l k_{2l}$$
$$+ z_3 z_1 k_{31} + z_3 z_2 k_{32} + z_3 z_3 k_{33} + \ldots + z_3 z_l k_{3l}$$
$$+ \ldots$$
$$+ z_l z_1 k_{l1} + z_l z_2 k_{l2} + z_l z_3 k_{l3} + \ldots + z_l z_l k_{ll},$$

we have

$$W(z_1, z_2) = z_1 d_1 + z_2 d_2 - \frac{1}{2}\left[z_1^2 k_{11} + z_2^2 k_{22} + 2 z_1 z_2 k_{12} \right]$$

$$- z_1 \sum_{j=3}^{l} z_j k_{1j} - z_2 \sum_{j=3}^{l} z_j k_{2j} - \frac{1}{2C} z_1^2 - \frac{1}{2C} z_2^2 + const.$$

Define

$$v_1 := \sum_{j=3}^{l} z_j k_{1j}, \quad v_2 := \sum_{j=3}^{l} z_j k_{2j}.$$

Then we have

$$W(z_1, z_2) = z_1 d_1 + z_2 d_2 - z_1 v_1 - z_2 v_2$$
$$- \frac{1}{2}\left[z_1^2 k_{11} + z_2^2 k_{22} + 2z_1 z_2 k_{12}\right] - \frac{1}{2C} z_1^2 - \frac{1}{2C} z_2^2 + const.$$

Since $r = z_1 + z_2$, we have $z_1 = r - z_2$ and

$$W(z_2) = d_1(r - z_2) + d_2 z_2 - v_1(r - z_2) - v_2 z_2$$
$$- \frac{1}{2}\left[k_{11}(r - z_2)^2 + k_{22} z_2^2 + 2k_{12}(r - z_2)z_2\right]$$
$$- \frac{1}{2C}(r - z_2)^2 - \frac{1}{2C} z_2^2 + const$$
$$= -d_1 z_2 + d_2 z_2 + v_1 z_2 - v_2 z_2$$
$$- \frac{1}{2}\left[k_{11}(r^2 - 2rz_2 + z_2^2) + k_{22} z_2^2 + 2k_{12} rz_2 - 2k_{12} z_2^2\right]$$
$$- \frac{1}{2C}(r^2 + z_2^2 - 2rz_2) - \frac{1}{2C} z_2^2 + const$$
$$= -\frac{1}{2}\left(k_{11} + k_{22} - 2k_{12} + 2C^{-1}\right)z_2^2$$
$$+ \left[-d_1 + d_2 + v_1 - v_2 + k_{11}r - k_{12}r + C^{-1}r\right]z_2 + const$$
$$= -\frac{1}{2}kz_2^2 + gz_2 + const,$$

where

$$k := k_{11} + k_{22} - 2k_{12} + 2C^{-1},$$
$$g := -d_1 + d_2 + v_1 - v_2 + k_{11}r - k_{12}r + C^{-1}r.$$

Setting $dW/dz_2 = 0$ yields $0 = -kz_2^{unc} + g$, implying $kz_2^{unc} = g$.

Define the current prediction errors as (here z_1 and z_2 actually mean z_1^{old} and z_2^{old}, respectively)

$$e_1 := f(x_1) - d_1 = \sum_{j=1}^{l} z_j k_{1j} + b - d_1$$

$$= z_1 k_{11} + z_2 k_{12} + \sum_{j=3}^{l} z_j k_{1j} + b - d_1$$

$$= z_1 k_{11} + z_2 k_{12} + v_1 + b - d_1,$$

$$e_2 := f(x_2) - d_2 = \sum_{j=1}^{l} z_j k_{2j} + b - d_2$$

$$= z_1 k_{12} + z_2 k_{22} + \sum_{j=3}^{l} z_j k_{2j} + b - d_2$$

$$= z_1 k_{12} + z_2 k_{22} + v_2 + b - d_2.$$

Hence we obtain

$$e_1 - e_2 = d_2 - d_1 + v_1 - v_2 + \left(z_1 k_{11} + z_2 k_{12} - z_1 k_{12} - z_2 k_{22} \right),$$

where

$$z_1 k_{11} + z_2 k_{12} - z_1 k_{12} - z_2 k_{22}$$
$$= \left(r - z_2 \right) k_{11} + z_2 k_{12} - \left(r - z_2 \right) k_{12} - z_2 k_{22}$$
$$= r\left(k_{11} - k_{12} \right) - \left(k_{11} + k_{22} - 2k_{12} \right) z_2^{old}$$
$$= r k_{11} - r k_{12} - \left(k_{11} + k_{22} - 2k_{12} + 2C^{-1} \right) z_2^{old} + 2C^{-1} z_2^{old}$$
$$= r k_{11} - r k_{12} - k z_2^{old} + 2C^{-1} z_2^{old}.$$

Hence we obtain

$$e_1 - e_2 = d_2 - d_1 + v_1 - v_2 + \left(r k_{11} - r k_{12} - k z_2^{old} + 2C^{-1} z_2^{old} \right)$$
$$= g - C^{-1} r - k z_2^{old} + 2C^{-1} z_2^{old},$$
$$g = e_1 - e_2 + C^{-1} r + k z_2^{old} - 2C^{-1} z_2^{old}$$
$$= k z_2^{old} + e_1 - e_2 + C^{-1} \left(z_1^{old} + z_2^{old} \right) - 2C^{-1} z_2^{old}$$
$$= k z_2^{old} + e_1 - e_2 + C^{-1} z_1^{old} - C^{-1} z_2^{old},$$
$$k z_2^{new} = g = k z_2^{old} + \left[\left(e_1 - e_2 \right) + C^{-1} \left(z_1^{old} - z_2^{old} \right) \right],$$

i.e.,

$$z_2^{new} = z_2^{old} + k^{-1} \left[\left(e_1 - e_2 \right) + C^{-1} \left(z_1^{old} - z_2^{old} \right) \right],$$

which is the desired result.   Then z_1^{new} is obtained as

$$z_1^{new} = z_1^{old} + z_2^{old} - z_2^{new}.$$

The main loop of the algorithm for updating z_1 and z_2 can be summarized as follows.

Step 1: $k \leftarrow k_{11} + k_{22} - 2k_{12} + 2C^{-1}$.

Step 2:   Determine the current bias b.

Step 3:   Determine the current fitted values $f(x_1)$ and $f(x_2)$.

Step 4: $r \leftarrow z_1 + z_2$.

Step 5:   Calculate   the   current   errors $e_1 \leftarrow f(x_1) - d_1$ and

          $e_2 \leftarrow f(x_2) - d_2$.

Step 6: $z_2 \leftarrow z_2 + k^{-1}\left[(e_1 - e_2) + C^{-1}(z_1 - z_2)\right]$

Step 7: $z_1 \leftarrow r - z_2$.

7.5 SMO for 1-norm Soft Regressor

Let $X \subseteq \mathfrak{R}^n$ and $Y \subseteq \mathfrak{R}$. Suppose we are given the training set

$$S := \left\{(x_q, d_q)\right\}_{q=1}^{\ell} \subseteq X \times Y.$$

Let $K(x, z)$ be a given kernel on $X \times X$. In the following, we will list an SMO algorithm for designing the 1-norm soft regressors. The derivation is very similar to that of the previous section.

Consider the following dual optimization problem:

(D1')   maximize $\displaystyle\sum_{q=1}^{\ell} z_q d_q - \varepsilon \sum_{q=1}^{\ell} |z_q| - \frac{1}{2} \sum_{q=1}^{\ell} \sum_{j=1}^{\ell} z_q z_j K(x_q, x_j)$

            subject to $\displaystyle\sum_{q=1}^{\ell} z_q = 0, \; -C \le z_q \le C, \; q \in \underline{\ell}.$

Suppose z_q, $q \in \underline{l}$, is the current value of the dual variable. Then the current predictive function is given by

$$f(x) = \sum_{q=1}^{l} z_q K(x_q, x) + b,$$

where

$$b = d_k - \varepsilon - \sum_{q=1}^{l} z_q K(x_q, x_k) \text{ for any } 0 < z_k < C,$$

or

$$b = d_k + \varepsilon - \sum_{q=1}^{l} z_q K(x_q, x_k) \text{ for any } -C < z_k < 0.$$

In the SMO algorithm, suppose we choose z_1 and z_2 for maximizatiom with other variables unchanged. Then we must have

$$z_1 + z_2 = r = const = z_1^{old} + z_2^{old}, \quad -C \le z_1, z_2 \le C.$$

Without loss of generality, the SMO algorithm first computes z_2^{new} and then obtains z_1^{new}. It is required that the updated z_2 lies in the interval $[U, V]$ because of the box constraints.

Define the current prediction errors as

$$e_1 := f(x_1) - d_1 = \sum_{j=1}^{l} z_j K(x_j, x_1) + b - d_1,$$

$$e_2 := f(x_2) - d_2 = \sum_{j=1}^{l} z_j K(x_j, x_2) + b - d_2,$$

and

$$k := k_{11} + k_{22} - 2k_{12}, \quad k_{qj} = K(x_q, x_j) = K(x_j, x_q) = k_{jq}.$$

The main loop of the algorithm for updating z_1 and z_2 can be summarized as follows.

Step 1: $k \leftarrow k_{11} + k_{22} - 2k_{12}$.
Step 2: Determine the current bias b.
Step 3: Determine the current fitted values $f(x_1)$ and $f(x_2)$.

Step 4: $r \leftarrow z_1 + z_2$.

Step 5:   Determine appropriate intervals $[U,V]$ used for clipping z_2.

Step 6:   Calculate   the   current   errors $e_1 \leftarrow f(x_1) - d_1$ and
$e_2 \leftarrow f(x_2) - d_2$.

Step 7: $z_2 \leftarrow z_2 + k^{-1}[(e_1 - e_2) + \varepsilon(\text{sgn}(z_1) - \text{sgn}(z_2))]$.

Step 8:   Clipping z_2 to $[U,V]$.

Step 9: $z_1 \leftarrow r - z_2$.

In Step 7, if we define $s := \text{sgn}(z_1) - \text{sgn}(z_2)$, then we have

$s = 0$ if we search the maximum in the first quadrant;
$s = -2$ if we search the maximum in the second quadrant;
$s = 0$ if we search the maximum in the third quadrant;
$s = 2$ if we search the maximum in the fourth quadrant.

The determination of the range $[U,V]$ is provided in the following. See Figure 7.5.1 for illustration.

Case 1: Suppose $r = 2C$. In this case, $z_1 = C$ and $z_2 = C$. No further search is possible and we may find another $-C < z_1 < C$ to continue the algorithm or simply ignore this case.

Case 2: Suppose $C \le r < 2C$. Only the first quadrant is involved. We set

$$z_2 \in [r - C, C], \quad s = 0.$$

Case 3: Suppose $0 < r < C$. Then the first, second, and fourth quadrants are involved.

(1) Look for maximum in the first quadrant: set $z_2 \in [0, r]$, $s = 0$.
(2) Look for maximum in the second quadrant: set $z_2 \in [r, C]$, $s = -2$.
(3) Look for maximum in the fourth quadrant: set $z_2 \in [r - C, 0]$, $s = 2$.

Choose the one that maximizes the payoff W.

Case 4: Suppose $r = 0$. Then the second and the fourth quadrants are involved.

(1) Look for maximum in the second quadrant: set $z_2 \in [0, C]$, $s = -2$.
(2) Look for maximum in the fourth quadrant: set $z_2 \in [-C, 0]$, $s = 2$.

Choose the one that maximizes the payoff W.

Case 5: Suppose $-C < r < 0$. Then the second, third, and fourth quadrants are involved.

(1) Look for maximum in the third quadrant: set $z_2 \in [r, 0]$, $s = 0$.
(2) Look for maximum in the second quadrant: set $z_2 \in [0, r + C]$, $s = -2$.
(3) Look for maximum in the fourth quadrant: set $z_2 \in [-C, r]$, $s = 2$.

Choose the one that maximizes the payoff W.

Case 6: Suppose $-2C < r \leq -C$. Only the third quadrant is involved. We set

$$z_2 \in [-C, r + C], \quad s = 0.$$

Case 7: Suppose $r = -2C$. In this case, $z_1 = -C$ and $z_2 = -C$. No further search is possible and we may find another $-C < z_1 < C$ to continue the algorithm or simply ignore this case.

In each of Case 3 to Case 5, we have to calculate the payoff W which is the objective function in problem (D1'). This can conveniently be done as follows. Let z_1^{temp} and z_2^{temp} be the temporary values of z_1 and z_2. First, compute

$$g = kz_2^{old} + e_1 - e_2,$$

and then the payoff W can be computed as

$$W\left(z_1^{temp}, z_2^{temp}\right) = -2^{-1}k\left(z_2^{temp}\right)^2 + gz_2^{temp} - \varepsilon\left|z_1^{temp}\right| - \varepsilon\left|z_2^{temp}\right| + const.$$

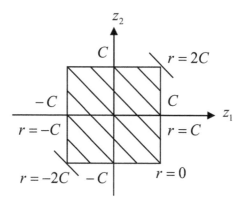

Figure 7.5.1: Illustration for seven cases.

7.6 SMO for 2-norm Soft Regressor

Let $X \subseteq \mathfrak{R}^n$ and $Y \subseteq \mathfrak{R}$. Suppose we are given the training set

$$S := \left\{(x_q, d_q)\right\}_{q=1}^{l} \subseteq X \times Y.$$

Let $K(x, z)$ be a given kernel on $X \times X$. In the following, we will list an SMO algorithm for designing the 2-norm soft regressors.

Consider the following dual optimization problem:

(D2')   maximize

$$\sum_{q=1}^{l} z_q d_q - \varepsilon \sum_{q=1}^{l} |z_q| - \frac{1}{2}\sum_{q=1}^{l}\sum_{j=1}^{l} z_q z_j K(x_q, x_j)$$
$$-\frac{1}{2C}\sum_{q=1}^{l} z_q^2$$

        subject to

$$\sum_{q=1}^{l} z_q = 0.$$

Suppose z_q, $q \in l$, is the current value of the dual variable. Then the current predictive function is given by

$$f(x) = \sum_{q=1}^{l} z_q K(x_q, x) + b,$$

where

$$b = d_k - \varepsilon - C^{-1} z_k - \sum_{q=1}^{l} z_q K(x_q, x_k) \quad \text{for any } z_k > 0$$

or

$$b = d_k + \varepsilon - C^{-1} z_k - \sum_{q=1}^{l} z_q K(x_q, x_k) \quad \text{for any } z_k < 0.$$

In the SMO algorithm, suppose we choose z_1 and z_2 for maximizatiom with other variables unchanged. Then we must have

$$z_1 + z_2 = r = const = z_1^{old} + z_2^{old}.$$

Without loss of generality, the SMO algorithm first computes z_2^{new} and then obtains z_1^{new}. It is required that the updated z_2 lies in the interval $[U, V]$.

Define the current prediction errors as

$$e_1 := f(x_1) - d_1 = \sum_{j=1}^{l} z_j K(x_j, x_1) + b - d_1,$$

$$e_2 := f(x_2) - d_2 = \sum_{j=1}^{l} z_j K(x_j, x_2) + b - d_2,$$

and

$$k := k_{11} + k_{22} - 2k_{12} + 2C^{-1}, \quad k_{qj} = K(x_q, x_j) = K(x_j, x_q) = k_{jq}.$$

The main loop of the algorithm for updating z_1 and z_2 can be summarized as follows.

Step 1: $k := k_{11} + k_{22} - 2k_{12} + 2C^{-1}$.

Step 2:   Determine the current bias b.

Step 3:   Determine the current fitted values $f(x_1)$ and $f(x_2)$.

Step 4: $r \leftarrow z_1 + z_2$.

Step 5:   Determine appropriate intervals $[U, V]$ used for clipping z_2.

Step 6:   Calculate   the   current   errors $e_1 \leftarrow f(x_1) - d_1$ and
$e_2 \leftarrow f(x_2) - d_2$.

Step 7: $z_2 \leftarrow z_2 + k^{-1}[(e_1 - e_2) + C^{-1}(z_1 - z_2) + \varepsilon(\operatorname{sgn}(z_1) - \operatorname{sgn}(z_2))]$.

Step 8:   Clipping z_2 to $[U, V]$.

Step 9: $z_1 \leftarrow r - z_2$.

In Step 7, if we define $s := \operatorname{sgn}(z_1) - \operatorname{sgn}(z_2)$, then we have

$s = 0$ if we search the maximum in the first quadrant;
$s = -2$ if we search the maximum in the second quadrant;
$s = 0$ if we search the maximum in the third quadrant;
$s = 2$ if we search the maximum in the fourth quadrant.

The determination of the range $[U, V]$ is provided in the following. See Figure 7.6.1 for illustration.

Case 1:   Suppose $r > 0$.   Then the first, second, and fourth quadrants are involved.

(1) Look for maximum in the first quadrant: set $z_2 \in [0, r]$, $s = 0$.

(2) Look for maximum in the second quadrant: set $z_2 \in [r, \infty)$, $s = -2$.

(3) Look for maximum in the fourth quadrant: set $z_2 \in (-\infty, 0]$, $s = 2$.

Choose the one that maximizes the payoff W.

Case 2:   Suppose $r = 0$.   Then the second and the fourth quadrants are involved.

(1) Look for maximum in the second quadrant: set $z_2 \in [0, \infty)$, $s = -2$.

(2) Look for maximum in the fourth quadrant: set $z_2 \in (-\infty, 0]$, $s = 2$.

Choose the one that maximizes the payoff W.

Case 3: Suppose $r < 0$. Then the second, third, and fourth quadrants are involved.

(1) Look for maximum in the third quadrant: set $z_2 \in [r, 0]$, $s = 0$.
(2) Look for maximum in the second quadrant: set $z_2 \in [0, \infty)$, $s = -2$.
(3) Look for maximum in the fourth quadrant: set $z_2 \in (-\infty, r]$, $s = 2$.

Choose the one that maximizes the payoff W.

In each of Case 1 to Case 3, we have to calculate the payoff W which is the objective function in problem (D2'). This can conveniently be done as follows. Let z_1^{temp} and z_2^{temp} be the temporary values of z_1 and z_2. First, compute

$$g = kz_2^{old} + e_1 - e_2 + C^{-1}\left(z_1^{old} - z_2^{old}\right),$$

and then the payoff W can be computed as

$$W\left(z_1^{temp}, z_2^{temp}\right) = -2^{-1}k\left(z_2^{temp}\right)^2 + gz_2^{temp} - \varepsilon\left|z_1^{temp}\right| - \varepsilon\left|z_2^{temp}\right| + const.$$

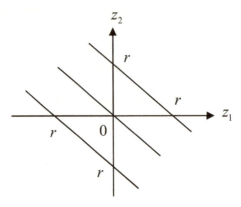

Figure 7.6.1: Illustration for three cases.

7.7 Illustrative Examples

In this section, we present some illustrative examples for support vector classification (SVC), support vector regression (SVR), and ridge regression (RR). We will use the SMO techniques presented in this chapter to numerically solve the nonlinear learning problems.

Example 7.7.1: Consider the data set of Example 5.6.1, where true discriminant function is given by the fractional power function

$$g(x_1, x_2) = x_2 - x_1^{2/3}, \quad x_1 \in [-2, 2], \quad x_2 \in [0, 2].$$

The parameter settings and simulation results for 1-norm SVC (SVC1) and 2-norm SVC (SVC2), all with Mahalanobis kernels, are shown in Table 7.7.1. Together with the true decision boundary, the decision boundaries thus determined for corrupted data are shown in Figure 7.7.1. With such highly corrupted data, the decision boundaries are reasonable.

Table 7.7.1: Parameter settings and simulation results in Example 7.7.1.

	SVC1	SVC2
C	2	4
(σ_1^2, σ_2^2)	$(1.0, 0.2)$	$(1.0, 0.5)$
Estimated maximal payoff	47.5122	57.8120
No. of misclassifications	8	10

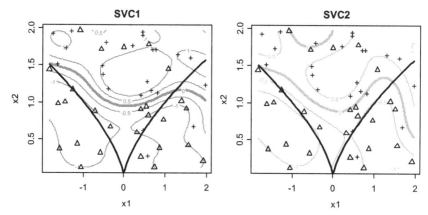

Figure 7.7.1: Decision boundaries in Example 7.7.1.

Example 7.7.2: Consider the data set of Example 5.6.2, where true regression function is given by the sinc function

$$g(x) = \begin{cases} 1, & x = 0, \\ \sin(x)/x, & x \neq 0, \end{cases} \quad x \in [-10, 10].$$

The parameter settings and simulation results for 1-norm SVR (SVR1), 2-norm SVR (SVR2), and ridge regressor (RR), all with Gaussian kernels, are shown in Table 7.7.2. Together with the true function, the predictive functions thus determined for corrupted data are shown in Figure 7.7.2. The performances of all learning machines are excellent.

Table 7.7.2: Parameter settings and simulation results in Example 7.7.2.

	SVR1	SVR2	RR
C	0.5	1	2
ε	0.03	0.02	none
σ^2	8	8	8
Estimated maximal payoff	4.2496	2.7633	5.2279
Mean squared error (MSE)	0.1051	0.0950	0.0885
Mean absolute deviation (MAD)	0.1707	0.2028	0.1956

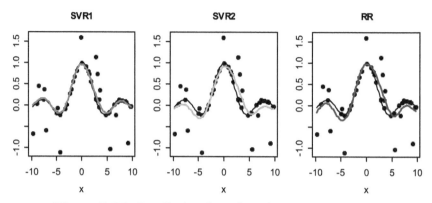

Figure 7.7.2: Predictive functions in Example 7.7.2.

Example 7.7.3: Consider the data set of Example 5.6.3, where true regression function is given by the Hermite function

$$g(x) = 1.1 \cdot \left(1 - x + 2x^2\right) \cdot e^{-x^2/2}, \quad x \in [-5, 5].$$

The parameter settings and simulation results for 1-norm SVR (SVR1), 2-norm SVR (SVR2), and ridge regressor (RR), all with Gaussian kernels, are shown in Table 7.7.3. Together with the true function, the predictive functions thus determined for corrupted data are shown in Figure 7.7.3. Again, the performances of all learning machines are excellent.

Table 7.7.3: Parameter settings and simulation results in Example 7.7.3.

	SVR1	SVR2	RR
C	10	10	50
ε	0.01	0.02	none
σ^2	3	3	3
Estimated maximal payoff	90.6484	28.0508	130.1047
Mean squared error (MSE)	0.1123	0.1060	0.0968
Mean absolute deviation (MAD)	0.1713	0.2291	0.2176

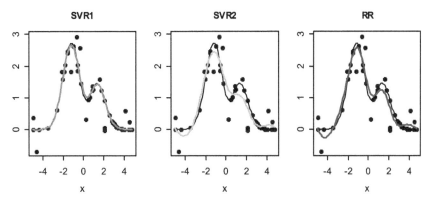

Figure 7.7.3: Predictive functions in Example 7.7.3.

7.8 Exercises

Exercise 7.8.1: Derive the updating law $z_2 \leftarrow z_2 + k^{-1} y_2 (e_1 - e_2)$ for the 1-norm soft margin classifier in Section 7.2.

Exercise 7.8.2: Derive the updating law $z_2 \leftarrow z_2 + k^{-1} y_2 [(e_1 - e_2) + C^{-1}(y_1 z_1 - y_2 z_2)]$ for the 2-norm soft margin classifier in Section 7.3.

Exercise 7.8.3: Derive the updating law $z_2 \leftarrow z_2 + k^{-1} [(e_1 - e_2) + \varepsilon(\mathrm{sgn}(z_1) - \mathrm{sgn}(z_2))]$ for the 1-norm soft regressor in Section 7.5.

Exercise 7.8.4: Derive the updating law

$$z_2 \leftarrow z_2 + k^{-1} [(e_1 - e_2) + C^{-1}(z_1 - z_2) + \varepsilon(\mathrm{sgn}(z_1) - \mathrm{sgn}(z_2))]$$

for the 2-norm soft regressor in Section 7.6.

Exercise 7.8.5: Consider the data set of Exercise 5.7.8, where the true discriminant function is given by the Hermite function

$$g(x_1, x_2) = x_2 - 1.1 \cdot (1 - x_1 + 2x_1^2) \cdot e^{-x_1^2/2},$$
$$x_1 \in [-5, 5], \quad x_2 \in [-1, 3].$$

The parameter settings for 1-norm SVC (SVC1) and 2-norm SVC (SVC2) with Mahalanobis kernels are shown in Table 7.8.5.

Table 7.8.5: Parameter settings in Exercise 7.8.5.

	SVC1	SVC2
C	0.5	0.5
$\left(\sigma_1^2, \sigma_2^2\right)$	$(8, 0.5)$	$(6, 0.4)$

Draw the decision boundaries thus determined and discuss whether these machine parameter settings are appropriate.

Exercise 7.8.6: Consider the data set of Exercise 5.7.9, where the true discriminant function is given by the sinc function

$$g(x_1, x_2) = \begin{cases} x_2 - 1, & x_1 = 0, \\ x_2 - [\sin(x_1)/x_1], & x_1 \neq 0, \end{cases}$$
$$x_1 \in [-10, 10], \quad x_2 \in [-2, 2].$$

The parameter settings for 1-norm SVC (SVC1) and 2-norm SVC (SVC2) with Mahalanobis kernels are shown in Table 7.8.6.

Table 7.8.6: Parameter settings in Exercise 7.8.6.

	SVC1	SVC2
C	2	2
$\left(\sigma_1^2, \sigma_2^2\right)$	$(2, 2)$	$(12, 8)$

Draw the decision boundaries thus determined and discuss whether these machine parameter settings are appropriate.

Exercise 7.8.7: Consider the data set of Exercise 5.7.10, where the true regression function is given by the fractional power function

$$g(x) = x^{2/3}, \quad x \in [-2, 2].$$

The parameter settings and simulation results for 1-norm SVR (SVR1), 2-norm SVR (SVR2), and ridge regressor (RR), all with Gaussian kernels, are shown in Table 7.8.7.

Table 7.8.7: Parameter settings and simulation results in Exercise 7.8.7.

	SVR1	SVR2	RR
C	3	3	1
ε	0.01	0.01	none
σ^2	3	3	3

Draw the predictive functions thus determined and discuss whether these machine parameter settings are appropriate.

Exercise 7.8.8: Consider a system with 4 input variables and 1 output variable. Suppose that 200 training examples are generated from a simple function with 5% corruption as follows:

$$g(x_1, x_2, x_3, x_4) = 0.2 \times \left[x_1 \sin(4x_1) + x_2 \sin(2x_2) + x_3 \cos(2x_4) \right]$$
$$+ 5\% \text{ corruption,}$$
$$-2 \le x_i \le 2, \ i \in \underline{4}.$$

The 40 testing examples are corruption-free. Find the predictive functions based on 1-norm SVR (SVR1) and 2-norm SVR (SVR2) with $C = 2$, $\varepsilon = 0.01$, and $\sigma^2 = 3$ in Gaussian kernel. Calculate the mean squared errors (MSEs) and the mean absolute deviations (MADs) for the training data and testing data.

7.9 Notes and References

For original paper on sequential minimal optimization, see Platt (1999). The SMO algorithms for 1-norm soft margin classifiers and 1-norm soft regressors can also be found in Cristianini and Shawe-Taylor (2000). There are also good numerical algorithms for solving the machine learning optimization problems. See, for instance, Luenberger (1984), Fletcher (1987), Bazaraa, Sherali, and Shetty (1993), Sundaram (1996), Bertsekas (1999), Boyd and Vandenberghe (2004), and Nocedal and Wright (2006). It should be noted that the kernel-based machine learning optimization problems can also be solved via the penalty and augmented Lagrangian methods; see Bertsekas (1999).

At each iteration of the algorithm, the usual SMO (two-parameter SMO, abbreviated as 2PSMO) algorithm jointly optimizes only two chosen parameters. That is, the optimization is performed at each iteration of the 2PSMO algorithm on a line segment. It is interesting, at least theoretically, to know if we may generalize the 2PSMO algorithm to 3PSMO (three-parameter SMO) algorithm, which jointly optimizes three chosen parameters at each iteration. That is, the optimization is performed at each iteration of the 3PSMO algorithm on a region consisting of infinitely many line segments. Simulation results in Lin etc (2011) show that 3PSMO algorithm is about twice as fast as the 2PSMO algorithm.

Bazaraa, M., D. Sherali, and C. Shetty (1993). Nonlinear Programming: Theory and Algorithm. Second Edition. Wiley, New York.

Bertsekas, D.P. (1999). Nonlinear Programming. Second Edition. Athena Scientific, Massachusetts.

Boyd, S. and L. Vandenberghe (2004). Convex Optimization. Cambridge University Press, Cambridge, United Kingdom.

Cristianini, N. and J. Shawe-Taylor (2000). An Introduction to Support Vector Machines. Cambridge University Press, Cambridge, United Kingdom.

Fletcher, R. (1987). Practical Methods of Optimization. Second Edition. Wiley, Chichester, United Kingdom.

Lin, Y.L., J.G. Hsieh, H.K. Wu, and J.H. Jeng (2011). Three-parameter sequential minimal optimization for support vector machines. Neurocomputing, Vol. 74, Issue 17, pp. 3467-3475.

Luenberger, D.G. (1984). Introduction to Linear and Nonlinear Programming. Second Edition. Addison-Wesley, Massachusetts.

Nocedal, J. and S.J. Wright (2006). Numerical Optimization. Second Edition. Springer, New York.

Platt, J. (1999). Fast training of support vector machines using sequential minimal optimization, in: B. Schölkopf, C.J.C. Burges, A.J. Smola (Eds.), Advances in Kernel Methods–Support Vector Learning, MIT Press, Cambridge, Massachusetts, pp. 185-208.

Sundaram, R.K. (1996). A First Course in Optimization Theory. Cambridge University Press, Cambridge, United Kingdom.

Chapter 8   Model Selection

Every learning problem has some (machine) parameters to be specified in advance. This is the problem of model selection. For instance, the number of hidden nodes in an artificial neural network or a generalized radial basis function network, or the number of fuzzy rules in a fuzzy neural network, must be specified before solving the associated optimization problem. Similarly, in the design of a kernel-based support vector machine, the kernel parameters, the regularization parameter C, and/or tolerance size ε must be prescribed in advance. In this chapter, we will use two commonly used evolutionary computation methods, i.e., genetic algorithms and particle swarm optimization algorithms, to perform the task of model selection. It should be kept in mind that only experimental data (or observational data) are available at hand. The key idea for model selection is the constructive and full use of all experimental data at hand.

Any procedure for the model selection problem in general involves some form of cross validation. Five techniques of cross validation in general use are the k-fold, leave-one-out, jackknife, deleted-d, and bootstrap (Good, 2006). In applying cross validation to determine the parameters of an SVM, a goodness-of-fit (GOF) metric (or statistic) must be pre-specified. Standard choice of the GOF metric is the G-statistic defined to be the ratio of the sum of squared residuals for testing data over that for the training data (Good, 2006). Two other popular choices are the sum of squared residuals (LS metric) and sum of absolute deviations of the residuals (LAD metric). See Good (2006) and the references therein.

The genetic algorithm (GA), originally developed by Holland over the course of the 1960s and 1970s, is a biologically motivated search technique mimicking natural selection and natural genetics. It is a general population-based search method in between exhaustive search and traditional search methods. When the fitness landscape (or cost surface) of the problem is unclear or riddled with many local optima, the genetic algorithm usually has good searching capability since the candidate solutions will not get stuck at the local optima. The genetic algorithm has been successfully applied to many fields of science and engineering.

The particle swarm optimization (PSO), originally developed by

Kennedy and Eberhart over the 1990s, is also a biologically motivated general search technique mimicking fish schooling, birds flocking, and bugs swarming. Swarm intelligence provides a useful paradigm for implementing adaptive systems. It was observed that human intelligence results partly from social interaction. PSO is also a population-based search method with each particle associated with a velocity. Therefore, particles in the swarm are flying through the search space. It is very easy to implement the PSO algorithm. The PSO algorithm has also been successfully applied to many areas of science and engineering.

Certainly, the GA and PSO are not used only for model selection. They can also be applied to find the connection weights of the neural networks. In the exercises, they are applied to standard optimization problems and the design of support vector regressors.

8.1 Genetic Algorithm

The genetic algorithm (GA) starts with a population of possible solutions or candidate solutions, called chromosomes, to the problem at hand. A prescribed fitness function or objective function is defined for chromosomes. Then highly fit chromosomes are selected for reproduction. After the genetic operations of crossover and mutation, a new generation of possible solutions is formed. This process is repeated until some convergence criterion is met. The whole process is illustrated in Figure 8.1.1.

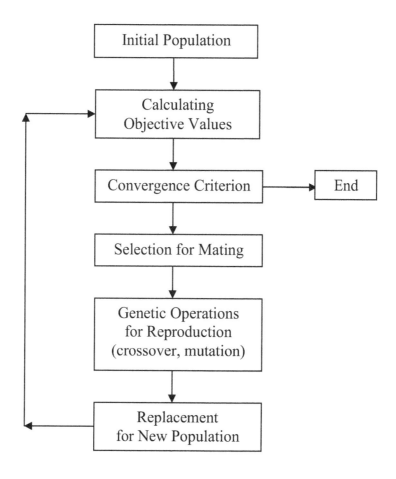

Figure 8.1.1: The process of genetic algorithm.

To prepare for the details of GA, we first list some basic terms in Table 8.1.1. See Haupt and Haupt (1998) and Mitchell (1996) for more details.

Table 8.1.1: Some basic terms in GA.

Terms	Definition
Evolution	a series of genetic changes in which living organisms acquire the characteristics that distinguish it from other organisms
Natural selection	The fittest individuals reproduce, passing their genetic information on to their offspring.
Encoding	the way in which the parameters are encoded
Genes	the encoding of a single parameter
Chromosomes	an array of parameters or genes representing candidate solution to the problem at hand
Fitness function	the function to be maximized
Fitness landscape	the hypersurface of the fitness function as a map of the points in the search space
Population	a group of individuals that interact (breed) together
Generation	one iteration of the genetic algorithm
Seeding	placing good guesses to the optimum parameter values in the initial population
Mating pool	a subset of the population selected for potential parents
Elitism	retaining some number of the best chromosomes at each generation
Selection	process of choosing parents for reproduction
Crossover	a reproduction operator that forms a new chromosome from two parent chromosomes by combing part of the information from each
Building block hypothesis	GAs attempt to find highly fit solutions to the problem at hand by the juxtaposition of the "good building blocks."
Mutation	a reproduction operator that randomly alters the values of genes in a chromosome
Convergence criterion	the stopping criterion for GA
On-line performance	the average of all fitness values up to the present generation
Off-line performance	the running average of the fitness of the best individual up to the present generation

Fitness function is the objective function to be maximized. The fitness value of a chromosome measures how good a chromosome is. One may also define a cost function to be minimized. The cost value a chromosome measures how bad a chromosome is. Selections are made essentially according to the fitness values.

Commonly used encoding schemes for parameters include binary encoding, Gray encoding, real encoding, and tree encoding. In binary encoding, each gene of a chromosome is a binary number, i.e., 0 or 1. That is, a chromosome is a string of binary numbers. In the real encoding, each gene of a chromosome is a real number. Initial population is randomly generated in general.

Selection is a process of choosing parents and putting them into the mating pool for reproduction. Chromosomes of larger fitness values will be selected with higher probability. Commonly used selection schemes include fitness-proportionate selection (roulette wheel selection, or stochastic sampling with replacement), stochastic sampling without replacement, stochastic universal sampling, random selection, elitism, Boltzmann selection, rank selection (from top to bottom), steady-state selection, and tournament selection.

In the fitness-proportionate selection, the number of times an individual chromosome is expected to reproduce is equal to its fitness value divided by the average of fitness values in the population. The elitism means to retain some number of the best chromosomes at each generation. The purpose of the rank selection is to prevent too-quick convergence (i.e., to avoid premature). The chromosomes in the population are ranked according to their fitness values, and the expected number of times that a given chromosome is selected depends on its rank rather than on its absolute fitness value.

We have particularly been interested in the tournament selection because of its computational efficiency, which can be described as follows:

Step 1: Randomly select two chromosomes from the population, say z_1 and z_2. Choose the "dad" by performing:

if $fitness[z_1] \geq fitness[z_2]$, then dad:= z_1; else dad:= z_2.

Step 2: Randomly select two chromosomes from the population, say z_3 and z_4. Choose the "mom" by performing:

$$\text{if } fitness[z_3] \geq fitness[z_4], \text{ then mom}:=z_3 \text{ ; else mom}:=z_4.$$

It is common practice to have low selection pressure in initial generations to avoid premature and maintain diversity, and high selection pressure in final generations to speedup the convergence.

Crossover is a reproduction (or genetic) operator that forms a new chromosome from two parent chromosomes by combing part of the information from each, controlled by a parameter P_c called crossover probability, with the hope to generate better offspring. Commonly used crossover schemes include single-point crossover, two-point crossover, uniform crossover, and parameterized uniform crossover.

The parameterized uniform crossover can be described as follows:

Data: parents:

$$z_d := \begin{bmatrix} z_{d1} & z_{d2} & \cdots & z_{d,l-1} & z_{dl} \end{bmatrix}$$
$$z_m := \begin{bmatrix} z_{m1} & z_{m2} & \cdots & z_{m,l-1} & z_{ml} \end{bmatrix}$$

Result: offspring:

$$z_b := \begin{bmatrix} z_{b1} & z_{b2} & \cdots & z_{b,l-1} & z_{bl} \end{bmatrix}$$
$$z_s := \begin{bmatrix} z_{s1} & z_{s2} & \cdots & z_{s,l-1} & z_{sl} \end{bmatrix}$$

Step: For each $i \in l$,

if $Rand(\cdot) > threshold\_x$, then

$$z_{bi} = z_{mi} - rand(\cdot)(z_{mi} - z_{di});$$
$$z_{si} = z_{di} + rand(\cdot)(z_{mi} - z_{di});$$

else $z_{bi} = z_{di}$; $z_{si} = z_{mi}$.

Here, $threshold\_x$ is a pre-specified parameter, say 0.25 or 0.75, and $Rand(\cdot)$, $rand(\cdot)$ are two generators giving random numbers between

$[0, 1]$. Note that if $rand(\cdot) = 0$, then $z_{bi} = z_{mi}$ and $z_{si} = z_{di}$, whilst if $rand(\cdot) = 1$, then $z_{bi} = z_{di}$ and $z_{si} = z_{mi}$.

Mutation is a reproduction (or genetic) operator that randomly alters the values of genes in a chromosome, controlled by a parameter P_m called mutation probability, with the hope to escape from the local optima (or leapfrog over the sticking points) of the fitness landscape. In its simplest form, some randomly selected genes of chromosomes are flipped in binary genetic algorithm, or replaced by new random numbers in real genetic algorithm, with probability P_m. Commonly used mutation schemes include point mutation, uniform mutation, and parameterized uniform mutation.

The parameterized uniform mutation can be described as follows:

For each $i \in l$,

> if $rand(\cdot) > threshold\_m$,
>> then z_i is replaced by a random number;
> else z_i is maintained.

Here, $threshold\_m$ is a pre-specified parameter, say 0.01 or 0.25, and $rand(\cdot)$ is a generator giving a random number in $[0, 1]$.

To stop the algorithm, we need a convergence criterion, i.e., the stopping criterion. The algorithm may be terminated when an acceptable solution has been obtained, or when the pre-specified maximum number of iterations has been reached, or there is no significant improvement of fitness values over prescribed runs.

There are many variants of the genetic algorithms. We now describe a simple version of the real genetic algorithm which we have used frequently in our research.

Let N_{ip} be the initial population size. After the initial random seeding, only N_p highly fit chromosomes, according to their fitness values, are kept for the next generation, i.e., N_p is the population size after the initial generation. Then N_g highly fit chromosomes are kept directly for the next generation (elitism). These chromosomes form the mating pool for reproduction. The rest N_b chromosomes, where $N_p = N_g + N_b$, are simply thrown away. The tournament selection is utilized for mating. The parameterized uniform crossover is performed on N_g highly fit chromosomes for generating N_b temporary offspring chromosomes. Let λ_j be the prescribed mutation rate in generation j. The number of times for mutation is given by $k_j := \lambda_j * N_p * l$, where l is the length of the chromosome. First, we randomly select one locus of a randomly chosen chromosome from N_b temporary offspring chromosomes. Then, the parameter at this locus is replaced by a random number. The N_g highly fit chromosomes and the N_b chromosomes after crossover and mutation operations form the population for the next generation.

In practice, we may need to apply the genetic algorithm several times to find a reasonably well approximate solution.

If GA is used to approximate the optimal connection weights of a neural network, then each connection weight becomes a gene of a chromosome.

8.2 Particle Swarm Optimization

The particle swarm optimization (PSO) algorithm starts with a population of candidate solutions, called particles, to the problem. A prescribed fitness function or objective function is defined for particles. The velocity of each particle is updated according to two factors, the cognitive factor and the social factor. The cognitive part of a particle requires the recording of its best previous position up to the present, reflecting its own memory of the past. The social part requires the recording of the particle giving the best objective value of all particles up to the present, representing the sharing of the experience of the whole swarm. After the velocity of a particle has been updated, its new position can be determined. The updating process aims at directing the particles of the swarm targeting the global optimum. The objective values of particles are calculated at each iteration of the process until the pre-specified convergence criterion is met. The whole process is illustrated in Figure 8.2.1.

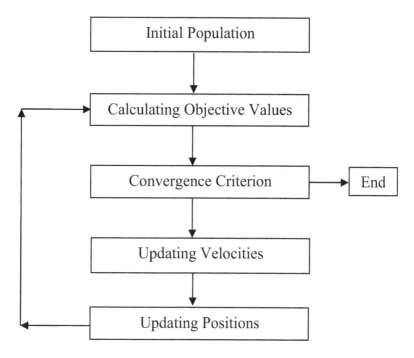

Figure 8.2.1: The process of PSO algorithm.

Let x_{ij} be the jth position component of the ith particle and v_{ij} the jth velocity component of the ith particle. The updating formulae for velocity and position of the ith particle are given by, respectively,

$$v_{ij} \leftarrow w * v_{ij} + c_1 * r_{ij}^{(1)} * \{bestx_{ij} - x_{ij}\} + c_2 * r_{ij}^{(2)} * \{bestx_{champion,j} - x_{ij}\};$$
$$x_{ij} \leftarrow x_{ij} + v_{ij}.$$

Here, $bestx_{ij}$ is the jth component of the best previous position of the ith particle, *champion* is the particle giving the best objective value of all particles up to the present, w is the inertia weight balancing local and global searches, c_1 and c_2 are two pre-specified constants, sometimes called the individuality and sociality coefficients, respectively, and $r_{ij}^{(1)}$, $r_{ij}^{(2)}$ are two random numbers in $[0, 1]$.

In many practical cases, it is preferable to put bounds on the velocities v_{ij}'s and/or positions x_{ij}'s. Moreover, we may need to apply the particle swarm optimization algorithm several times to find a reasonably well approximate solution.

If PSO is used to approximate the optimal connection weights of a neural network, then each connection weight becomes a component of a particle.

8.3   GA-based SVM Parameter Settings

In this section, we propose two general GA-based frameworks for determining the parameters of a support vector learning problem.   It should be kept in mind that only experimental data (or observational data) are available at hand.   Constructive and full use of all experimental data at hand is a natural approach for model selection.   Both the training errors and testing errors may be taken into account in these two frameworks.

Suppose we want to design a soft margin classifier or a soft regressor as described in Section 6.3 and Section 6.4, respectively.   Assume that we use the Mahalanobis kernel

$$K(x, z) := \exp\left[-\sigma_1^{-2}(x_1 - z_1)^2 - \ldots - \sigma_n^{-2}(x_n - z_n)^2\right].$$

The parameters for support vector classification (SVC) are C, σ_1^2, ..., and σ_n^2, in which case a chromosome for SVC is given by $z := \begin{bmatrix} C & \sigma_1^2 & \ldots & \sigma_n^2 \end{bmatrix}$ and each component z_i, $i \in \underline{n+1}$, is a gene. Possible fitness value of a chromosome in SVC is the number of testing data that are correctly classified.   The parameters for support vector regression (SVR) are C, ε, σ_1^2, ..., and σ_n^2, in which case a chromosome for SVR is given by $z := \begin{bmatrix} C & \varepsilon & \sigma_1^2 & \ldots & \sigma_n^2 \end{bmatrix}$ and each component z_i, $i \in \underline{n+2}$, is a gene.   Possible fitness value of a chromosome in SVR is the negative (or reciprocal) of the mean squared error (MSE) or the mean absolute deviation (MAD) for testing data.

Framework 1 for model selection as shown in Figure 8.3.1 may be viewed as a generalization of the method of cross validation (specifically, the k-fold method). In each generation of Framework 1, the training examples of fixed size are randomly selected from experimental data set with the remaining as the testing examples. Because of the random selection of training examples, the fitness values of the same chromosome are different for different rounds.

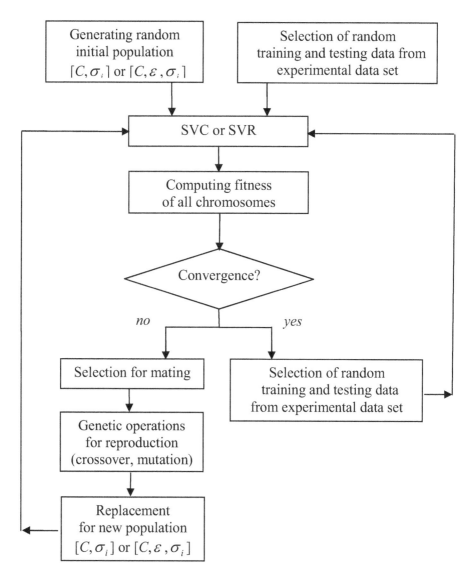

Figure 8.3.1: GA-based Framework 1 for SVM parameter settings.

It is our experience that the experimental data that is likely to stump the learning machine should be kept in the training data set for full training of the learning machine. This motivates our Framework 2 for model selection as shown in Figure 8.3.2.

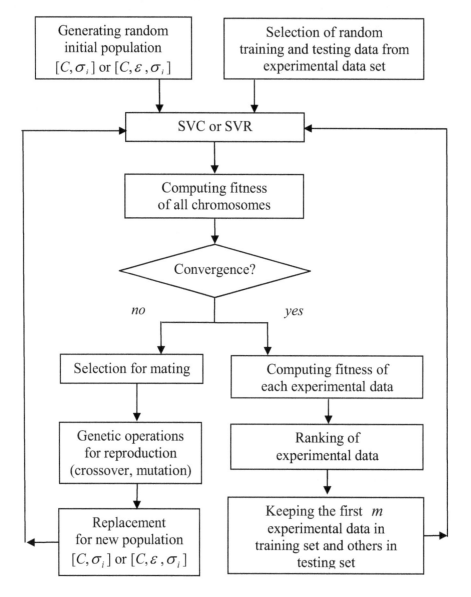

Figure 8.3.2: GA-based Framework 2 for SVM parameter settings.

The main feature of Framework 2 is that both the chromosomes, representing the possible parameters of the learning problem, and the experimental data are assigned the fitness values. In SVC, possible fitness value of a chromosome is the number of testing data that are correctly classified and that of an experimental data is the number of misclassifications made by chromosomes in the current population. In SVR, possible fitness value of a chromosome is the negative (or reciprocal) of the mean squared error (MSE) or the mean absolute deviation (MAD) for testing data and that of an experimental data is the MSE or MAD made by chromosomes in the current population. The experimental data with higher fitness values are kept in the training data set for the next generation.

It is a characteristic of the genetic algorithm that upon termination of the algorithm, multiple possible candidates for the solution of the problem are provided. Thus we must devise some ways to choose a final solution among those possible candidates, i.e., the final choice of the parameters of the learning problem. A natural criterion is the **life time** of a chromosome, i.e., the number of generations that a given chromosome lives. The chromosome with the longest life time is chosen as our final solution. Another reasonable criterion is the "**life score**" of a chromosome, which is the average score over generations of a given chromosome. In this approach, scores are assigned in descending order to only top m, say top 5, chromosomes. For other chromosomes, the scores are set to be zero. The chromosome with the highest life score is chosen as our final solution.

8.4 PSO-based SVM Parameter Settings

As in the previous section, we may provide two PSO-based frameworks for determining the parameters of a support vector learning problem, as shown in Figure 8.4.1 and Figure 8.4.2. The fitness functions are defined as those in the previous section. The particle giving the best objective value of all particles up to the termination of the algorithm is chosen as our final solution.

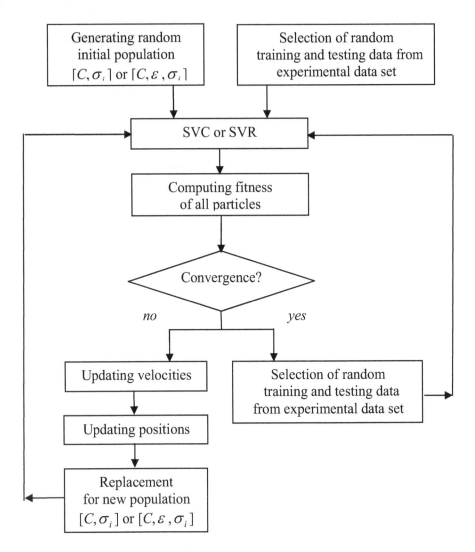

Figure 8.4.1: PSO-based Framework 1 for SVM parameter settings.

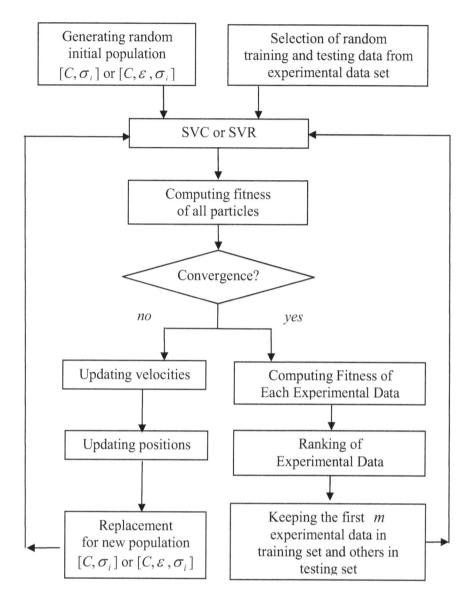

Figure 8.4.2: PSO-based Framework 2 for SVM parameter settings.

8.5 Illustrative Examples

In this section, we provide some numerical examples to illustrate the use of the PSO-based framework 1 for SVM parameter settings of the support vector classification and regression problems.

At each iteration of the following simulations, the number of training examples is 30 and the number of testing examples is 20. The fitness function is taken as the number of testing examples that are correctly classified in the classification cases and the fitness function is taken as the negative mean absolute deviation for the testing examples in the regression cases.

Example 8.5.1: Consider the data set of Example 5.6.1, where true discriminant function is given by the fractional power function

$$g(x_1, x_2) = x_2 - x_1^{2/3}, \quad x_1 \in [-2, 2], \quad x_2 \in [0, 2].$$

The parameter settings and simulation results for 1-norm SVC (SVC1) and 2-norm SVC (SVC2), all with Mahalanobis kernels, are shown in Table 8.5.1. The true decision boundary and the decision boundaries determined by SVC1 and SVC2 are shown in Figure 8.5.1. With such highly corrupted data, the decision boundaries are reasonable.

Table 8.5.1: Parameter settings and simulation results in Example 8.5.1.

PSO	SVC1	SVC2
Number of generations	100	100
Length of each particle	3	3
Population size	40	40
Searching region of particle components	$C \in [1, 5]$	$C \in [1, 5]$
	$\sigma_1^2 \in [0.5, 2]$	$\sigma_1^2 \in [0.5, 2]$
	$\sigma_2^2 \in [0.1, 0.5]$	$\sigma_2^2 \in [0.1, 1]$
Range of particle velocities	$[-0.1, 0.1]$	$[-0.1, 0.1]$
Inertia weight w	0.6	0.6
Individuality coefficient c_1	1.7	1.7
Sociality coefficient c_2	1.7	1.7
Final parameters	$C = 2.3582$	$C = 2.2473$
	$\sigma_1^2 = 1.6596$	$\sigma_1^2 = 1.8049$
	$\sigma_2^2 = 0.3061$	$\sigma_2^2 = 0.1184$
Estimated maximal payoff	58.3450	29.4912
Number of misclassifications	8	7

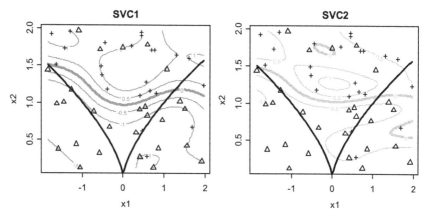

Figure 8.5.1: Decision boundaries in Example 8.5.1.

Example 8.5.2: Consider the data set of Example 5.6.2, where true regression function is given by the sinc function

$$g(x) = \begin{cases} 1, & x = 0, \\ \sin(x)/x, & x \neq 0, \end{cases} \quad x \in [-10, 10].$$

The parameter settings and simulation results for 1-norm SVR (SVR1) and 2-norm SVR (SVR2), all with Gaussian kernels, are shown in Table 8.5.2. The true function and the predictive functions determined by SVR1 and SVR2 are shown in Figure 8.5.2. The predictive function determined by SVR1 is almost identical to the true regression function.

Table 8.5.2: Parameter settings and simulation results in Example 8.5.2.

PSO	SVR1	SVR2
Number of generations	100	100
Length of each particle	3	3
Population size	40	40
Searching region	$C \in [0.2, 1]$	$C \in [0.5, 2]$
of particle components	$\varepsilon \in [0.01, 0.5]$	$\varepsilon \in [0.01, 0.5]$
	$\sigma^2 \in [4, 12]$	$\sigma^2 \in [4, 12]$
Range of particle velocities	$[-0.1, 0.1]$	$[-0.1, 0.1]$
Inertia weight w	0.6	0.6
Individuality coefficient c_1	1.7	1.7
Sociality coefficient c_2	1.7	1.7
Final parameters	$C = 0.7272$	$C = 0.5$
	$\varepsilon = 0.01$	$\varepsilon = 0.01$
	$\sigma^2 = 8.2913$	$\sigma^2 = 4$
Estimated maximal payoff	6.2577	1.6294
Mean squared error (MSE)	0.1063	0.0985
Mean absolute deviation (MAD)	0.1623	0.2015

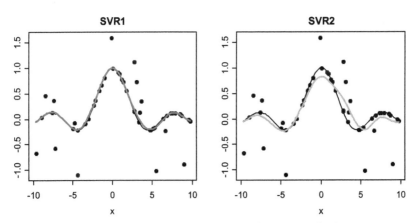

Figure 8.5.2: Predictive functions in Example 8.5.2.

Example 8.5.3: Consider the data set of Example 5.6.3, where true regression function is given by the Hermite function

$$g(x) = 1.1 \cdot (1 - x + 2x^2) \cdot e^{-x^2/2}, \quad x \in [-5, 5].$$

The parameter settings and simulation results for 1-norm SVR (SVR1) and 2-norm SVR (SVR2), all with Gaussian kernels, are shown in Table 8.5.3. The true function and the predictive functions determined by SVR1 and SVR2 are shown in Figure 8.5.3. The predictive function determined by SVR1 is almost identical to the true regression function. Note that the parameters in this example are quite different from those in Example 7.7.3.

Table 8.5.3: Parameter settings and simulation results in Example 8.5.3.

PSO	SVR1	SVR2
Number of generations	100	100
Length of each particle	3	3
Population size	40	40
Searching region	$C \in [1, 2]$	$C \in [1, 2]$
of particle components	$\varepsilon \in [0.01, 0.05]$	$\varepsilon \in [0.01, 0.05]$
	$\sigma^2 \in [2, 4]$	$\sigma^2 \in [0.5, 2]$
Range of particle velocities	$[-0.1, 0.1]$	$[-0.1, 0.1]$
Inertia weight w	0.6	0.6
Individuality coefficient c_1	1.7	1.7
Sociality coefficient c_2	1.7	1.7
Final parameters	$C = 2$	$C = 2$
	$\varepsilon = 0.01$	$\varepsilon = 0.01$
	$\sigma^2 = 2$	$\sigma^2 = 0.5$
Estimated maximal payoff	20.1013	6.7287
Mean squared error (MSE)	0.1100	0.0765
Mean absolute deviation (MAD)	0.1679	0.2085

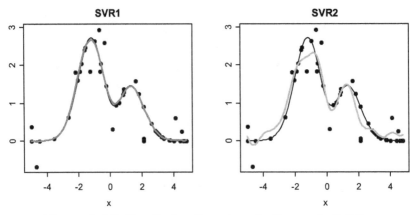

Figure 8.5.3: Predictive functions in Example 8.5.3.

8.6 Exercises

Exercise 8.6.1: Consider the non-smooth function

$$g(x, y, z) = (x - 1)^2 + (y - 2)^2 + |z - 3|,$$

which has the obvious global minimizer $x^* = 1$, $y^* = 2$, $z^* = 3$. Use a genetic algorithm with population size 40 to approximate the minimizer.

Exercise 8.6.2: Consider the function in Exercise 8.6.1. Use a particle swarm optimization algorithm with population size 40 to approximate the minimizer.

Exercise 8.6.3: Consider the data set of Exercise 5.7.8, where the true discriminant function is given by the Hermite function

$$g(x_1, x_2) = x_2 - 1.1 \cdot (1 - x_1 + 2x_1^2) \cdot e^{-x_1^2/2},$$
$$x_1 \in [-5, 5], \quad x_2 \in [-1, 3].$$

Use the PSO-based framework 1 to determine the parameters of the 1-norm SVC (SVC1) with Mahalanobis kernel. Draw the decision boundary thus determined and discuss whether these machine parameter settings are appropriate.

Exercise 8.6.4: Consider the data set of Exercise 5.7.9, where the true discriminant function is given by the sinc function

$$g(x) = \begin{cases} 1, & x = 0, \\ \sin(x)/x, & x \neq 0, \end{cases} \quad x \in [-10, 10].$$

Use the PSO-based framework 1 to determine the parameters of the 1-norm SVC (SVC1) with Mahalanobis kernel. Draw the decision boundary thus determined and discuss whether these machine parameter settings are appropriate.

Exercise 8.6.5: Consider the data set of Exercise 5.7.10, where the true regression function is given by the fractional power function

$$g(x) = x^{2/3}, \quad x \in [-2, 2].$$

Use the PSO-based framework 1 to determine the parameters of the 1-norm SVR (SVR1) with Gaussian kernel. Draw the predictive function thus determined and discuss whether these machine parameter settings are appropriate.

In the following two exercises, we investigate the possibilities of applying the genetic algorithm and particle swarm optimization algorithm to solve the 1-norm support vector regression problem.

Let $X \subseteq \mathfrak{R}^n$ and $Y \subseteq \mathfrak{R}$. Suppose we are given the training set

$$S := \left\{ (x_q, d_q) \right\}_{q=1}^{l} \subseteq X \times Y.$$

Let $K(x, z)$ be a given kernel on $X \times X$. Consider the following optimization:

(D1')   maximize $\displaystyle \sum_{q=1}^{l} z_q d_q - \varepsilon \sum_{q=1}^{l} |z_q| - \frac{1}{2} \sum_{q=1}^{l} \sum_{j=1}^{l} z_q z_j K(x_q, x_j)$

              subject to $\displaystyle \sum_{q=1}^{l} z_q = 0, \quad -C \leq z_q \leq C, \quad q \in \underline{l}.$

Exercise 8.6.6:

(a) Devise a genetic algorithm that will not violate the linear equality and box constraints.

(b) Discuss whether the genetic algorithm or the particle swarm optimization algorithm can do any better than the sequential minimal optimization algorithm.

We may also transform the constrained optimization (D1') to an optimization problem without the linear equality constraint, which is easier to solve. Note that the linear equality is easily violated by operations such as crossover and mutation of the genetic algorithm. To resolve this, we may transform the program (D1') to the following program via the exterior penalty function method:

(D1P')   maximize

$$\sum_{q=1}^{l} z_q d_q - \varepsilon \sum_{q=1}^{l} |z_q| - \frac{1}{2} \sum_{q=1}^{l} \sum_{j=1}^{l} z_q z_j K(x_q, x_j) - M \left| \sum_{q=1}^{l} z_q \right|$$

subject to

$$-C \le z_q \le C, \quad q \in \underline{l}.$$

Here the penalty parameter M is a big positive number. As is clear from the problem formulation of (D1P'), any violation of linear equality constraint will be highly penalized. Of course, we must guarantee that the box constraints are satisfied, which is easy to do.

Exercise 8.6.7:

(a) Devise a genetic algorithm that will not violate the box constraints.

(b) Discuss whether the genetic algorithm or the particle swarm optimization algorithm can do any better than the sequential minimal optimization algorithm.

8.7 Notes and References

For original paper on GA, see Holland (1962). Other good references are Davis (1991), Goldberg (1989), Haupt and Haupt (1998), Holland (1975), and Mitchell (1996). For the parameterized uniform crossover, see Spear and De Jong (1991) and Haupt and Haupt (1998). For the application of GA and PSO in fractal image compression, see Wu, Jeng, and Hsieh (2007) and Jeng, Tseng, and Hsieh (2009).

For original papers on PSO, see Eberhart and Kennedy (1995) and Kennedy and Eberhart (1995). Their recent book, Kennedy and Eberhart (2001), is very readable. For exterior penalty function method in the exercises, see Bazaraa, Sherali, and Shetty (1993) and Nocedal and Wright (2006).

For GA-based and PSO-based model selection, see Hsieh (2007).

There are some other successful metaheuristic algorithms for optimization. For Differential Evolution algorithms (DE), see Storn and Price (1997) and Price and Storn (1997). For Artificial Bee Colony algorithms (ABC), see Karaboga and Basturk (2007a, 2007b). For Cuckoo Search algorithms, see Yang and Deb (2009) and Yang and Deb (2010).

Bazaraa, M., D. Sherali, and C. Shetty (1993). Nonlinear Programming: Theory and Algorithm. Second Edition. Wiley, New York.

Davis, L. (Ed.) (1991). Handbook of Genetic Algorithms. Van Nostrand Reinhold, New York.

Eberhart, R.C. and J. Kennedy (1995). A new optimizer using particle swarm theory. Proceeding of the Sixth International Symposium on Micro Machine and Human Science, Nagoya, Japan, pp. 39-43.

Goldberg, D.E. (1989). Genetic Algorithms in Search, Optimization, and Machine Learning. Addison-Wesley, Massachusetts.

Good, P. I. (2006). Resampling Methods. Third Edition. Birkhauser, Boston.

Haupt, R.L. and S.E. Haupt (1998). Practical Genetic Algorithms. Wiley, New York.

Holland, J.H. (1962). Outline for a logical theory of adaptive systems.

Journal of the Association for Computing Machinery, Vol. 3, pp. 297-314.

Holland, J.H. (1975). Adaptation in Natural and Artificial Systems. University of Michigan Press, Michigan.

Hsieh, J.G. (2007). A simple guide to machine learning and soft computing (tutorial session speech). Proceeding of 14th International Conference on Intelligent System Applications to Power Systems (ISAP 2007), Kaohsiung, Taiwan, pp. 1-10 (Tutorial).

Jeng, J.H., C.C. Tseng, and J.G. Hsieh (2009). Study on Huber fractal image compression. IEEE Transactions on Image Processing, Vol. 18, Issue 5, pp. 995-1003.

Karaboga, D. and B. Basturk (2007a). Artificial bee colony (abc) optimization algorithm for solving constrained optimization problems. in Advances in Soft Computing: Foundations of Fuzzy Logic and Soft Computing, P. Melin et al., Eds., IFSA 2007, LANI, Springer- Verlag, Berlin, Vol. 4529/2007, pp. 789-798.

Karaboga, D. and B. Basturk B (2007b). A powerful and efficient algorithm for numerical function optimization: artificial bee colony (abc) algorithm. Journal of Global Optimization, Vol. 39, No. 3, pp. 459-471.

Kennedy, J. and R.C. Eberhart (1995). Particle swarm optimization. Proceeding of IEEE International Conference on Neural Networks, Perth, Australia, Vol. 4, pp. 1942-1948.

Kennedy, J. and R.C. Eberhart (2001). Swarm Intelligence. Morgan Kaufmann, San Francisco, California.

Mitchell, M. (1996). An Introduction to Genetic Algorithms. MIT Press, Cambridge, Massachusetts.

Nocedal, J. and S.J. Wright (2006). Numerical Optimization. Second Edition. Springer, New York.

Price, K. and R. Storn (1997). Differential evolution: Numerical optimization made easy, Dr. Dobb's Journal, Vol. 22, No. 4, pp. 18-24.

Spear, W.M. and De Jong, K.A. (1991). On the virtues of parameterized uniform crossover. In R.K. Belew, and L.B. Booker (Eds.), Proceedings of the 4th International Conference on Genetic Algorithms, pp. 279-286. Morgan Kaufmann, California.

Storn, R. and K. Price (1997). Differential evolution–a simple and efficient heuristic for global optimization over continuous spaces. Journal of Global Optimization, Vol. 11, pp. 341–359. doi:10.1023/A:1008202821328

Wu, M.S., J.H. Jeng, and J.G. Hsieh (2007). Schema genetic algorithm for fractal image compression. Engineering Applications of Artificial Intelligence, Vol. 20, pp. 531-538.

Yang, X.S. and S. Deb (2009). Cuckoo search via Levy flights. Proceedings of World Congress on Nature & Biologically Inspired Computing (NaBIC 2009), India, IEEE publications, USA, pp. 210-214.

Yang, X.S. and S. Deb (2010). Engineering optimization by cuckoo search. International Journal of Mathematical Modeling and Numerical Optimization. Vol. 1, No. 4, pp. 330-343.

Chapter 9   Wilcoxon Learning Machines

Robust and nonparametric smoothing is a central idea in statistics that aims simultaneously to estimate and model the underlying structure without much influence by the outliers.   One important method belonging to this category is the Wilcoxon approach to linear (parametric) regression problems.   The resulting regressors are usually robust against (or insensitive to) outliers.   This motivates us to include the Wilcoxon approach to nonlinear machine learning problems.

In this chapter, we study the newly developed Wilcoxon learning machines.   These machines are quite robust against (or insensitive to) outliers.   First, we introduce the score functions and Wilcoxon norms. Then we introduce the Wilcoxon approach to artificial neural networks, generalized radial basis function networks, and fuzzy neural networks, together with the weights updating rules.   The resulting networks are called   Wilcoxon   artificial   neural   networks   (WANNs),   Wilcoxon generalized radial basis function networks (WGRBFNs), and Wilcoxon fuzzy neural networks (WFNN), respectively.   Finally, motivated by the support vector machines, we investigate the kernel-based Wilcoxon machines (KWMs).

9.1 Wilcoxon Norm

Before investigating the Wilcoxon learning machines, we first introduce the Wilcoxon norm of a vector, which will be used as the objective function for all Wilcoxon learning machines.   See Hogg, McKean, and Craig (2005).

To define the Wilcoxon norm of a vector, we need a score function. A **score function** is a function $\varphi(u):[0,1] \to \Re$ which is non-decreasing (i.e., increasing) such that

$$\int_0^1 \varphi^2(u)du < \infty .$$

Usually, the score function is standardized so that

$$\int_0^1 \varphi(u)du = 0 \quad \text{and} \quad \int_0^1 \varphi^2(u)du = 1.$$

The **score** associated with the score function φ is defined by

$$a_\varphi(i) = \varphi\left(\frac{i}{l+1}\right), \quad i \in \underline{l}.$$

Hence we have

$$a_\varphi(1) \le a_\varphi(2) \le \dots \le a_\varphi(l).$$

It can be shown that the following function is a pseudo-norm (or semi-norm) on $\mathfrak{R}^l$:

$$\|v\|_W := \sum_{i=1}^l a(R(v_i))v_i = \sum_{i=1}^l a(i)v_{(i)}, \quad v := [v_1 \quad \dots \quad v_l]^T \in \mathfrak{R}^l,$$

where $R(v_i)$ denotes the rank of v_i among $v_1, \dots, v_l$, $v_{(1)} \le \dots \le v_{(l)}$ are the ordered values of $v_1, \dots, v_l$, $a(i) := \varphi[i/(l+1)]$, and $\varphi(u) := \sqrt{12}(u - 0.5)$. We call $\|v\|_W$ the **Wilcoxon norm** of v.

It is easy to show that the Wilcoxon norm satisfies the following properties for a pseudo-norm:

(a) $\|v\|_W \ge 0$ for all $v \in \mathfrak{R}^l$;

(b) $\|\alpha v\|_W = |\alpha| \cdot \|v\|_W$ for all $\alpha \in \mathfrak{R}$ and $v \in \mathfrak{R}^l$;

(c) $\|u + v\|_W \le \|u\|_W + \|v\|_W$ for all $u, v \in \mathfrak{R}^l$.

Moreover, $\|v\|_W = 0$, $v := [v_1 \quad \dots \quad v_l]^T \in \mathfrak{R}^l$, implies that $v_1 = \dots = v_l$. Further, it can be shown that the Wilcoxon norm can be written as

$$\|v\|_W = \frac{\sqrt{3}}{2(l+1)} \sum_{i=1}^l \sum_{j=1}^l |v_i - v_j|, \quad v := [v_1 \quad \dots \quad v_l]^T \in \mathfrak{R}^l,$$

or equivalently as

$$\|v\|_W = \frac{\sqrt{3}}{l+1}\sum_{i<j}|v_i - v_j|, \quad v := \begin{bmatrix} v_1 & \cdots & v_l \end{bmatrix}^T \in \mathfrak{R}^l.$$

Note that there are other score functions available, which can be used in different situations. For instance,

$$\varphi_2(u) = \text{sgn}(2u - 1) = \begin{cases} -1, & 0 \le u \le 1/2, \\ 1, & 1/2 < u \le 1, \end{cases}$$

$$\varphi_3(u) = \begin{cases} \sqrt{6}(4u - 1), & 0 \le u \le 1/4 \\ 0, & 1/4 < u \le 3/4, \\ \sqrt{6}(4u - 3), & 3/4 < u \le 1, \end{cases}$$

$$\varphi_4(u) = \begin{cases} \sqrt{\dfrac{12}{5}}\left(4u - \dfrac{3}{2}\right), & 0 \le u \le 1/2, \\ \sqrt{\dfrac{12}{5}} \cdot \dfrac{1}{2}, & 1/2 < u \le 1. \end{cases}$$

It is noted that

$$\sum_{i=1}^{l} a(R(v_i)) = \sum_{i=1}^{l} \varphi\left(\frac{i}{l+1}\right) = \sum_{i=1}^{l} \sqrt{12}\left(\frac{i}{l+1} - 0.5\right)$$

$$= \frac{\sqrt{12}}{l+1}\sum_{i=1}^{l} i - \frac{\sqrt{12}}{2} \times l = \frac{\sqrt{12}}{l+1} \times \frac{l \times (l+1)}{2} - \frac{\sqrt{12}}{2} \times l = 0.$$

9.2 Linear Wilcoxon Regressor

In this part, we consider the linear Wilcoxon regressors. The delta learning rule updates the weights and bias of a linear least squares regressor with correcting terms which are proportional to the errors or differences between the actual outputs the predicted outputs. On the other hand, the weights of a linear Wilcoxon regressor are updated according to the ranks of the residuals, but not the magnitudes of the residuals.   See Hogg, McKean, and Craig (2005).

Let $X \subseteq \mathfrak{R}^n$ and $Y \subseteq \mathfrak{R}$.   Suppose we are given the training set

$$S := \left\{ \left(x_q, d_q \right) \right\}_{q=1}^{l} \subseteq X \times Y.$$

The linear predictive function is given by

$$f(x) = \langle w, x \rangle + b.$$

The residual due to the qth example is defined by

$$e_q := d_q - \langle w, x_q \rangle - b, \quad q \in \underline{l}.$$

The Wilcoxon approach is to choose weight vector w and b that minimize the Wilcoxon norm of the residuals given by

$$\|e\|_W := \sum_{q=1}^{l} a \left(R(e_q) \right) e_q = \sum_{q=1}^{l} a(q) e_{(q)}, \quad e := \begin{bmatrix} e_1 & \cdots & e_l \end{bmatrix}^T \in \mathfrak{R}^l.$$

However, note that

$$
\begin{aligned}
\|e\|_W &:= \sum_{q=1}^{l} a \left(R(e_q) \right) e_q = \sum_{q=1}^{l} a \left(R(e_q) \right) \left(d_q - \langle w, x_q \rangle - b \right) \\
&= \sum_{q=1}^{l} a \left(R(e_q) \right) \left(d_q - \langle w, x_q \rangle \right) - b \sum_{q=1}^{l} a \left(R(e_q) \right) \\
&= \sum_{q=1}^{l} a \left(R(e_q) \right) \left(d_q - \langle w, x_q \rangle \right) - 0 \\
&= \sum_{q=1}^{l} a \left(R(e_q) \right) \left(d_q - \langle w, x_q \rangle \right) \\
&= \sum_{q=1}^{l} a \left(R(\rho_q) \right) \rho_q \\
&= \sum_{q=1}^{l} a(q) \rho_{(q)},
\end{aligned}
$$

where

$$\rho_q := d_q - \langle w, x_q \rangle, \quad q \in \underline{l}, \text{ and } \rho := \begin{bmatrix} \rho_1 & \cdots & \rho_l \end{bmatrix}^T \in \mathfrak{R}^l.$$

This shows that $\|e\|_W$ is not a function of the bias b. Thus, it is equivalent to consider minimizing

$$\|\rho\|_W := \sum_{q=1}^{l} a(R(\rho_q))\rho_q = \sum_{q=1}^{l} a(q)\rho_{(q)}, \quad \rho := \begin{bmatrix} \rho_1 & \cdots & \rho_l \end{bmatrix}^T \in \mathfrak{R}^l.$$

Taking the gradient with respect to w and setting it to zero, we have

$$0 = \frac{\partial}{\partial w} \|\rho\|_W = -\sum_{q=1}^{l} a(q) x_{(q)}.$$

Hence the estimating equations are given by

$$\sum_{q=1}^{l} a\!\left(R\!\left(d_q - \langle \hat{w}, x_q \rangle\right)\right) x_q = 0.$$

The bias or the intercept parameter is given by the median of the residuals, i.e.,

$$\hat{b} = \operatorname*{med}_{1 \le q \le l}\{d_q - \langle \hat{w}, x_q \rangle\}.$$

Since the gradient of $\|\rho\|_W$ is given by

$$\frac{\partial}{\partial w} \|\rho\|_W = -\sum_{q=1}^{l} a(R(\rho_q)) x_q,$$

the updating law based on the steepest decent is given by

$$w_k \leftarrow w_k + \eta \sum_{q=1}^{l} a(R(\rho_q))(x_q)_k, \quad k \in \underline{n},$$

where $(x_q)_k$ is the kth component of the qth data x_q, and $\eta > 0$ is the learning rate. The bias or the intercept parameter b is given by the median of the residuals, i.e.,

$$b = \underset{1 \le q \le l}{med}\{\rho_q\}.$$

Example 9.2.1: We are given 20 training data, with about half skewed outliers, as shown in Figure 9.2.1. The true function is $y = 3x + 2$. The linear least squares estimate is $y = 3.4383 \cdot x + 2.6463$, and the linear Wilcoxon estimate, with the slope parameter minimizing the Wilcoxon norm of residuals, is $y = 3.0001 \cdot x + 2.0$, which is essentially the same as the true function. Figure 9.2.2 gives visualization of the function $w \mapsto \|\rho\|_w$, where w is the slope parameter and $\|\rho\|_w$ is the corresponding Wilcoxon norm of residuals. This confirms that the minimum occurs at $w = 3$. This example shows that the linear Wilcoxon regressor is quite robust against outliers. That is, the Wilcoxon norm of residuals might be a better robustness indicator than the usual l_2-norm.

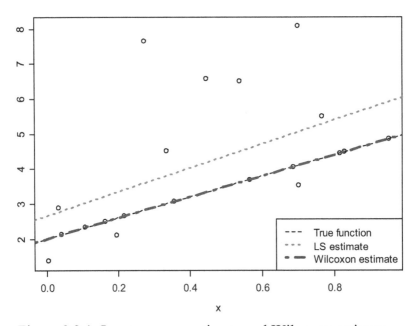

Figure 9.2.1: Least squares estimate and Wilcoxon estimate.

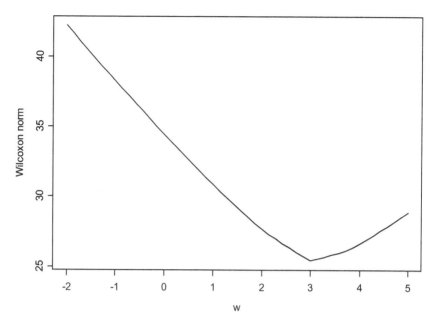

Figure 9.2.2: Graph of the function $w \mapsto \|\rho\|_W$.

It is a good place here to compare how the residuals are penalized in cost functions of commonly used approaches. Let the linear predictive function be given by

$$f(x) = \langle w, x \rangle + b.$$

In the least squares (LS) approach, the cost function to be minimized is the MSE (mean squared errors) given by

$$\frac{1}{l}\|e\|_{LS}^2 := \frac{1}{l}\sum_{q=1}^{l} e_q^2 = \sum_{q=1}^{l}\left(e_q/l\right)\cdot e_q,$$

where e_q is the residual due to the qth example. It is desired that $e_q \approx 0$. It can be seen that positive (resp., negative) residual gets a positive (resp., negative) "score" (or penalizing weight) e_q/l in a linear way. Thus, larger deviations of the residuals from zero get heavier penalizing weights.

In the least absolute deviations (LAD) approach, the cost function to be minimized is the MAD (mean absolute deviations) given by

$$\frac{1}{l}\|e\|_{LAD} := \frac{1}{l}\sum_{q=1}^{l}|e_q| = \sum_{q=1}^{l}[\operatorname{sgn}(e_q)/l]\cdot e_q .$$

It is desired that $e_q \approx 0$. It is obvious that positive (resp., negative) residual gets $1/l$ (resp., $-1/l$) "score" (or penalizing weight) in a uniform fashion. Thus, all residuals are penalized equally.

In the Wilcoxon approach, the cost function to be minimized is given by

$$\|e\|_W := \sum_{q=1}^{l} a(R(e_q))e_q = \sum_{q=1}^{l} \sqrt{12}\left(\frac{R(e_q)}{l+1} - 0.5\right)e_q ,$$

It is desired that $e_q \approx e_{med}$, where e_{med} is the median of all the residuals. The residual e_q strictly greater (resp., smaller) than the median e_{med} gets a positive (resp., negative) score according to its rank. Thus, larger deviations of the residuals from the median get heavier penalizing weights. The result of Example 9.2.1 gives us a hint that the Wilcoxon norm of the residuals might be a good robustness indicator (against outliers) than other cost functions.

9.3 Wilcoxon Artificial Neural Network

As shown in the last section, the linear Wilcoxon regressor is quite insensitive (or robust) against outliers. This motivates us to consider the Wilcoxon artificial neural networks (WANNs). Consider the artificial neural network as shown in Figure 9.3.1. There is a single input layer with $n+1$ nodes, a single hidden layer with $m+1$ nodes, and a single output layer with p nodes. We also have p bias terms at the output nodes.

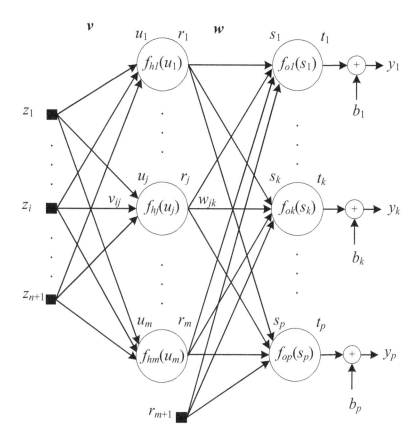

Figure 9.3.1: Wilcoxon artificial neural network.

Let the input vector be

$$x := \begin{bmatrix} x_1 & \cdots & x_n \end{bmatrix}^T \in \Re^n,$$

or

$$z := \begin{bmatrix} z_1 & \cdots & z_n & z_{n+1} \end{bmatrix}^T = \begin{bmatrix} x_1 & \cdots & x_n & 1 \end{bmatrix}^T \in \Re^{n+1},$$

i.e.,

$$z_i := x_i, \quad i \in \underline{n}, \quad z_{n+1} := 1.$$

Let v_{ij} denote the connection weight from ith input node to the input of the jth hidden node. Then the input and output of the jth hidden node are given by, respectively,

$$u_j = \sum_{i=1}^{n+1} v_{ij} z_i, \quad z_{n+1} := 1, \quad r_j = f_{hj}(u_j), \quad j \in \underline{m},$$

where f_{hj} is the activation function of the jth hidden node.

Let w_{jk} denote the connection weight from the output of the jth hidden node to the input of the kth output node. Then the input and output of the kth output node are given by, respectively,

$$s_k = \sum_{j=1}^{m+1} w_{jk} r_j, \quad r_{m+1} := 1, \quad t_k = f_{ok}(s_k), \quad y_k = t_k + b_k, \quad k \in \underline{p},$$

where f_{ok} is the activation function of the kth output node and b_k is the bias.

Let $X \subseteq \mathfrak{R}^n$ and $Y \subseteq \mathfrak{R}^p$. Suppose we are given the training set

$$S := \{(x_q, d_q)\}_{q=1}^{\vee} \subseteq X \times Y \quad \text{or} \quad S := \{(z_q, d_q)\}_{q=1}^{\vee} \subseteq \mathfrak{R}^{n+1} \times \mathfrak{R}^p.$$

In the following, we will use the subscript q to denote the qth example. For instance, x_{qi} denotes the ith component of the qth pattern $x_q \in \mathfrak{R}^n$, $q \in \underline{l}$, $i \in \underline{n}$.

In a Wilcoxon artificial neural network, the approach is to choose network weights that minimize the Wilcoxon norm of the total residuals

$$\Psi_{total} = \sum_{k=1}^{p} \sum_{q=1}^{l} a(R(\rho_{qk})) \rho_{qk} = \sum_{k=1}^{p} \sum_{q=1}^{l} a(q) \rho_{(q)k},$$

$$\rho_{qk} := d_{qk} - t_{qk}, \quad q \in \underline{l}, \quad k \in \underline{p}.$$

Here, $R(\rho_{qk})$ denotes the rank of the residual ρ_{qk} among $\rho_{1k}, \ldots, \rho_{lk}$, $\rho_{(1)k} \le \ldots \le \rho_{(l)k}$ are the ordered values of $\rho_{1k}, \ldots, \rho_{lk}$, and $a(i) := \varphi[i/(l+1)]$ is a score function with $\varphi(u) := \sqrt{12}(u - 0.5)$.

The Wilcoxon norm of residuals at the kth output node is given by

$$\Psi_k := \|\rho_k\|_W := \sum_{q=1}^{l} a(R(\rho_{qk})) \rho_{qk} = \sum_{q=1}^{l} a(q) \rho_{(q)k},$$

$$\rho_k := \begin{bmatrix} \rho_{1k} & \rho_{2k} & \cdots & \rho_{lk} \end{bmatrix}^T \in \mathfrak{R}^l.$$

Then we have

$$\Psi_{total} = \sum_{k=1}^{p} \Psi_k.$$

The artificial neural network used here is the same as that used in standard artificial neural network, except the bias terms at the output nodes. The main reason is that the Wilcoxon norm is not a usual norm, but a pseudo-norm (or semi-norm). In particular,

$$\|v\|_W = 0, \quad v := \begin{bmatrix} v_1 & \cdots & v_l \end{bmatrix}^T \in \mathfrak{R}^l,$$

implies that $v_1 = \ldots = v_l$. This means that, without the bias terms, the resulting predictive function with small value of the Wilcoxon norm of total residuals may deviate from the true function by constant offsets.

Now we introduce an incremental gradient descent algorithm. In this algorithm, Ψ_k's are minimized in sequence. From the definition of Ψ_k, we have

$$\Psi_k := \|\rho_k\|_W = \sum_{q=1}^{l} a(q) \left[d_{(q)k} - t_{(q)k} \right] = \sum_{q=1}^{l} a(q) \left[d_{(q)k} - f_{ok}\left(s_{(q)k} \right) \right].$$

First, we propose an updating rule for w_{jk}, which is given by

$$w_{jk} \leftarrow w_{jk} - \eta_w \frac{\partial \Psi_k}{\partial w_{jk}}, \quad j \in \underline{m+1}, \quad k \in \underline{p},$$

where $\eta_w > 0$ is a learning rate. Since

$$\frac{\partial \Psi_k}{\partial w_{jk}} = \sum_{q=1}^{l} a(q)(-1) f'_{ok}\left(s_{(q)k} \right) r_{(q)j} = -\sum_{q=1}^{l} a\left(R(\rho_{qk}) \right) f'_{ok}\left(s_{qk} \right) r_{qj},$$

the updating rule becomes

$$w_{jk} \leftarrow w_{jk} + \eta_w \cdot \sum_{q=1}^{l} a\left(R\left(\rho_{qk}\right)\right) f'_{ok}\left(s_{qk}\right) r_{qj} \, .$$

Next, we propose an updating rule for v_{ij}, which is given by

$$v_{ij} \leftarrow v_{ij} - \eta_v \frac{\partial \Psi_k}{\partial v_{ij}}, \quad i \in \underline{n+1}, \quad j \in \underline{m},$$

where $\eta_v > 0$ is a learning rate. Since

$$\frac{\partial \Psi_k}{\partial v_{ij}} = \sum_{q=1}^{l} a(q)(-1) f'_{ok}\left(s_{(q)k}\right) w_{jk} f'_{hj}\left(u_{(q)j}\right) z_{(q)i}$$

$$= -\sum_{q=1}^{l} a\left(R\left(\rho_{qk}\right)\right) f'_{ok}\left(s_{qk}\right) w_{jk} f'_{hj}\left(u_{qj}\right) z_{qi} \, ,$$

the updating rule becomes

$$v_{ij} \leftarrow v_{ij} + \eta_v \sum_{q=1}^{l} a\left(R\left(\rho_{qk}\right)\right) f'_{ok}\left(s_{qk}\right) w_{jk} f'_{hj}\left(u_{qj}\right) z_{qi} \, .$$

The bias term b_k, $k \in \underline{p}$, is given by the median of the residuals at the kth output node, i.e.,

$$b_k = \underset{1 \leq q \leq l}{med}\left\{d_{qk} - t_{qk}\right\}.$$

The details of the whole algorithm are left for interested readers.

Note the similarities and differences between the updating rules for Wilcoxon artificial neural networks and standard artificial neural networks investigated in Section 5.2.

9.4 Wilcoxon Generalized Radial Basis Function Network

In this section, we discuss the Wilcoxon generalized radial basis function networks (WGRBFNs). In particular, we will only consider a commonly used class of approximating functions $g : \mathfrak{R}^n \to \mathfrak{R}^p$ with Gaussian basis functions, which can be represented as a feed-forward network shown in Figure 9.4.1. In this network, there is a single input layer with n nodes, a single hidden layer with m nodes, and a single output layer with p nodes. We also have p bias terms at the output nodes.

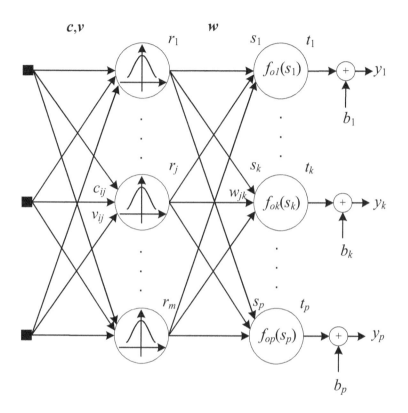

Figure 9.4.1: Wilcoxon generalized radial basis function network.

Let

$$x := \begin{bmatrix} x_1 & \cdots & x_n \end{bmatrix}^T \in \mathfrak{R}^n$$

be the input vector. Let $c_j := \begin{bmatrix} c_{1j} & c_{2j} & \ldots & c_{nj} \end{bmatrix}^T$, $j \in \underline{m}$, be the center of jth basis function and v_{ij} be the ith "precision" of jth basis function, with $v_{ij} := 1/(2\sigma_{ij}^2) > 0$, $i \in \underline{n}$. Then the output of the jth hidden node is given by

$$u_j = \sum_{i=1}^{n} \left(x_i - c_{ij} \right)^2 v_{ij}, \quad r_j = \exp\left(-u_j \right).$$

Let w_{jk} denote the connection weight from the output of the jth hidden node to the input of the kth output node, and let b_k be the bias term. Then the input and output of the kth output node are given by, respectively,

$$s_k = \sum_{j=1}^{m} w_{jk} r_j, \quad t_k = f_{ok}(s_k), \quad y_k = t_k + b_k, \quad k \in \underline{p},$$

where f_{ok} is the activation function of the kth output node.

The predictive function $f_k(x)$ is a nonlinear map given by

$$y_k = f_k(x) = f_{ok}\left(\sum_{j=1}^{m} w_{jk} \exp\left[-\sum_{i=1}^{n} \left(x_i - c_{ij} \right)^2 v_{ij} \right] \right) + b_k, \quad k \in \underline{p}.$$

Let $X \subseteq \mathfrak{R}^n$ and $Y \subseteq \mathfrak{R}^p$. Suppose we are given the training set

$$S := \left\{ \left(x_q, d_q \right) \right\}_{q=1}^{l} \subseteq X \times Y.$$

In the following, we will use the subscript q to denote the qth example. For instance, x_{qi} denotes the ith component of the qth pattern $x_q \in \mathfrak{R}^n$, $q \in \underline{l}, \ i \in \underline{n}$.

In a Wilcoxon generalized radial basis function network, the approach is to choose network weights that minimize the Wilcoxon norm of the total residuals

$$\Psi_{total} = \sum_{k=1}^{p} \sum_{q=1}^{l} a\left(R\left(\rho_{qk} \right) \right) \rho_{qk} = \sum_{k=1}^{p} \sum_{q=1}^{l} a(q) \rho_{(q)k},$$

$$\rho_{qk} := d_{qk} - t_{qk}, \quad q \in \underline{l}, \ k \in \underline{p}.$$

Here $R(\rho_{qk})$ denotes the rank of the residual ρ_{qk} among $\rho_{1k}, \ldots, \rho_{lk}$, $\rho_{(1)k} \leq \ldots \leq \rho_{(l)k}$ are the ordered values of $\rho_{1k}, \ldots, \rho_{lk}$, and $a(i) := \varphi[i/(l+1)]$ is a score function with $\varphi(u) := \sqrt{12}(u - 0.5)$.

The Wilcoxon norm of residuals at the kth output node is given by

$$\Psi_k := \|\rho_k\|_W := \sum_{q=1}^{l} a(R(\rho_{qk}))\rho_{qk} = \sum_{q=1}^{l} a(q)\rho_{(q)k},$$

$$\rho_k := [\rho_{1k} \quad \rho_{2k} \quad \cdots \quad \rho_{lk}]^T \in \mathfrak{R}^l.$$

Then we have

$$\Psi_{total} = \sum_{k=1}^{p} \Psi_k.$$

Now we introduce an incremental gradient descent algorithm. In this algorithm, Ψ_k's are minimized in sequence. From the definition of Ψ_k, we have

$$\Psi_k := \|\rho_k\|_W = \sum_{q=1}^{l} a(q)[d_{(q)k} - t_{(q)k}] = \sum_{q=1}^{l} a(q)[d_{(q)k} - f_{ok}(s_{(q)k})].$$

First, we propose an updating rule for w_{jk}, which is given by

$$w_{jk} \leftarrow w_{jk} - \eta_w \frac{\partial \Psi_k}{\partial w_{jk}}, \quad j \in \underline{m}, \quad k \in \underline{p},$$

where $\eta_w > 0$ is a learning rate. Since

$$\frac{\partial \Psi_k}{\partial w_{jk}} = \sum_{q=1}^{l} a(q)(-1)f'_{ok}(s_{(q)k})r_{(q)j} = -\sum_{q=1}^{l} a(R(\rho_{qk}))f'_{ok}(s_{qk})r_{qj},$$

where s_{qk} is the kth component of the qth vector s_q and r_{qj} is the jth component of the qth vector r_q, the updating rule for w_{jk} becomes

$$w_{jk} \leftarrow w_{jk} + \eta_w \cdot \sum_{q=1}^{l} a\big(R\big(\rho_{qk}\big)\big) f'_{ok}\big(s_{qk}\big) r_{qj}, \quad j \in \underline{m}, \quad k \in \underline{p}.$$

By similar derivation, the updating rules for c_{ij} and v_{ij} are given, respectively, by

$$c_{ij} \leftarrow c_{ij} - \eta_c \frac{\partial \Psi_k}{\partial c_{ij}}$$

$$= c_{ij} + \eta_c \cdot \sum_{q=1}^{l} a\big(R\big(\rho_{qk}\big)\big) f'_{ok}\big(s_{qk}\big) r_{qj} w_{jk} \cdot 2\big(x_{qi} - c_{ij}\big) v_{ij},$$

$$v_{ij} \leftarrow v_{ij} - \eta_v \frac{\partial \Psi_k}{\partial v_{ij}}$$

$$= v_{ij} - \eta_v \cdot \sum_{q=1}^{l} a\big(R\big(\rho_{qk}\big)\big) f'_{ok}\big(s_{qk}\big) r_{qj} w_{jk} \big(x_{qi} - c_{ij}\big)^2,$$

$$i \in \underline{n}, \quad j \in \underline{m},$$

where $\eta_c > 0$ and $\eta_v > 0$ are learning rates.

The bias term b_k, $k \in \underline{p}$, is given by the median of the residuals at the kth output node, i.e.,

$$b_k = \operatorname*{med}_{1 \le q \le l} \big\{d_{qk} - t_{qk}\big\}.$$

The details of the whole algorithm are left for interested readers.

9.5 Wilcoxon Fuzzy Neural Network

In this section, we discuss the Wilcoxon fuzzy neural networks (WFNNs). In particular, we will only consider the approximating functions $g : \Re^n \to \Re^p$ with normal Gaussian fuzzy sets in the IF parts and normal fuzzy sets in the THEN parts, which can be represented as a feed-forward network shown in Figure 9.5.1. Note that we have p bias terms at the output nodes.

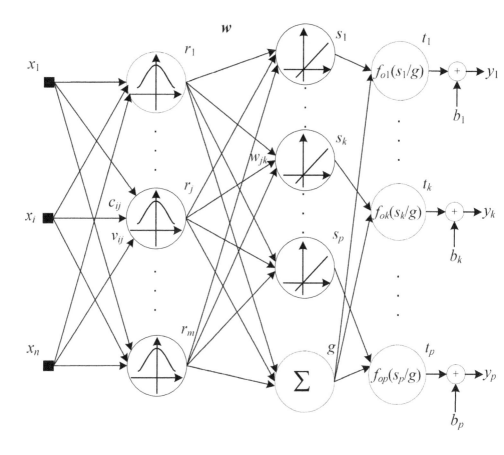

Figure 9.5.1: Wilcoxon fuzzy neural network.

Let c_{ij} and v_{ij}, with $v_{ij} := 1/\left(2\sigma_{ij}^2\right) > 0$, $i \in \underline{n}$, $j \in \underline{m}$, be the center and "precision" of the ith normal Gaussian fuzzy set A_{ij} of IF part in the jth rule, respectively. Further, let w_{jk} be the center of the kth normal fuzzy set B_{jk} of THEN part in the jth rule, and let b_k be the bias term.

Define, for $i \in \underline{n}$, $j \in \underline{m}$, and $k \in \underline{p}$,

$$x := \begin{bmatrix} x_1 & \cdots & x_n \end{bmatrix}^T \in \mathfrak{R}^n,$$

$$u_j = \sum_{i=1}^{n}\left(x_i - c_{ij}\right)^2 v_{ij},$$

$$r_j = \exp(-u_j), \quad s_k = \sum_{j=1}^{m} w_{jk} r_j, \quad g = \sum_{j=1}^{m} r_j, \quad t_k = f_{ok}(s_k/g)$$

then

$$y_k = t_k + b_k.$$

Here, f_{ok} is the activation function of the kth output node.

The predictive function $f_k(x)$ is a nonlinear map given by

$$y_k = f_k(x) = f_{ok}\left(\frac{\sum_{j=1}^{m} w_{jk} \exp\left[-\sum_{i=1}^{n}(x_i - c_{ij})^2 v_{ij}\right]}{\sum_{j=1}^{m} \exp\left[-\sum_{i=1}^{n}(x_i - c_{ij})^2 v_{ij}\right]}\right) + b_k, \quad k \in \underline{p}.$$

Let $X \subseteq \mathfrak{R}^n$ and $Y \subseteq \mathfrak{R}^p$. Suppose we are given the training set

$$S := \{(x_q, d_q)\}_{q=1}^{l} \subseteq X \times Y.$$

In the following, we will use the subscript q to denote the qth example. For instance, x_{qi} denotes the ith component of the qth pattern $x_q \in \mathfrak{R}^n$, $q \in \underline{l}$, $i \in \underline{n}$.

In a Wilcoxon fuzzy neural network, the approach is to choose network weights that minimize the Wilcoxon norm of the total residuals

$$\Psi_{total} = \sum_{k=1}^{p} \sum_{q=1}^{l} a(R(\rho_{qk}))\rho_{qk} = \sum_{k=1}^{p} \sum_{q=1}^{l} a(q)\rho_{(q)k},$$

$$\rho_{qk} := d_{qk} - t_{qk}, \quad q \in \underline{l}, \quad k \in \underline{p}.$$

Here $R(\rho_{qk})$ denotes the rank of the residual ρ_{qk} among $\rho_{1k}, \ldots, \rho_{lk}$, $\rho_{(1)k} \leq \ldots \leq \rho_{(l)k}$ are the ordered values of $\rho_{1k}, \ldots, \rho_{lk}$, and $a(i) := \varphi[i/(l+1)]$ is a score function with $\varphi(u) := \sqrt{12}(u - 0.5)$.

The Wilcoxon norm of residuals at the kth output node is given by

$$\Psi_k := \|\rho_k\|_W := \sum_{q=1}^{l} a(R(\rho_{qk}))\rho_{qk} = \sum_{q=1}^{l} a(q)\rho_{(q)k},$$

$$\rho_k := \begin{bmatrix} \rho_{1k} & \rho_{2k} & \cdots & \rho_{lk} \end{bmatrix}^T \in \Re^l.$$

Then we have

$$\Psi_{total} = \sum_{k=1}^{p} \Psi_k.$$

Now we introduce an incremental gradient descent algorithm. In this algorithm, Ψ_k's are minimized in sequence. From the definition of Ψ_k, we have

$$\Psi_k := \|\rho_k\|_W = \sum_{q=1}^{l} a(q)[d_{(q)k} - t_{(q)k}] = \sum_{q=1}^{l} a(q)\left[d_{(q)k} - f_{ok}\left(\frac{s_{(q)k}}{g_{(q)}} \right) \right].$$

First, we propose an updating rule for w_{jk}, which is given by

$$w_{jk} \leftarrow w_{jk} - \eta_w \frac{\partial \Psi_k}{\partial w_{jk}}, \quad j \in \underline{m}, \quad k \in \underline{p},$$

where $\eta_w > 0$ is a learning rate. Since

$$\frac{\partial \Psi_k}{\partial w_{jk}} = \sum_{q=1}^{l} a(q)(-1)f_{ok}'\left(\frac{s_{(q)k}}{g_{(q)}} \right)\frac{r_{(q)j}}{g_{(q)}} = -\sum_{q=1}^{l} a(R(\rho_{qk}))f_{ok}'\left(\frac{s_{qk}}{g_q} \right)\frac{r_{qj}}{g_q},$$

the updating rule for w_{jk} becomes

$$w_{jk} \leftarrow w_{jk} + \eta_w \cdot \sum_{q=1}^{l} a(R(\rho_{qk}))f_{ok}'\left(\frac{s_{qk}}{g_q} \right)\frac{r_{qj}}{g_q}, \quad j \in \underline{m}, \quad k \in \underline{p},$$

where s_{qk} is the kth component of the qth vector s_q and r_{qj} is the jth component of the qth vector r_q.

By similar derivation, the updating rules for c_{ij} and v_{ij} are given, respectively, by

$$c_{ij} \leftarrow c_{ij} - \eta_c \frac{\partial \Psi_k}{\partial c_{ij}}$$

$$= c_{ij} + \eta_c \cdot \sum_{q=1}^{l} a\big(R\big(\rho_{qk}\big)\big) f'_{ok} \left(\frac{S_{qk}}{g_q}\right) \frac{r_{qj}}{g_q}\left(w_{jk} - \frac{S_{qk}}{g_q}\right) \cdot 2\big(x_{qi} - c_{ij}\big) v_{ij} \,,$$

$$v_{ij} \leftarrow v_{ij} - \eta_v \frac{\partial \Psi_k}{\partial v_{ij}}$$

$$= v_{ij} - \eta_v \cdot \sum_{q=1}^{l} a\big(R\big(\rho_{qk}\big)\big) f'_{ok} \left(\frac{S_{qk}}{g_q}\right) \frac{r_{qj}}{g_q}\left(w_{jk} - \frac{S_{qk}}{g_q}\right) \cdot \big(x_{qi} - c_{ij}\big)^2$$

$$i \in \underline{n}, \quad j \in \underline{m},$$

where $\eta_c > 0$ and $\eta_v > 0$ are learning rates.

The bias term b_k, $k \in \underline{p}$, is given by the median of the residuals at the kth output node, i.e.,

$$b_k = \operatorname*{med}_{1 \leq q \leq l}\big\{d_{qk} - t_{qk}\big\}.$$

The details of the whole algorithm are left for interested readers.

9.6 Kernel-based Wilcoxon Machine

In this section, we first introduce the kernel-based Wilcoxon classifiers (KWCs). Let $X \subseteq \mathfrak{R}^n$ and $Y := \{1, -1\}$. Suppose we are given a non-trivial training set

$$S := \big\{\big(x_q, d_q\big)\big\}_{q=1}^{l} \subseteq X \times Y.$$

Let $K(\cdot, \cdot)$ be a given kernel on $X \times X$. Motivated by the 2-norm support vector classifier (SVC), suppose the discriminant function is given by

$$f(x) = \sum_{j=1}^{l} z_j d_j K(x_j, x) + b, \quad z_j \geq 0, \quad j \in \underline{l}.$$

The KWC can be represented as a feed-forward network as shown in Figure 9.6.1. Note that when we use the usual Euclidean inner product as the kernel, the KWC becomes a linear classifier.

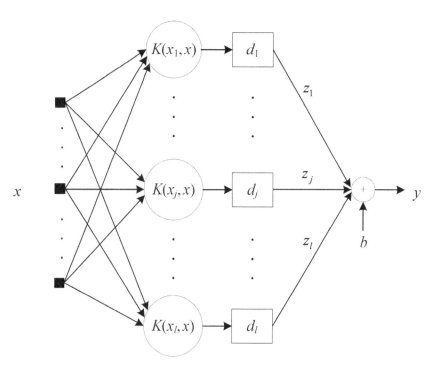

Figure 9.6.1: Kernel-based Wilcoxon classifier.

The residual due to the qth example is defined by

$$\rho_q := d_q - \sum_{j=1}^{l} z_j d_j K(x_j, x_q), \quad q \in \underline{l}.$$

The Wilcoxon approach is to choose z_j, $j \in \underline{l}$, that minimize the Wilcoxon norm of the residuals given by

$$\|\rho\|_W := \sum_{q=1}^{l} a(R(\rho_q))\rho_q = \sum_{q=1}^{l} a(q)\rho_{(q)}, \quad \rho := [\rho_1 \quad \cdots \quad \rho_l]^T \in \Re^l.$$

Here, $R(\rho_q)$ denotes the rank of the residual ρ_q among $\rho_1, \ldots, \rho_l$, $\rho_{(1)} \le \ldots \le \rho_{(l)}$ are the ordered values of $\rho_1, \ldots, \rho_l$, and $a(i) := \varphi[i/(l+1)]$ is a score function with $\varphi(u) := \sqrt{12}(u-0.5)$.

Note that the Wilcoxon norm $\|\rho\|_W$ can also be written as

$$\|\rho\|_W := \frac{\sqrt{3}}{2(l+1)} \sum_{q=1}^{l} \sum_{m=1}^{l} |\rho_q - \rho_m|$$

$$= \frac{\sqrt{3}}{2(l+1)} \sum_{q=1}^{l} \sum_{m=1}^{l} \left| (d_q - d_m) - \sum_{j=1}^{l} z_j d_j \left[K(x_j, x_q) - K(x_j, x_m) \right] \right|.$$

Thus, $\|\rho\|_W$ is a piecewise linear continuous function of z_j, $j \in \underline{l}$, since the sum of piecewise linear continuous functions is still a piecewise linear continuous function. Further, since each summand is a convex function of z_j, $j \in \underline{l}$, and a positive linear combination of convex functions is again convex, the Wilcoxon norm $\|\rho\|_W$ is a convex function of z_j, $j \in \underline{l}$. Thus, we are faced with a convex optimization problem. This allows an easy way to compute the Wilcoxon norm $\|\rho\|_W$ by using any least absolute deviations (LAD) routine.

Taking the gradient of $\|\rho\|_W$ with respect to z_j, $j \in \underline{l}$, we have

$$\frac{\partial}{\partial z_j} \|\rho\|_W = -\sum_{q=1}^{l} a(R(\rho_q)) d_j K(x_j, x_q) = -d_j \sum_{q=1}^{l} a(R(\rho_q)) K(x_j, x_q).$$

Then, the updating law based on the gradient projection method is given by, $k \in \underline{l}$,

$$\hat{z}_k \leftarrow z_k + s \cdot d_k \sum_{q=1}^{l} a(R(\rho_q)) K(x_k, x_q),$$

$$\bar{z}_k \leftarrow \begin{cases} 0, & \hat{z}_k < 0, \\ \hat{z}_k, & \hat{z}_k \ge 0, \end{cases}$$

$$z_k \leftarrow z_k + \eta\left(\bar{z}_k - z_k\right) \quad \text{(or} \quad z_k \leftarrow \left(1-\eta\right)z_k + \eta \cdot \bar{z}_k\text{)},$$

where $s > 0$ is a step size and $\eta > 0$ is the learning rate. The bias term b is given by the median of the residuals, i.e.,

$$b = \underset{1 \leq q \leq l}{med}\left\{\rho_q\right\}.$$

Next, we introduce the kernel-based Wilcoxon regressors (KWRs). Let $X \subseteq \mathfrak{R}^n$ and $Y \subseteq \mathfrak{R}$. Suppose we are given the training set

$$S := \left\{\left(x_q, d_q\right)\right\}_{q=1}^{l} \subseteq X \times Y.$$

Motivated by the 2-norm support vector regressor (SVR), suppose the predictive function is given by

$$f(x) = \sum_{j=1}^{l} z_j K\left(x_j, x\right) + b.$$

The KWR can be represented as a feed-forward network as shown in Figure 9.6.2. Note that when we use the usual Euclidean inner product as the kernel, the KWR becomes a linear regressor.

The residual due to the qth example is defined by

$$\rho_q := d_q - \sum_{j=1}^{l} z_j K\left(x_j, x_q\right), \quad q \in \underline{l}.$$

The Wilcoxon approach is to choose z_j, $j \in \underline{l}$, that minimize the Wilcoxon norm of the residuals given by

$$\|\rho\|_W := \sum_{q=1}^{l} a\left(R\left(\rho_q\right)\right)\rho_q = \sum_{q=1}^{l} a(q)\rho_{(q)}, \quad \rho := \left[\rho_1 \quad \cdots \quad \rho_l\right]^T \in \mathfrak{R}^l.$$

Again, we are faced with a convex optimization problem.

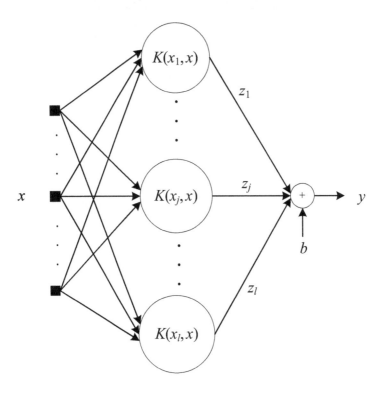

Figure 9.6.2: Kernel-based Wilcoxon regressor.

Taking the gradient of $\|\rho\|_W$ with respect to z_j, $j \in \underline{l}$, we have

$$\frac{\partial}{\partial z_j}\|\rho\|_W = -\sum_{q=1}^{l} a\big(R(\rho_q)\big)K\big(x_j, x_q\big).$$

Then, the updating law based on the steepest decent is given by

$$z_k \leftarrow z_k + \eta\sum_{q=1}^{l} a\big(R(\rho_q)\big)K\big(x_k, x_q\big), \quad k \in \underline{l},$$

where $\eta > 0$ is the learning rate. The bias term b is given by the median of the residuals, i.e.,

$$b = \underset{1 \le q \le l}{med}\big\{\rho_q\big\}.$$

We wish to point out that the kernel parameters for kernel-based Wilcoxon learning machines can also be determined by genetic algorithm and particle swarm optimization techniques, as we have done in Sections 8.3 and 8.4 for the parameters of the support vector machines.

9.7 Illustrative Examples

In this section, we present some illustrative examples for Wilcoxon learning machines.

In the first example on nonlinear classification, the activation functions of the hidden nodes and output node of WANN are all bipolar sigmoidal functions. The Mahalanobis kernel is used in KWC with "variances" σ_1^2 and σ_2^2.

Example 9.7.1: Consider the data set of Example 5.6.1, where true discriminant function is given by the fractional power function

$$g(x_1, x_2) = x_2 - x_1^{2/3}, \quad x_1 \in [-2, 2], \quad x_2 \in [0, 2].$$

The parameter settings and simulation results for WANN and KWC are shown in Table 9.7.1. For WANN, we the initial weights v_{ij} and w_{jk} are randomly generated 100 times, each resulting in a trained WANN. We then choose the best WANN according to the cost value. Together with the true decision boundary, the decision boundaries thus determined for corrupted data are shown in Figure 9.7.1. With such highly corrupted data, the decision boundaries are reasonable. WANN provides a simpler decision boundary.

Table 9.7.1: Parameter settings and simulation results in Example 9.7.1.

		WANN	KWC
Parameters		No. of hidden nodes $= 4$	$\left(\sigma_1^2, \sigma_2^2\right) = \left(1.2, 0.2\right)$
Initialization		$v_{ij} \in \left[-1, 1\right]$	SVC2
		$w_{jk} \in \left[-1, 1\right]$	$\left(\sigma_1^2, \sigma_2^2\right) = \left(1.2, 0.2\right)$
			$C = 8$
Estimated minimal cost		24.8621	26.6760
No. of misclassifications		8	5

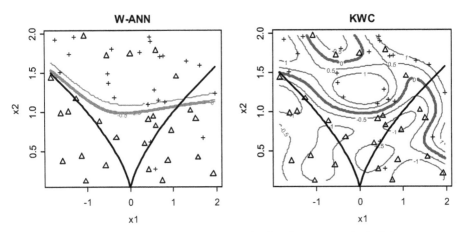

Figure 9.7.1: Decision boundaries in Example 9.7.1.

In the next two examples on nonlinear regression, the activation functions of the output nodes for WGRBFN and WFNN are linear functions with unit slope. The Gaussian kernel is used in KWR with "variance" σ^2.

Example 9.7.2: Consider the data set of Example 5.6.2, where true regression function is given by the sinc function

$$g(x) = \begin{cases} 1, & x = 0, \\ \sin(x)/x, & x \neq 0, \end{cases} \quad x \in \left[-10, 10\right].$$

The parameter settings and simulation results for WGRBFN and KWR are shown in Table 9.7.2. For WGRBFN, we the initial weights

c_{ij}, v_{ij}, and w_{jk} are randomly generated 20 times, each resulting in a trained WGRBFN. We then choose the best WGRBFN according to the cost value. Together with the true function, the predictive functions thus determined for corrupted data are shown in Figure 9.7.2. The performance of KWR is better than that of WGRBFN.

Table 9.7.2: Parameter settings and simulation results in Example 9.7.2.

	WGRBFN	KWR
Parameters	No. of hidden nodes $= 4$	$\sigma^2 = 0.3$
Scaling on x	none	unit normal
Initialization	$c_{ij} \in [-5, 5]$	SVR2
	$v_{ij} \in [0.01, 4]$	$\sigma^2 = 0.3$
	$w_{jk} \in [-2, 2]$	$C = 0.5$
		$\varepsilon = 0.01$
Estimated minimal cost	11.2357	12.0840
Mean squared error (MSE)	0.0890	0.1074
Mean absolute deviation (MAD)	0.1526	0.1612

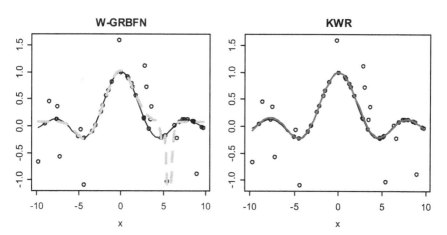

Figure 9.7.2: Predictive functions in Example 9.7.2.

Example 9.7.3: Consider the data set of Example 5.6.3, where true regression function is given by the Hermite function

$$g(x) = 1.1 \cdot \left(1 - x + 2x^2\right) \cdot e^{-x^2/2}, \quad x \in [-5, 5].$$

The parameter settings and simulation results for WFNN and KWR are shown in Table 9.7.3. For WFNN, we the initial weights c_{ij}, v_{ij}, and w_{jk} are randomly generated 20 times, each resulting in a trained WFNN. We then choose the best WFNN according to the cost value. Together with the true function, the predictive functions thus determined for corrupted data are shown in Figure 9.7.3. The performances of both learning machines are excellent.

Table 9.7.3: Parameter settings and simulation results in Example 9.7.3.

	WFNN	KWR
Parameters	No. of hidden nodes $= 4$	$\sigma^2 = 1$
Initialization	$c_{ij} \in [-5, 5]$ $v_{ij} \in [0.01, 4]$ $w_{jk} \in [-2, 2]$	SVR2 $\sigma^2 = 1$ $C = 0.5$ $\varepsilon = 0.01$
Estimated minimal cost	12.0571	12.1360
Mean squared error (MSE)	0.0988	0.1061
Mean absolute deviation (MAD)	0.1665	0.1625

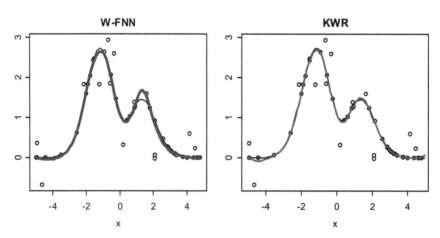

Figure 9.7.3: Predictive functions in Example 9.7.3.

9.8 Exercises

Exercise 9.8.1: Prove that the Wilcoxon norm of $v \in \mathfrak{R}^l$

$$\|v\|_W := \sum_{i=1}^l a(R(v_i))v_i = \sum_{i=1}^l a(i)v_{(i)}, \quad v := \begin{bmatrix} v_1 & \cdots & v_l \end{bmatrix}^T \in \mathfrak{R}^l,$$

can be written as

$$\|v\|_W = \frac{\sqrt{3}}{2(l+1)} \sum_{i=1}^l \sum_{j=1}^l |v_i - v_j|, \quad v := \begin{bmatrix} v_1 & \cdots & v_l \end{bmatrix}^T \in \mathfrak{R}^l.$$

Exercise 9.8.2: Prove that the score functions $\varphi_2(u)$, $\varphi_3(u)$, and $\varphi_4(u)$ all satisfy the standardizing conditions:

$$\int_0^1 \varphi(u)du = 0 \quad \text{and} \quad \int_0^1 \varphi^2(u)du = 1.$$

Exercise 9.8.3: Let $X \subseteq \mathfrak{R}^n$ and $Y := \{1, -1\}$. Suppose we are given a non-trivial training set

$$S := \{(x_q, d_q)\}_{i=1}^{\mathcal{U}} \subseteq X \times Y.$$

Let $K(\cdot,\cdot)$ be a given kernel on $X \times X$. Motivated by the 1-norm support vector classifier, suppose the discriminant function is given by

$$f(x) = \sum_{j=1}^l z_j d_j K(x_j, x) + b, \quad 0 \leq z_j \leq C, \quad j \in \underline{l}.$$

Develop an updating rule for z_j, $j \in \underline{l}$, by minimizing the Wilcoxon norm of the residuals.

Exercise 9.8.4: Let $X \subseteq \mathfrak{R}^n$ and $Y \subseteq \mathfrak{R}$. Suppose we are given a non-trivial training set

$$S := \{(x_q, d_q)\}_{i=1}^{\mathcal{U}} \subseteq X \times Y.$$

Let $K(\cdot,\cdot)$ be a given kernel on $X \times X$. Motivated by the 1-norm support vector regressor, suppose the predictive function is given by

$$f(x) = \sum_{j=1}^{l} z_j K(x_j, x) + b, \quad -C \le z_j \le C, \quad j \in \underline{l}.$$

Develop an updating rule for z_j, $j \in \underline{l}$, by minimizing the Wilcoxon norm of the residuals.

Exercise 9.8.5: Consider the data set of Exercise 5.7.8, where the true discriminant function is given by the Hermite function

$$g(x_1, x_2) = x_2 - 1.1 \cdot \left(1 - x_1 + 2x_1^2\right) \cdot e^{-x_1^2/2},$$
$$x_1 \in [-5, 5], \quad x_2 \in [-1, 3].$$

In this exercise, we use a Wilcoxon artificial neural network with 4 hidden nodes and a kernel-based Wilcoxon classifier with $\sigma_1^2 = 1.2$ and $\sigma_2^2 = 2$ in Mahalanobis kernel. Draw the decision boundaries thus determined. Discuss whether these machine parameter settings are reasonable.

Exercise 9.8.6: Consider the data set of Exercise 5.7.9, where the true discriminant function is given by the sinc function

$$g(x_1, x_2) = \begin{cases} x_2 - 1, & x_1 = 0, \\ x_2 - [\sin(x_1)/x_1], & x_1 \ne 0, \end{cases}$$
$$x_1 \in [-10, 10], \quad x_2 \in [-2, 2].$$

Assume that the data have been normalized on x_1 and x_2 by the unit normal scaling. In this exercise, we use a Wilcoxon generalized radial basis function network with 4 hidden nodes and a kernel-based Wilcoxon classifier with $\sigma_1^2 = 1$ and $\sigma_2^2 = 1$ in Mahalanobis kernel. Draw the decision boundaries thus determined. Discuss whether these machine parameter settings are reasonable.

Exercise 9.8.7: Consider the data set of Exercise 5.7.10, where the true regression function is given by the fractional power function

$$g(x) = x^{2/3}, \quad x \in [-2, 2].$$

Draw the predictive functions determined by a Wilcoxon fuzzy neural network with 4 hidden nodes and a kernel-based Wilcoxon regressor with $\sigma^2 = 1$ in Gaussian kernel.

9.9 Notes and References

For Wilcoxon norms and linear Wilcoxon regressors, see Hogg, McKean, and Craig (2005). For original paper on Wilcoxon learning machines, see Hsieh, Lin, and Jeng (2008). For optimization techniques of least absolute deviations (LAD) problems, see Bloomfield and Steiger (1983) and Pinkus (1989).

Bloomfield, P. and W.L. Steiger (1983). Least Absolute Deviations. Birkhauser, Boston.

Hogg, R.V., J.W. McKean, and A.T. Craig (2005). Introduction to Mathematical Statistics. Sixth Edition. Prentice-Hall, New Jersey.

Hsieh, J.G., Y.L. Lin, and J.H. Jeng (2008). Preliminary study on Wilcoxon learning machines. IEEE Transactions on Neural Networks, Vol. 19, No. 2, pp. 201-211.

Pinkus, A. (1989). On L^1-approximation. Cambridge University Press, Cambridge, United Kingdom.

Index

activation function 37, 46, 58, 97, 165
active set 23
adaptive linear neuron (Adaline) 11, 23, 97, 101
affine function 18
Armijo rule 175
artificial neural network (ANN) 2, 161, 164, 168, 172

back propagation (BP) 161, 169, 185, 199, 205
bias-variance dilemma (tradeoff) 9
bipolar sigmoidal function 165, 166, 167, 183, 198
box constraint 76, 132, 138, 266, 277

canonical form 193
canonical hyperplane 64
chromosome 292, 294, 295, 296, 297
classification learning 4
cluster analysis 5
cognitive factor 298
compact set 14, 15, 168
complementarity conditions 24, 25
concave function 18, 19, 20
convex program 22, 64, 74, 130
convex combination 16, 19, 20, 196
convex function 13, 18, 20, 21, 35
convex set 13, 15, 16, 17, 19
cost surface 172, 173, 291
Cover's Theorem 161, 162, 163, 216
critical point 24, 32, 33, 34
cross validation 10, 174, 291, 301
crossover 292, 294, 296, 298, 312
curse of dimensionality 163, 221, 235

defuzzifier 192, 193, 194, 195, 196
delta learning rule 11, 97, 101, 102, 114
density estimation 5
discriminant function 39, 42, 47, 48, 52
dual function 26, 30, 64, 75, 83

dual problem 26, 28, 30, 64, 65
duality gap 28, 70, 80, 123

elitism 294, 295, 298
epigraph 18, 19,
equality constraint 21, 22, 23, 24, 25
evolution 2, 10, 11, 216, 291
evolutionary computation (EC) 2, 10, 216, 291
evolutionary programming (EP) 10, 11
evolution strategy (ES) 10, 11
exterior penalty function method 312, 313
extreme point 16, 17, 20

feasible point 21, 22, 23, 24, 26
feasible region 21, 22, 26, 30
feasible set 15, 21, 22, 23, 31
feasibility gap 70, 80, 87, 95, 123
feature composition 9
feature map 58, 59, 94, 110, 221
feature selection 9
feature space 54, 55, 58, 59, 94
Fisher scoring algorithm 179
fitness function 292, 294, 298, 303, 306
function learning 5, 127, 169
functional margin 42, 43, 60, 64, 67
fuzzifier 192, 193, 194, 195, 196
fuzzy inference engine 192
fuzzy neural network (FNN)196, 198, 212, 216, 347
fuzzy rule base 192, 193
fuzzy system 191, 192, 193, 194, 195

gene 295, 298, 300
generalization error 2, 7
generalized delta learning rule11, 169, 185, 199
generalized linear model (GLM) 178
generalized radial basis function network (GRBFN) 161, 212, 213, 215
genetic algorithm (GA) 2, 10, 11, 216, 291
genetic programming (GP) 10, 11
geometric margin 42, 43, 44, 63, 64
global minimizer 13, 20, 29, 31, 32
growing method 174

hard limiting function 46
heavy ball method 177
hidden layer 58, 161, 164, 182, 238
Hilbert space 223, 227,
Hyperplane 37, 39, 40, 41, 42
hyperbolic tangent function 165, 166, 167, 183, 198

individuality coefficient 306, 308, 309
inductive bias 9
inequality constraint 21, 22, 23, 24, 25
input layer 164, 182, 324, 329
insensitive 125, 317, 324

kernel
    Gaussian 59, 182, 188, 190, 193
    Polynomial 7, 8, 59, 61, 62
    Mahalanobis 59, 232, 284, 288, 300
    radial basis function 2, 11, 161, 182, 183
kernel-based
    Wilcoxon classifier (KWC) 346
    Wilcoxon regressor (KWR) 319, 322, 324, 347
kernel trick 221
KKT conditions 24, 25, 29, 31, 32
KKT Theorem 13, 24
k-means 190
knowledge discovery in databases (KDD)

Lagrangian 23, 28, 29, 30, 31
Landscape 172, 216, 291, 294, 297
law of sufficiency 10
least absolute deviation (LAD) 323, 338, 347
least squares support vector machine (LS-SVM) 112, 160
life time 303
life score 303
linear independence constraint qualification (LICQ) 23
linear program 13, 21, 22, 24, 33
linearly separable 37, 42, 43, 44, 45
link function 165, 178

maximal margin hyperplane 43, 44, 63, 64, 67
maximal margin classifier (MMC) 37,62, 68, 73, 87
mean absolute deviation (MAD) 286, 300, 303, 306, 308
mean squared error (MSE) 172, 188, 203, 209, 210
measure of dissatisfaction 69, 80, 87, 136, 140
membership function 193, 194, 195, 196
Mercer's Theorem 221, 223, 226, 256
Mercer kernel 226
Minimizer 13, 20, 24, 29, 31
model matrix 100
model selection 9, 205, 291, 292, 300
multi-class classification 221, 249, 251, 255, 256
mutation 292, 294, 297, 298, 312

natural selection 291, 294
natural genetics 291
nearest mean classifier (NMC) 88, 89, 96
neural network 2, 10, 11, 37, 46
normal equation
        for least squares regression 101
        for ridge regression 114
Novikoff's Theorem 49, 51, 53, 92, 96

objective function 15, 21, 22, 26, 31
one-versus-one (OVO) 251
one-versus-rest (OVR) 251
optimal hyperplane 43, 67, 75, 83
optimal solution 21, 22, 26
outlier 54, 73, 76, 109, 205
output layer 164, 182, 324, 329
overfitting 7, 173

parameter setting 206, 207, 208, 209, 210
particle swarm optimization (PSO) 2, 10, 12, 216, 291
pattern recognition 4, 217, 221, 256
perceptron 11, 37, 46, 47, 48
predictive function 2, 7, 8, 99, 102
preference learning 5
primal problem 26, 28, 29, 156
pruning method 174

quadratic program 22, 30, 124, 259

recursive least squares (RLS) algorithm 97, 105, 154, 160, 189
recursive ridge algorithm 117
regression estimation 5
regularization parameter 113, 213, 291
reinforcement learning 4, 5, 12
replacement 295
reproduction 292, 294, 295, 296, 297
residual 46, 100, 168, 184, 199
ridge regression 97, 109, 113, 114, 115
ridge regressor (RR) 117, 152, 154, 239, 272
robust 2, 37, 43, 44, 96
robust regression 2, 109, 217, 219,
Rosenblatt's algorithm 51, 54, 88, 92, 93

saddle point 28, 172, 216
score 303, 317, 318, 319, 323
score function 317, 318, 319, 326, 331
selection 9, 175, 190, 205, 291
sensitivity theorem 25
sequential minimal optimization (SMO) 87, 152, 259, 290, 312
sigmoidal function 165, 166, 167, 183, 198
single-layer neural network 37, 46, 58, 97, 99

slack variable for classification 70
slack variable for regression 125
Slater's condition 29
smoothing parameter 113, 180, 213, 232
social factor 298
sociality coefficient 299, 306, 308, 309
soft computing 1, 3, 10, 11, 12
soft margin classifier
    1-norm (SVC1) 89, 90, 284, 288, 306
    2-norm (SVC2) 89, 90, 284, 288, 306
    υ-soft margin classifier 96
soft regressor
    1-norm (SVR1) 152, 155, 156, 285, 286
    2-norm (SVR2) 152, 156, 285, 286, 288
    υ-soft regressor 157
Sparseness 67

strong duality theorem 28
subgraph 19, 20
supervised learning 4, 5, 6, 7
support vector 2, 12, 35, 37, 67
support vector classification (SVC) 284, 305
support vector machine (SVM) 12, 238, 248, 256
support vector regression (SVR) 97, 284, 300, 311

testing error 7, 10, 174, 300
tolerance size 291
training error 7, 8, 52, 174, 208
tournament selection 295, 298
two-layer neural network 57, 58

underfitting 7, 8
parameterized uniform crossover 296, 298, 313, 314
parameterized uniform mutation 297
unipolar logistic function 165, 166, 167, 183, 197
unit normal scaling 156, 346
universal approximation property 168, 184, 193, 194
universal approximator 168, 184, 193, 196, 218
unsupervised learning 4, 5

weak duality theorem 26, 27
Weierstrass Theorem 13, 14, 15, 31, 35
weighted least squares 159
Widrow-Hoff algorithm 97, 101, 102, 104, 105

Wilcoxon
    artificial neural network (WANN) 317, 324, 325, 326, 328
    fuzzy neural network (WFNN) 347
    generalized radial basis function network (WGRBFN) 346
    learning machine 2, 317, 341, 347
    norm 317, 318, 320, 322, 324

Woodbury inversion formula 107, 118

ε -insensitive 125

邁向機器學習與軟計算之路（國際英文版）
Pathways to Machine Learning and Soft Computing

作　　者╱謝 哲 光　鄭 志 宏　林 義 隆　郭 英 勝　聯 合 編 著
（Jer-Guang Hsieh, Jyh-Horng Jeng, Yih-Lon Lin, and Ying-Sheng Kuo）

出版者╱美商 EHGBooks 微出版公司

發行者╱美商漢世紀數位文化公司

臺灣學人出版網：http://www.TaiwanFellowship.org

印　　刷╱漢世紀古騰堡®數位出版 POD 雲端科技

出版日期╱2018 年 7 月

總經銷╱Amazon.com

臺灣銷售網╱三民網路書店：http://www.sanmin.com.tw

　　　　　三民書局復北店

　　　　　地址╱104 臺北市復興北路 386 號

　　　　　電話╱02-2500-6600

　　　　　三民書局重南店

　　　　　地址╱100 臺北市重慶南路一段 61 號

　　　　　電話╱02-2361-7511

　　　　　全省金石網路書店：http://www.kingstone.com.tw

定　　價╱新臺幣 570 元（美金 19 元 / 人民幣 125 元）